Gender Divisions and Working Time in the New Economy

GLOBALIZATION AND WELFARE

Series Editors: Denis Bouget, *MSH Ange Guépin, France*, Jane Lewis, *Barnett Professor of Social Policy, University of Oxford, UK* and Peter Taylor-Gooby, *Darwin College, University of Kent, Canterbury, UK*

This important series is designed to make a significant contribution to the principles and practice of comparative social policy. It includes both theoretical and empirical work. International in scope, it addresses issues of current and future concern in both East and West, and in developed and developing countries.

The main purpose of this series is to create a forum for the publication of high quality work to help understand the impact of globalization on the provision of social welfare. It offers state-of-the-art thinking and research on important areas such as privatization, employment, work, finance, gender and poverty. It includes some of the best theoretical and empirical work from both well established researchers and the new generation of scholars.

Titles in the series include:

Restructuring the Welfare State
Globalization and Social Policy Reform in Finland and Sweden
Virpi Timonen

The Young, the Old and the State
Social Care Systems in Five Industrial Nations
Edited by Anneli Anttonen, John Baldock and Jorma Sipilä

Solidarity Between the Sexes and the Generations
Transformations in Europe
Edited by Trudie Knijn and Aafke Komter

The Third Sector in Europe
Edited by Adalbert Evers and Jean-Louis Laville

The OECD and European Welfare States
Edited by Klaus Armingeon and Michelle Beyeler

Poverty and Subsidiarity in Europe
Minimum Protection from an Economic Perspective
Didier Fouarge

Gender Divisions and Working Time in the New Economy
Changing Patterns of Work, Care and Public Policy in Europe and North America
Edited by Diane Perrons, Colette Fagan, Linda McDowell, Kath Ray and Kevin Ward

Gender Divisions and Working Time in the New Economy

Changing Patterns of Work, Care and Public Policy in Europe and North America

Edited by

Diane Perrons
Director, Gender Institute and Reader in Economic Geography and Gender Studies, London School of Economics

Colette Fagan
Co-Director, European Work and Employment Research Centre and Professor of Sociology, University of Manchester

Linda McDowell
Professor of Human Geography, School of Geography and the Environment, University of Oxford and Professorial Fellow, St John's College

Kath Ray
Research Fellow, Policy Studies Institute, London

Kevin Ward
Reader in Geography, University of Manchester

GLOBALIZATION AND WELFARE

Edward Elgar

Cheltenham, UK • Northampton, MA, USA

Published by
Edward Elgar Publishing Limited
Glensanda House
Montpellier Parade
Cheltenham
Glos GL50 1UA
UK

Edward Elgar Publishing, Inc.
136 West Street
Suite 202
Northampton
Massachusetts 01060
USA

A catalogue record for this book
is available from the British Library

Library of Congress Cataloguing in Publication Data

Gender divisions and working time in the new economy : changing patterns of work, care and public policy in Europe and North America / edited by Diane Perrons ... [et al.].
    p. cm. – (Globalization and welfare)
  Includes bibliographical references.
  1. Sexual division of labor–United States. 2. Sexual division of labor–Europe. 3. Hours of labor–United States. 4. Hours of labor–Europe. 5. Work and family–United States. 6. Work and family–Europe. 7. United States–Economic conditions. 8. Europe–Economic conditions. I. Perrons, Diane. II. Series.

HD6060.65.U5G46 2006
306.3'615'091821—dc22

2005049823

ISBN-13: 978 1 84542 020 8 (cased)
ISBN-10: 1 84542 020 9 (cased)

Printed and bound in Great Britain by MPG Books Ltd, Bodmin, Cornwall

Contents

Figures, tables and boxes

FIGURES

TABLES

BOXES

Contributors

EDITORS

Diane Perrons is director of the gender institute and a reader in economic geography and gender studies at the London School of Economics. Her research focuses on social and spatial divisions in the new global economy, paying particular attention to gender and regional inequalities. She is author of *Globalization and Social Change; People and Places in a Divided World* (Routledge, 2004) and co-editor of *Making Gender Work* (Open University Press, 1996). She is a coordinator of the ESRC seminar series 2005–2007 on Gender, Work and Life in the New Global Economy.

Linda McDowell is professor of human geography in the School of Geography and the Environment at the University of Oxford and Professorial Fellow at St John's College. Her research interests are in the intersection of economic restructuring, labour market change and new class and gender divisions in contemporary Britain. She has undertaken several studies of labour market change in Britain including *Capital Culture* (Blackwell, 1997), *Redundant Masculinities?* (Blackwell, 2003) and *Hard Labour* (UCL Press, forthcoming). She is a coordinator of the ESRC seminar series on Gender, Work and Life in the New Global Economy, with Diane Perrons.

Colette Fagan is co-director of the European Work and Employment Research Centre and professor of sociology at the University of Manchester. Her research focuses on gender relations in employment and domestic life, with a particular focus on cross-national comparative analysis. Her publications include *Part-time Prospects: an International Comparison* (edited with Jackie O'Reilly, 1998, Routledge), *Women's Employment in Europe: Trends and Prospects* (with Jill Rubery and Mark Smith, 1999, Routledge) and various papers on work-time issues including 'The temporal re-organisation of employment and household rhythm of work schedules: the implications for gender and class relations'. The American Behavioural Scientist (2001) and 'Gender and working-time in industrialised countries' (in J. Messenger (ed.), *Finding the Balance: Work Time and Workers' Needs and Preferences*, Milton Park: Routledge).

Kath Ray is a research fellow at the Policy Studies Institute. Her research interests include welfare to work policies, gender and work-life balance, race equality policies and gender and racialized identities. She completed her PhD at the University of Manchester in 2000 and has since held research positions at the University of Manchester and University College, London.

Kevin Ward is reader in geography at the School of The Environment and Development of the University of Manchester. He is co-author of *Spaces of Work. Global Capitalism and the Geographies of Labour* (SAGE Publications, 2003), *Urban Sociology, Capitalism and Network Modernity* (Macmillan, 2003) and *Managing Employment Change: The New Realities of Work* (Oxford University Press, 2002). He is also a co-editor of *City of Revolution: Restructuring Manchester* (Manchester University Press, 2002) and over 30 articles and book chapters. His research interests are state reorganization, the politics of urban development, territorial governance, and labour market restructuring.

CONTRIBUTORS

Susan Baines is a senior research associate in the Centre for Social and Business Informatics, University of Newcastle upon Tyne. She has more than ten years' experience of applied social research and evaluation. Her work has been broadly concerned with economic restructuring, technological innovation and family life, and she has published extensively on those themes. She was principal investigator of a study on the work–life balance for self-employed parents under the Joseph Rowntree Foundation Work and Family Life Programme.

Ann Bergman is a senior lecturer in working life science at the University of Karlstad. Her research area is gender and work. In her dissertation she studied processes of segregation and integration in different types of organisations and job structures.

Jean-Yves Boulin is a sociologist, a researcher at the National Centre for Scientific Research (CNRS) and based at the Interdisciplinary Research Institute in Socio-Economy (IRIS) at the Paris-Dauphine University. His research interests focus on a broad range of working-time and time-related issues, including regulation of working time, the relations between working time and the other social times, time use studies, social organization of time and local time policies. He is member of the editorial committee of the ETUI journal *Transfer*, and of *Futuribles*, a French journal of future studies.

Berit Brandth is a professor at the Department of Sociology and Political Science at the Norwegian University of Science and Technology in Trondheim, Norway. She is also affiliated with the Norwegian Centre for Rural Research. Her research focuses on gender, work and care politics, where one important focus has been fathers and parental leave. She is the author (with Elin Kvande) of the book *Flexible Fathers* (in Norwegian), and co-editor of *Gender, Bodies and Work* (Ashgate Publishing, 2005). Her research topics also include gender in agriculture- and forestry-based work which she has studied through such inroads as technology, organization, family and the agricultural media.

Michaela Brockmann completed her MSc in Comparative Social Research at the University of Oxford in 1998. She is now a research officer at the Thomas Coram Research Unit, Institute of Education, University of London. Her main interests include the integration of paid work and the family over the life course and she has been working on a number of cross-national research projects, funded by the EU, the Department of Health, and the ESRC. She is currently undertaking a PhD, examining the work and family 'careers' of childcare workers in Britain and Germany.

Brendan Burchell is a senior lecturer in the Faculty of Social and Political sciences at the University of Cambridge. His main research area concerns the interdisciplinary study of the relationship between labour markets and individual well-being, in particular job insecurity and work intensification. His publications include the book *Job Insecurity and Work Intensification* (Routledge, 2002).

James Cornford is a senior lecturer in the University of Newcastle upon Tyne Business School and co-director of the Centre for Social and Business Informatics. His research is focused around a number of themes including: the design, development and deployment of information systems in the public realm (including higher education and local government); the implications of the uptake and use of information and communication technologies for urban and regional development; and the industrial structure of the media industries.

Rosemary Crompton is professor of sociology at City University London. Her previous books include *Restructuring Gender Relations and Employment* (Oxford University Press, 1999), *Women and Work in Modern Britain* (Oxford University Press, 1997) and *Renewing Class Analysis* (Blackwell, 2000). Her current project, Class, Gender, Employment and Family, is part of the ESRC GeNet network (www.genet.ac.uk).

Simon Duncan is professor in comparative social policy at the University of Bradford. His current research interests lie in the area of family lives and social policy, especially in parenting, partnering and the work–life balance; marriage, cohabitation and the law; and in the comparative analysis of gender inequality in welfare states. Before this he worked on the relative success and failure of different European housing systems. Recent books include *Marriage, Cohabitation and the Law* (Hart, 2005, with A. Barlow, G. James and A. Park) and *Analysing Families* (Routledge, 2003, edited with A. Carling and R. Edwards).

Jeanne Fagnani is Research Director at the Centre National de la Recherche Scientifique (MATISSE, University of Paris 1). She is currently the French partner of the European team 'Transitions' which is conducting a three-year cross-national comparative research. Her latest publications include *Fathers and Mothers: Dilemmas of the Work–Life Balance, A Comparative Study in Four European Countries* (with M. Fine-Davis, D. Giovannini, L. Hojgaard and H. Clarke, Kluwer Academic Publishers, 2004) and 'Schwestern oder entfernte Kusinen? Deutsche und französische Familienpolitik im Vergleich', in W. Neumann (ed.), *Welche Zukunft für den Sozialstaat? Reformpolitik in Frankreich und Deutschland* (Leske und Budrich, 2004).

Melissa Fisher is assistant professor of Anthropology in the Department of Sociology and Anthropology at Georgetown University. She received her PhD in cultural anthropology from Columbia University. For her dissertation Dr Fisher conducted ethnographic fieldwork and archival research in New York City where she examined the career, networking and mentoring practices of the first generation of Wall Street women. She is currently transforming her study into a book. She is also the co-editor of a volume entitled *Frontiers of Capital: Ethnographic Reflections on the New Economy* (Duke University Press, 2006).

Lena Gonäs is professor of working life science at Karlstad University. Her research area is in labour market relations, gender segregation and employment policies. She has for many years been working at the National Institute for Working Life and is the scientific leader for a large multidiciplinary research project on Gender and Work, that is being reported during 2005.

Irene Hardill is professor of economic geography at the Graduate School, College of Business, Law and Social Sciences, Nottingham Trent University. Her research concerns the juggling of paid and unpaid work (unpaid caring activity as well as voluntary action) and household decision making. Recent publications include *Gender, Migration and the Dual Career Household* (Routledge, 2002).

Hazel Johnstone has a BA in Social Anthropology and Sociology from Hull, an MSc in Social Anthropology from LSE and has been the manager of the Gender Institute at LSE since its inception. She oversaw the practical arrangements for the seminar series Work, Life and Time in the New Economy, as well as helping with the production of this book. She is also managing editor of the *European Journal of Women's Studies* in her spare time.

Elin Kvande is a professor in work and organization studies at the Department of Sociology and Political Science at the Norwegian University of Science and Technology in Trondheim, Norway. Her research focuses on gender, work and organization, where she especially has written about flexible time cultures and gendered organizations. She is co-editor of *Gender, Bodies and Work* (Ashgate Publishing, 2005). Her research topics also include welfare state policies, where one important focus has been fathers and parental leave. She is the author (with Berit Brandth) of the book *Flexible Fathers* (in Norwegian).

Marie-Thérèse Letablier is a sociologist and research director in the Centre National de la Recherche Scientifique in Paris. Her main research interests include work, family and gender issues from a European and a comparative perspective. She has been involved in several European research networks. Her publications include *Families and Family Policies in Europe* (with Linda Hantrais, Longman, 1996), *Familles et travail: contraintes et arbitrages* (with J. Fagnani, la Documentation Française, 2001) and 'Work and family balance: a new challenge for politics in France', in J.Z. Giele and H. Holst (eds), *Changing Life Patterns in Western Industrial Societies* (Elsevier, 2003).

Joost van Loon is professor of media analysis at the Institute for Cultural Analysis at Nottingham Trent University. His research concerns risk, media, technology, culture and everyday spaces. He has over 60 international publications, among which are *Risk and Technological Culture* (Routledge, 2002) and *The Risk Society and Beyond* (co-edited with Barbara Adam and Ulrich Beck, Sage, 2000). He is also co-editor of *Space and Culture*.

Jo Morris is senior equality and employment rights officer at the Trades Union Congress with more than 20 years experience of equality work in Britain and Europe, specializing in equal pay, part-time work, sexual harassment, working time organization and work–life balance. Jo combines a deep experience of policy-making roles – from the first UK legal challenge that established rights for part-time workers in 1982 to being a member of the social partner negotiating team for the European Directive on Part-time Work

– with 20 years' practical experience of implementing innovative working-time arrangements in the public and private sectors. Jo has had a particular interest in developing mutually beneficial working-time models, particularly in the context of the gendered division of labour, and has managed work–life balance projects in local government, the Inland Revenue and other public sector organizations.

Anita Nyberg has been working at the National Institute for Working Life, Stockholm, Sweden since 1998, as a professor in gender perspective on work and economy. In 1995 she was appointed secretary of a governmental committee on the distribution of economic power and economic resources between women and men. This committee worked for three years between 1995 and 1998 and resulted in 13 different reports. She has been working as a lecturer in economics in the Economics Department and as a researcher at Theme Technology and Social Change at the University of Linköping. Her main areas of interest is women's and men's paid and unpaid work and their incomes.

Jane Pillinger is an independent researcher and policy advisor working in the areas of equality and diversity, working time and public service quality and is currently advising a number of Irish public sector agencies in the areas of equality, disability, health and homeless services. She has taught at Leeds University and Leeds Metropolitan University and was formerly the head of trade union studies at Northern College. Jane has been a specialist advisor to the House of Commons Select Committee on Employment and the Select Committee on Trade and Industry with a particular emphasis on flexible working time. In the last few years she has been working with the Public Services International and the International Labour Organisation on gender pay equity. She is author of *Feminising the Market: Women's Pay and Employment in the European Community* (Macmillan, 1992), *Working Time in Europe* (ETUI and EPSU, 2002), and *Quality in Public Services* (European Foundation for the Improvement of Living and Working Conditions, 2001).

Silvia Posocco is tutorial fellow at the LSE Gender Institute. She was recently awarded her PhD in Secrecy, Subjectivity and Sociality: an ethnography of conflict in Petén, Guatemala (1999–2000). Her research interests lie in the areas of anthropological theory, notably epistemology, hermeneutics, ontology, nihilism; anthropology of secrecy; anthropology of Guatemala; violence and conflict; anthropology of development/governmentality; the anthropology of gender and sexualities; gender theory. Silvia designed and managed the web page for the ESRC seminar series Work, Life and Time in the New Economy, where early drafts of some of these papers were presented.

Harriet B. Presser is distinguished university professor in the Department of Sociology, University of Maryland, College Park. She is Past President of the Population Association of America (1989). In 2002, Professor Presser was elected a fellow of the American Association for the Advancement of Science 'for innovative research on issues of population, labour force, gender, and social inequality; for exceptional institution building; and for outstanding service to demographic and sociological societies'. In addition to conducting basic research in social demography, Professor Presser studies population and family policy issues from a national and international perspective. Her recent publications include: *Working in a 24/7 Economy: Challenges for American Families* (Russell Sage Foundation, 2003) and 'The female share of weekend employment: a study of 16 countries' (with Janet C. Gornik), *Monthly Labor Review*, 128 (August 2005): 41–53.

Teresa Rees is a pro vice-chancellor at Cardiff University where she is also a professor in the School of Social Sciences. Her research focuses on gender mainstreaming in education, training and labour market policies. More recently she has conducted work on women and scientific careers in the European Union, acting as rapporteur for a number of European Commission high-level expert groups. She was a co-author of the Greenfield report on women in science, engineering and technology in the UK 'SET Fair'. She also advises the National Assembly for Wales on equality policies and is a member of the DTI's Commission for Equality and Human Rights Steering Group. She was elected an academician of the Academy of Social Sciences in 2002 and awarded a CBE for services to higher education and equal opportunities in 2003.

Kerstin Rosenberg is senior lecturer in gender studies at the University of Karlstad. She has a PhD in business economics and in her dissertation she studied the results from different job evaluation projects in Sweden. Her research areas are gender and wage formation with special reference to job evaluation.

Sarah Walsh is a research associate in the Centre for Social and Business Informatics, University of Newcastle upon Tyne. She largely focuses on qualitative research methods, specializing in ethnography. Her research includes the perceptions and expectations of technology within health and social care settings; user-perspectives on public services and multi-agency working within the public sector, specifically within children's services.

Acknowledgements

The editors wish to thank the Economic and Social Research Council (ESRC award R45126511) for funding the series on which this collection is based, all those who presented and contributed to the discussions in the six seminars and the authors who have contributed their text with special thanks to those writing in their second language. We all wish to thank Ralph Kinnear for 'English proofing' the final text; Hazel Johnstone, Gender Institute, London School of Economics for her administrative support with the seminar series and with the preparation of the final typescript; Claudia Soares, University of Urbino for help collating references, Silvia Posocco for designing and managing the web page that accompanied the seminar series and, finally, special thanks to Catherine Elgar for her support and encouragement to produce this collection.

We are grateful to Lawrence Erlbaum Associates, New Jersey for granting us permission to reprint Harriet Presser's chapter which originally appeared as 'Employment in a 24/7 Economy: Challenges for the Family' in Ann C. Crouter and Alan Booth (eds) *Work–Family Challenges for Low-Income Parents and Their Children*. Duke University Press granted permission to print Melissa Fisher's chapter, which appears as 'Navigating Wall Street Women's Gendered Networks in the New Economy' in *Frontiers of Capital: Ethnographic Reflections on the New Economy* (copyright 2006, Duke University Press, all rights reserved). Every effort has been made to contact copyright holders for their permission to reprint materials in this book. The publishers would be grateful to hear from any copyright holder who is not here acknowledged and will undertake to rectify any errors or omissions in future editions of this book.

The usual disclaimers apply.

1. Introduction: work, life and time in the new economy

Diane Perrons, Linda McDowell, Colette Fagan, Kath Ray and Kevin Ward

The organization and composition of paid work and the structure of families have changed dramatically in recent decades and so too has the context within which individuals and families organize their lives. Contemporary times are characterized by the widespread, albeit uneven, use of information and computing technologies and greater economic, political and social communications between peoples and between states. As a consequence states in Northern and Western Europe have become more homogenous and moved closer to the United States in terms of their economies and working patterns. The service sector has become dominant, paid work has become feminized and more flexible and families are more varied in their composition. The significance of the male breadwinner, female caregiver model, dominant in the mid-twentieth century, has declined in both Europe and the United States, but the ensuing care deficit has not been resolved and to varying degrees growing numbers of both dual- and single-earning households struggle to find time to combine paid work with caring (Heyman, 2000). These changes result from the interrelations between the shifting economic and political context, in particular a more competitive and global economic environment and changing lifestyle preferences with regard to living and working arrangements.

In advanced industrial societies new lifestyles, forms and patterns of work became increasing apparent towards the end of the twentieth century and terms such as 'the risk society', 'late modernity', 'knowledge society' and 'new economy' were used to portray the new era. The global dimension of change was also noted and increasing references were made to concepts such as 'one world', 'globalization', 'global economy' and 'global transformation' to depict the increasing interconnections between people and places, and to varying degrees the implications of such relations (Perrons, 2004a). While overall there have been massive increases in wealth, especially in Western nations, attention has also been drawn to some of the negative consequences of these changes in terms of widening economic inequalities between and within countries (Milanovic, 2002; Wade, 2001; Piketty and Saez, 2003; Rifkin, 2004) and the suffering endured by many people, especially women and children in poorer countries (Bhavani et al., 2003; UNICEF, 2004).

Collectively we refer to these phenomena as the 'new economy' and this book aims to explore how these macro-level changes are affecting the micro organization of daily life, with particular reference to working patterns and gender divisions in Northern and Western Europe and the United States. We also consider the various policy responses to these changes and the extent to which they promote greater gender equity, recognizing the potentially heterogeneous gender interests of different groups of women and men as well as the diverse patterning of gender relations and divisions across different social domains.

This introduction identifies some of the key issues, and outlines the context in which all countries have experienced change to a greater or lesser degree. The issues are explored in depth in the chapters, which consist of case studies of specific countries – France, Norway, Sweden, the UK and the USA – and thematic comparative studies, across Europe and the US. The majority of the chapters derive originally from the ESRC seminar series on Work, Life and Time in the New Economy',[1] and reflecting these contributions the collection is focused on the analysis of Western societies.

THE NEW ECONOMY

The last ten years have seen academics in a range of disciplines, as well as the press, begin to use the term the 'new economy'. However, there is little agreement about what is meant by it. Orthodox economists use the term narrowly to refer to the mid- to late-1990s boom, which fuelled and was fuelled by the growth of dot.com companies, but in contrast to the past, wage increases were only moderate, generating a unique period of inflation-free growth (Greenspan, 1998). With the slowdown in the rates of economic growth and the collapse of the dot.com boom this interpretation has been rather discredited but the idea of a high-technology knowledge-based 'new economy' remains important, with writers such as Manuel Castells (2000) and Diane Coyle and Danny Quah (2002) emphasizing how ICTs (information and communication technologies) have revolutionized the organization of business and commerce. Promotion of 'knowledge' work as crucial to economic success remains a central tenet of EU policy most clearly expressed in the Lisbon Strategy (European Parliament, 2000).

More pessimistic interpretations of the new economy however refer to growing risk and insecurity (Beck, 2000), falling fertility (Esping-Andersen, 2002), the fragmentation of communities (Sennett, 1998), and the erosion of traditional social rhythms and practices, as the boundaries around work dissolve, raising the intensity of work as people are never 'off-line'.

Danny Quah (1996) analytically links the positive and negative dimensions of the new economy, and argues that its emergence is associated with widening social divisions. In his analysis some of the essential characteristics of the knowledge-based economy which contribute to economic growth, also increase economic inequality. For Quah, a knowledge good is anything that can in principle be digitized and people producing these goods are knowledge workers. Thus pop and rock singers as well as architects, to the extent that their designs can be digitized, are knowledge workers as well as those working more directly with ICTs. Knowledge goods are infinitely expansible, that is they can be replicated at very low cost; and they are non-rival – thus one person's consumption does not prevent another's. These properties should tend to generate greater equality. However as Quah (1996) explains, knowledge goods are also characterized by increasing economies of scale because although they can be replicated and thus have very low marginal costs, the cost of the first product, for example a new computer game, can be very high, thus large firms tend to dominate the market and having done so they create a range of related products, locking consumers in to their particular brand. A further property is the superstar effect, which refers to consumers' preferences for products of greater renown even though they may be barely distinguishable from competitors. Given the weightlessness of knowledge products there are few constraints on market size so the producers can capture an increasing share of the market. As knowledge goods and knowledge workers become more important in the economy, social and spatial inequalities will tend to increase. Qhah implies that these inequalities are rather random and in the new economy social mobility is greater such that the poor have chances of becoming rich. However, ethnicity, sexual orientation, class and gender typically code work, so the widening social divisions are likely to reinforce existing structural inequalities in the labour force. Gender inequalities are particularly likely to be intensified in the new economy owing to the expansion of carework to replace women's domestic labour as they enter employment in growing numbers.

Carework is typically low paid in market economies because it is highly labour intensive with limited scope for productivity gains, which perhaps helps to explain why, despite the proliferation of work–life balance policies, gender inequality in the labour market continues (Perrons, 2004b). In the case of marketized domestic services, class divisions arising from the working class servicing the middle class also generate divisions between women. In addition to these changes relating to the composition of employment, there have been contradictory changes in the contractual status of employees associated with the implementation of protective employment legislation on the one hand and deregulation and individualized contracts on the other. These developments are associated with neo-liberalism but the outcomes are contingent, hence the value of comparative empirical investigation.

One of the drivers of contemporary change is the worldwide supremacy of neo-liberalism or the Washington consensus,[2] referring collectively to trade liberalization, economic deregulation (though in the area of gender equity there is more regulation – see Walby, 2002), privatization, active labour market policies and fiscal discipline in conjunction with the spread of formal democracy. States adhering to this philosophy are then constrained in terms of their freedom to manage their economies, and firms are compelled to operate within the intensely competitive global market, which shapes their internal working patterns and practices.

Competition is pervasive; neither private firms nor the state can afford any slack or porosity in their organizations. Firms trading internationally have to be competitive in global markets and so make similar demands on their suppliers, including the state, prompting pressure for cost savings, privatization and rationalization of public sector services (Streeck, 1999). Indeed these competitive pressures have contributed to widening economic inequality and social divisions within and between states as well as to new forms of work and the feminization of employment.

In all sectors the regularly employed workforce is pared down to a minimum, supplemented by more flexibly employed workers, whose working times vary with fluctuations in demand. Correspondingly work intensity has increased in terms of the speed of work and tightness of deadlines (Green, 2003).

Contemporary management practices can internalize the pressures by, in effect, turning employees into their own managers who are 'held responsible for their sales, their products, their branch, their store, etc. as though they were independent contractors, even though in reality they are simple wage labourers' (Bourdieu, 1998: 2) which intensifies the working environment and contributes to ideas about the time squeeze. Thus employees also experience pressure from their colleagues as well as clients (Burchell, this volume); and as Julia Brannen (2005) comments, as we seemingly take more control over our time, so time takes control of us and our apparent control over working time only means that we spend longer working. More polemically it has been suggested that 'the very best workers are now those who never sleep, never consume, never have children, and never spend time socialising outside of work' (Carnoy, 2000: 143). While fertility has fallen and remains below replacement level in the EU25 at 1.6 (US, 2.07) (Eurostat, 2004b) and remains a policy concern in terms of the future labour supply, in reality contemporary workers, especially the middle-aged, are likely to have caring responsibilities for either children or the elderly and in many cases for both, generating a potential caring deficit as women, the traditional carers, have become more active in the labour market.[3]

All of these changes in the conditions under which people live and labour make it more difficult to realize equal opportunities or family-friendly policies as people feel under pressure not to exercise their entitlements to breaks, time off or holidays. For those on non-permanent contracts, the choice is often a more straightforward one, as they may have few, if any, entitlements to exercise.

These arguments have so far been presented in rather abstract terms and as though changes largely reflect market logic, but all markets operate within social and political frameworks and institutions. Correspondingly they are open to modification by prevailing cultural norms and political and social pressures, including state legislation and regulation as well as action by trade unions. In the European Union these social and political frameworks are shaped both by supranational strategies relating to economic stability, growth and employment, as well as by country-specific policy regimes and institutional arrangements.[4] Thus while European Union countries may share some ideals relating to the European Social Model, which differs from the more neo-liberal philosophy prevailing in the Unites States, the actual policies and frameworks in different states will continue to vary and are discussed in more detail in the context of specific countries in the chapters to follow.

STATE POLICIES

As a consequence of this more competitive environment the sustainability and desirability of the European Social Model, which sought to combine market efficiency with social solidarity, is being challenged. While social cohesion remains in parts of the political vocabulary, the driving force of policy is undoubtedly productivity and economic growth. The European Union compares its performance negatively with the US[5] in respect of employment and growth, and with Asia, especially China and India, where productivity can be similar but wages a minute fraction of those in the West. To promote growth the European Union developed and subsequently endorsed the Lisbon Strategy (2000) through which it sought to become 'the most dynamic and competitive knowledge based economy in the world, capable of sustaining economic growth with more and better jobs and greater social cohesion and respect for the environment' (EC, 2004a). However this strategy was to run alongside the Growth and Stability Pact adopted in 1997, which is directed towards securing budgetary discipline and the short-term stability of the currency, and it is not clear that these strategies are compatible (see Arnaud, 2003). The Growth and Stability Pact is focused on the nominal economy and issues such as low inflation, balanced budgets and limited public expenditure, while the Lisbon strategy is oriented towards growth and employment expansion. Employment targets are specific: expanding the overall employment rate to 70 per cent, and the female rate to 60 per cent by 2010. To realize the female rate, further targets for childcare were set in 2002 of 90 per cent for children between three years old and the statutory school age, and 33 per cent for children under three.[6] Clearly such targets are likely to require an increase in public expenditure, something limited by the growth and stability policy.

Thus contradictions exist within economic policy and between economic and social policies at the supranational level and it has been argued that 'if we want to preserve and improve our social model we have to adapt it'. This statement was made in the Kok (2004) report, which makes renewed arguments for further liberalizing the EU economy and the labour market through increased adaptability or flexibility. The old European social model in terms of more regulated employment relations therefore seems to be waning and displaced by a growing similarity, especially in terms of flexible and more intensive working patterns, with the United States, where there has been little tradition of collaboration between the social partners.

At the same time however, and apparently running against this trend, EU social policy is also expanding into new areas. For example the EU is extending its area of competency into the family by developing a number of policies concerned with reconciling paid work and family life, an area previously considered outside of its remit. In addition to the targets for childcare the EU Strategy for Gender Equality (EC, 2000b) has implemented gender mainstreaming, which requires that all policies be examined for their gender differentiated effects, in addition to more specific actions concerned with the gender pay gap, civil rights and gender stereotypes. In this respect the EU is similar to other supranational institutions including the United Nations, the World Bank and the OECD, all of which have expressed concern about gender equality and women's empowerment and, in the case of the latter, reconciling paid work and family life, something also highlighted in the EU's gender equality strategy.[7]

It is likely that these measures are motivated as much by the economic concern for an expanded workforce together with demographic unease about low fertility and aging as by an intrinsic desire for gender equity. For example the OECD (2002) in its series of reports, 'Babies and Bosses' recognizes that family-friendly policies can increase the living standards of parents and children and thus are a goal in themselves in terms of enhancing gender equality and child development, but nevertheless clearly states that: 'getting the right policy in place will promote other societal goals ... [in particular will] ... allow aggregate labour supply and employment to be increased' (OECD,

2002: 5). Likewise firms in both the US and EU have commercial reasons for pursuing diversity strategies (see Fisher, this volume).

The unresolved tension or conflict between economic and social policy remains however, as increasing care provision in a more liberal, competitive and global economy would require significant increases in public expenditure owing to the inherent characteristics of carework, in particular its low productivity as described in traditional neo-classical terms (Himmelweit, 2005: Himmelweit and Perrons, 2005). Consequently carework tends to be underprovided in market economies or restricted to an elite able to meet the high costs. Thus to achieve the childcare targets state-subsidized provision will almost certainly be required. Yet the state has difficulty raising funds from the private sector given the competitive environment, and is limited in its capacity to raise debt given the restrictions on government spending and budget deficits in the Growth and Stability Pact, or in the case of the US from its adherence to neo-liberalism in general and the preference for regressive cuts in taxation exercized during the Bush presidency (from 2001 to the present).

From a feminist perspective neither changes in work organization and family composition nor the introduction of apparently gender-aware policies are entirely unambiguously positive developments. Whilst on the one hand, policies that take a holistic view of the economy by taking cognisance of reproductive work (Elson, 1998) and genuinely empower women by enabling them to lead 'lives they have reason to value' (Sen, 2000: 3) are clearly welcome, it is not clear that the contemporary interest in care by national and supranational organizations meets these aspirations. Indeed it is important to consider whether current policies are driven as much by the desire to expand the employment rate and enhance economic growth in the quest for a competitive knowledge-based economy as by a desire for equality, and to consider what implications this has for achieving gender equity. The measures would seem to be progressive for women; however it is important to consider what the outcomes are for different groups of women (and men) positioned differently in economic terms. Without wider and more deep-seated changes in the gender composition of employment, in particular in relation to segregation and the monetary rewards given to jobs disproportionately done by women, in the valuation of carework and care relations and in the domestic division of labour between women and men, increasing female employment may lead to widening inequalities between women and to an increase in women's overall workload.

GENDER DIVISIONS IN CARING AND PAID WORK

Research on gender patterns in working time shows that men in households with children tend to work longer hours than men in general, and typically their wives or partners work less, even when employed full-time (Fagan, 2001; Anxo and Boulin, 2004). Nevertheless if paid work and caring work are combined, women on average work longer hours than men and it is almost invariably women that make the compromises necessary to fit paid work around the family and who experience the anxiety and stress of combining these roles (Moen, 2003; Eurostat, 2004; McDowell et al., 2005 and Crompton and Brockmann, this volume). The details of this picture vary within and between European countries and between these countries and the United States, but the broad trends are consistent (Messenger, 2004). The experiences of individuals also vary depending on their actual working hours and the level of employer and state support, both of which vary between countries. There are additional variations between employers and regions within the same country, as the policies of firms vary and are only partly conditioned by the national context, and the application of national and firm policies can vary regionally depending on the actual resources available.

In terms of paid employment gender divisions are also persistent. Both vertical and horizontal employment segregation remain entrenched. Segregation in employment builds upon and probably reinforces gender stereotypes, with women being seen as naturally suited to caring work but out of place in jobs dealing with complex machinery, involving physical labour, or in managerial positions, especially as the managers and supervisors of men. Only 21 per cent of the EU15 workforce has a woman as their immediate superior while 63 per cent have a man, the remainder having no immediate supervisor. Women managers and supervisors are much more likely to be supervising other women, and less than 10 per cent of employed men have a woman manager (Fagan and Burchell, 2002). In terms of horizontal segregation women are over-represented in activities relating to nurturing, care, clerical work and sales, while men are over-represented in sectors and occupations involving money, management and machinery. For example women hold 66 per cent of clerical and sales jobs, while men hold 80 per cent or more of jobs in the armed services, craft and related trades, plant and machine operators, and 66 per cent of skilled agricultural and fishery jobs. Further, while women have been gaining entry into professional jobs, segregation also exists among the professions, with men being over-represented in mathematical and engineering professions and women over-represented in health and education. These statistics are for the EU15 as a whole, and while the degree of segregation varies between member states, all share this general pattern (Fagan and Burchell, 2002; Rubery et al., 1999). Similar patterns of vertical and horizontal segregation exist in the USA and in both cases contribute to the continuing gender pay gap between women and men (Anker, 1998).

In the USA the drift to the right in politics has led to successive cuts in welfare expenditure and taxes, as a consequence of which, although employment rates are high, wages have not increased by a corresponding amount, leading to an expansion of the working poor, many of whom are single mothers pressed into the labour market through the Welfare To Work programme. Work has become more flexible by contract and in terms of working hours, and despite lack of formal maternity provision the US has higher female participation rates compared to European countries. However a glass ceiling remains. Women hold only eight CEO-ships, 13.6 per cent of board seats and 15.7 per cent of top executive jobs in the Fortune 500. These statistics formed the essence of the '85 Broads campaign' and the idea of holding a women's 'buycot day' in order to demonstrate the economic power that women could exert as consumers, given that 85 per cent of all purchases in the USA are either made or influenced by women[8] (see Fisher, this volume). Similarly in Norway there was a campaign for women to stop work from mid October each year to reflect the fact that women on average continue to earn only 86 per cent as much as men.

Given this situation it is clear that simply expanding the female employment rate without addressing issues of employment composition and pay will not by itself resolves gender inequality. Similarly developing flexible hours and flexible services (Boulin; Morris and Pillinger this volume) may better enable people to combine paid work with caring, but not be sufficient to challenge gender divisions of labour in work and at home and thus promote more deep-seated gender equality.

While many states are now assuming an adult citizen rather than a male breadwinner model in terms of their policies (see Lewis, 2002) examining the actual position of women in the labour market makes it clear that the reality is more likely to be a one-and-a-half earner model with women dispropor-tionately making the career compromises and putting at risk their long-term economic well-being. At the same time however, even with many women devoting a considerable part of their time to caring, a deficit nevertheless remains and these concerns are intensified by the changing composition of the family which has been the traditional source of care.

CARE DEFICIT

Concern about the caring deficit has been heightened by dramatic changes in family composition. The statistics almost speak for themselves. To varying degrees across the European Union the numbers divorcing, the proportion of children born outside marriage, and the proportion of one-person households have been increasing while the numbers marrying have declined. In the EU the average divorce rate is 1.9 per 1000 but there are wide variations, with low levels in Southern Europe and higher levels elsewhere. For example the divorce rate was 0.9 per cent in Spain, compared to 3 per cent in Belgium in 2002, which is closer to the US figure of 3.9 (2004) where nearly 50 per cent of marriages end in divorce (National Statistics, 2004; NVSS, 2004; Whitehead and Popenoe, 2004). In fact in the US the divorce rate is now declining following a peak in the early 1980s, but this is partly because fewer people marry. These changes can be viewed positively, as people are less bound by tradition and freer to author their own lives (see Hardill and van Loon, this volume), or negatively in terms of heralding a crisis in the family, both intrinsically and because of the role played by the family as the traditional provider of care regardless of normative values about the family as an institution.

Changes in household and family structures also include an increase in dual-earning households which are now the dominant form among those of working age in the EU15, and the rate of increase in dual-earning households with at least one child has been particularly marked in most states during the 1990s (Eurostat, 2002). In the EU the modal pattern among these households (with and without children) is for the man to work long full-time hours (40+) and the woman to work long part-time hours (20+). However there are significant variations between countries, with the UK having a highly polarized gender division with men working very long hours and women very short hours (Fagan, 2001; Bishop, 2004). France has a more balanced distribution and the smallest proportion of men working over 40 hours, partly as a consequence of the 35-hour week (see Fagnani and Letablier, this volume). There has also been an increase in the number of single-parent earner households; all of these changes reflecting the social expectation that all people will be labour market active. In the United States there has been an increase in the diversity of working hours with more people working very few and more people working very many hours, as well as greater variation in the times that people work (Presser, this volume). In fact the number of hours worked by dual-earner households with children there has remained stable between 1992 and 2002, averaging at 79 a week, but there has been an increase in the number of these households as well as in single-parent earner households (EPF, 2004). These are the households that experience time pressures and in some cases greater stress, even though gender divisions in working hours remain.

Thus families are becoming increasingly fluid and household working hours have been increasing. This has resulted in a growing recognition that the male breadwinner, female caregiver model is no longer a social reality and is neither economically desirable nor sustainable (Esping-Andersen, 1999; Lewis, 2001). Nevertheless the costs of providing care are considerable, especially in the context of public sector financial stringency. How this ensuing care deficit is addressed varies between countries and this has different implications for the gender division of labour and for gender equity. Some of these implications are drawn out in the chapters that follow.

COMPARATIVE ANALYSIS

Although many of the processes in terms of the organization of work and work-life balance policies discussed above are universal in their existence, they are not universal in terms of their effects, and so rigorous and differentiated academic inquiry is required to document how these patterns vary over time and between countries. Even though the power of nation-states may have been redefined in the context of a global economy with supranational institutions, economic and social policy continues to be nationally differentiated. State policies reflect different national traditions, cultures and contexts and thus influence working patterns, family choices and gender roles in different ways. These differences have significant implications for the overall levels of economic inequality within states, the degree of gender equity, and on a more practical level the actual working times, provision of eldercare and childcare: factors which shape the specific context in which contemporary families negotiate their household strategies and gender division of labour between paid and unpaid work.

While there may be some trends towards convergence in social policies emanating from adherence to the neo-liberal consensus, exploring continuing differences between states provides an important challenge to the idea that the move to neo-liberalism is inevitable irreversible and undifferentiated. In reality, commitment to the neo-liberal model varies and is far more diluted in countries rooted in corporatist and social democratic traditions that lie behind the European Social Model in comparison to the UK or the US. The contributions to this book examine a range of issues such as the degree of work inequality, the patterning of working hours, degrees of work intensity and stress, cultures of parenting, the provision of childcare, and equal opportunities policies across different countries of the EU and the US. They thus contribute to our understanding of spatial variations in gender divisions and how these are shaped by different state responses to women's labour market participation across Europe and the US.

THE CHAPTERS

To explore these issues this book includes a range of studies examining how these broader changes are experienced in daily life in different national contexts. The focus is on changing working patterns and how families in different nation-states manage their reproduction from one day to the next and over time, assessing in particular what the impact has been on gender divisions. Potentially the new economy extends the temporal and spatial boundaries of paid work, and correspondingly potentially widens the opportunities for people seeking paid work, especially those with caring responsibilities (though with the risk of work becoming boundless). In reality however, as the more detailed studies indicate, the effects are more complex and differentiated.

The case studies do not address identical issues nor do they address them in the same way. While there are common themes, including new forms of work, new working times, feminization of employment, gender divisions and ways of combining paid work with caring, the national case studies are framed within debates and issues that reflect their specific contexts and consequently highlight the implicit differences between states in terms of social, cultural and political traditions, the existing provision of state supportive care services and contemporary concerns.

The Nordic countries in particular are framed within a social democratic welfare tradition with an adult citizen model and only a weak male breadwinner ethos. Nevertheless the Swedish case studies indicate that gender inequality in pay systems is pervasive and is likely to reappear when the more liberal and individualized pay systems are added on to an existing corporatist collective bargaining framework (Gonäs, Bergman and Rosenberg, this volume). At the same time the ethos of care as a state obligation is clearly evident in both Sweden and Norway. In Sweden, care policies have been developing independently from, indeed almost counter to, the economic trends and continued to expand despite falling levels of employment following the economic crisis of the early 1990s and subsequent membership of the EU in 1995 and adherence to its policies (Nyberg, this volume). Likewise in Norway consistent efforts have been made through state policies to involve fathers in childcare (Brandth and Kvande, this volume). The French case also demonstrates the more corporatist tradition through the resistance to neo-liberal deregulation with the introduction of the 35-hour week,[9] although the reduction in paid work has not been sufficient to lead to any major changes in the gender division of labour outside of the workplace and the continuation of the 35-hour week is itself currently threatened (Fagnani and Letablier, this volume). By contrast the US and the UK reflect the greater flexibility and individualization found in the neo-liberal economies, though there are some structural constraints to degree of flexibility (see Duncan, this volume).

The book is divided into five parts, each preceded by a short introduction, which highlights some of the issues and brings a comparative perspective to bear on the chapters. The overarching themes from the five parts are then drawn together in the conclusion in Chapter 16. In this way we hope to have preserved the depth that single case studies provide while not overlooking the comparative dimension, which makes the different cases so interesting.

Part I explores the changing character of work and working times and whether the popular perceptions of increased intensity and insecurity are matched by quantitative and qualitative evidence and the implications of these changes for health and work–life balance. These issues are explored further in Part II, which also considers the implications of the increase in the feminization of employment in different national contexts for managing work life balance. It clearly demonstrates different national perspectives or responses to the destabilization of the male breadwinner, female carer model, but also how work–life balance issues can be affected by other national policies, in the case of France for example by the reduction in working time motivated by concern with high levels of unemployment. This part also considers the impact of new working times and new employment relations on work–life balance and stress.

The chapters in Part III pursue these issues by focusing on decision making at the household level and the influence of social class, geographical context and state policy in influencing the gender division of labour within the household. Part IV takes a rather different direction by examining the ways in which new technologies and city time policies can be used to deliver local government services more effectively to match the needs of a more feminized and flexible workforce, given both the spatial mismatches between work-places, homes, schools and nurseries, and the associated tensions between the different time schedules of these activities. These spatial and temporal coordination issues become more complex as the number of children in the household increase (Jarvis, 2005; Skinner, 2003). Finally, Part V focuses more directly on policies and processes that promote or impede progress towards gender equality (Rees, this volume).

In the Conclusion we try to draw together the implications of the different case studies and reflect more generally on whether and in what ways contemporary changes in the labour market have altered gender divisions. We try to draw out the significance of different national policies in the context of greater economic homogenization. Although in many ways everyone is inextricably integrated into the global economy, the form of that integration still varies significantly between nation-states and examining the experiences of people in different countries helps to identify the opportunities and tensions in different policy approaches for moving us towards a position of greater gender equity. We argue that this requires a focus on outcomes for different groups of men and women in different structural positions as well as on the possibly contradictory gender effects of policies in different social arenas. In this sense policies are required that not only enable people (women in particular) to meet their practical interests to manage work and life, but also meet more strategic interests of gender equity such as challenging the gendered division of responsibilities for social reproduction; which would allow fathers to share in caring for their children and allow women to be engaged in paid work which is necessary to ensure their economic welfare, given the increase in likelihood that they will at some point in their lives have to be economically independent.

Finally we consider in a more speculative way what kind of social or spatial agenda would promote a sustainable and equitable work–life balance in knowledge-based economies. Are we too trapped or conditioned by our own world and current patterns to envisage a system in which there is a genuinely greater sharing of roles? Or is the current division of labour by task between women and men – although not the association with unequal monetary rewards – the preferred one? Public policies in a wide range of nation-states have changed significantly in terms of their rhetoric, in the range of issues that they now consider within their 'competency' and in terms of practical policies. By exploring the experiences of different countries it is possible to see how divisions of labour between household members, men and women, and between the family, the state and the private sector, vary and the extent to which the different division of responsibilities facilitates a society where differentiation may remain but where differentiation by tasks does not lead to differentiation in economic well-being.

NOTES

1. The exception is the chapter by Harriet Presser. Other papers from the series – Brannen, Doogan, Jarvis, and Rubery, Ward, Grimshaw and Beynon – together with an introduction by the editors which reflects on the different understanding of the new economy, have been published in a special issue of *Time and Society* (2005).
2. See Williamson (2004).
3. Ruth Emerek refers to this as the 'sandwich generation'; see Emerek (1998).
4. These strategies and their associated targets, for example for levels of employment or childcare, are negotiated by member states through the Open Method of Coordination which commits member states to work together towards shared goals but does not seek to homogenize their inherited policy regimes and institutional arrangements.
5. Recent data shows that the EU's employment rate grew at a rate of 0.2 per cent in 2003 compared to 0.9 per cent in the US, the EU employment rate is 63 per cent compared to 69.9 per cent in the US and the unemployment rate is higher 9.1 per cent compared to 6 per cent in the US (European Commission, 2004b).
6. These targets were set in the Barcelona council of 2002.
7. See for example the Millennium Development Goals (UNDP (2003), empowerment strategies and the European Union's Strategy for Gender Equality (EC, 2000b), see also OECD (2002).
8. 85 Broads was originally founded in 1999 as a network for current and former Goldman Sachs women professionals and is now a wider group with women MBAs from the leading graduate business schools and colleges, and women professionals from over 450 companies. The name of the group is a word play on GS's HQ address which is 85 Broad St., New York.

9. In December 2004 some relaxation of the 35-hour working week was introduced with the amount of permitted overtime per year being raised by 40 hours from 180 to 220, and employees will also be encouraged to sell back to their employer the compensatory days off they earn by working more than 35 hours.

PART I

Social and spatial divisions and work–life management in the new economy

While the definition and identification of the new economy remains contested and clearly takes different forms in different states, as this collection illustrates, it is clear that waged work has achieved a currently unsurpassed centrality in the twenty-first century in the economies of the advanced industrial world and in the everyday lives of their inhabitants. Waged work or employment is now seen as important for woman as well as for men, whether these women are or are not mothers. This is a significant shift from the long acceptance that for married women and for mothers it is their unpaid work in the family that defines their economic role. Nowadays many women both want to and expect to work, influenced by rising educational standards, equality agendas and new forms of support mechanisms, both human and technical. And governments increasingly expect women to work, and increasingly welfare state entitlement for women in their roles as mothers or wives is conditional on labour market participation. The nature and resources attached to this expectation varies between welfare state regimes.

This expectation has been explicit for some time in the Nordic social democratic regimes, where labour market participation is explicitly linked to citizenship and comprehensive welfare benefits, including relatively generous parental leave and public childcare systems to support the 'weak breadwinner' gender arrangement (Lewis, 1992), in conjunction with active labour market policies of job creation and training for the unemployed. However welfare reforms in the liberal regimes of the USA and the UK have meant that welfare entitlements are increasingly contingent on labour market participation, but where the policy emphasis on 'welfare-to-work' is more punitive and not underwritten by the same level of public funding of family leave, childcare and other social infrastructure as is found in the Nordic regimes. Between these contrasting examples, a similar shift in government expectations has also emerged in policy reforms in many EU member states – influenced at least in part by the European Employment Strategy policy guidelines to raise women's employment rates – where for example there are increased obligations on single parents and partnered mothers in low-income households to seek employment. The shift in these states too from manufacturing-dominated labour markets to 'new' economies where the service sector is now predominant has also encouraged rising female labour participation rates as the service sector is more typically a female-employing sector than was manufacturing. Thus in most of the 'old' EU nations (the 15 pre-May 2004 states) including the UK, women are now almost half the waged labour force.

The changing sectoral and gender composition of the labour market however is not a singular story of women's advance. The lineaments of the new economy, like the old, are marked by social and spatial inequalities as different places and particular groups of people fare more or less well as economic restructuring transforms class, gender and geographical inequalities. It is clear that labour market participation remains unequal: men as a group work longer hours than women, as the majority of women, especially in Britain, work fewer hours and for less financial reward. A gender pay gap seems to be a persistent and universal feature of the new economy, even in the more equitable Nordic countries where women's greater propensity to be employed in public sector occupations excludes them from the highest-paying jobs of all, which tend to be in the private sector, but nevertheless provides many of them with reasonable wages. This sectoral segregation is mirrored by continuing occupational segregation as women continue to be concentrated into those jobs where employers rely on their 'traditional' skills: the old stereotypical notions that women are 'naturally' kinder, calmer, more caring but less rational than men and so are suited for certain types of work, and do not deserve equal remuneration. Despite women's growing participation, their escape from female ghettos and their continuing assault on the 'old' professions (law, medicine, the City) and the new occupations (the media, cultural industries, high-tech industries, business), the levers of power and the marks of status remain solidly concentrated in the hands of men, as do the extremely high salaries associated with the new 'superstars' of global corporations and media networks.

But inequalities take a class as well as a gendered form in the new economies of Europe and the USA. The reorganisation of work into new patterns – more flexible, less secure, undertaken on a 24/7 basis – in the new consumer-focused economy has increased the concentration of the lowest-paying, least secure forms of 'servicing' work, undertaken by both men and women, often on insecure contracts with few benefits such as paid holidays and sickness benefits. Young men who might once have expected to follow their fathers, or perhaps it is now their grandfathers, into relatively secure and reasonably well-paid manufacturing jobs now have to look for work in the service economy where often women, assumed to be more deferential and less unreliable, as well as cheaper to employ, may be the preferred employees. The old heavy industrial areas of national economies have been particularly adversely affected by manufacturing decline and often fail to attract any but poorly paid service sector jobs as replacements. Middle-aged and elderly men then may find themselves reliant on unemployment or sickness benefits, where eligible, or among the poorest residents of these localities. The highest-paying professional jobs of the new economies tend to be spatially concentrated in other regions, often those with more favourable climates, less ravaged landscapes and, especially, close to the centres of power and influence, often in the capital cities where the banks, stock markets, cultural industries and seats of government produce a concentration of the most affluent individuals and households within a nation-state, as well as attracting the movers and shakers of global industries and the cosmopolitan opinion-formers.

Some of these new patterns of inequalities and their social consequences are the focus of the three chapters in Part I. Others are discussed elsewhere in the collection. Indeed the analysis of the uneven structure and implications of current economic changes runs throughout all of the chapters, building a complex picture of the changing patterns of work. In Chapter 2 Brendan Burchell provides a succinct yet comprehensive review of the ways in which not only new patterns of work, in terms of longer or antisocial hours for example, affect working people and their families, but also work intensification – the increased intensity of work – adds to daily and lifetime stress for workers and their households. He assesses the utility and validity of different measures of stress, and assesses the differences between 12 member states of the European Union. Stress of course is hard to measure, and comparing different types of jobs raises complicated questions, but as Burchell shows, it seems that white-collar employees, in the UK at least, may currently be reporting a decline in their stress levels, perhaps reflecting the growth of more rewarding jobs. It may be too that stress is an 'artificial' factor in the sense that employees may be influenced by media reporting or the new 'therapy' or 'blame' culture to respond differently than in the past to questions about what constitutes high-pressure work. The causes of stress and their relationship to different types of work are discussed further in Chapter 7. Nevertheless it seems evident that if more people in each household and family than previously are now engaged in waged work, then the organization of daily life, both at home and in the workplace, must be more stressful than previously.

In Chapter 3, Harriet Presser addresses exactly this issue, where she focuses on the growing temporal diversity of working hours in the USA and its effect on family life. One of the most significant temporal trends of working in the new economy is the rise of the 24/7 society where increasing numbers of employees' working hours diverge from the old standard 9–5 day (which was incidentally a male rather than a female norm as women have long worked 'non-standard' hours, often to fit in which family commitments). These changing patterns of work for growing numbers of people bring not only stress for the individuals who may have to cope with changing shift patterns or antisocial hours, but also increased strains for family scheduling and for the organization of all those tasks necessary for daily well-being. Presser draws on her own and others' work to identify these problems, which are especially daunting for low-income families who are less able to replace their own domestic efforts with those of others or with market-based goods and services. She concludes her chapter by laying out a challenging research agenda for future work.

In the final chapter of Part I, the focus shifts away from low-income families struggling to manage different work schedules to what initially seem to be an extremely privileged group: women who have clambered up the greasy pole to reach the higher echelons of the (still male-dominated) investment banks on Wall Street. These are young women who surely are able to 'have it all', working in some of the most prestigious and well-paid institutions right in the core of the global economy. And yet, as Linda McDowell (1997) found ten years earlier in the City of London, women remain disadvantaged in the institutions of global money, marked by their gender as 'out of place', as 'broads' (a term ironically adopted as the label for a network of female employees of Goldman Sachs established in 1999) rather than 'one of the guys'. Through case-study work, Melissa Fisher explores the *raison d'être* and function of a women-only network on Wall Street, assessing the extent of transformations in Wall Street women's organizational identity and the ways they talk about themselves at work given shifts in the structure of financial markets, in corporate cultures and in feminist politics since the Second World War but especially since the 1980s deregulation of financial markets. She ends with some tantalizing glimpses into why many of these women seem unhappy despite their evident privilege, looking for their 'true selves' or greater meaning in their lives outside the corporate workplace. Thus these three chapters, in their diverse foci and different approaches, illustrate something of the new stresses and strains that accompany the transition to a 'new' economy for men and for women, for individuals and for households and for the least-well and best-paid workers therein.

2. Work intensification in the UK

Brendan Burchell

INTRODUCTION

The long-hours culture of the UK has become common knowledge across Europe. This chapter investigates a less obvious but more insidious change in the labour market – work intensification, or the increasing effort that employees put into their jobs during the time that they are working. Research suggests that the intensification of work may be a greater problem in terms of stress, psychological health and family tension than long working hours. This chapter will start with a consideration of the evidence that there has been a change in employee effort in the past quarter-century. This in turn means considering how the effort that an employee expends on their job might be measured, and an evaluation of the evidence available at various points in time. I will then briefly review the literature considering the effects of work intensification on the well-being of employees and their families. The reasons for the increased intensity of work, and its possible recent decline, will be discussed. Finally, the chapter will consider the influence of trade unions, the courts and the media on the rate of work intensification.

THE 1970s AND 1980s

In a recent review of the literature on work intensification, Green (1999) suggests a number of ways in which effort might be measured. Apart from self-reporting, he also considers quantifiable proxy (for instance industrial accidents), case-studies, productivity and a measure called the Percentage Utilization of Labour (PUL) index based on work-study.

The attempt by Bennett and Smith-Gavine (1987) to measure the intensity of work of the British workforce by the PUL methodology was a formidable project. It involved a longitudinal survey of over 100 employers representing more than 100 000 employees. For each task that operatives were undertaking, a standard time that the tasks should have taken was compared to the actual time taken to complete the tasks, and a ratio of the two measures purported to show the extent to which labour was being used to its maximum efficiency. Care was taken to ensure that index was comparable from year to year, and an index was produced for the period 1971 to 1988. During that time there was an increase in the index from about 97 per cent to 104 per cent, with most of that increase occurring in the period 1980–83. Taken at face value, this seemed to vindicate the theory that the Thatcherite revolution, starting with the election of the Conservative Party in 1979, had indeed increased the efficiency of British industry, curbing the excesses of the 'lazy' British worker.

However a detailed critique of the PUL index by Guest (1990) demonstrates convincingly that there may have been a number of faults with the conception and enacting of the PUL methodology that limits both the accuracy and the relevance of the findings. The PUL methodology is based on the idea of scientific management, studying operative workers in manufacturing, whose jobs are specified and understood by their managers. As such a small proportion of employees in Britain today fall into this category, it can no longer purport to give an indication of the labour force as a whole. Other changes in the labour market away from the hierarchically organized management of operatives have further reduced the relevance of PUL. The sharp distinction between the knowledge of managers and the labour of workers has been rejected, and it is now widely acknowledged that workers understand their jobs at least as well as managers. Indeed the movement towards quality circles and autonomous teams is based on the idea that efficiency and quality of output are improved by empowering employees to draw upon their knowledge of the work to improve efficiency (Guest, 1990).

As well as being unsuited to measuring work as it is practiced outside traditional factories, Guest argues that the PUL methodology suffered other flaws that also detracted from its credibility. The extent to which it was measuring simply effort or the intensity of work was unclear; it is likely that the index was also contaminated by many other factors such as the choice of workplaces included in the sample (and their replacement as factories closed during the decline of the manufacturing sector), the increasing reliability of machines and the professionalization of management (see Guest, 1990, for a comprehensive critique.

Unfortunately, both Guest (1990) and Green (1999) conclude, the PUL index is fundamentally flawed. Similarly, none of the other objective measures or proxy measures claiming to detect changes in the intensity of work over time is reliable or valid enough to be useful. There are too many other variables, apart from effort, which influence them. For instance industrial accidents are also strongly influenced by health and safety regulation and enforcement as well as the culture of reporting or downplaying accidents. And while economists claim to be able to measure productivity accurately, it is a function of employee skill, managerial efficiency and reliability of machinery, as well as effort.

This leaves only self-report measures as a reliable indicator of work intensification. Up until the 1990s there were no repeated cross-sectional surveys that could be used to give an indication of changes in the intensity of work. The best self-report evidence that was available relied on respondents making judgements about their current levels of effort or speed of work compared to, say, their effort or speed of work five years ago. For instance in 1986 the Social Change and Economic Life Initiative (SCELI) survey asked questions about increased effort and pace of work in the past five years. The sample included over 3000 employees drawn from six towns in England and Scotland. Taken at face value, the findings produced evidence of an extensive increase in both effort and speed: 56 per cent and 38 per cent of the 3000 employees reported increases respectively, compared to only 8 per cent on both measures who reported a decrease.

Batstone and Gourlay (1986) obtained similar evidence from a 1984 survey of shop stewards, who concurred in the worker's view that there had been a major increase in the effort levels of workers over the previous five years. Further analysis of the SCELI data suggests that this perceived increase in effort was not limited to manual workers; in fact it was white-collar workers that reported the greatest increase in the intensity of their work. There was a marked social class effect (using the registrar-general's 1980 scheme to classify occupations into six groups), as shown in Figure 2.1: 64 per cent of professional and intermediate white-collar workers reported having to increase effort, compared to only 45 per cent of semi-skilled manual workers and 39 per cent of 'unskilled' manual workers.

Similar questions to these 'retrospective changes in effort' questions continue to be used, for instance in the 1998 Job Insecurity and Work Intensification Survey (JIWIS) data,[1] and the Institute of Management survey (Wheatley, 2000). The results are similar to those found in SCELI, showing a sizable majority of the sample reporting an intensification of work: in both cases over 60 per cent of respondents have reported an intensification of their work, compared to only 4 and 5 per cent respectively who reported a reduction in effort. This pattern of results seems to occur regardless of the time-period asked about; in the Wheatley case respondents were only asked about the past 12 months.

But this cross-sectional survey methodology has its problems. The net increases may at least in part be attributable to either life-cycle effects (that is, employees having to work harder as they get promoted into positions of greater responsibility), or to distortions in recall (perhaps viewing the past with rose-tinted spectacles). As I sit writing this chapter, I could easily list a dozen other urgent jobs competing for my time. If I think back five years, it is

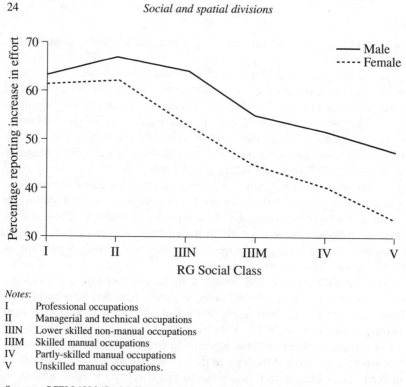

Notes:

I   Professional occupations
II   Managerial and technical occupations
IIIN   Lower skilled non-manual occupations
IIIM   Skilled manual occupations
IV   Partly-skilled manual occupations
V   Unskilled manual occupations.

Source: SCELI 1986 (Social Change and Economic Life Initiative Survey).

Figure 2.1   Change in effort by sex and social class

difficult for me to remember which overdue tasks were pressurizing me then, so it is tempting to say that the past year was my busiest ever. Yet taking a more considered view, I judge that my level of work has remained about constant for over ten years now; I cannot remember the nature of the pressures on me five years ago, so it is tempting to say that I am busier now. But in reality it is difficult for me, or for any respondent, to accurately compare their level of work intensity now and five years ago. Whilst the phenomenology of perceived increases in pressure is itself interesting, and something I will return to later in this chapter, this sort of evidence is not reliable as a way of monitoring changes in the intensity of work over time. Luckily there now exists repeated cross-sectional data, which overcomes this problem.

Before we move on, what do we know about changes in the intensity of work during the 1970s and 1980s? There is some circumstantial and imperfect evidence that there was intensification. The flawed PUL index shows an increase, and there seems to have been a consensus amongst both employees and trade union officials that work had intensified. Furthermore this intensification of work seems plausible, and there was indeed an explicit attempt in the Thatcherite reforms of the labour market to increase productivity by creating a cowed workforce and weakened trade unions. But despite the general consensus that work intensity increased over those two decades, the evidence is equivocal.

THE EARLY 1990s

The 1990s brought an important resource to the study of the intensity of work in the UK and the rest of Europe: the European Working Conditions Survey. Through a repeated cross-sectional analysis of the EU workforce, at last it was possible to obtain a more accurate picture of the way in which the speed of work was changing over time.

The survey has been conducted three times: in 1991, 1995–96 and 2000. The 1991 version was a relatively short questionnaire that has been lengthened in the subsequent waves. The sample size started at 1000 per country in 1991, and was increased to 1500 in 2000, giving adequate power to detect change over time. Fortunately the questions on the speed of work and tightness of deadlines have remained constant over the three waves, leading to a useful time-series. The questions were a little unusual, to make them compatible with the rest of the questionnaire. Respondents in each of the European Union countries were asked, in two consecutive questions, how much of the time in their jobs they had to work (1) at speed, or (2) to tight deadlines. They responded on seven-point scales from all of the time to never.[2] One could argue that, as 'tight deadlines' and 'working at speed' are somewhat subjective constructs, it may not be useful to compare workers from very different cultures. For example a Nordic worker with a regular lunchtime would have a very different template from the growing tradition in the UK for lunch-on-the-go. Likewise there may be differences across public or private sectors, between the regularly employed and agency workers and between occupations. Furthermore the translations of the questions between European languages resulted in different nuances to the terms 'speed of work', so comparisons between countries may also be compromized by this unavoidable methodological problem with international surveys. But when we compare each country with its own data from five years before, we can more safely chart the relative changes in work intensification between countries. Green and McIntosh (2001) performed a comprehensive analysis of the intensity of work over this period, and found that there had indeed been an increase in the speed of work and tightness of deadlines in most of the 12 EU member states.

Figure 2.2 (see Burchell et al., 2002) shows, on the horizontal and vertical

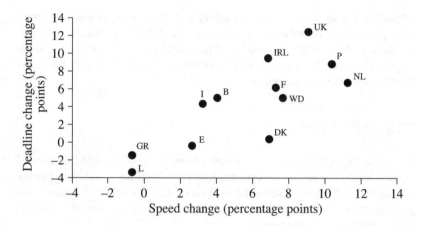

Note: Change in percent of respondents working at speed and to tight deadlines all or almost all
          of the time.

Source: EWCS (European Working Conditions Surveys).

Figure 2.2   Changes in the intensity of work, 1991–96

dimensions respectively, the changes in the proportion of workers in each
country working at speed and to tight deadlines most or all of the time. The
general trend in all European counties has been up, but the rate of change
varies considerably between countries. Some countries, such as Greece and
Luxembourg, seem to have experienced little or no change. But one country
stands out as having experienced work intensification more than any other
country – the UK.

The UK was also unusual in another respect: in all other EU countries (12
at the time) the increased intensification was greater in the private sector, but
in the UK the increase was greatest in the public sector. This finding comes as
no surprise to UK public sector employees themselves; there had been several
attempts by the Conservative government to increase the quality of the public
sector services, such as the introduction of league tables for schools,
universities and hospitals. At the same time, there was an unwillingness to
increase costs or staffing levels, so the increased productivity came largely
from increasing the intensity of work for the employees (sometimes referred
to euphemistically by government ministers as 'efficiency savings').

Green went beyond simply describing these changes to explaining them in
terms of the proximate causes. Amongst the correlates of work intensification
were the use of computers and the weakening of trade unions; strict
demarcations between workers were one (albeit crude) way in which
employees could guard against relentless work. These barriers have often been

removed, and given way to multi-skilling, increasing management's ability to utilize labour more intensively (Green, 1999; Burchell et al., 2002).

When employees were asked about the sources that drove their pace of work, there were notable changes in the UK between 1986 and 1997. The two most dramatic changes were the increase in pressure from 'clients or customers' and from 'fellow workers or colleagues'. These responses, coming from employees, reflect their perspectives. In the JIWIS data, employers were also asked about the causes of intensification. Although not incompatible with the proximate causes found in supply-side data, managers give a different, 'higher-order' set of explanations for the intensification of work, including increased globalized competition and the demands from shareholders for short-term profits, and reduced Treasury funding in the public sector, leading to downsizing but with an expectation that the reduced number of employees would still achieve the same or a higher quantity and quality of work (Burchell et al., 2002).

THE LATEST EVIDENCE ON THE INTENSITY OF WORK, 1996–2000

The third wave of the European Working Conditions Survey was completed in 2000. A comparison of the 1995–96 and the 2000 data shows that there has been a further increase in the intensification of work, but a much smaller increase than in the previous five-year period. The UK data is virtually unchanged, and some countries have displayed a decrease (especially Portugal and Austria). The greatest increases in intensification took place in Belgium, Italy, France, Luxembourg and Sweden (Fagan and Burchell, 2002).

Breaking this data down by gender, collar and UK vs. the rest of Europe shows some unexpected results. Like making comparisons between countries, it is difficult (if not impossible) to make direct comparisons of effort between very different jobs. How could we possible objectively compare the effort expended by, say, a busy labourer on a building site and a busy midwife? The former uses his muscles more, and expend more calories each hour, but the latter might feel more 'drained' by her work and feel that the job is more relentless. But we can explore the ways in which the effort required of different occupations has changed over time.

As Figure 2.3 shows, the slight rise in the intensity of work in Europe was far from uniform. In the UK, there was a slight decline in the intensity of work for white-collar men and women, but a dramatic increase in intensity for male and female blue-collar workers. In the rest of the EU, there was a small decrease in work intensity for white-collar males, and a small increase for all other categories of workers.

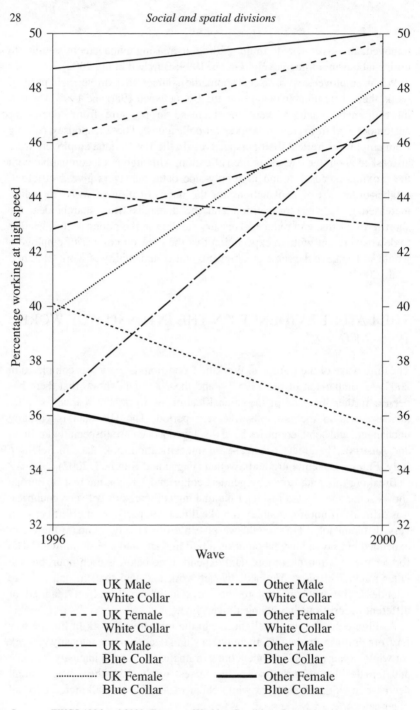

Source: EWCS 1996 and 2000 (European Working Conditions Surveys).

Figure 2.3   Changes in the intensity of work, 1996–2000

This levelling off of work intensity in the EU was not predicted, either by academics or other social commentators, so if the only evidence for it were one survey, it would be reasonable to question the accuracy of that one set of results. But fortunately there are other repeated surveys that provide very similar patterns of stability. Gallie (2004) analysed surveys carried out for DG Employment in 1996 and 2001. He constructed a 'Work Pressure Index' by aggregating four self-report variables, and found no significant change over this period in the UK or any other member state except for Germany, which showed a marked decline in the intensity of work. Green's analysis of the Employment in Britain surveys in 1992, 1997 and 2001 also confirms the pattern of a rise in the early 1990s, but a levelling off in the latter period. With three independent surveys all giving remarkably similar findings, this levelling off of work intensity in the late 1990s does seem to be supported by reliable evidence.

REASONS FOR THE REDUCED INTENSITY OF WORK FOR UK WHITE-COLLAR WORKERS

Like many changes in the labour market, there has probably been more than one force driving the change in work effort in the UK. Up to the mid-1990s, many possible culprits for the change in the intensity of work were identified. As well as those identified above, other changes, more difficult to measure, may also have been responsible. It could be that management are now much better trained and highly skilled at managing the flow of work; previously one heard of employees having to spend much of their working days idle waiting for plant, materials, maintenance workers or supervisors to arrive. New management techniques, such as flatter hierarchies and autonomous teams, may have made workers take more responsibility for their own productivity. Perhaps increased wage differentials acted as a motivator for individual advancement, urging employees to work themselves harder to achieve promotions. Or it could be simply that jobs are more rewarding now than in the past, and so employees are more self-motivated than they used to be.

These all seemed to be plausible explanations for the unidirectional intensification of work observed up to the mid-1990s. But none of these assumed causes have reversed direction for UK white-collar workers, so how can we explain this reversal of the trend?

Firstly, it is difficult to know what the current trend is. We have observed a levelling off, but until new data becomes available we do not know whether the trend has reversed or simply levelled off. If it is a simple levelling of work intensity, albeit at a higher level than the level in the 1970s or 1980s, then perhaps the intensification of work was not inevitably being driven upwards by some processes inherent in capitalism (see Fairris, 2004 for a historical account), but had rather been through a one-off rise, and had restabilized.

Alternatively, if the evidence of the EWCS downturn in the intensification of work is borne out with a continued decline for some or all categories of workers, then a quite different set of causes for its decline might be needed. But before speculating on the reasons for this, I will briefly explore three other aspects of work intensity: the effects on health and well-being, the legal response to stress at work, and the media coverage of work intensity.

WORK INTENSITY, HEALTH AND WELL-BEING

If, as President Ronald Reagan stated, 'Hard work never killed anyone', should we not welcome this as a sign of increased efficiency and competitive advantage? Unfortunately there is now a large body of evidence that the intensification of work poses an enormous challenge to health and work–family balance. Wichert (2002) used data from both the 1996 EWCS and 1998 JIWIS to investigate the relationship between work intensification and well-being. She finds that self-reported health problems caused by employment are often two or three times higher for employees working at high speed more than 75 per cent of the time, compared to employees working at high speed only 25 per cent of the time or less; backaches, headaches, anxiety, skin problems, stomach aches, sleeping problems and muscular pains were particularly strongly associated with the speed of work. Burchell and Fagan (2004) find a gender difference, such that women are more susceptible to the negative health effects of work intensity than men. Furthermore Wichert (2002) found the effect of pressure of the sheer quantity of work on GHQ scores (a measure of mild anxiety and depression) was marked (a much stronger relationship than for instance with job insecurity).

Nolan (2002) used the JIWIS data to investigate the relationship between the intensity of work and work–life balance. Respondents working intensively were much more likely to report that their work had a negative effect on their marriage or relationship. Qualitative analyses revealed that employees were well aware of the negative effects that workload pressures had on their relationships with their partners and children. Other international evidence is also reviewed extensively by Nolan, and paints a bleak picture of the effects of work intensification on family life. Boisard et al. (2003) express concern over the longer-term effects of work intensity, leading employees to question their employability until normal retirement ages. So, even if death by overwork is not a common phenomenon in the West, there is certainly an abundance of evidence that it has a negative effect on quality of life.

INCREASED STRESS AT WORK AND THE LEGAL RESPONSE

In the year 2000 in the UK there were 512 new work-related stress court cases brought by employees against employers. In 2001 this figure increased twelvefold to 6428. What caused such a dramatic rise?

Even if we believe that this rise in court cases reflects an increase in stress at work, caused by the intensification of work, it is implausible that it is caused directly by the modest rise in work intensification over the late 1990s. The EWCS data suggest that the increase in the intensity of work has been a gradual change over several years, not a spectacular rise in one year.

The most plausible explanation for this striking rise is probably that work intensity and the resulting stress levels had been rising slowly for at least ten years. Trade unions had, during that time, become weaker and lost their niche in bargaining for collective wage increases, and were starting to feel as if their role was disappearing. In response to this threat, trade unions started to redefine their role as being guardians of individuals' working conditions and advocates in individual dispute cases. There were a few high-profile cases of employees wining sizable compensation claims against their employers where high levels of stress at work had been claimed as the cause of psychological problems. Suddenly this ability to make claims against employers caught the public imagination and with trade unions there to publicize, politicize and press the charges, there followed an avalanche in cases. This in turn may have made employers more concerned about their vulnerability to legal claims, leading them to moderate their pressure to increase employees' workloads.

THE ROLE OF THE MEDIA

The case of the link between the intensification of work and stress at work, one can see a new sort of relationship arising between social scientists, the media and the lay public, different from the relationship that has existed with other labour market research. This in turn might provide an explanation for the recent levelling off of the intensity of work, and even for the reduction amongst white-collar workers in the UK.

It is interesting to compare the phenomenon of the intensification of work with other labour market problems such as low wages and job insecurity. In those cases social scientists also demonstrated convincingly that job insecurity and low wages were linked with poor well-being, and these research findings were effectively disseminated. However the important difference in those cases was that the research findings are hardly actionable by employees themselves. No doubt the vast majority of employees on low wages would agree that their quality of life would improve if their wages were increased, and the majority of insecure employees would similarly like to be in secure jobs. But in both cases the employees, acting individually, are powerless to improve their own situation; collective action by trade unions, or labour market regulation by governments or the EU, are the principal ways in which change can be implemented.

In the case of work intensification, there is no obvious lever that trade unions or the state can act upon to moderate the market. Because of the difficulty of assessing the intensity of individual jobs, health and safety legislation is unlikely to be effective (Ladipo et al., 2003). But unlike many other forms of labour market disadvantage, there is at least some voluntary control over the intensification of work by the employees themselves. The causes for the intensification of work at the individual level are complex, and impossible to divide simply into cases where the intensity of work is determined by the employee, and cases where it is determined primarily by the employer. For instance some of the reasons that employees give for their speed of work is that if they did not work so intensively, they would fail to provide an adequate service for their customers, patients or students; that they would increase the workload of their team-mates; or that their work would then fall below acceptable professional standards. For each of these cases the employee's explanation for their intensified work suggests that they have accepted, to some extent, that they have made a personal decision to work intensively. Yet it is simultaneously the case that if the employer had provided a higher level of staffing, the employees would not have been forced into working so intensively.

Nevertheless it does suggest that one way in which the level of work intensity might be reduced would be to make employees aware of the adverse consequences or work intensification for their health and their work–life balance, so the dissemination of the research findings on the cost to the individual of work intensification might plausibly be one route towards reducing the intensification of work.

There is plenty of evidence that the dissemination of research finding (either directly or via journalists) has been a widespread phenomenon. Newspaper and magazine articles and television documentaries linking the intensification of work to individual, family and social costs have become very common. Whereas the linking of speed of working to health might have been an unorthodox position ten or 20 years ago, it has now become a widely held social representation.

There have also been a number of books on the subject, aimed at the popular as well as the academic market. For instance Madeleine Bunting, a journalist, launched a book that created many public debates in the media: *Willing Slaves: How the Overwork Culture is Ruling our Lives* (2004). She describes, using interviews, statistics and anecdotes, a bleak picture of the ubiquitous nature of overwork amongst the exploited workforce of the UK. The back cover of the book declares, 'Work-related stress is soaring. Over a third of the British workforce is so exhausted at the end of a day's work that they can only slump on the sofa.'

Similarly, Tom Hodgkinson's book *How to be Idle* (2004) is an attempt at inspiring readers to 'take it easy in a work-obsessed world' (inside sleeve). The intensity of work has also entered government discourses, for instance in the *Work and Parents* Green Paper (Department of Trade and Industry, 2000).

So perhaps the reason for the levelling or decline in work intensity is a consequence of journalists and academics encouraging lay people to be more mindful of the negative consequences of overwork, which in turn has influenced both employees' behaviour, and also the culture within organizations. Whereas social researchers are used to studying media and culture as a determinant of social change, in this case perhaps those same researchers have brought about social change as their findings have been disseminated beyond the academic publications into the mass media.

The role of the media may also explain the differential directions of change between white- and blue-collar employees. White-collar workers may not only be more aware of the media debates concerning work intensity, but they may also be in a more powerful position in their organizations to control their own workloads.

Paradoxically the publication of Hodgkinson's and Bunting's books comes a few years after the end of white-collar work intensification in the UK. But as was discussed in considering the way in which retrospective recall methods may overestimate work intensification, it is highly likely that individuals may continue to discuss the ubiquitous nature of work intensification long after the labour market has stabilized. Furedi (2004) goes so far as to claim that the current obsession with stress is caused by a 'therapy culture' and an attempt to redefine ordinary setbacks in life such as disappointment, tiredness or depression as needing to be discussed publicly and medicalized. In a similar vein, Wainwright and Calanan (2002) conclude that in order to understand the way in which the discourse around work intensification and stress have increased exponentially, we must understand the ways in which individuals have been encouraged to take on the role of 'work stress victim'. Problems at work that used to be enacted between trade unions and employers within the realms of industrial disputes have now become individualized as problems of mental health. In these disputes, the rhetoric of grievance has become entwined with the rhetoric of stress and illness.

But this is only speculation. Whilst there is good evidence that the intensity of white-collar work has stabilized since the mid-1990s, two things remain uncertain. What caused this levelling, and what does the future hold? Has the intensity of work in the UK peaked, or are we just experiencing a temporary respite before a further period of intensification of work?

NOTES

1. The JIWIS data was collected from employers and employees in 25 case-study companies in the UK in 1997–98. It is described in detail in Burchell et al. (2002).
2. This response scale, from 'all of the time' to 'never', may seem like a strange way to measure intensity of work. It was used throughout the questionnaire to measure many aspects of working conditions; using the same response scale for many questions made the questionnaire more economical to administer, even if it was not ideal in all cases.

3. Employment in a 24/7 economy: challenges for the family*

Harriet B. Presser

INTRODUCTION

Over recent decades, the US labour force has been experiencing greater diversity in the nature of employment. The total number of weekly hours people are employed has been spreading to both ends of the continuum, so that more people are working very few as well as very many hours (Smith, 1986; US Department of Labor, 2002). Which hours people are working has also been changing, with flexitime on the rise (Golden, 2001; US Department of Labor, 1998), and more people working the 'fringe times' of the traditional 9–5 working day (Hamermesh, 1999). Interestingly, the increasing diversity in work hours has been occurring while the cumulative number of weekly hours people are employed has remained virtually unchanged between 1970 and 2001 (Rones et al., 1997; US Department of Labor, 2002).[1]

An important but often neglected aspect of temporal diversity is employment that occurs mostly in the evening or night, or on a rotating basis around the clock. Although we do not have comparable data over time to rigorously assess the trend in non-day work shifts, there are strong indications that such employment is on the rise as we move toward a 24-hour, 7-days-a-week economy. As of 1997, only 29.1 per cent of all Americans worked mostly during the daytime, 35–40 hours per week, Monday to Friday – the 'standard' working week. Removing the limitation of 35–40 hours, and including those working part-time and overtime, the percentage increases to 54.4 per cent – a bare majority (Presser, 1999).

As consumers, we witness the movement toward a 24/7 economy by observing that stores are increasingly open evenings and nights, it is easier to make travel reservations or order goods with a live voice on the phone at any time of the day or week, and we increasingly expect medical care and other services to be available to us at all times. A new phrase, '24/7', has quickly become common parlance to denote around-the-clock availability. From a consumer perspective, there seem to be few complaints about 'colonizing the world after dark,' to borrow Murray Melbin's (1987) phrase.

But what does this expansion of economic activity around the clock mean for workers who provide their labour in the evenings, nights and at weekends? And what does it mean for families? While there is a considerable body of research on the individual consequences of shift work, particularly its health consequences (for reviews, see US Congress, 1991; Wedderburn, 2000), there is a paucity of research on the family consequences of late-hour shifts and weekend employment – what I mean by non-standard schedules.

In this chapter, I document the prevalence of non-standard work schedules among employed Americans and consider what this implies for the functioning and stability of family life. I do this drawing primarily upon findings from my recent book *Working in a 24/7 Economy: Challenges for American Families*, and my earlier publications, along with reviewing the work of others. The challenges that families with preschool and school-aged children face when parents work non-standard schedules is discussed in the context of these findings, particularly as they relate to low-income families. I also list some important research needs to fill major gaps in our knowledge.

It is important to acknowledge at the outset that the temporal nature of work life for families is being driven primarily by factors external to the family. As I have described elsewhere (Presser, 1999), there are at least three interrelated factors that increase the demand for Americans to work late or rotating shifts and weekends: a changing economy, changing demography and changing technology. The growth of the service sector of the economy (which has higher proportions working non-standard schedules than the goods-producing sector) is a critically important factor underlying all of these changes. This growth has been remarkable: in the 1960s, employees in manufacturing greatly exceeded those in service industries, whereas by 1999, the percentage was over twice as high in services as in manufacturing (Hatch and Clinton, 2000; Meisenheimer II, 1998). A related change has been the dramatic increase in women's labour force participation during this period, especially among married women with children, 70 per cent of whom are now employed (US Census Bureau, 2001, Table 578). Not only have women moved disproportionately into the service sector, responding to the growing demand for such workers, but also their increased employment in all sectors contributed to this growing demand, as people needed more services at late hours and weekends. For example the decline in full-time homemaking with greater daytime employment of women has generated an increase in the extent to which family members eat out and purchase other homemaking services. (For elaboration of other relevant factors, see Presser, 2003.)

We have then a process whereby macro changes external to the family affect the temporal nature of employment, offering more job opportunities at late and rotating hours as well as on weekends. Out of necessity or preference (and the data suggest mostly the former: see Presser, 1995), employees increasingly take such jobs, which in turn affect the temporal nature of family life, particularly the 'at home' structure of American families in the evenings, nights and at weekends. This is the context in which we should view the challenges of American families generated by the 24/7 economy.

PREVALENCE OF NON-STANDARD WORK SCHEDULES: MAY 1997 CURRENT POPULATION SURVEY

National studies describing the prevalence of US shift workers – those who work most of their hours in the evening or night – go back to the early 1970s and are based primarily on special supplements added to the US Census Bureau's Current Population Surveys (CPS; see for example Hedges and Sekscenski, 1979). These surveys are based on very large samples (over 50 000 households), making them ideal for assessing prevalence. However, over the years the way the work schedule questions have been asked and the response options allowed have often changed, precluding a rigorous determination of trends over time in the prevalence of work schedules.[2] Also weekend employment was not asked about until 1991. I report here what we know about the prevalence of non-standard work schedules – both with regard to shifts and weekend employment – for the most recent year data are publicly available, 1997.

Definitions of Work Schedules

First, an important note about defining work schedules. As used in this chapter, work shifts refer to when people work most of their hours. Accordingly, people who work mostly in the day, but also in the evening or night, are considered here to be daytime workers. Estimates of the extent to which people work evenings and nights, whether or not they primarily work days, would be substantially larger than the estimates for evening and night shifts shown here. I prefer to use work shifts denoting most hours, as this provides a sharper distinction between various patterns of employment around the clock, differences that are expected to substantially alter the temporal nature of family life.

In determining what constitutes a specific shift, I have modified the definition used by the Bureau of Labour Statistics (Hedges and Sekscenski, 1979; US Department of Labour, 1981) to include the 'hours vary' response option used in 1997:[3]

- Fixed day: At least half the hours worked most days in the prior week fall between 8 a.m. and 4 p.m.
- Fixed evening: At least half the hours worked most days in the prior week fall between 4 p.m. and midnight.
- Fixed night: At least half the hours worked most days in the prior week fall between midnight and 8 a.m.
- Rotating: Schedules change periodically from days to evenings or nights.
- Hours vary: An irregular schedule that cannot be classified in any of the above categories.

I define persons as working non-standard hours when they work other than fixed-day schedules the previous week on their principal job.[4] (The percentage employed who are multiple job holders is 7.6 per cent; inclusion of the hours of employment on secondary jobs would make little difference in designating shifts, since the definition refers to most hours.)

The specific days of the week worked were asked for the principal job, although no reference to 'last week' or 'usual week' is included in the question.[5] However, this information was asked after other questions relating to the usual week. Specific weekday or weekend combinations categorize the specific workdays. Those who work non-standard days (weekends) are defined as working on Saturday and/or Sunday.

It should be noted that we are not addressing here the issue of flexitime, in which employees are given the option to vary their beginning and ending hours within a confined range according to their personal preferences. Rather, we are considering the work shift that is typically mandated by employers.

Estimates of Prevalence

Table 3.1, based on these definitions, shows the prevalence of non-day employment for all employed Americans aged 18 and over in 1997. One-fifth of the employed do not work a fixed daytime schedule on their principal job. Two-fifths of the employed do not work five days a week, Monday to Friday. Part-time workers (fewer than 35 hours a week on all jobs) are more likely than full-time workers to work non-standard hours and days. Most of the diversity in work schedules however is contributed by full-timers because part-timers make up less than one-quarter of all employed.

Although the labour force is highly segregated occupationally by gender (Reskin and Roos, 1990), gender differences in work schedule behaviour among all those employed are not great. With regard to hours, men are somewhat more likely than women to work other than fixed daytime schedules (21.1 per cent and 19.6 per cent, respectively). The gender difference is seen specifically in the higher percentages of men than women working fixed nights and variable and rotating hours. There is no gender difference in the prevalence of evening work (both 8.1 per cent). Among part-time workers of both sexes, substantial proportions work evenings (15.2 per cent of men and 14.0 per cent of women). Part-time workers are the subgroup showing the highest percentages with variable hours.

As for work days, men are only slightly more likely than women to work during non-standard times – that is, other than a five-day work week, Monday to Friday (40.3 per cent and 38.9 per cent, respectively). The distribution of non-standard workdays, however, varies considerably by gender. In particular, men are more likely than women to work weekends (34.9 per cent and 27.9 per cent, respectively); women are more likely than men to work weekdays but fewer than five days a week (11.0 per cent vs. 5.3 per cent, respectively). Very few employed Americans, men or women, work weekends only. As might be expected, workdays are most likely to be non-standard when people work part-time.

When work hours and days are combined, Table 3.1 shows the figure cited earlier – that only 54.4 per cent of employed Americans work Monday to Friday, five days a week, on a fixed-day schedule. The counterpart is that 45.6 per cent do not – 47.1 per cent of men and 43.8 per cent of women. Moreover, the large majority of part-timers work other than this five-day weekday pattern.

If individuals have this high prevalence of non-standard schedules, it follows that couples as a unit – with both spouses 'at risk' of working such schedules – will have a higher prevalence. We see in Table 3.2 that almost one-quarter (23.8 per cent) of all couples with at least one earner have at least one spouse who works a non-day shift. The percentages are higher for those with children, and particularly those with preschool-aged children (30.6 per cent).

When focusing on dual-earner couples only, the prevalence of non-day shifts is higher than for all couples, since either spouse is 'at risk' of working non-days. Over one-quarter (27.8 per cent) of dual-earner couples have a spouse who works a non-day shift. Again, those with children are most likely to have such a schedule, and particularly those with preschool-aged children (34.7 per cent). Rarely do both spouses work non-day shifts. Although there are usually some overlapping hours of employment among couples with one spouse working non-days, there is considerable non-overlap, and thus it is appropriate to characterize such couples as essentially working 'split shifts'. (An alternative term used is 'tag-team'.)

Single mothers (non-married and separated) are more likely to work non-standard schedules than married mothers – as well as longer hours. For single mothers with children under age 14, 20.8 per cent work non-standard hours

Table 3.1 The work schedules of employed Americans age 18 and over by gender and number of hours employed (May 1997, CPS)

Work schedules	Total			Males			Females		
	Total	>= 35 hours	< 35 hours	Total	>= 35 hours	< 35 hours	Total	>= 35 hours	< 35 hours
Hours:									
Fixed day	80.1%	83.0%	70.4%	78.9%	81.1%	67.5%	81.4%	85.9%	72.0%
Fixed evening	8.1	6.3	14.4	8.1	6.9	15.2	8.1	5.5	14.0
Fixed night	4.1	4.3	3.7	4.5	4.5	4.5	3.7	3.9	3.3
Hours vary	4.2	3.2	7.7	4.4	3.7	8.5	3.9	2.5	7.2
Rotating*	3.6	3.2	3.8	4.1	4.0	4.4	2.8	2.2	3.5
Number	49,570	38,272	11,201	25,916	22,067	3,800	23,654	16,205	7,401
Days:									
Weekday only, 5 days	60.3	65.7	42.4	59.7	62.3	45.6	61.1	70.6	40.6
Weekday only, <5 days	8.0	3.6	22.9	5.3	3.4	16.1	11.0	3.9	26.6
7 days	7.9	7.7	8.0	8.7	8.4	9.5	6.9	6.7	7.2
Weekday and weekend,									
<7days	23.1	22.9	24.3	25.7	25.8	26.2	20.1	18.7	23.3
Weekend only, 1 or 2 days	0.7	0.1	2.4	0.5	0.1	2.6	0.9	0.1	2.2
Number	50,275	37,827	10,771	26,167	21,802	3,635	24,108	16,025	7,136

Combination:

Fixed weekday, 5 days	54.4	59.6	36.5	52.9	55.5	38.6	56.2	65.4	35.3
Rotators or hours vary and weekend*	5.3	4.6	7.2	5.9	5.4	8.6	4.5	3.5	6.5
All others	40.3	35.8	56.3	41.1	39.2	52.8	39.3	31.1	58.2
Number	48,672	37,813	10,765	25,469	21,790	3,631	23,203	16,203	7,134

Notes:

* This includes 74 individuals designated as 24-hour workers.

The total number of cases is more than the sum of those working 35 or more hours last week and less than 35 hours because of missing data on the number of hours worked last week on all jobs. Also, differences in number of cases by type of work schedules are due to missing data for these variables. All percentages are weighted for national representativeness; the number of cases reports unweighted samples for each category. Percentages may not add exactly to 100 because of rounding.

Source: Presser (1999).

41

Table 3.2   Percentage of married couples with at least one spouse who works non-day shifts, by family type, and age of youngest child (May 1997, CPS)

Family type and age of youngest child	% non-day
At least one earner*	23.8
At least one earner and:	
Child <age 14	25.8
Child <5	30.6
Two earners only**	27.8
Two earners and	
Child <age 14	31.1
Child <5	34.7

Notes:
Non-day shifts include work schedules in which the hours most days of the reference week were between 4 p.m. and 8 a.m., rotating hours, and those too variable to classify.
*Couples with at least one employed spouse on the job during the reference week in non-agricultural occupation, including all rotators, and both spouses aged 18 and over.
**Couples with both spouses on the job during the reference week, including all rotators, both in non-agricultural occupations, and both aged 18 and over.

and 33.2 per cent work weekends; for married mothers with children under age 14, it is 16.4 per cent and 23.9 per cent, respectively (Presser, 2003). For both marital statuses, having younger children as well as having low individual earnings increases the percentages.

With such widespread prevalence of non-standard work schedules among American families, what do we know about the consequences? I address this issue first with regard to the existing literature, and then report on some findings from my previous research.

SOCIAL CONSEQUENCES OF NON-STANDARD SCHEDULES: LITERATURE REVIEW

Although there is an abundant literature on the effect of women's employment per se on family life, particularly relating to issues of marital quality, childcare and child well-being, there is a paucity of research on the effects of employment at non-standard work schedules (by either employed mothers or fathers) on the family. The following reviews many of these findings for the US, although it is not meant to be exhaustive.[6]

Quantitative Studies

The most thorough national study, and one that considered weekend employment as well as non-day shifts, is based on data now 25 years old, the 1977 US Quality of Employment Survey (Staines and Pleck, 1983). The authors found that for all married couples as well as dual-earner couples specifically, shift work was associated with difficulties in scheduling family activities; moreover working weekends and variable days was linked with less time in family roles and higher levels of work–family conflict and family adjustment. Some of the negative family outcomes were reduced when a worker's control over his or her work schedule was taken into account.[7] This study was an ambitious effort to explore the impact of work schedules on families, although the way non-day shifts were defined and grouped together is problematic as well as the different sampling procedures for main respondents and spouses.[8]

Other less intensive national studies that consider the relationship between non-standard work schedules and family life include the longitudinal study on the effects of shift work on marital quality and stability by White and Keith (1990), based on a 1980 survey, with a follow-up component in 1983 (White and Keith, 1990). This study also has definitional problems.[9] The study found that marital happiness, sexual problems, and child-related problems were negatively affected by shift work, although the effects were of relatively low magnitude. The longitudinal analysis revealed that among marriages that remained intact over the three-year period, entry into shift work significantly increased marital disagreements and entry out of shift work significantly increased marital interaction and decreased child-related problems. Looking specifically at marital break-up, the investigators found that being a shift-work couple in 1980 significantly increased the likelihood of divorce by 1983 – from 7 per cent to 11 per cent.

Neither of these two studies were designed to study shift work in depth; rather, they were secondary analyses of surveys undertaken for more general purposes. Another secondary analysis by Blair (1993), based on the National Survey of Families and Households (the same data source to be reported in the next section), considered the effects of employment (and family) characteristics on various dimensions of marital quality for both husbands and wives, and included shift status as one aspect of employment. The operational definition of shift status (a dichotomous variable) is not provided, but having a shift was found to significantly reduce marital quality only in terms of 'daily contact', not other measures considered. A smaller longitudinal study of 92 working-class dual-earner couples recruited from prenatal classes at hospitals in Western New England (about one-half with spouses working the same shift and one-half different shifts; Perry-Jenkins and Haley, 2000) showed that during the first year of parenthood, working different shifts helped couples manage childcare but often had negative consequences for the mental health of the parents and their marital relationship.

Empirical studies designed specifically to study the impact of shift work on employees, while not national in scope, suggest some negative family effects. The most extensive US study of this type dates back to the early 1960s (Mott et al., 1965), and was designed to investigate the social, psychological and physical consequences of shift work for white, blue-collar men in selected continuous processing industries. Analysing three dimensions of marital quality, the investigators concluded that shift work led to 'some reduction in marital happiness and an even greater reduction in the ability to coordinate family activities and to minimize strain and friction among family members' (Mott et al., 1965: 146).

More recently, some empirical studies have addressed issues of parent–child interaction and childcare use as related to non-standard work schedules in studies about family life for certain populations. With regard to parent–child interaction, the 1999 National Survey of America's Families (Phillips, 2002), which focuses on low-income households, found that married couples with children aged 6–11 who worked late hours were more likely to be involved in their children's school, but the children of such parents were less likely to be engaged in extracurricular activities. This study does not distinguish the type of shift, defining 'night hours' as employment mostly from 6 p.m. to 6 a.m. Another study, more broadly inclusive of all married couples (not just low-income), is based on the 1981 Study of Time Use; this study found little relationship between work schedules – the amount of minutes husband and wife are employed within certain ranges of hours around the clock – and the amount of parental time with children, but children here include all those under age 20 (Nock and Kingston, 1988).

The type of childcare arrangements that people working non-standard hours make for their children has been studied at the national level, showing a heavy reliance on relative care. Among dual-earner couples, much of this relative care is by resident fathers (Brayfield, 1995; Casper, 1997; O'Connell, 1993; Presser, 1986). This is essentially 'split-shift' parenting, whereby mothers and fathers work very different hours: one mostly days and the other mostly non-days. While mothers are more likely than fathers to report 'better childcare arrangements' as their main reason for working non-standard hours, only a minority of either spouse do so; most parents report reasons related to their jobs, not their families (Presser, 1995).

We know very little about child outcomes related to shift work, from either quantitative or qualitative studies. A cross-tabular analysis of data from the National Longitudinal Survey of Youth (Heymann, 2000), without controls, showed that school-aged children who had poor educational outcomes in 1996 were more likely to have parents who worked evening shifts some or all of their working years between 1990 and 1996 than were other children. (Evening shifts are self-defined by respondents without specification of which hours this encompasses.)

A three-city study (Boston, Chicago, and San Antonio) of low- and moderate-income families in 1999 found more problem behaviours and fewer positive behaviours among children aged 2–4 when parents worked non-standard hours or weekends (grouped together) compared to fixed daytime schedules (Bogen and Joshi, 2001). Multivariate analyses suggested that non-standard schedules might affect children directly as well as have a small indirect effect on children by increasing parenting challenges (decreasing satisfaction and increasing stress).

Qualitative Studies

Qualitative studies on how families cope when one or both parents work non-standard schedules are rare. Rubin (1994), in her study of 162 working-class and lower-middle class families in the US, discusses the pressures on time for both husbands and wives when they work different shifts (about one-fifth of her couples). She notes the lack of childcare options that result in each parent caring for their children while the other is employed.

Other qualitative studies offer a mixed message about positive and negative aspects of parents working non-standard schedules. For example, Deutch's study of 30 dual-earner couples working different shifts finds parents speaking positively about such work schedules allowing both spouses to rear their children and have a joint income. Yet the author concludes, 'the loss of time together was a bitter pill to swallow. The physical separation symbolized a spiritual separation as well' (Deutsch, 1999: 177).

Garey's (1999) interviews with seven nurses working the night shift full-time indicated that these mothers liked the fact that this late work schedule allowed them to maximize family time and do traditional maternal tasks at home, as though they were full-time 'at-home moms'. Such tasks included helping with homework and being able to participate or facilitate children's school and extracurricular activities. Moreover, they preferred the night to evening shifts because they were able to supervise dinner and bedtime and, for those married, have more time with their spouses. The cost to these mothers, which they were all willing to assume, was considerable sleep deprivation (most getting about four to five hours a night).

Problems of sleep deprivation among shift workers and the desire to be a 'good mother' by working late hours are also relayed in interviews with women in the Midwest (sample size not provided; Hattery, 2001a). Another qualitative study of 90 male security guards on rotating shifts found that many fathers also deprived themselves of sleep in order to participate in family life, eating meals with their family 'out of sync with their biological rhythm' (Hertz and Charlton, 1989: 502).

SOCIAL CONSEQUENCES OF NON-STANDARD WORK SCHEDULES

The National Survey of Families and Households, 1986–87 and 1992–94

Building on this body of research, I have analysed data from the National Survey of Families and Households (NSFH) on the relationship between non-standard work schedules and family life. I present here some highlights of these findings (for more details, see the references cited).

First, a note on the NSFH. This representative survey of all American families was conducted in two waves: the first interview during the years 1987 to 1988 ($N = 13007$); the second between 1992 and 1994 ($N = 10007$). Spouses and partners were asked to complete a separate questionnaire, so one can obtain couple data on selected variables.[10] The findings reported here are based on Wave 1, with an analysis of Wave 2 when considering marital instability, and relies on data from both spouses among those married. The shift definition is the same as that reported earlier for the CPS, except that the 'hours vary' is not a response option and thus all non-standard work shifts are 'non-day' (see note 4). For some analyses, non-day shifts had to be combined as a single group because of the small numbers in each type of shift. In analyses that permit a separate examination of different non-day shifts, the results typically present a complex picture.

Marital quality

Four dimensions of marital quality at Wave 1 were examined as separate dichotomous dependent variables in regressions: general marital unhappiness, low quality time, marriage in trouble, and assessment of an even or higher chance of divorce. The shift patterns of the couples (non-days grouped) and the family type were key independent variables. Control variables included the number of hours each spouse worked, the education of both spouses, the number of times each spouse has been married, whether husband or wife cohabitated, the difference in age between the spouses, the duration of marriage, whether there were children less than age 19 in the household, and for some models the gender ideology of each spouse and the age of the wife. The results can be summarized as follows, separately for married single-earner couples (one-fifth of these single earners are wives), and dual-earner couples.

Among single-earner couples, non-day shifts and weekend employment seem to pose a risk to the quality of the marriage relative to daytime employment – but only when it is the wife who is the single earner, not the husband. The negative relationships for wives are stronger when children are present.

Among dual-earner couples, couples with a spouse working non-standard hours generally have higher levels of marital dissatisfaction relative to those in which both spouses work fixed days, but these relationships are specific to certain couple work schedules and certain indicators of marital quality. In most instances the relationships are stronger when children are present. Interestingly, adding the control for gender ideology of the spouses did not significantly alter these relationships for couples with or without children. Weekend employment was not significantly associated with marital dissatisfaction.

Marital instability

Among couples married at Wave 1, their marital status at Wave 2 – about five years later – was assessed in regression analyses that considered the work shifts and weekend employment of both spouses (with similar controls as above). It was found that only for couples with children did non-standard work schedules increase the likelihood of marital instability – and only when the husband or wife worked the night shift (there are some additional conditions relating to duration of marriage; see Presser, 2000). One could speculate that this result occurs because spouses who choose to work late night hours are especially likely to be in troubled marriages before making this decision, but a separate analysis of the quality of marriages among those who enter into non-day shifts between Waves 1 and 2 does not support this view (Presser, 2000).

Gender Division of Household Labour

The NSFH data suggest that the functioning as well as the stability of family life is affected by non-standard work schedules. An important family function is household labour. Focusing specifically on dual-earner households, regression analyses show that when husbands work a non-daytime or rotating shift and their wives work a day shift, the men are significantly more likely to do traditionally female household tasks than couples in which both spouses work day shifts. These tasks include: preparing meals, washing dishes and cleaning up after meals, cleaning the house, and washing, ironing, and mending clothes (Presser, 1994). The control variables included the husband's education, occupation and earnings, both absolute and relative to his wife, the gender ideologies of both spouses, and their stage in the life course, including the number of preschool and school-aged children.

Parent–Child Interaction

Other aspects of family functioning include the frequency of parent–child interaction. In the NSFH, data are available on the extent to which parents eat meals with their children and do various one-to-one activities together.

As for meals, having dinner together is an especially important day-to-day ritual in most families. Both mothers and fathers who work evenings and rotating shifts are significantly less likely to have dinner with their children than parents who work days. Working nights, however, does not show less frequent family involvement in dinner relative to days (Presser, 2001). In contrast, non-standard work schedules are associated with greater frequency in which parents eat breakfast with their children, but which non-standard schedule has this relationship differs by gender of parent and whether a single or married mother (Presser, 2003).

As for one-to-one parent–child interaction, the NSFH asked questions about the frequency of the following parental activities with children ages 5–18: leisure activities outside the home, work on projects, private talks, and help with homework. Overall there is a mixed picture, with differences evident by gender of parent and marital status of mothers. The findings (Presser, 2003) suggest the following. With regard to the frequency of leisure activities outside the home, working nights may minimize this for mothers, both single and married; rotating shifts seem to do this for married fathers and single mothers. With regard to parents working on projects with children, the frequency is higher when dual-earner mothers work rotating shifts and single mothers work evenings, as compared to days; shift status is not associated with this activity for fathers, with the exception of one near-significant relationship. As for the frequency of private talks, single, but not married, mothers show a relationship to shift status (more frequent when they work evenings and nights rather than days, less frequent when they rotate); married fathers show a reverse pattern from single mothers (less frequent with evening work and more frequent with rotating shifts). As for help with homework, the significant relationships for mothers of both marital statuses are negative when they are on rotating shifts, and positive for fathers when they work night shifts. The few significant or near-significant relationships with regard to weekend employment also show a mixed picture, with only some activities seemingly related and differences in direction by gender of parent. This is very much a complex set of results, suggesting that non-day shifts matter for parent–child interaction both positively and negatively, but the different effects of different shifts, as well as the gender differences, are hard to interpret and need further study.

Childcare arrangements

Parents who work non-standard hours and weekends rely more heavily on relatives for childcare for their preschool-aged children when mothers are employed. When mothers are married and working non-standard schedules, the most frequent 'relative' providing care is the child's father, clearly increasing that form of parent–child interaction. When mothers are not married and are working non-standard schedules, the most frequent relative providing care is the grandparent. While this greater reliance on relatives when working non-standard hours has been shown with other national data sources, as previously noted, analysis of the NSFH data takes into account weekend employment as well as work shifts and also considers patterns of multiple childcare use. Those working non-standard schedules, weekends as well as non-day, are more likely to make multiple arrangements (Presser, 2003). This fact, along with the heavier reliance on informal providers, makes for more complex childcare arrangements for such parents, both married and single.

Among school-aged children 5–11, the presence of parents at home when children leave for and return from school is generally enhanced when mothers work evenings and nights, a clear advantage of such schedules. This relationship obtains for single mothers, but the overall presence of a parent at home during such times is less than for married mothers – which is to be expected given that the child's father is usually not living in these non-married households. For both family types, we do not know if the parents working late hours are awake or asleep before and after school. Typically, other childcare arrangements are made when parents are not present. However, about 15 per cent of parents report their children aged 5–11 in self-care before school, and about 10 per cent after school. Self-care is reported less by parents who work late rather than work daytime hours, but if parents working nights are more likely to be asleep when the child leaves and returns from school, parental supervision of children may be lacking and self-care of such children may be greatly underestimated.

IMPLICATIONS FOR LOW-INCOME FAMILIES

Both the existing research and my new NSFH findings summarized here suggest that employment at non-standard times presents some major challenges to US families. While there may be advantages, the data suggest that in many ways employment at non-standard hours and weekends adds extra stress to families with children, and with regard to night work, may substantially increase the risk of separation or divorce among the married. There has been no research to date that rigorously assesses how low-income families cope with non-standard schedules relative to those with higher incomes. Indeed, there is little research that rigorously assesses how those working non-standard schedules cope relative to those working at standard times, regardless of income. Some of the qualitative studies are insightful but they report on too few cases to draw conclusions.

We know that although employment at non-standard times occurs at all levels of income, it is disproportionately found among those with low incomes. For example, the top five occupations of non-day workers are cashiers, truck drivers, waiters and waitresses, cooks, and janitors/cleaners. It is not just that these jobs are low-paying in general – they are even more low-paying if you have these occupations and work at non-standard times (Presser, 2003). Thus people who work non-standard hours have to deal with the joint stresses of managing with such low pay and with being 'out of sync' temporally with other family members, including their children. As noted earlier, it does not appear that parents who work non-standard schedules generally find this the preferred mode of child rearing, despite the advantage of reduced childcare costs and greater involvement of fathers. Single mothers of low income who generally do not benefit from sharing childcare with fathers would seem to find working non-standard schedules especially problematic.

It thus seems appropriate to conclude that while some parents may prefer such schedules, employment at non-standard times is driven by demand and generally recruits those with limited job possibilities. This includes mothers moving from welfare to work who often experience a misfit between their required hours and days of employment, and the availability of formal childcare, and have to put together a patchwork of informal arrangements to hold onto their jobs. My analysis of mothers in the labour force in 1997 with characteristics similar to those moving from welfare to work (high school education or less, aged 18–34, at least one child under age 14) revealed that about two-fifths of these employed mothers did not work a fixed-day schedule on weekdays only (Presser, 2003). Moreover, many of those working fixed days had hours that extended into the 'fringe' – that is, they started very early in the morning or ended in the evening, times when formal daytime childcare is typically not available.

The minimal attention to such issues reflects the general lack of attention in the social policy arena to the temporal frictions between work and family life that occur as a consequence of the widespread engagement of employed parents in non-standard schedules. Two-parent families often look much like one-parent families in terms of parent–child interaction, and single-parent families much like no-parent families. Presumably 'intact' families often are comprised of spouses who hardly see one another. We need to be concerned about the special needs such situations generate for low-income families and how they might be addressed. One way to find this out is to do research that focuses specifically on this issue.

RESEARCH NEEDS

It is clear from the research to date that investigating the social consequences of non-standard work schedules for individuals and their families is not an easy task. There are different work shifts, there is weekend employment, and the cumulative number of hours people work needs to be taken into account. Moreover, the consequences may be different for families with children versus no children, and between those with preschoolers versus older children. On top of such considerations are the special problems of low-income parents, particularly single mothers. And there is the question of short-term versus long-term costs and benefits (for example, enhancing father–child interaction when spouses work split shifts, but increasing the odds of divorce if one of the spouses works nights).

Such considerations reflect complex situations that need further study, and there are many ways to approach this. I offer my assessment of some important considerations for future research as specified in my recent book (Presser, 2003), recognizing that we need many studies with multiple approaches.

1. The need to do focused studies on the costs and benefits of working non-standard schedules. As we have seen, most of the research to date on the consequences of working non-standard schedules has been based on large-scale surveys or on qualitative studies that were not designed with this focus. Thus we know very little about why people work these schedules, their perceived trade-offs, and the perceived impact on their lives and those of family members. It would be highly relevant to consider gender differences here as well as distinctions between single and married mothers, particularly with regard to the trade-offs being made.
2. The need to distinguish different work shifts in studies of the consequences of non-standard work schedules. As the findings presented in this chapter suggest, different non-standard work shifts may have different effects on family life and on children. To more adequately assess this, we need large-scale studies that oversample those working non-standard shifts so that there are sufficiently large numbers to make comparisons between those working evenings, nights and rotating shifts, as well as days.

3. The need to have precise measures of work shifts. It has been noted that many of the shift work studies use ambiguous definitions of work shifts, often self-defined by the respondent without clear instruction from the interviewer. It would seem best to ask people the specific hours their work begins and ends (daily or for most days during a reference week), plus whether they rotate, and leave the derivation of the day, evening and night shifts to the investigator (which is then reported with the findings). This approach would also allow investigators to compare different studies by deriving similar definitions of work shifts.

4. The need to study the movement of employees in and out of different work schedules. Studies of shift work have generally been cross-sectional rather than longitudinal, yet there is undoubtedly considerable flow in and out of different work schedules. It is important to know the duration of shift work for employees, and particularly employed parents, and how movement in and out of non-standard work shifts relates to family concerns, employer demands, and the lack of alternative daytime job opportunities.

5. The need to explore the effects of non-standard work schedules on the physical and emotional health of individuals and how these effects on individual well-being interact with the functioning of family life. Given the paucity of knowledge on this interaction, it would seem appropriate to start with intensive qualitative studies of families working late and rotating shifts. It would be especially interesting to explore the extent to which those working such schedules suffer from sleep deprivation, and the process by which this may interact with family functioning, affecting the quality and stability of marriages as well as the care of children. In the latter regard, it is important to know how well preschool-aged children are being cared for during the day by parents who work nights or rotating shifts.

6. The need for research on married fathers who care for their children during most of the hours that mothers are employed. It would be revealing to know how distinctive these fathers are from other fathers and the consequences (positive and negative) that they perceive for themselves of having taken on this responsibility as well as the actual consequences. In the latter context, it would be especially interesting to have longitudinal data to assess change over time.

7. The need for intensive research on the reasons for working non-standard work schedules, particularly those of parents with children. To date, we rely on one question in the CPS for our knowledge of reasons people work non-standard hours. Qualitative studies refer to some couples that report either positive or negative consequences of shift work, but we have no research that probes in depth as to why substantial numbers of parents

have chosen these schedules. In addition to some preferring to arrange childcare this way, there may be other care giving reasons that merit exploration (for example, better arrangements for the care of disabled persons and the elderly). Also, it would be good to know what people really mean when they say their main reason is that it is a job requirement, and if there are gender differences in this meaning.

8. The need for more research on the effects of non-standard work schedules on children, including their development and school achievement. While we have moved forward over the past decade in better understanding the effect of child care on child development, we have generally ignored the issue of how the non-standard work schedules of parents, and the more complex child care arrangements this generates, affects child outcomes. This issue calls for studies of the children in addition to the parents, and both the frequency and quality of parent-child interactions as well as child care quality. Such research would require substantial sample sizes in order to consider children of different ages and the different work schedules of parents. Good measures of child outcomes are also important.[11]

FUTURE EXPECTATIONS

Filling these research needs is important not only to better understand today's families, but to better anticipate the future, as the number of American households with parents working non-standard hours increases. I predict this increase will be experienced disproportionately by all employed women, and to a lesser extent by employed black and Hispanic men. This prediction is supported by job growth projections between 2000 and 2010, although I recognize that such projections essentially are educated guesses subject to error.

Table 3.3 shows the top ten occupations in 2000 that, according to the Bureau of Labour Statistics, are projected to have the largest job growth between 2000 and 2010 (Hecker, 2001 Table 4). Using the May 1997 CPS data, I have calculated the percentage in these top growth occupations that work non-standard schedules. (As noted in the table's footnote, given the difference in occupational codes used for the projections and for the CPS, the matching of some occupations is not precise, and for one not possible.)

We see that most of these occupations – namely, food preparation and serving workers, registered nurses, retail salespersons, cashiers, security guards, and waiters and waitresses – are disproportionately high on the percentage working other than a fixed day (far exceeding the overall average for all occupations of 19.9 per cent). The same occupations that are

Table 3.3 Largest projected job growth occupations 2000–2010, their work schedule, gender and race characteristics

Job growth rank	Occupation[b]	Employment (in 1000s)		% in occupation working non-standard schedules, May 1997 CPS			% of group in occupation May 1997 CPS		
		2000	2010[a] (projected)	% other than fixed day (a)	% weekend (b)	% (a) or (b) (c)	% female (all occs = 46.0)	% non-Hispanic black (all occs = 10.5)	% Hispanic (all occs = 9.8)
1	Food preparaton and serving workers, including fast food[c]	2206	2879	45.8	55.0	68.0	51.5	11.8	24.2
2	Customer service representatives[d]	1946	2577	NA	NA	NA	NA	NA	NA
3	Registered nurses	2194	2755	34.6	42.9	55.1	94.5	7.5	3.2
4	Retail salespersons	4109	4619	32.2	62.9	70.6	55.3	7.7	8.7
5	Computer support specialists[e]	506	996	20.0	15.9	26.5	56.1	19.9	3.1
6	Cashiers, except gaming	3325	3799	50.4	71.0	80.1	77.2	15.6	12.3
7	Office clerks, general	2705	3135	16.2	15.7	23.5	76.3	13.6	8.9
8	Security guards[f]	1106	1497	57.0	55.8	73.9	22.8	19.4	13.0

| | 9 | Computer software engineers, applications g | 380 | 760 | 5.2 | 13.5 | 16.9 | 31.5 | 6.6 | 2.4 |
| | 10 | Waiters and waitresses | 1983 | 2347 | 65.1 | 79.0 | 89.5 | 78.8 | 3.1 | 12.6 |

Notes:
a Projections are derived by the Bureau of Labor Statistics (Hecker, 2001, Table 4).
b The BLS occupational classification for job projections is based on the National Industry-Occupation Employment Matrix (NIOEM) and does not always correspond exactly with the CPS occupational classification, as noted in the footnotes below.
c This category includes Kitchen Workers, Food Preparation, and 'Misc. Food Preparation Occupations' in the CPS.
d There is no separate classification in the CPS for this category.
e This category corresponds to 'Computer Equipment Operators' in the CPS.
f This category includes 'Guards and Police, Except Public Service' and 'Protective Service Occupations, n.e.c' in the CPS.
g This category includes 'Computer System Analysis and Scientists' and 'Operations and Systems Researchrs and Aanlysts' in the CPS.

Source: Presser (2003).

55

disproportionately high on non-standard hours are disproportionately high on weekend employment.

We also see in Table 3.3 (far right) the per cent female, the per cent black, and the per cent Hispanic in these top growth occupations. These percentages can be compared with the percentages in all occupations for the respective groups shown in the column headings. When the percentages for specific occupations exceed that for all occupations, the subgroups are disproportionately in those occupations.

This comparison reveals that the top growth occupations high on non-standard work schedules are also high on percent female, with the one exception being security guards. The picture is more mixed for blacks and Hispanics, who are over-represented in the top growth occupations of food preparation and servers, cashiers, and security guards, and for Hispanics, of waiters and waitresses. Hispanics are under-represented as registered nurses; blacks, as waiters and waitresses.

In conclusion, employment in a 24/7 economy presents many challenges for US families. The research to date hints at many of these, but we have much more to learn. We should not be turned away by the complexity of the issue. Indeed, I contend that when work and family research does not take into account the non-standard work schedules of employed family members, it is likely to be missing some important explanatory variables for the outcomes of interest. Moreover, work and family policies cannot continue to ignore the temporal diversity of working families, especially those of low income. Failure to explicitly acknowledge such diversity compromises the effectiveness of such policies, as exemplified by the misfit between childcare availability and the work hours of many mothers moving from welfare to work.

The movement toward a 24/7 economy, in my view, will not be reversed in the decades ahead. It may be slow in pace or even stalled by a weakening economy, but I believe the long-term trend is toward more employment around the clock, particularly in the service sector. I hold this view because the 24/7 economy is driven by factors external to the family that are not likely to change in the foreseeable future. For better or worse, families will increasingly need to respond to these challenges. And so will we as scholars.

NOTES

* I am grateful to Kei Nomaguchi and Lijuan Wu for their very able research assistance in generating the data both for this chapter and for my other publications upon which this chapter draws. The analysis of the NSFH data summarized here was supported in large part by the W.T. Grant Foundation and a visiting scholarship at the Russell Sage Foundation. This chapter is reprinted from Ann C. Crouter and Alan Booth (eds), *Work-Family Challenges for Low-Income Parents and Their Children*, New Jersey: Lawrence Erlbaum.

1. As Jacobs and Gerson (1998) note, the changes in cumulative work time have been essentially in the number of weeks worked per year, and the extent of this increase is under considerable debate.
2. For example, between 1973 and 1980, people were asked the hours they began and ended worked most days in the prior week, but there was no question as to whether they are rotators that happen to be on the day shift in the prior week. Since about one-third of those who work other than fixed daytime schedules are rotators, this seriously underestimates the prevalence of non-day shifts. Changes in the CPS were made in 1980 asking specifically about shift rotation, but the response options on the hours work began and ended varied in other ways in the special CPS supplements on work schedules that followed (1985, 1991, 1997), presenting comparability problems. Ignoring this issue, the data have been presented to show there has been little change in shift work between 1985 and 1997 (Beers, 2000). I do not believe one can draw this conclusion from these data.
3. The BLS used these shift definitions when analysing only full-time wage and salary workers. I use this designation for all workers, both full- and part-time and both self-employed and wage and salary workers.
4. The shift definition used for my analysis of data from the National Survey of Family Growth, to be discussed later in this chapter, excludes 'hours vary', as detailed information on work schedules for every day of the week were provided without this response option, permitting the allocation of individuals into the other categories as appropriate.
5. The question reads: 'Which days of the week (do you/does [name]) work [On this job/for this business] [Only]? (Check all that apply.)'
6. For a more extensive review of the literature on shift work, separately by topic, see Presser (2003).
7. Using the same data source, Nock and Kingston (1988) found among dual-earner couples that there was no strong relationship between the combined number of hours couples worked or the amount of time one or both spouses worked, and marital or family satisfaction. (This study excludes those who work 'irregular hours', and thus presumably excludes rotators.)
8. Those working afternoon schedules were combined with evening and night workers, and together were categorized as non-day shift workers. (Those working in the morning were among the day workers.) The effects of different non-day shifts were not separately considered (nor the gender of the shift worker). Also, the main respondents in the sample were eligible only if they worked at least 20 hours a week, but the number of hours of employment was not restricted for spouses.
9. The researchers asked respondents if they were shift workers but did not define the range of hours that constitute a shift nor the type of shift.
10. For further methodological details, see Sweet, et al. (1988), and http://ssc.wisc.edu/nsfh/home.htm.

4. Enterprising women: remaking gendered networks on Wall Street in the new economy[1]

Melissa Fisher

In 1954, the Eisenhower Bull Market ushered in a new period of economic prosperity for the nation and an unprecedented growth spurt on Wall Street. Corporate expansion, aggressive stock selling and increased consumer activity contributed to the financial climate. In 1957, in the wake of these changes, the *New Yorker* (1957) ran an article about a group of 27 female security analysts. Susan Zuger, the group's president and founder, told the reporters the story of the creation of the Young Women's Investment Association (YWIA). She and her female friends wanted to join the Investment Association of New York – an organization of young financial men – to help them make 'Street contacts' to find better jobs. Barred from entry because of their gender, they chose to form their own organization. These female entrepreneurs were convinced that 'the Association is definitely a growth situation' (the *New Yorker*, 1957). Indeed by 2004 the YWIA now known as the Financial Women's Association of New York (FWA) had developed into 'a leading executive organization of 1100 members committed to shaping leaders in business and finance with a special emphasis on the role and development of women' (http://www.fwa.org).

Forty-plus years after the creation of the FWA, the nation was again flush with enthusiasm, this time around about the 'new economy'. 'Flatter hierarchies', 'global networks', and 'startups' were part of the vocabulary of business. In October 1999, the *New York Times* ran an article entitled, 'A network of their own: from an exclusive address, a group for women only'. According to the piece, two years earlier, Janet Hanson, president and CEO of Milestone Capital, the country's first women-owned firm to specialize in managing institutional money market funds, had invited a group of Goldman Sachs female alumnae to meet at the Water Club in New York City. The women discussed their lives since leaving the firm. Some, like Hanson, a veteran of Goldman Sachs, had launched their own businesses. Others were full-time mothers living in the suburbs. Yet in spite of the intervening years and geographical distances between them, the women all, Hanson told the reporter, still 'spoke the language of Wall Street'.

In 1999 Hanson decided to recreate the reunion atmosphere online. Based out of her firm's headquarters in Westchester, New York, this new economy female entrepreneur called the first Wall Street women's network in cyberspace '85 Broads' – a play on the address of Goldman Sachs, 85 Broad Street in Manhattan, and the colloquial term 'broads' for women. The group is composed of women currently working at Goldman Sachs and female corporate refugees from the firm.

WALL STREET WOMEN'S NETWORKS

I highlight these two stories about networks because I am interested in locating transformations in Wall Street women's organizational identity in relation to shifts in post-World War II financial markets, corporate structures and feminist politics. The FWA emerged during the heyday of the Eisenhower Bull Market (1954–69). The period of the extended post-war economic expansion witnessed the shift from the partnership to the corporation as the predominant organizational form on Wall Street. The hierarchical authority structure, the linchpin of modern bureaucracies, dominated the ways managers thought about the world and about themselves (Jackall, 1988: 17). Striving for success, in corporations, entailed moving up or getting ahead in a single organization.

Buoyed by the feminist movement's struggle to open up formerly male professions, women in finance began their careers in the area of research during the late fifties and sixties (Fisher, 2004). The primary goal of the FWA, however, from its inception in 1956, was occupational mobility, insuring that women move up the corporate ranks on Wall Street. FWA women viewed the network as an elite female financially focused entity defined by business principles, rather than a pro-feminist organization oriented toward fighting gendered discrimination and sexual harassment in the workplace.[2]

But by the 1990s, the vision of a Manhattan-based female corporate network, void of a gendered political agenda, began to appear difficult to sustain. Legal battles over sexual discrimination on Wall Street, emerging in the 1970s, gathered momentum in the last decades of the twentieth century as increasing numbers of women entered the workforce. Hence in contrast to the group's formative years, a financial women's community, without any feminist perspective, became a source of struggle among the FWA's leadership's ranks.

At the same time, rigid work structures that provided lifelong career stability gave way to a more fluid new economy, driven by technology and the globalization of markets. Corporate bureaucracies became more flexible and less secure institutions (Sennett, 2000: 1). The assumptions of successfully building a lifelong career in one firm or even set of firms on Wall Street – working hard, making a lot of money, and becoming a managing director – began to disappear. As Linda McDowell notes, 'for increasing numbers of workers ... there is an expectation of a career that is discontinuous and interrupted, marked by successive contracts rather than the life-time tenure of a single occupation' (McDowell, 1997: 33). Indeed one out of every ten employees in the securities industry has been relieved of responsibility since April 2001 (Kolker, 2003: 24). The number of women working in New York City's financial industry dropped by more than 20 per cent in the first two years of the new century, to an estimated 60 000 from more than 70 000 (Gandel, 2002: 1). This is a significant reversal in Wall Street women's fortunes after two decades of advancement in the industry (Gandel, 2002). Lay-offs however are not the only factor responsible for the decline. In the wake of September 11th, more and more women have decided to walk away from Wall Street, in search of alternative career paths (Gandel, 2002: 2).

Reflecting these cultural, political and economic shifts, contemporary Wall Street women's networks consist of a series of disparate projects and agendas. Some focus on occupational mobility, others on life outside of work; some address diversity in the workplace, and still others centre on philanthropic endeavours. In recent years for example the FWA has added a diversity committee advocating and recruiting African-American, Asian American and other 'minority' women to FWA membership, programs, committees and speakers. 85 Broads provides a cyber forum for former and current Goldman Sachs women to make contacts as they make career transitions in the new information-based business environment. Miles To Go, a non-profit organization established by 85 Broads, raises, manages and distributes charitable funds in support of primarily gendered humanitarian, philanthropic, and educational causes around the world.

The cornerstone of the FWA was (and still is) pushing women's occupational mobility. A key mission of 85 Broads is also helping women advance in their careers. However by the turn of the millennium these women's networks are dealing with new issues and obstacles: calls for diversity in business, a loss of permanent work, and a search for the meaning of success in an increasingly post-corporate world. What is novel, I suggest, in Wall Street women's networks in the new economy is the lack of any clear hegemonic logic to their projects. A series of challenges from both within and outside of the financial women's community – the feminist movement, the globalization of markets, and the virtualization of and sometimes disappearance of work – have destabilized the ordering principles of women's networks. I want to explain this process of decentring, and why it occurred, in some detail. What does Wall Street women's talk about themselves and their networks reveal about the ways shifts in success ideology register and respond to historically engendered cultural tensions? What does their discourse disclose about transformations in the ways women relate to the market, workplace, and feminism over time? And what might all of these changes tell us about the political trajectory of financial women's networks?

CONSTRUCTING SUCCESSFUL FEMALE BUSINESS ICONS AND MOBILITY NARRATIVES IN THE FWA

To begin to address these questions requires taking a look at internal discussions over definitions of professional success and mobility. Beginning in the mid-1980s, the FWA began to pay homage to famous female figures within the Wall Street community, a practice that they continue to engage in to this day. The board initially focused their attention on women who had attained at least the senior vice-presidential level, and were well known throughout the industry. They created a list of eight criteria for selecting award recipients. Below is a partial list of their guidelines:

> Activities, particularly social or philanthropic, are not particularly important. However, a long-standing commitment to helping women succeed in business is a vital element to her ultimate selection. *She should be someone we would all want to have as a mentor or that we could point to and say, 'This is my idea of a successful woman!'* ...

> While not a requirement, *evidence that she has risen above strife and 'against all odds' might be another part of her background that would make her a viable candidate* ...

> *There should be evidence of some 'balance' and 'multifacedness' to this woman's life, i.e. Work should not be the only activity upon which her world revolves.* (FWA Award Recipient Guidelines; emphasis added)

By attempting to select a woman who had 'risen above strife' and 'against all the odds', the 1980s FWA was wedding the 'American Dream' narrative – the belief that anyone with talent can make it regardless of their gender, race or class – to the biographies of Wall Street women. Moreover they were constructing particular, iconic types of female executives to register with the historical moment in capitalism. In effect the women drew on traditional ideas of the American self-made man and turned that figure into a contemporary corporate woman. Success heroes are radical individuals. They transform themselves and their situation through personal initiative (Traube, 1992: 72). By celebrating these types of figures, the FWA subtly valued the challenges of individual achievement over forging a collective movement to advance women's causes.

What is especially interesting is that the discourse of the FWA was rooted in American notions of inclusion. However their practices ran counter to it. At its best, FWA practices provided women with 'successful' female business role models. But at its worst, they hardened the boundaries of its network, effacing differences of class and race amongst women. In this sense the FWA built a gendered network of distinction, a network based not only on a member's economic capital, but their symbolic or cultural capital as well (Bourdieu, 1984). A woman's participation in philanthropic endeavours was not especially valued. This lack of emphasis on women's charitable practices would shift during the next several decades. However, already by the 1980s, a corporate woman's identity beyond the world of work, a notion that would become central to Wall Street women's subject formation in the new economy, was beginning to emerge.

The FWA constructed female business icons and gendered mobility narratives. Equally important, they created female financial subjects. Specifically the network provided a space for women slowly to take on a corporate habitus. Through participating in FWA events, women gradually developed a system of bodily movements, gestures, expressions, eating habits and ways of dressing that helped distinguish them as professional-managerial classed women (Bourdieu, 1984: 192). For example in March 1996 I attended an event entitled 'Celebrating Women's History: Defining Moments in the Lives of Five Leaders.' During the panelists' discussions of career success they alluded to an historical process of habitus making in the FWA. Specifically an audience member asked the panelists – women who had been active FWA members in the late 1970s and throughout the 1980s – if they had any female role models during these early days. Linda Super, a former high-ranking financial professional provided the following response:

> There were no women role models for the corporate paradigm. There was no one around to tell if you if it was ok to wear nail polish to the office, what office dress meant, if black tie meant your dress could be cocktail length or if it had to be an evening gown. There were no women to show you how to stand, to watch what they did, to explain and define all of the cues. There were no women to tell you how much to drink, to order white or red wine, or if you should laugh at a bad joke. You did not have someone to talk to about these things. But, the FWA is great because you have women to talk to, to be around. You can find out where something fits in, what is corporate behaviour, and things that are not easy to define. Subtle cues make a difference. The glass ceiling revolves around these issues. (From field notes)

Within the ranks of the professional-managerial class, bureaucratization throughout most of the twentieth century has traditionally affected criteria for advancement (Traube, 1992: 73). Hard work is a necessary but not sufficient means by which successfully climbing the corporate hierarchy is achieved. Mastery of the techniques of self-presentation, particularly in the top echelons of institutions, is equally essential. Properly managing one's external appearance – face, dress and speech – provide crucial signals to one's peers and superiors that one is willing to undertake other forms of self-adaptation required in the business world (Jackall, 1988: 46–7). Indeed body image and maintenance is an increasingly essential part of performance in financial service work (McDowell, 1997). Normally one learns the managerial codes in the course of repeated, long-term social interaction with other managers and one's superiors, especially a mentor (Jackall 1998: 38, 61). However historically women have encountered difficulty in securing a mentor to show them the 'corporate' ropes (Kanter, 1977). Participating in FWA events therefore provided an alternative means for women to attempt becoming proficient in the rules of survival and success required in moving up the executive ladder.

REMAKING SUCCESS AND THE CORPORATE SELF IN THE NEW ECONOMY

85 Broads women are constructing a new script for success in the new economy moment marked by the precariousness of work. Indeed the network is a response to the ways flexible, short-term work and downsizing are destroying the signposts that people traditionally use to define success in the workplace (Sennett, 2000: 2). Loyalty and sacrifice to a collective entity – the firm – are vanishing in the wake of these developments. The 'old' narrative of steadily moving up the business and social ladder in a single institution is no longer viable. Indeed the goals of 85 Broads are driven by the women's concerns over their next move in a world void of clear-cut career paths. Hanson elaborates on these concerns in the description of her motives for building the network:

> The driving passion for me [in creating 85 Broads] was in realizing what can happen to people after they leave Goldman Sachs because the Goldman Sachs bond is so strong it might just as well be woven into the DNA. When people leave the firm it's a similar experience to leaving graduate school or any major institutional experience in your life. You have a shared identity with the people you work with in close quarters under intense circumstances. So, I think of 85 Broads as a giant Outward-Bound adventure. It can be grim to be out there on your own after being in such a team-oriented culture like Goldman Sachs. My original objective was to make the women that left Goldman Sachs not feel like they had fallen off a cliff – at any age. After you leave the workplace and also when you decide to re-enter the workforce after any time away, your confidence in yourself can diminish. (From fieldwork interview, January 2003)

In an article entitled 'The new political economy and its culture', Richard Sennett writes about the new 'dispensable self'. When labour becomes dispensable, workers feel that they 'can simply disappear from view' (Sennett, 2000: 5). Individuals must struggle for security and a coherent sense of self (Sennett, 2000: 10). 85 Broads not only provides a site for the reconstitution of a 'diaspora' for Wall Street female refugees in the new economy; it also provides a site for identity reconstruction. Some of the women have quit, left or been laid off by Goldman Sachs. However the fact that they are no longer official employees of Goldman Sachs does not matter because the women now carry the firm in their DNA. Financial knowledge, something that one acquired by working on Wall Street, once defined membership in the FWA. Surface appearance once sufficed to signal one's membership in the corporate order. Now a contemporary biological metaphor – DNA deep within the molecular structures of the self – defines the category of the female financial subject.

Yet, once again, the women's talk about their network is embedded in American discourse. Hanson equates the network to a 'giant Outward Bound adventure'. Outward Bound programmes emphasize personal growth through experience and challenge in the wilderness. In the spirit of independence and self-reliance, 85 Broads women exhibit their kinship with the American frontiersman, whose self-transformation takes the form of mastering the savage in the name of civilization (Slotkin, 1986: 86–7, cited in Traube, 1992: 72). However in the contemporary moment, the frontier is no longer located within nature. It is rooted directly in mastering the new global economy of technology, the unknown, and self-realization.

In contrast to the FWA's weekly events held in New York City, 85 Broads stages all-day conferences approximately every six months for its members in various global cities: New York City, San Francisco, Frankfurt, Tokyo and London. Unlike a number of the FWA meetings that examine being successful in finance, 85 Broad events centre on key questions, echoing the focus of Oprah Winfrey's self-styled television programme, such as 'What's Your Destiny?' and 'What's Your Gift?' Indeed it is not all together surprising that in an interview with a younger member of 85 Broads, the woman called Janet Hanson 'Oprahesque'. Janet, 'like Oprah', she told me, 'is all about asking what's your life about – what our destiny means to us'.

The notion of the self, articulated in these events, is not about mastering surface appearances, but rather an essence to develop and cultivate. This version of success as self-fulfilment and empowerment – embodied in new age thought – promises compensation for the degradation of or loss of work. Its roots are in the 1950s American definition of success as the product of a partial retreat from work into a familial world of leisure (Traube, 1992: 74). In the new economy, one in part trades traditional career advancement for the emotional fulfilment of finding one's inner gift and destiny.

Goldman Sachs managing director Jacki Hoffman-Zehner drew on the idea of 'destiny' throughout the speech she gave during the event – What's Your Destiny? – held on 16 May 2001. In her talk she wove together American gendered notions of destiny, survival and power into a single narrative to contextualize her decision to leave Goldman Sachs. She plans to pursue her 'personal destiny' to make a movie about 'women who are going to change the world'. According to Hoffman-Zehner, 'I never thought I was *destined* to be a mortgage bond trader, but I do feel that I *am* destined to help empower women' (Hoffman-Zehner, 2001: 3).

The new economic rhetoric in play today – 'informational competence', 'flexible labour', and the like – 'shifts the focus from impersonal conditions like the possession of capital to more personal matters of competence' (Sennett, 2000: 6). When the successful fall from grace, it places the responsibility for failure on the individual. Building a career, as discussed earlier, is thus no longer exclusively about determining the criteria required in advancing within a single bureaucratic hierarchy. In the new economy each individual must direct his or her career trajectory. Such a process entails managing the entrepreneurial self for the current challenge, including accumulating skills as best one can in order to prepare for the next moment (McRobbie, 2002: 100). Success depends upon inner willpower and the discipline to dust oneself off when one falls down. The possibility and, indeed, reality of failure is now written into the new formula for the contemporary successful corporate self. The purpose of Wall Street women's networks – moving women up the career ladder – has indeed been partially destabilized in the new post-corporate world of work.

FINANCE AND FEMINISM: QUANDARIES OF IDENTITY AND ALLIANCE MAKING

Both the FWA and 85 Broads are built around their members' shared identity as women in finance. Moreover the women not only want to unite on the basis of who they are as women, but also want to assert a certain social status, and to insist on the particularity of their industry, and in the case of 85 Broads, their firm. Historically they do not add issues of race or ethnicity to the mix; their self-definition is extremely narrow. As women they could not have entered the workforce, without the feminist movement's insistence on the opening up of formerly male professions such as law, medicine and management. Indeed as professional-managerial class women they have incorporated mainstream feminism's strategy for assimilation. As a result they have focused on how to 'make it' in the business world (Ehrenreich, 1989: 216). However the more radical agendas of the movement – revolution, overthrowing the corporate order and improving the plight of poor or African American women – have proved far more problematic for financial women and their networks to incorporate into their identity and mission. Given women's uneasy relationship to the more radical dimensions of feminism, we need to closely look at the process by which the women's movement has influenced the politics of financial women's networks over time. Accordingly, I want to re-examine the histories of the FWA and 85 Broads as a series of steps in identity reformation and political alliance-making. Notably, FWA leaders attempted to strategically incorporate parts of the women's movement agenda into their mission without making a public stance on their point of view.

The first FWA board meeting of the 1981–82 calendar year started off with debates over the public and private relationship of the organization to women's politics. Officially the association took the standpoint that the FWA was a professional not a political or feminist group. Dealing with women's issues however proved to become increasingly complicated in the wake of the feminist movement and anti-discrimination suits on Wall Street in the 1970s and 1980s. During the meeting on 2 September 1981, FWA women debated if the FWA would sponsor a march on Washington in support of the ERA. 'It was concluded that this activity was too political and had the potential of a disastrous outcome. However, although the FWA would not become involved as a sponsor, mention could still be made in the newsletter that the BPW has announced that it is undertaking this activity' (FWA Board Minutes, 2 September, 1981: 1, 3).

The women's talk about the FWA's relationship to the ERA reveals their anxieties about deciding which facets of their multiple identities they were going to continue to build their network around. Having initially chosen to construct it around 'women' they were then pulled toward the ERA and feminist politics by the unfolding logic of their identities' implication in the network. Yet by electing not to take a public stand on women's political issues they attempted to control the ramifications of drawing on 'femaleness' as a foundation for solidarity. Making sense of their decision requires examining the conservative national and political forces of the 1980s shaping Wall Street women. Anthropologist Elizabeth Traube, in her book *Dreaming Identities: Class, Gender, and Generation in 1980s Hollywood Movies*, writes that during this era, 'Hollywood joined New Right Leaders in directing socially rooted discontents against independent upwardly mobile women. Movies as well as political discourse attacked uncontrolled, ambitious women in the cause of a moral crisis that, given its definition, called for a stronger authoritarian patriarchy' (Traube, 1992: 20).

The FWA 'solved' the problem of becoming aligned with women's politics and issues by creating indirect and less overt ways to lend support. For example they decided to publicize the ERA March in the newsletter, but to ensure that it was clear that the FWA were not the sponsors. Hiding behind the political cloak of other women's organizations became a common FWA strategy. This was also especially true of the FWA's early relationship with other national associations of professional women. In October 1981, several FWA board members travelled to a Northeast city to participate in a meeting of a national network of executive women. The FWA president reported to the board in November that the national group 'is still substantially less sophisticated and professional than the FWA. Therefore the FWA is placed in the position of sharing its resources with them without the likelihood, at this time, of receiving reciprocal benefits of equal value'. Notably, the FWA president did not suggest that the FWA withdraw its support or involvement with the group. Rather she concluded that the network's 'potential does seem to be in the area of Washington representation and of being able to take a political stance on certain issues on the national level and thereby reduce the pressure the FWA experiences to take political positions on the local level' (FWA Board Minutes, November 4, 1981: 2).

The women's frustration regarding the lack of power, leadership and resources available in other executive women's networks in the nation had some serious consequences for their political alliance-building strategies. In the end, they used their affiliations with women's national networks in order to avoid taking official political stances on women's issues. Furthermore they chose to focus on making international connections, rather than national ones, to cement their identification with other financial women and to by-pass dealing with feminist issues at 'home'. Indeed during the same meeting in November 1981, the value of international networking over the national became a major source of interest. The FWA president drew the board's attention to their sister organization – the Hong Kong FWA, an association composed of 100 members, many of whom held financial positions and were associated with the FWA of New York. She 'suggested that the existence of such an organization provides the potential for an international scope, which may prove a more fertile direction than the national organization efforts of the Alliance' (FWA Board Minutes, 4 November 1981: 2). The board immediately pursued a tighter bond with the Hong Kong FWA by inviting the president of the sister FWA organization to meet the board.

Throughout the 1980s, the FWA continued to privilege international networking over national alliance building. It also maintained its strategy of creating links with women who shared their financial identity. Groups of about 30 FWA women travelled to visit the (women's) financial community in

London in 1985, followed by a trip to Tokyo, Peking and Hong Kong a year later.

THE LOGIC OF FINANCIAL WOMEN'S NETWORK FORMATIONS

The cultural logic of women's network formation must first be understood in relation to the logic of financial capitalism. Beginning in the 1980s, Wall Street began to witness major changes. There was a huge expansion of employment in the financial services industry in the United States, as well as Britain and Japan (Sassen, 2001). The growth and globalization of the industry forced institutions to enlarge their managerial structures and emphasize partnership and leadership (Eccles and Crane, 1988). Indeed as markets and firms went global, a new global power structure in finance emerged. High-status and well-paid jobs in the higher echelons of management became increasingly concentrated in global cities such as New York, London and Tokyo (Sassen, 2001).

The FWA women's decision to privilege the local and international must therefore be analysed in reference to the shifting geography of power operating within New York City and globally. In her book *The Global City*, Saskia Sassen argues that New York, Tokyo and London have become central nodes in the new financial economy, strategic sites for the concentration of top-level control and management of spatially dispersed global market activity. One effect has been that such cities have gained in importance and power relative to nation-states. Flows of capital, people and information have bound global cities in networks, creating a global city web whose constituent cities and city-actors become 'global' through the networks in which they participate (Sassen, 2001). Sassen's emphasis on cities allows us to identify concrete local effects and instantiations of globalization. Her analysis also provides the basic scheme to explain why FWA women made decisions to privilege, at least partly, incorporating themselves into circuits of financial women that were operating on an international scale.

Given that the overarching goal of the FWA was moving women into positions of power in finance, the women's networking decisions were generated by and made in relation to the masculine-dominated geography of global city managerial power. It therefore is no coincidence that the women found themselves frustrated with the lack of power, leadership and resources available in the national networks of executive women. Indeed it is not surprising that they turned their entrepreneurial attention towards making links with New York City corporate women engaged in finance and women's groups in Hong Kong and London. The women working in these financial areas were after all also participating within the new circuit of transnational financial power embedded in their global cities.

The FWA's networking strategies must also however be understood in terms of the women's relationship to feminism. Privileging alliances with financial women in global cities produces a network that separates wealthy transnational female professionals (those in the 'group') from underpaid and poor women to whom they have some responsibility in the public space of the nation. Through this separation the FWA builds a constituency for the global mobility of women in finance. In this light, the organization's move to international over national connections provides a way to by-pass feminist issues at home that could be divisive among members, or place the group members in a position where they might not benefit as much from networking. The FWA does not for example build alliances with other American women's groups that might potentially force them to deal with problems facing 'other' women such as poverty. Forming these kinds of connections might pull the association away from focusing on its agenda to push women up the career ladder in finance. The FWA in the 1980s, as a result, created new arenas of financial all-female sociality that drew on but extended local forms in transnational directions and produced global female financial subjects.

DIVERSITY AND PHILANTHROPY IN NEW MILLENNIAL WALL STREET WOMEN'S NETWORKS

In the new millennium calls for diversity on Wall Street are further transforming the relationship between the FWA and feminism. Indeed FWA leaders have responded to these movements by beginning to shift their organization's mission away from an exclusive focus on gender to one to that incorporates the language of diversity and multiculturalism. Specifically in 2002 FWA president Joan Green named diversity as a key priority for the FWA. Accordingly the FWA, in an historic move, created a Diversity Committee. The committee focuses on 'increasing [their] visibility with diverse groups such as the Urban Bankers and Asian Women in Business; ensuring that women of colour are represented as speakers, members, and FWA leaders; and partnering with corporate sponsors to support their internal diversity efforts' (FWA Newsletter, March 2003).[3]

The emerging multicultural logic of Wall Street women's networking practices must be understood in relation to contemporary institutional logics in global finance. It is tempting to suggest that the recent incorporation of diversity efforts by Wall Street women's networks implies that (predominantly white) executive women are finally building alliances with professional women of colour that acknowledge that women are caught up in hierarchies of gender as well as race or ethnicity and class. Here a more utopian read of these developments might argue that while corporate women have historically focused on individual achievement, the time may have come for them to join forces in a collective movement. While I have no doubt that there are individual managers, organizational communities and firms on Wall Street devoted to improving equality in the workplace, I believe that their practices must be viewed in relation to the business of finance, including especially the management and development of a 'diverse' workforce. In that light I want to turn attention to the rapid growth and proliferation of employee networking groups.

During the 1990s Wall Street began to implement worldwide diversity efforts. Firms such as heritage J.P. Morgan developed policies to define and deal with forms of difference. Today part of that effort includes the participation of more than 18 000 employees 'worldwide', approximately 90 affinity groups at what is now named J.P. Morgan Chase (J.P. Morgan Chase: Diversity: Workplace Initiatives). While the women's network boasts one of the largest memberships (around 5000), a wide range of networks based on race, cultural heritage, gender, sexual orientation, disability and/or other defining criteria are sprouting up. For example network groups now include African-Americans, Asian-Pacific Americans, generational-over 40, as well as lesbian, gay, bisexual and transgender employees (J.P. Morgan Chase: Diversity: Workplace Initiatives). Thus if we are to make sense of the new 'multicultural' approach taken by female financial organizations such as the FWA, we cannot ignore the ways in which such practices are directly tied to the recent history of the business of identity politics in financial corporations.

Philanthropic activities are also serving as an avenue for Wall Street women's networks for dealing with issues of race or ethnicity, gender and public participation. 'Miles to Go', a non-profit organization established by 85 Broads, supports humanitarian, philanthropic and educational causes around the world. Projects supported include Room to Read, an organization devoted to educating children in poverty; StreetSquash, a youth enrichment programme in Harlem; Junior Achievement of Nigeria, an organization devoted to children's welfare; and the National Council for Research on Women, an alliance of 95 leading women's research and policy centres involved in scholarship, advocacy and programming on behalf of women and girls worldwide (Miles to Go). Notably, the 21st FWA International Conference took place in the Dominican Republic in March 2005. Here part of the trip focused 'on the economic prospects for this country, with special emphasis on the role of microfinance for women seeking to lead their families out of poverty' (FWA News, September 2004).

Wall Street women's giving operates in a fashion that is consistent with traditional gendered forms of philanthropy practiced amongst American elites. Historically women of the upper class have dedicated major gifts to causes that are related to their life, concerns, and priorities as women (Ostrower, 1995: 73). There is continuity in financial women's current support for social services. Like elite women before them, members of 85 Broads focus on providing funds for youth and women. In this sense the network continues to build their identity around the category of women. However, philanthropy is also a mark of class status that contributes to defining the women as part of the new economy elite (ibid: 6). Thus, even as Wall Street women integrate feminism into their organizational practices, they construct themselves as elite female subjects.

CONCLUSIONS

In this chapter I have drawn attention to the way transformations in Wall Street women's networked organizational identities and politics are grounded in larger historical frameworks of various sorts. These include: epochal shifts (the globalization of financial capitalism), the virtualization and sometimes disappearance of permanent corporate work, social movements (feminism), and women's 'own imaginings and practices in relation to cultural conceptions of "success" and self' (Ortner, 2003: 1).

First, I have tried to show how the two narratives about women's success on Wall Street draw on and refashion two competing American styles and notions of the work ethic. Specifically, I have illuminated the ways in which Wall Street women's talk about themselves, and their network, reveal the ways shifts in success ideology register and respond to historically engendered cultural tensions. On the one hand, dominant success narratives produced in the FWA (during the 1980s) represent a traditional 'old economy' emphasis on the organizational work ethic. Here, as Paul Heelas argues, 'work is valued as a means to the end of professional or community status and career advancement, as defined by the organization' (Heelas, 2002: 80). On the other hand, 85 Broads women's articulation about finding 'their destiny' reveals the ways in which a new generational network of financial women are elaborating upon a more 'new economy' exploratory type of self-work ethic (Heelas, 2002: 80). Here in an increasingly post-corporate era, work becomes more broadly defined and is 'taken to provide the opportunity to "work" on oneself; to grow; to learn ("the learning organization"); to become more effective *as* a person' (du Gay, 1996, cited in Heelas, 2002: 83).

Notably, while my analysis points to the ways these different notions of success and work ethics articulate with different stages of the economy, I want to make sure to emphasize that these are ideal-type differentiations. In contemporary everyday life these distinctions may collapse, collide, and/or contradict one another' (Heelas, 2002: 81). Indeed for example in the autumn of 2002 I attended a political women's group event held in the penthouse of a New York City department store. The evening event, composed of many of the earlier generation of FWA women, focused on how to 'rewire' your life. Here some of these former high-ranking executive women spoke about their recent experience leaving the street and trying to create a new career that was more connected to their true sense of self. Hence I suspect we are in the midst of witnessing attempts by Wall Street women to reach some kind of cultural consensus of the meaning of success, in a work world fraught with economic change and uncertainty.

Second, I have illuminated how a closer look at the different narrative constructions of success helps us to sort out the shifting gendered politics of Wall Street women, and illuminate the cultural backdrops to debates over the relationship between financial women's networks, Wall Street firms, feminism and society at large. On the one hand, historically the FWA has taken a rather conservative approach to corporate feminist politics. Building upon the older organizational work ethic, FWA women have traditionally viewed their network as an elite organizational entity defined by business principles, rather than a pro-feminist institution oriented toward overtly fighting gendered and/or racial forms of discrimination. Hence the network up until relatively recently has focused most of its energy on moving women (who have been by and large white) up the corporate ladder. It is only recently that they have begun to address diversity issues, in light of the current emphasis on diversity in the securities industry as a whole.

On the other hand, 85 Broads has infused the more contemporary exploratory self-work ethic with what we might call an emergent professional managerial class New Age feminism. Here 85 Broads women espouse an ideology in which if they are to ever achieve their real potential (as women) they must effectively search for the meaning of life and success in themselves beyond the borders of the corporation. This belief then takes form for example in their turn to charitably raising money for the benefit of 'other' women both at home and across the globe. Thus, we seem to be observing the ways in which, in the new economy, a significant number of professional managerial class women are becoming somewhat disillusioned with what the "primary" institutions (particularly the workplace) 'have to offer with the regard to the meaning of life' (Heelas, 2002: 92). What is clear is that changes in the nature of the corporation as well as feminism are producing shifts in the ways women (and presumably men) relate to the workplace, and consequently construct their sense of personhood, success and political practice (Guthey, 2004: 325).

NOTES

1. This research was supported in part by a grant from the Alfred P. Sloan Foundation's programme on Workplace, Workforce and Working Families. Wall Street women may disagree with some of the interpretations of their experiences suggested here, but I have tried to capture the complexities, ambiguities and anxieties of their world. A note on style: quotations that are reconstructed from my field notes are not verbatim transcriptions; these passages are indicated with 'from fieldwork interview' or 'from field notes'. Lastly, I have changed and disguised the names of Wall Street women as well as some of the professional women's organizations cited in the FWA archives.
2. Notably, as Helen McCarthy points out in her study of professional women's groups in the United Kingdom, 'despite the history of networks being intertwined with that of the women's movement, few networks explicitly espouse feminist or equality goals' (McCarthy, 2004: 42). For a further discussion of the FWA's primary mission as focused on moving women up in finance rather than addressing feminist concerns, see also Sastry and Lee (2000). For works on gender in international finance, see McDowell (1997), Fisher (2003) and Czarniawska (2004).
3. The Urban Bankers is an organization devoted to serving the needs of minorities in the financial services industry.

PART II

Work, time and the work–life balance

The male breadwinner model is disappearing statistically as the female employment rate rises in Europe and the United States. Working times are also becoming more varied as information and communication technologies (ICTs) expand the temporal and spatial boundaries of work, and this is cumulative as social expectations about collective rhythms of work erode. The growth in the number of dual-earner households with children is often associated with the idea of time squeeze or time pressure and stress. Nevertheless the ease with which paid work and caring can be combined and the impact on the well-being of parents and children vary considerably across states, depending partly on the form and extent of work–life balance and family-friendly policies and traditions, especially regarding working hours.

Changing working times and especially longer working hours affect all social groups and not just those with children or other caring responsibilities. In the UK the concept of work–life balance was introduced partly in response to the long-hours culture and the ways in which paid work could and perhaps should be combined with other aspects of life including studying and leisure as well as caring. It was designed to reflect the diverse interests of workers and thereby be more inclusive than family-friendly, and also has more normative connotations by conveying the idea of harmony between paid work and these other life dimensions. While some firms have introduced leave or sabbaticals for a range of purposes, the connotations of work–life balance remain tied to caring, leave and flexible working, and in practice to policies that enable people to combine paid work and care. Indeed the terms 'family-friendly' and 'work–life' balance are often used interchangeably in the UK and the US, while in continental Europe and EU policy the terms 'family-friendly' and 'reconciliation of work and family life' are currently more prevalent.

In the UK work–life balance policies together with flexible working practices do enable people combine caring with paid work, but often in ways that lead to long overall working days rather than the implied harmonious equilibrium. Alternatively the policies entail career compromises, as reduced hours and periods of leave generally have negative implications for career progression. The ways in which households resolve work–life issues also have implications for social divisions more generally. More highly qualified women are more likely to retain greater attachment to the labour market, work full-time and develop careers. They are also more likely to be in dual high-earning households owing to associative matching between similarly qualified women and men. By contrast people in less well-paid occupations requiring lower qualifications, manage caring by one partner, typically the woman, reducing their working time and taking advantage of the highly flexible working patterns that have been introduced especially since the 1990s which enable them to fit their jobs around their caring responsibilities. This subordination of women's paid work not only complies with traditional expectations about gender roles, but the opportunity cost of women subordinating paid work to the family is also typically far lower.

Women in low-paid and even middle-range jobs with partners in the UK often welcome the chance to work in the evening, at night and at weekends when their partner with more traditional working hours can care for their children. For single parents and couples who both work flexible hours, the issues are more complex and contingent on precise arrangements. In the US, by contrast, flexible working was found not to be so welcome as it prevented people from using the formal childcare (see Presser) an issue also important in France (see Fagnani and Letablier, this volume). Thus precise patterns vary with the different provisions made by different states to facilitate work caring combinations.

The chapters in Part II are case-studies from three European countries with rather different welfare regimes: the liberal market UK, corporative France and social democratic Sweden. Each case-study focuses on a different dimension of work–life balance reflecting different preoccupations in the different countries.

The first case-study by Jeanne Fagnani and Marie Thérèse Letablier explores the differential implications of the reduced working time law (RWT) on the gendered division of labour in France and again how this in turn varies by social class. Their study is situated within a country with a more corporatist tradition in terms of the relations between the social partners, and specifically within a history of state concern with and influence over working hours. While the specific measure they examine, the introduction of the 35-hour week, was motivated by concerns about unemployment and thus not explicitly concerned with work–life balance, the authors examine its impact on managing work and care. In particular they consider how the new working patterns and workers' control of flexibility varies between different sectors and how gender and social class influence use of the time saved.

In Sweden there is a more established tradition of and public support for the adult citizen model – dual-earning dual-carer households. However during the past decade, and especially in the early 1990s, there has been a similar concern about the unprecedented levels of unemployment. Thus the second case-study by Anita Nyberg examines the sustainability of the dual-earner, dual-carer model in a period of economic crisis with not only high levels of unemployment but also declining employment and large budget deficits. In order to do so she provides a detailed investigation of the changes in childcare and parental leave policies from 1990 to 2003 and more specifically discusses how the entitlements to childcare for women and men and the duration and funding for different forms of leave have changed. Additionally she examines how the form, scale and quality of publicly funded childcare have changed during this period of economic crisis when expanding the female employment rate was not therefore a priority.

Part II continues with a case-study of the UK by Rosemary Crompton and Michaela Brockman and uses both quantitative and qualitative data to provide a detailed analysis of the relationship between new working patterns and stress. More specifically they explore how work life stress varies by gender, social class and worker aspirations in the context of new more individualized social relations in the UK workplace. The study also comments on the widening social inequalities in the UK and how these are reinforced by the patchy provision of affordable childcare, which in turn sustains a division of labour between women and men, the extent of which varies by occupational class.

Thus each of the case studies illustrates the differential work–life balance provisions and it becomes clear that these not only reflect the different welfare traditions or systems of social regulation but also potentially reinforce these patterns. In the France and the UK the forms of provision in their existence and their absence have a greater tendency to reinforce inequality by social class, while in the Swedish case the continuing commitment to wider-scale provision of care in and for itself promotes more comprehensive provision and facilitates greater attachment to the labour market for all social groups. What becomes clear however is that while work–life balance or family-friendly policies undoubtedly facilitate increases in the female employment rate, one of the rationales for their introduction at national and EU level, they nevertheless generate some new concerns because they can also reinforce gender divisions both at work and in the home. So while they contribute to the short-term agenda of bringing about greater equality between women and men in terms of employment participation, they may be more limited in terms of bringing about deeper forms of gender equality.

5. The French 35-hour working law and the work–life balance of parents: friend or foe?

Jeanne Fagnani and Marie Thérèse Letablier

The reduction of working time has long been on the political agenda in France, particularly for left-wing governments. Policy aims and objectives have varied over time, but the precipitative factor for change in the 1990s was the increase in the unemployment rate; fighting it became a public priority. An additional motive for this policy was to increase flexibility in the work organization, impelling collective bargaining and improving the work and life balance, especially for parents with young children. The proposal tabled in 1997, when a socialist government came to power, was more comprehensive than previous legislation in that it set out to ensure that other aspects of time structuring were addressed. In comparison to 1936 and the 1980s, the focus was on both the reduction of working time and the negotiation of work-time organization at workplace level. Arrangements were to be brought more into line with individual preferences. The position of France is unique in Europe because it is an example of working time being reduced by law and applying to all workers.

Although the reduction of working time is no longer on the agenda in France, nor any other EU country, this chapter examines the outcome of this policy, especially as it relates to the work and life balance issue. Although this issue was not the main priority of the measures, it deserves attention because parents had to deal with more complex childcare arrangements. Against the background of the development of flexible work schedules, and an increase in workload, parents are clearly facing growing difficulties in managing their everyday life. First, to set these laws in their historical context, we will look at the role of these laws in the creation of working time norms since the nineteenth century. We will then focus on the ways the 'Aubry laws' have been implemented, along with their practicalities. In the third section, their impact on the everyday life of working parents with young children is examined. This is partly to answer the following question: does the reduction in working time (RWT) make it easier for parents to balance paid work with family responsibilities, when we take into account that among the majority of dual-earner families in France, both partners work full-time? We then turn our attention to the effect the measures have had on gender relations.

REGULATING WORKING TIME BY LAW: A FRENCH TRADITION

France is the only country in Europe whose government has used legislation to impose a collective RWT: the 35-hour laws that cut the maximum working week by four hours with no loss of pay. Such a procedure had been used in the past; therefore reforms in the late 1990s are first of all set in the context of past state regulation in this field.

An Historical Background to the Reduction of Working Time

France has a long tradition of strong central government and to understand the current laws on the reduction of working hours we must look back to the nineteenth century (Fridenson and Reynaud, 2004). If the decisive social battles over reduction of working hours took place in the twentieth century, it is as a direct result of the multiplicity of actors, and the objectives they pursued, in the preceding century.

The struggle to reduce working hours began largely as a result of militant actions taken by physicians; working from within the establishment, their social and economic goals were achieved in successive stages alongside an emerging, and at the time novel, idea of 'public health'. The law of 1841, which reduced the working hours of children, was obtained by an industrialist's concern about children's moral and religious education. Following this was the law of 1892 that reduced the hours worked by women. Among the main promoters of this law figured the labour unions, which were trying to remove women from jobs made increasingly scarce by a poor economic climate. Additionally other workers, most notably from the business sector, began to agitate for a halt to the practice of working on Sundays and the attendant disruption this caused to their families. The Church also intervened in the debate, standing firmly in defence of keeping the Sabbath day holy as a means of upholding religious standards.

Nevertheless the distance between judicial norms and actual practice remained considerable. This was due to a combination of factors: weak supervision and control of the measures, a lack of effective sanctions and a notable absence of any political will. The law of 1919 instituted the eight-hour workday, 'which seems to have been the first law concerning working hours that was actually put into practice on some level' (Chatriot et al., 2003: 16). In

1936 legislation was drafted for a 40-hour working week. Although suspended throughout the war years, these measures became law in 1946.

Tough Social and Economic Times for Employees except those in the Public Sector

The reduction in working time was part of the Left coalition government's legislative programme in the 1990s. When the Left returned to power in 1997, it was one of the Jospin government's four key elements of social policy, along with universal health cover, youth employment programmes and elderly care reforms. While most employers were ambivalent towards a reduction in working time and strongly opposed the government's view, a first law was passed in 1998, and a second one in 2000. These laws, designated 'Lois Aubry I and II', reduced the legal standard of working time from 39 to 35 hours per week. As employers were obliged to come to terms with the implementation of the law, a bargaining process was launched within most firms. Employers received financial compensation as a way of alleviating the increases in operating costs caused by both a reduction in working time and the need to recruit and hire new employees. To further reduce employer cost, government-mandated social contributions for low-wage earners[1] were also reduced. Additionally many collective agreements stipulated that wage increases would be frozen for a certain period of time.

These laws produced a climate that encouraged modernization in the workplace, by giving firms more latitude to increase work flexibility. All of this took place against the background of unbalanced power relationships between employers and employees. At the time the law was drafted, unemployment was running extremely high at 12 per cent, and trade union membership was historically low at less than 10 per cent of the workforce. It should therefore come as no surprise that sometimes unions have been compelled to accept flexible working schedules and practices to which they have traditionally been opposed.

Revising the 35-hours Law

The Conservative government, in place since June 2002, made amendments to the 35-hour law in order to attenuate its rigidity and introduce more flexibility in implementation. Against a background of growing economic uncertainty and increasing competition, the 35-hour laws were widely believed to have brought mayhem to work organization, generating extra costs both for companies and the state. The revision of the law was part of President Jacques Chirac's election platform when he was competing for the elections in 2002 as the representative of the right wing. His express aims were to give more freedom to firms, to weaken state power and to rehabilitate work values. In fact for the right, the 35-hour laws reveal a threefold mistake: firstly, in principle because it is not the state's responsibility to decide how work should be organized in firms; secondly, in economic perspective because their impact on employment is judged to be too weak; and lastly, in social impact because they have generated inequalities between workers.

Following reforms made in 2003 a new level of flexibility has been introduced in the implementation of the 35-hour laws. A new law (17 January 2003) stipulates an annualization of the measurement of working time. In addition, the number of overtime hours authorized for each employee has been progressively increasing, from 130 to 180 hours per year. During the summer of 2004, the 35-hours question was again on the political agenda. Some members in the government want to go all the way and completely abrogate the legal controls over working time, giving full responsibility to private firms. Nicolas Sarkozy, the former finance minister, has been pushing for more reform, while arguing that international competition demands more working time from employees. In this context and with some firms threatening to relocate abroad, many 35-hour agreements have been renegotiated, extending hours of work without any increase in wages. Similar trends can be observed in Germany.

Objectives of the Aubry Laws

The 'Aubry I' law passed in 1998 abrogated the measures set out in the 'Robien' law of 1996, which instituted compensations for companies who reduced working time in an effort to generate more jobs. The 'Aubry' laws went further than anything previously by settling the legal duration of working time at 35 hours per week from 1 January 2000 for companies with more than 20 employees, and from January 2002 for all others. The first law made provisions for financial incentives from the state for firms that introduced the law before the stipulated date and used it to create jobs. These benefits were subject to the signature of a convention with the state, following an agreement between social partners. Companies that linked the RWT to an increase in the size of the workforce also benefited from a cut in social contributions (6 per cent for a reduction in working time of 10 per cent, and 9 per cent for a reduction of 15 per cent). Relief was also given to companies facing economic difficulties that kept staff on instead of laying them off.

The second law ('Aubry II', 2000) included new measures regarding work and time organization. There was regulation of overtime hours, length of leave and various forms of part-time and temporary work. Time-saving accounts were introduced which allowed workers to vary their working hours over the space of a year and 'save up' time. Special provisions were made for managers and professionals with long working hours. Additionally the second law put forward a broader range of options for reducing working hours. Incentives for employers included reductions in social contributions to encourage implementation. Employees, for their part, were forced to accept a moderation of the increase in their wages as a counterpart of the RWT.

Additional objectives of the laws were to increase flexibility in work organization, to reactivate collective bargaining, especially at firm level, and to improve the work–life balance. From the 1970s onwards, the right to a healthy work and life balance became a social issue and a rather popular demand expressed both by trade unions and the social movement. Slogans such as '*Du temps pour vivre*' (more time for everyday life) expressed widespread aspirations. This spirit emerged in a context where dual-earner families were becoming the norm, and where part-time work did not receive much consideration from either the trade unions or the feminist movement. During the 1990s, the concern *vis-à-vis* unemployment growth and job creation returned the issue to the political agenda of left-wing parties.

Once again, researchers were investigating the work and life balance in an attempt to promote the idea of a more family-friendly and more gender-equal society (Méda, 2001). In such an environment it was assumed that working time regulations could free up parents' caring time by limiting normal employment hours to 35 per week, whatever the form of reduction. Some feminist scholars concluded from their research that shortening working time for all workers may be the most promising tool for achieving a gender-egalitarian redistribution of domestic labour and parental responsibilities.[2] (Letablier, 2004). Nevertheless implementation of the laws was complex, and diversity has been the rule in introducing new forms of work organization.

HOW WAS THE POLICY ORGANIZED AND DELIVERED? WHAT WAS AT STAKE?

The RWT was carefully prepared, and social partners were invited to participate in a dialogue to elaborate its various measures. Initially few of them supported the idea. Advocates of the reform argued that it would lead to greater work sharing and encourage social dialogue in the workplace, while also providing an opportunity for workers to have more free time for personal activities. Opponents advocated, as an alternative to wage restraint, allowing workers the freedom to make an individual choice between reductions in the length of working hours or an increase in salaries.

Restructuring Working Time

The legislative process involved lengthy negotiations between employers and unions at workplace level, which aimed to fix the conditions of the reduction (in particular wage conditions), and the implementation of new schedules. The process of negotiation successfully produced a series of workplace agreements. Not only have working hours been reduced, but work-time arrangements have also been revised. Previously, many workers had little opportunity to reorganize working time on a daily, weekly, monthly or annual basis. The new law has led to greater flexibility in working time arrangements, for both employers and employees.

Large and Small Firms: a Strong Divide

Three out of four full-time employees worked less than 36 hours a week in 2004; however broad variations are to be observed between small and large firms. In general, implementation of the laws was easiest in large firms. Small companies were more reluctant *vis-à-vis* the RWT and had difficulty coping with the complexity of implementation. Indeed for small firms, the shift towards 35 hours means an increase in work costs (Pham, 2003).

By the end of the year 2002, roughly 75 per cent of employees were working in firms where the 35-hour week had already been implemented. It is noteworthy that over 80 per cent of employees in large firms (500 employees or more) were affected by the 35-hour week while only 52 per cent of the employees in small firms (10 to 20 employees) have had their working time reduced, in spite of a legal obligation to do so since January 2002.

Due to the demands of business, and the strong desire to increase competitiveness, some large companies reorganized working hours and introduced more flexible work schedules as a way to offset the extra costs of the RWT. Therefore employees had little choice but to accept more flexibility at the workplace. For instance automobile industry giant Renault secured flexible working practices – weekend shifts, night work – in return for a shorter week. Caterpillar adopted a seven-day working week. Across differing organizations a broad range of options was offered to reduce working time.

Whereas a number of small firms suggested only one means of reduction of working hours to their employees, the majority were offered several options. For most of these employees, working time reduction has taken the form of days off, often combined with a time account (*modulation/annualisation*), which means it is possible to make hours of work vary over the length of the year. Around 33 per cent have a half-day off every week, or one day off every two weeks; 25 per cent have opted for a reduction in hours worked each day, most of them being blue-collar workers. Some employees combine two options.

Most part-time workers continue to work part-time, their hours of work having been reduced in line with the reduction accorded to full-time workers. In general, manual workers are more enthusiastic about a daily reduction of hours of work (38 per cent) whereas only a minority (8 per cent) among employees at management and supervisory level have been able to opt for this pattern of reduction. A longer vacation was by far the most widespread option for highly qualified employees at management level who have on average a supplement of 13.5 days off per year (Afsa et al., 2003).

Employees' Positive Judgement despite Harder Working Conditions

The trade union CFDT (Confédération Française du Travail) carried out a survey at the very beginning of the implementation of the RWT: 58 per cent of the respondents reported the positive impact of the implementation of the measures on their own situation, and 57 per cent were supportive towards the agreement passed in their firm. Whereas a large majority (81 per cent) of the respondents reported no major changes in their work organization, 15 per cent reported that their working conditions had become worse after the implementation of the measure (CFDT, 1999). Additionally, 48 per cent of the respondents reported an intensification of work in their firm because they have to perform the same work in a shorter time span. Most of the respondents had their working time schedules reorganized. Rhythms of work[3] have become more variable and less predictable, especially for low-skilled employees, among which women are over-represented.

Thus as far as working schedules are concerned, the gap between employees has been increasing. This has been confirmed by other studies: 40 per cent of full-time employees have regular working hours whereas 20 per cent have irregular and unforeseeable working schedules (Estrade and Ulrich, 2003). In his research on the implementation of the 35-hour law, Jérôme Pelisse also provides evidence of increasing inequalities between employees, in terms of financial compensation, organizational constraints and ability to control time off (Pelisse, 2002).

IMPACT ON THE WORK–LIFE BALANCE: AMBIVALENT OUTCOMES

It was assumed that the 35-hour law would contribute to improving working parents' daily life management. However a state-of-the-art literature review shows the heterogeneity of the impact of this law on the work–life balance.

A 2000 onwards survey of wage earners (with or without children), working in companies that had implemented this law for at least one year, showed 57 per cent of employees reporting that their everyday life had not changed with the RWT; 34 per cent reported that it had made it easier to combine work and family life (32 per cent of men and 38 per cent of women). The proportion is significantly higher for women with children aged less than 12 years (Méda and Orain, 2002). As far as parents with children under 12 years are concerned, 63 per cent of the women reported that they had been spending more time with their children since the reduction of their working hours compared to 52 per cent of men. More precisely, fathers as well as mothers reported that they devoted more 'quality time' to their children than before (respectively 21 per cent and 25 per cent).

The survey on the reconciliation of work and family life by parents of young children (the youngest aged under six years), which we carried out in 2000 (Fagnani and Letablier, 2004), provides additional analysis on the perceptions of working parents with regard to the effects of the RWT on their daily lives. Among the respondents (fathers or mothers), who had their working hours reduced due to the implementation of the law, 58 per cent responded 'Yes' to the question: 'Do you feel that the law on the 35 hours has made it easier for you to combine your family life with your working life?' The figures were 59 per cent among women and 55 per cent among men respectively.

Our results confirm the dramatic role played by working conditions, working time schedules and the ways of introducing the RWT in the formation of respondents' opinions about the effect of the 35-hour week on family life. For instance almost half of the respondents had their working hours imposed on them, while the others were able to negotiate, either through their trade unions or by choosing the hours themselves. Parents viewed the effect of the RWT on their family life to be positive where it had been possible to negotiate the working hours. They were more frequently discontented when their working hours had been imposed.

The views of parents with young children also vary according to whether or not they have unsociable working hours. More than six in ten of parents with fixed and 'standard' working hours felt that the RWT had improved their daily lives, against 50 per cent of those who worked non-standard hours. In their research on the effect of the intensification of work for male and female employees, Fagan and Burchell (2002) confirm that unsociable hours (and long hours) have significant negative effects on the work–life balance: the greater the level of non-standard hours, the greater the dissatisfaction.

Positive perceptions of the 35-hour law would appear to be closely linked to whether an employer is perceived as being 'family-friendly'. On the other hand, those who are unhappy about the effects of the law express negative views of their companies, in particular with regard to working conditions and employers' attitude towards employees' family obligations.

Clearly it requires more than a simple reduction of hours worked for parents to feel comfortable with their work and family life balance. Other conditions are required, such as a conscientious organization of working time that is compatible with family needs and childcare arrangements. Additionally it is imperative that there exist positive conditions under which RWT can be introduced and negotiated within companies.

The methods used to implement the law have an enormous influence on the views of parents with young children. Those working in 'protected' and 'family-friendly' sectors – which benefited even before the law was passed from preferential conditions linked to their situation as working parents – declared more frequently than the others that the RWT, and the reorganization of work, had made it easier for them to combine their family life with their job.

Although a majority of parents expressed a positive opinion about the extra time off they have received, a not negligible proportion was disappointed and felt that the measures had had no significant impact on their family life, or indeed that the impact had been negative. Divergences between employees were to be seen whatever their profession and economic sector. The main beneficiaries are those who can take full advantage of the RWT within the framework of standard, predictable and manageable working hours. The losers in this system are those who are unable to take full advantage of increased time off as they are subject to working time calculated on a yearly basis (with implied periods of long working hours), or to unsociable work schedules badly synchronized with the daily routine of young children.

Other research confirms that attitudes towards the RWT depend heavily on the way work is reorganized in the firm and on the restructuring process, especially with regards to the bargaining process (Lallement, 2003). Insofar as these factors are concerned, employees of the public sector could be said to be rather privileged.

The Public Sector: a Family-friendly Workplace

Numerous studies have shown that the conditions for workers in the public sector (or sectors considered as such) are generally superior to those in the private sector with regards to working time. This would help explain the strong attraction the public sector holds for women, in particular for the most qualified. Aside from a high level of job security, there is the power to request a leave of absence (particularly when children fall ill), the possibility to take Wednesday off (schools are closed on Wednesday) and the ability to obtain working hours that are adaptable to the demands of family life. Additionally the actual hours worked each week by both employees and management are less in the public sector than for those with similar positions in the private sector: in 2001, those working in the public sector worked on average 42 hours 45 minutes per week as opposed to 44 hours 55 minutes for those working in the private sector (Afsa et al., 2003).

We can observe a similar divergence between the public and private sector when we observe the effects of RWT on the personal life of employees with young children. State employees expressed a positive opinion of RWT more frequently than others: 68 per cent of them responded 'yes' to the question, 'Do you feel that the law on the 35 hours has made it easier for you to combine your family life with your working life?' compared to only 55 per cent of those working in the private sector (Fagnani and Letablier, 2004).

Negotiations in the public sector or sectors considered as such (with the exception of hospitals and law enforcement where employees are subject to shift work), have unfolded in an environment more favourable to employees than the one that exists for their counterparts in the private sector. A number of factors have contributed to this phenomenon: high levels of unionization (union membership rates are higher in public than in private sector), a deeply held belief in the tradition of 'social dialogue', and a work organization which encourages flexibility and offers working hours that can adapt to the needs of employees with dependents.

A survey carried out among a representative sample of the 36 270 men and women employed by local Family Allowances Funds (in charge of managing family allowances) confirms that a large majority of employees in the public sector are very satisfied with the effects of the RWT on their work–life balance (Boyer et al., 2004). While their working time has been reduced, no change has been introduced in the working schedule; hours of work remain regular and entirely predictable. Eight out of ten employees reported the positive impact of the reduction on their private life because they enjoy having more free time: 80 per cent choose to continue to work 39 hours per week (five days) and to have 20 days off per year. Parents (87 per cent of mothers and 90 per cent of fathers) with young children under 12 responded that they spend more time with their children, especially on Wednesday when children do not attend school.

All of these results confirm that consequences for employees vary according to economic sector, the conditions of the agreement signed between social partners, and whether the company they work for is in dire straits or not. What is imperative to understand is that conditions under which the negotiations were carried out go back to the question of the balance of power between employers, trade unions and employees within firms, as well as to the quality of the 'social dialogue' that existed at the time of the negotiations.

The RWT was also supposed to promote a more equal sharing of paid and unpaid work between parents, in line with the new orientations in family policy, putting an emphasis on 'shared parenting' (Büttner et al., 2002). Did these laws contribute to promoting a more equal sharing of domestic chores and childrearing responsibilities?

Gendering Working Time Reduction

A major impact of the 35-hour law has been to reduce the working time gap between men and women. In France, household employment profiles differ from those observed in most European countries. Excepting the fact that it has one of the highest rates of dual-earner families among EU countries, it is also, with Denmark and Portugal, the country with the lowest gender gap in working time (Franco and Winqvist, 2002). Additionally the gap between men and women working full-time is lower than in many other countries worldwide.

Impact on Gender in Unpaid Work and Leisure

While the RWT tends to reduce the working time gap between men and women, no significant change was registered on the sharing of domestic and parental responsibilities. Although people appreciate having more free time, the use of this time remains highly gender-based. It is also noteworthy that 30 years ago, less-educated and lower-skilled workers had less leisure time than highly educated people; the reverse can be observed nowadays.

The Use of Time Surveys carried out by INSEE (Institut National de la Statistique et des Etudes Economiques) show that this development is mainly due to the greater risk of unemployment, and to the increase in part-time work among the working classes (INSEE, 2004). Nowadays highly educated and highly qualified people tend to work longer hours than less-educated people. Significantly, leisure practices vary with the level of education: travelling, reading and listening to music remain the preserve of the middle and upper classes, while the majority of the working-class population devotes a large part of their free time to watching television. Concerning time dedicated to leisure, women report that, following the reduction in their working time, they spend more time on personal care and reading or listening to music, while men spend more time on sport, gardening and pottering about. In addition, men and women say that they travel more than previously, especially during vacation periods and long weekends (Méda and Orain, 2002).

Nevertheless the RWT did not significantly affect the sharing of unpaid work: women continue to assume most of domestic duties while men are more involved in gardening, shopping and DIY. In addition, 42 per cent of the respondents to the RWT and Lifestyles Survey of the Minister of Employment reported changes in the timing of domestic work, part of it being performed during days off, leaving more time to care for children during the weekends (Méda and Orain, 2002). Likewise, according to the CFDT survey, 51 per cent of the respondents reported that the 35-hour laws had had a positive impact on their everyday life. However 30 per cent of women and 48 per cent of men devoted this time to leisure, while respectively 47 per cent and 27 per cent devoted it to family responsibilities (CFDT, 1999).

CONCLUSION

Time structuring is an important issue for family life as demonstrated by this state-of-the-art literature review. It is beginning to be addressed by policy makers in several EU countries. Although the reduction of legal working time might not be the best way to increase employment, it may be effective under certain conditions in reconciling paid work and family life. The French experience suggests that for a working time policy to be successful, it must enjoy public support, economic and social conditions must be conducive to change, and it must be able to deliver significant improvements in family living conditions, thus serving as a means to reinforce social cohesion.

NOTES

1. Employers did not have to pay for the social security contributions of their low-paid employees.
2. Eighty-five per cent of part-time jobs are held by women (Employment Survey, INSEE, 2002).
3. Defined by regularity and advanced-notice working schedules, and by employees' freedom to choose a working time schedule in line with their preference, as well as the timing of their holidays.

6. Economic crisis and the sustainability of the dual-earner, dual-carer model

Anita Nyberg

INTRODUCTION

The preconditions in the long run for the dual-earner, dual-carer model in Sweden are generally considered to be economic growth, balanced public finances and full employment. In the beginning of the 1990s, the Swedish economy failed badly on all three accounts. There was negative economic growth three years in a row, unemployment reached levels unimaginable since the 1930s, and employment was rapidly declining. While only 1991–93 saw negative economic growth, the whole decade can be considered as a period of crisis on the labour market. Even in 2005 unemployment is high, and despite some improvement in the area, employment is considerably lower than in 1990.[1] Negative economic growth has meant declining revenues and massive unemployment increased public expenditures, which together led to huge budget deficits. The government was under severe pressure to carry out adjustment measures and although agonizing, allowances were cut and the public sector and public expenditure were reduced (Kautto, 2000; Eklund, 2001, Chapter 17).

The combination of labour market restructuring and welfare state retrenchment suggests that policy support for the dual-earner, dual-carer model could face heightened scrutiny. We might well see a fading interest in policies that further women's, and especially mothers', integration into the labour market. Instead women might increasingly be defined through motherhood and caring, and men through employment and wages, which means a return to more traditional gender relations and a weakening of the dual-earner, dual-carer model.

The aim of this chapter is to investigate whether or not a deep economic crisis affects the dual-earner, dual-carer model, and if so, how. This is investigated by studying Swedish childcare and parental leave policies on national and sub-national levels from 1990 to 2003. Publicly financed childcare and parental leave are usually seen as cornerstones in the dual-earner, dual-carer model. First, central state policies are studied: did the legislation change? If so, did the new legislation weaken or strengthen the norm of the dual-earner, dual-carer model? Second, since it is actually provided by the municipalities, the provision of childcare at that level is also investigated: was the supply of childcare amended quantitatively or qualitatively, and was the price, in terms of childcare fees, altered? Third, on the individual level, did parents' use of childcare and parental leave change? The chapter ends with a discussion of the sustainability of the dual-earner, dual-carer model in a situation of massive unemployment, declining employment and large budget deficits.

PARENTAL LEAVE AND ALLOWANCE

It is generally accepted that parental leave has positive effects on the continuous labour market attachment of women. If women are guaranteed paid leave while their jobs are held open, they are more likely to enter the labour market and to build up the eligibility conditions before becoming pregnant (Sundström and Dufvander, 1998). And it may also promote fathers' participation in childcare.[2] However as the title of a monograph on the subject – *Parental Leave: Progress or Pitfall?* (Moss and Deven, 1999) – implies, parental leave can be problematic. If leave schemes offer long periods of leave – taken almost entirely by women – they may reinforce gendered divisions of labour in both employment and the family. Cash benefits for care may have the intention of supporting women's traditional role, postponing women's return to the labour market, and/or keeping female unemployment down (OECD, 1995). These tendencies can be especially strong in times of economic crisis. Further, if the situation on the labour market is unstable and insecure, fathers might be even less willing than usual to take parental leave.

Have regulations and the use of parental leave moved in that direction in Sweden since 1990? In 1974, maternity leave was replaced with parental leave, which meant that leave following the birth of a child was no longer reserved for the mother, but could also be used by the father. However the father could also transfer this right to the mother. In 1974 parental leave was six months. It was soon extended, and in the 1980s the Social Democrats wanted to extend parental leave to 18 months. But the economic crisis in the beginning of the 1990s and an unexpected baby boom around 1990 made this impossible. By 1990 the parental leave was 15 months and in 2005 is 16 months.[3]

In order to persuade fathers to exercise their right to the parental allowance, a 'father's month' (and 'mother's month') was introduced in 1995; one month of the parental leave could no longer be transferred to the other parent. In 2002 parental allowance was increased by another month, and neither can these days be transferred. This means that if parents want to use all 16 months of parental leave, each parent must take at least two months. However there is nothing to stop a parent from not using his (or her) leave (Jansson et al., 2003: 33).

As well as introducing the first father's months, the bourgeois coalition government also launched a childcare allowance in July 1994. The allowance was paid out for children aged one or two years. The parents could use the money to enable one parent to stay at home, or to pay for childcare. Parents could also choose between public and private forms of childcare, both of which were eligible for public subsidy (Bergqvist and Nyberg, 2002)[4]. After taking office in the fall of 1994, the Social Democrats abolished the childcare allowance. Thus it was only in force for roughly six months. The argument, especially from social democratic women, was that childcare allowance is a trap for women.

The Swedish parental leave system is very flexible. It is possible to choose between full, three-quarter, half, one-quarter or one-eighth (that is one hour) of a day. Parents have a right to full-time leave until the child is 18 months or as long as she or he is paid parental allowance. The parental allowance may be drawn at any time until the child has reached eight years old, or has finished the first year in school. Additionally, parents employed full-time are granted unpaid partial leave of absence up to three-quarters time until the child is eight years old, or has finished the first year in school. Many mothers use this opportunity, but very few fathers do.

In 1974, when parental leave was introduced, income replacement was raised to the level of sick pay – 90 per cent of earnings. At the same time the benefit became taxable and pensionable. In the wake of the 1990s economic crisis in Sweden the percentage level of parental leave was lowered to 80 per cent in 1995, to 75 per cent in 1996, and put back to 80 per cent in 1998 when the economy had recovered a little.[5] All the time there has been a ceiling of 7.5 times the basic amount. Because salaries have risen and income differences widened since 1990, the proportion of parents – especially fathers – with earnings above the ceiling (and who therefore receive less than 80 per cent in compensation) has increased. The highest amount a parent today (2004) can receive is 646 SEK per day (about 70 euros) (RFV, 2002a). Ninety days of the parental allowance are compensated by a low flat rate, which has been the same since 1987 (60 SEK, or about 6–7 euros, per day). Non-employed parents receive a guaranteed amount, which up until 2002 was the same as the flat-rate days, but since then been raised considerably, and is today SEK 180 (about 20 euros).[6]

It could be argued that the introduction of the father's month encourages fathers to take parental leave, and thereby supports the dual-earner, dual-carer

model. However, the lower compensation level works in the opposite
direction.

THE USE OF PARENTAL LEAVE

Almost all families with children make use of parental leave and parental
allowances. Ninety-seven per cent use some income-related days, and around
90 per cent at least some of the flat-rate days. The share of families that uses
all parental allowance days amounts to around 60 per cent (these data apply to
children born 1991–93) (RFV, 2002a: 12). Even if the parents can use the
parental leave until the child is eight years old, most parents take the majority
of the days during the first two years of the child's life. Women take parental
leave mainly until the child is about 12 months old, while men take parental
leave chiefly when the child is between 11 and 15 months (Jansson et al.,
2003: 18).

Of those who received parental allowance in 1990, fathers amounted to 26
per cent and mothers to the remaining 74 per cent. In 2003 the proportion of
fathers had increased to 43 per cent and the proportion of mothers then
declined to 57 per cent. Also, the proportion of days the fathers take of all
parental allowance days has increased from 7.7 in 1990 to 17.2 in 2003. An
overwhelming number of both mothers and fathers take whole days.

This shows the use of parental allowance days in a specific year. However
it might be more interesting to investigate this from the perspective of the child
and for the whole period of parental leave – especially to investigate if the
introduction of the father's month in 1995 made a difference. There is some
information on how many days of parental allowance fathers have used by the
time the child has turned four. About half of the fathers of the children born in
1993 and 1994 did not use a single day of parental allowance. This proportion
declined to 23–34 per cent for children born in 1995–99. The proportion that
took 30 days or more increased from not quite 30 per cent to 50 per cent
(Jansson et al., 2003). Another study compared the children born two weeks
before the introduction of the father's month with children born two weeks
after, and followed them until they were eight years old. It was found that
the share of fathers who did not use any parental allowance days at all,
decreased from 54 per cent to 18 per cent, and the proportion of fathers who
took around one month increased from 9 per cent to 47 per cent (Ekberg et al.,
2004).

Studies show that fathers in families with relatively poorer attachment to
the labour market, and relatively low incomes, used parental leave less
than other families (Jansson et al., 2003). The group of fathers that do not
use any parental allowance is however heterogeneous – it also includes

fathers who have incomes above the parental allowance ceiling. The contrasting group consists of parents in families with high incomes, but not above the father's ceiling – where the mother has high income and education. They share parental leave to a higher degree. However overall, the introduction of the father's month has had an impact on the use of parental allowance days by fathers and mothers in a way that seems to strengthen the dual-earner, dual-carer model. Fathers take more parental leave and mothers less.

PUBLICLY FINANCED CHILDCARE

The provision of public childcare services is understood to support parents, especially mothers, in managing the tension between paid work and care-giving responsibilities, and thereby furthers the dual-earner, dual-carer model (see Orloff, 1993; Sainsbury, 1994; Lewis, 1997a; Korpi, 1999; Siim, 2000; Daly and Rake, 2003). Here full provision of public childcare means quality, accessible, affordable publicly financed childcare, at least for children of employed or studying parents.

From a comparative perspective the Swedish welfare state is often described as universal, but in practice many social benefits are related to labour market participation. The right to childcare has been restricted to children whose parents were in paid work (or studying) or to children with special needs. That is, labour market participation, or need, has formed the basis for eligibility to publicly financed childcare.

A parliamentary decision in 1985 entitled all children aged between 18 months and school age with working or studying parents, or those with special needs, a place in municipal childcare by 1991. But municipalities were only obliged to include the expansion of childcare in their plans, which meant that in reality the growth in the number of places was too slow. Therefore in January 1995 new legislation came into force which specified the obligation on municipalities to provide childcare without unreasonable delay (that is 3–4 months) for children aged 1–12 years, where parents were working or studying or if the child had a special need (Bergqvist and Nyberg, 2002).

In 2001 a step towards universalism was taken when the parliament decided that the municipalities were obliged also to offer children of unemployed parents preschool care for at least 15 hours per week. This obligation was extended to include children of parents on parental leave with another child in 2002. In addition, pre-school activities for four- and five-year-olds were introduced in 2003 consisting of 15 hours childcare per week free of charge (Skolverket, 2002 p. 3).[7]

THE SUPPLY AND DEMAND FOR CHILDCARE

Today almost all children have a right to public childcare. To have the right is however not always the same thing as the supply being great enough to meet demand. Legislation also has to be supported by resources to make the expansion possible. In fact the supply of childcare has hardly ever matched the demand. Nowhere near all employed or studying parents have had access to the childcare they needed. Swedish mothers entered the labour market long before there was enough public childcare. In 1970 for example, half of the mothers with preschool children (0–6 years) were employed, while only 9 per cent of the preschool children were in public childcare. For a long time many parents arranged childcare in the informal sector (Nyberg, 2000).

Around 1990, a combination of a baby boom and more rigorous legislation meant a raised demand for public childcare. As can be seen in Figure 6.1 the proportion of two-, three-, four- and five-year-olds in childcare increased from around 55–65 per cent in 1990 to around 87–97 per cent in 2003. Hardly any children at all below the age of one are found in public childcare since they are at home with a parent on parental leave. This is also true for a large proportion of the one-year-olds since parental leave is longer than one year and can be spread out.

Towards the end of the 1990s the call for public childcare for children of working or studying parents was more or less fulfilled, but there was still a demand. Supply of childcare generated its own demand, and as many parents lost their jobs in the 1990s, many children also lost their place in childcare. This was a difficult experience for both parents and children, and parents demanded childcare even when they were unemployed. They did not consider it fair that the children should lose their place in childcare because they had lost their job. Of the children of unemployed parents a relatively large share went to preschool even before the change in the legislation 2001. In 1999 58 per cent of all children one to five years of age to unemployed parents went to preschool; three years later the proportion was 76 per cent.

The rules of the municipalities were less generous towards children of parents on parental leave. The largest number of children not having a place in public childcare was found in this category in 1999 (Skolverket, 2003b, Table 2.2), but this also changed. In 1999, 26 per cent of all one- to five-year-olds with a parent on parental leave were in preschool, three years later the proportion had nearly doubled to 47 per cent. It should be pointed out that a very small number of the children are more permanently at home with an 'at-home-parent', only about 2 per cent.

A very large proportion of six-year-olds (not seen in the diagram) were in public childcare in 1990 – however during the 1990s the activities for six-year-olds had been integrated into school activities. Preschool class has become a kind of school of its own. Therefore the six-year-olds are today found in preschool classes and in leisure-time centres. In 2003 more than 80

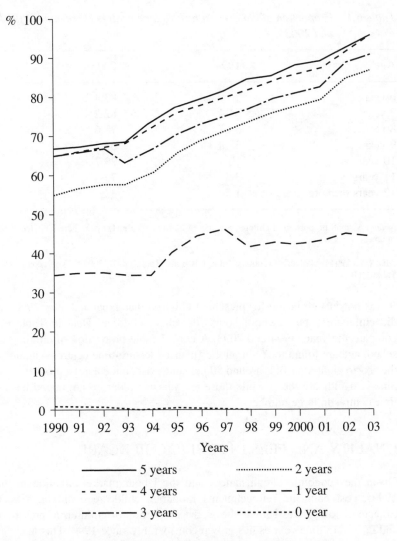

Note: Public childcare includes preschool, family daycare and leisure-time centres.

Source: 1990–93 calculated from data of the number of enrolled children and the number in each age-group in Statistisk årsbok; 1994–99 Skolverket (2000a); 2000–2003 Skolverket (2004).

Figure 6.1   Children in public childcare (percentages)

per cent of six-year-olds were in public childcare. Although children have been able to start school at the age of six since 1991, few children do so (see Table 6.1).

Table 6.1   *Proportion of children in leisure time centres (percentage, 1994 and 2003)*

Age	1994	2003
6 years	?	83.4
7 years	61.4	82.2
8 years	54.7	77.6
9 years	37.8	63.2
10 years	10.4	20.7
11 years	3.8	7.6
12 years or more	1.5	3.2

Note: A small proportion of children are also in family daycare. They are here included in the figures.

Sources: 1994 – Skolverket (2000a), Table 1.10B and Table 1.14B; 2003 – Skolverket (2004), Table 1.1B.

It was not just childcare for preschool children that expanded after 1990: so did childcare outside school hours for school children. Data in Table 6.1 compare the years 1994 and 2003. A considerable proportion of children of school age are found today in public-financed leisure-time centres – amongst the six- to eight-year-olds around 80 per cent. Also, quite a large proportion of nine-year-olds are there, while those ten years or older do not attend leisure time centres in large numbers.

QUALITY AND FEES IN PUBLIC CHILDCARE

Given the economic circumstances and the labour market situation in the 1990s, cost cuts and retrenchments in public childcare could have been expected. However as shown above, the proportion of children in preschool and in leisure-time centres has grown considerably since 1990. This leads us to ask what happened to quality and childcare fees in childcare.

Measuring the quality of childcare is no easy task and there is no general agreement as to how this should be done. However one possible way is by looking at the number of children per staff. In preschools in 1991 there were 4.2 children per staff, in 1997 and 1998 there was a peak of 5.7 and in 2003

5.4. Another way of measuring quality in childcare is group size. In 1990 the average group size was 13.8 children per group, in 2002 the number of children was 17.4 (Skolverket, 2003a, Table 4.1). In the leisure-time centres the number of children per staff increased during the whole period. The average number of children per annual equivalent worker more than doubled. In 1990 the number of children was 8.3 and in 2003 18.2 children (Bergqvist and Nyberg, 2001, Table 4; Skolverket, 2004, Table 1.16A). If quality is measured in this way, then quality in leisure-time centres has deteriorated considerably. Without doubt quality has deteriorated, but maybe not as much as the figures suggest. Leisure-time centres are today integrated into the schools in a way which was not the case in 1990; it is therefore hard to make comparisons.

Another dimension of quality is the educational level of the employees in public childcare, where higher educational level means higher quality. Almost 98 per cent of personnel working in preschool childcare are trained to work with children. Around half of the staff are university trained, while most of the remaining staff are qualified child-minders. In the leisure-time centres 56 per cent are university trained (2003) (Skolverket, 2004, Table 1.16A). The proportion of university-trained personnel is probably higher today in the beginning of the 2000s than in 1990, but lower than in the second half of the 1990s. One reason for this is the problem of finding qualified staff; another might be to reduce costs.

One way for the municipalities to handle the financial situation in the 1990s was to try to keep costs down by increasing the number of children per staff member, and increasing group size; another was to increase revenues by raising childcare fees. In 1990 parents paid 10 per cent of the total gross costs of childcare in childcare fees. By 2000 this proportion had increased to 19 per cent (Skolverket, 2001a: 10); that is, parents contributed a rising share of the costs. In the 1990s ever more municipalities examined the level and system of childcare fees and changed the design in order to shift some of the costs from the municipalities to the parents.

There was also a distinct tendency for fees to be used as a way to moderate demand. Almost all municipalities introduced some form of time-related fee, in extreme cases for the exact number of hours the child was in childcare. Ever more municipalities also tied the size of the childcare fee to the parents' income. However in 2002 the central government introduced a maximum childcare fee. This meant that a ceiling was set on the fees payable by parents for childcare. One important reason for this was the large difference in childcare fees between different municipalities. Another was to lower the level of the fees and also to eliminate the marginal effects of the childcare fees on parents' (mothers') income. The government's intention was to encourage women to work more, not less. After the introduction of the maximum fee almost all families pay lower fees (Skolverket, 2003b: 37, 41).

For the municipalities, the introduction of the maximum fee was voluntary. Municipalities that adopted the new system received compensation from the state for loss of income. The maximum fee was quickly introduced and by 2004 all municipalities applied the maximum fee (Skolverket, 2003b: 37).

In an inquiry towards the end of the 1990s, parents were asked if they found childcare adequate. A majority were satisfied, and most content were parents whose children had a place in public childcare (90 per cent). Of parents who were not satisfied (10 per cent), about half (5 per cent) would like to change from family daycare to a preschool, or the other way around; the other half (5 per cent) would like to be able to keep the child at home. Less satisfied were those parents (74 per cent) who did not have a place for their child in public childcare. In this category most parents would like to have a place in preschool (Skolverket, 2001b).

SUMMARY AND DISCUSSION

At the beginning of the 1990s Sweden found itself in a state of disintegration: government finances were in chaos, and unemployment was high while employment was decreasing. In such a situation it would not have been surprising if the interest in promoting publicly financed childcare and parental leave policies in order to further mothers' employment and fathers' care of children and the dual-earner, dual-carer model had wilted.

However as far as parental leave is concerned, it could be argued that an unintended effect of the economic crisis was to preserve the dual-earner, dual-carer model, at least if one believes that a lengthening of the parental leave – without any restrictions on the transferability of the leave – would have meant longer absences from the labour market, and longer presences at home for mothers, and thereby undermine the dual-earner, dual-carer model. The economic crisis interfered with plans to extend parental leave to 18 months, and the first father's month was introduced and has to be taken within the existing period of parental leave.

The most important changes in parental leave from 1990 until today are the introduction of the father's month, and the reduced level of the income compensation of the parental allowance. The first father's month was pushed through by the Liberal Party in the bourgeois government (1991–94), in 'exchange' for the introduction of the childcare allowance. When the Social Democrats came back to power they abolished the childcare allowance, but not the father's month, which they extended with another month in 2002.

Fathers use the months reserved for them to quite a large extent, but they do not use many transferable months. They are transferred to the mother, and the primary responsibility for dependent care work remains delegated to mothers.

There is an obvious risk that fathers' use of parental leave stops at one to two months (preferable in the summertime). Today a governmental investigation is looking into parental leave. Pressure is strong from some unions, political parties and women's organizations to divide the parental leave into three parts: one-third for the mother, one-third for the father and one-third which is transferable. There is also an ongoing discussion about raising the ceiling in the parental allowance.

Regarding publicly financed childcare, stricter legislation was introduced in 1995 which stated that all children with employed or studying parents, or children with special needs, who so wished, should without unreasonable delay have a place in public childcare. This legislation was in line with, and strengthened, the dual-earner, dual-carer model. This is also the case with the maximum fee, which was introduced in 2002. The maximum fee meant that the costs for childcare were reduced, and potential marginal effects on mothers' (parents') earnings were reduced, which meant that mothers were encouraged – if the opportunity was there – to work longer hours. Further steps were taken by parliament in the beginning of the 2000s to make childcare available to almost all children through decisions to introduce preschool activities for at least three hours per day for children of the unemployed and parents on parental leave, and all four- and five-year-olds.

At the municipality level the development was more ambiguous. As suppliers of childcare, the municipalities had to arrange childcare for a growing number of children, with shrinking resources. Demand for childcare has always been higher then supply and there has been pressure to accept more children per group and per adult. This became an urgent problem in the 1990s. After decades of considerable expansion, when quantitative supply of childcare was at the centre, the discussion in the beginning of the 2000s is about qualitative aspects, where there are some misgivings for the future.

However at present (2005) childcare is accessible and affordable to almost all children. This means that public childcare has become a universal right almost in the same way as school; however it is a right, not an obligation, but parents are keen to utilize this right. Furthermore the responsibility for childcare at the national level was moved from the Ministry of Health and Social Affairs to the Ministry of Education and Science in 1996, with the aim of strengthening the pedagogical profile of childcare. The government has decided that lifelong learning should be the cornerstone in the policy against unemployment. Sweden should be able to compete with high competence and this is to be imbued in the system of education – from preschool to university. Childcare is still central to the dual-earner, dual-carer model, but the dual-earner, dual-carer model is maybe not so central to childcare any more.

From the above we can conclude that the dual-earner, dual-carer model stood the test quite well in the 1990s at the state, the municipality and the parental level. The model seems to be rather sustainable and an economic crisis is not automatically a threat to the dual-earner, dual-carer model. This is not unique for Sweden. An explicit shift on the part of the governments in most Western European countries toward the assumption that women will be on the labour market has come in the 1990s, during a period of labour market and welfare state restructuring.

But parental leave and childcare policies that stop at facilitating women's employment often means allowing women to combine work with family responsibilities rather than achieving equality with men in the home and the labour market. Mothers with preschool children often work part-time in low-paid female-dominated occupations. More needs to be done, not only to increase women's rate of employment, but also to break up the gender segregation on the labour market and to advance the possibilities for women to obtain secure, well-paid, and if they so wish, full-time employment. Family-friendly policies need to aim more at facilitating fathers', rather than mothers', possibilities to combine work and care for children.

NOTES

1. In 1990 the unemployment rate for men (16–64 years) was 1.7 per cent and for women 1.6 per cent. For men a peak was reached in 1993 with 9.7 per cent and for women in 1997 with 7.5 per cent. In 2003 the unemployment rate for men is still 5.3 per cent and for women 4.4 per cent. In 1990 the employment rate for men was 85 per cent and for women 81 per cent and reached the lowest level for men in 1994 – 72 per cent – and for women in 1997 – 69 per cent. In 2003 it had increased to 76 per cent for men and 73 per cent for women (AKU, SCB).
2. See for example Kamerman and Kahn (1991), Lewis (1993, 1997a), Walby (1994), Siaroff (1994), Sainsbury (1994, 1996, 1999), Duncan (1996), Bergqvist et al. (1999), Esping-Andersen (1999), Korpi (1999), Siim (2000), Leira (2002), Daly and Rake (2003).
3. Parental leave can be taken without parental allowance being paid out, but there is a strong correlation between the leave and the allowance. Here the concepts are used as if they coincided.
4. The childcare allowance was 2000 SEK a month, which is far from sufficient to be able to support oneself.
5. Also unemployment and sickness allowances were lowered (Kautto, 2000: 57).
6. RFV = Riksförsäkringsverket = the National Insurance Board.
7. Skolverket = National Agency for Education.

7. Class, gender and work–life articulation

**Rosemary Crompton and
Michaela Brockmann**

INTRODUCTION

The 'mid 20th century social compromise', as described by Crouch (1999), appeared to have ameliorated endemic conflicts within advanced capitalist societies via measures such as the recognition of citizenship rights in welfare state arrangements, the regulation of employer–employee conflicts via developed systems of industrial relations, and economic stabilization via the application of broadly Keynesian policies.[1] However this model was underpinned by extensive gender segregation in both the public and private spheres of work. Men in full-time employment received a 'family wage' and related benefits; women gained benefits, often indirectly, as wives and mothers. Thus the relative 'decommodification' of the male employee was achieved in part as a consequence of the allocation of unpaid caring and domestic labour to women (Lewis, 1992). This division of labour between the sexes may not have been 'fair', but it served to ensure social reproduction (Folbre, 1994). A wide range of both external and internal factors have contributed to the destabilization of this 'compromise'. One major internal factor has been the growth of women's claims to equality, particularly in the sphere of employment, as women have increasingly entered the labour force. This has brought with it more pressures on households and families, as the necessity for caring work is no longer resolved by the domestication of women. Not surprisingly therefore, the question of work–life 'balance' has emerged as an important issue at the beginning of the twenty-first century, and there has been an increasing focus on the topic by both academic researchers and policy makers alike (for example Moen, 2003; Hochschild, 1997; Lewis and Lewis, 1996; DTI, 2000, 2003b).

However it may be suggested that there are parallel developments, associated with strategies and policies designed to assist economic regeneration, that render work–life balance increasingly problematic. Neo-liberal economic and labour market policies have both increased the extent of economic inequality, as well as increasing pressures on individual employees via work intensification and growing perceptions of job insecurity (Burchell et al., 2002; Gallie, 2002). Pressures on individuals to 'perform' at work will, other things being equal, leave fewer resources available for other dimensions of life (Hochschild, 1997). In this chapter, we cannot hope to address all of the issues raised by these recent developments. We will therefore focus on occupational class and gender variations in work–life stress, particularly the impact of aspirations for promotion on levels of stress. We will examine in some detail (via a case-study of a major supermarket chain) promotion procedures amongst a group registering a relatively high level of work–life stress – that is, routine and manual men who wish to be promoted. Through our investigation of these topics, we will raise a number of important questions relating to contemporary processes of class and gender equality.

Women's employment (in particular, that of mothers) has been rising in all OECD countries, although there is still considerable inter-country variation. For example in 1999 the employment rate of all mothers with a child under six was 61.5 per cent in the United States, and 55.8 per cent in Britain, but 41.8 per cent in Spain and 45 per cent in Australia. Nevertheless while the employment rate of mothers remains much lower than that of fathers, the gap has been closing quite rapidly, by around one percentage point per year over the 1990s (OECD, 2001: 133). There has been some tendency for empirical research on work–life issues to have had a focus on managerial and professional women in dual-earner households, not least because better-qualified women have a higher participation rate in the labour market (Blossfeld and Drobnic, 2001: 377; OECD, 2001). Indeed as such women are likely to be in partnerships with similar men, then as Blossfeld and Drobnic (2001: 381) have argued, 'the decrease in gender inequality in terms of labour-force participation is accompanied by an increase in social class inequalities'. As we shall see, the characteristic manner in which households negotiate work–life 'balance' do serve to deepen material inequalities, but levels of work–life stress would appear to run in the opposite direction.

It may be suggested that the concept of work–life 'balance' is itself somewhat problematic, in that the term 'balance' suggests that some kind of harmony has been achieved between the competing demands of employment and family life. Given the increase in women's employment, more households are combining more paid work with their family obligations, but this does not necessarily mean that a harmonious balance has been achieved. All too often, the topic of work–life balance is addressed largely in material terms. That is, if couples somehow or other manage to combine dual earning with caring responsibilities it is assumed that a 'balance' has been reached. However individuals and families have to struggle with many pressures and tensions in order to combine employment and family responsibilities. We prefer therefore to use the rather more neutral term 'work–life articulation' in our discussion.[2] The working-hour strategies employed by couples in order to achieve work–life articulation vary, both within and between nation states. As has been noted above, better-educated women more frequently remain in employment after childbearing (OECD, 2001; Rake et al., 2000). Less-educated women are more likely to withdraw from employment or to work part-time, leading to increased inequality at the level of the household. However non-employed or part-time women will have more time available for domestic work and childcare, thus the 'one-and-a-half breadwinner' mode of work–life articulation is likely to result in lower levels of work–life stress. The availability of part-time employment varies considerably between different countries, and in Britain, the focus of our discussions, there are extensive opportunities for part-time working.[3]

As Moen (2003: 20) has demonstrated for the US, the most common arrangement amongst couples with children is a 'neotraditional' modification of the male breadwinner, female homemaker 'template', where the man works longer hours than the woman. This reflects the fact that although women are increasingly moving into higher-level employment positions, many (indeed probably most) of these women also retain the major responsibility for domestic and family life, thus maintaining patterns of gender inequality in employment. Indeed at times when such women give priority to their families by resigning from high-profile, high-paying jobs, this is greeted in some quarters as evidence that women cannot 'have it all' and should make a choice between employment and family life.[4] On the other hand, women who remain in demanding jobs and buy in domestic services face another kind of opprobrium for their part in the oppression of other women (for example Ehrenreich and Hochschild, 2003). It has often been suggested that the 'problem' of work–life balance is largely a material one:

> Any sensible approach to work–life policies cannot ignore the … phenomenon of occupational class in the amount of access and take-up of work–life balance entitlements. Women in managerial and professional jobs with higher incomes and benefits are in a much better position to achieve a balance than their much lower-paid and insecure counterparts employed, for example, in the retail trade and textiles. (Taylor, n.d.: 18)

This statement therefore assumes that work–life balance is essentially a practical matter – that is, being able to make the arrangements for women to combine family and employment. Women with higher incomes will indeed be more enabled to purchase substitute services, and they are also more liable to have favourable employment conditions (see below). However, as we shall see, work–life articulation also has an important experiential dimension, as reflected in the perceived difficulties, as reflected in levels of stress, in achieving this 'balance'. On average managerial and professional women register more stress than women in lower-level occupations.

In the first part of this chapter, we report on the findings of a recent survey. Our discussion will demonstrate that levels of work–life stress, as measured by a series of attitudinal questions, appear to be relatively high in Britain, particularly amongst managerial and professional employees. We also explored the impact of aspirations for promotion on work–life stress. We found that women in managerial and professional occupations who hoped to move up the job ladder expressed higher levels of work–life stress than similar women who did not have promotion aspirations; but for managerial and professional men, promotion aspirations did not have a significant impact on work–life stress. Rather, besides professional and managerial women, the other group of employees for whom promotion aspirations had a negative impact on work–life stress were routine and manual men. In the second part of this chapter therefore, recently gathered qualitative data relating to careers, caring responsibilities and promotion procedures in a deskilled service sector organization – a major supermarket – is presented. Finally, we briefly discuss the implications of our findings.

Our analysis draws on the British Social Attitudes (BSA) survey, which in 2002 included the ISSP (International Social Survey Programme) Family 2002 (Family and changing gender roles) questionnaire.[5] The ISSP Family 2002 questionnaire included a series of questions on family, gender roles and work–life stress. Data were gathered both face-to-face and by self-completion questionnaires (Park et al., 2003: 283). Our analysis focuses on employees only. The ISSP Family 2002 modules were administered to all participants in the BSA survey. Versions B and C of the BSA generated 2312 cases, 1094 of who were in employment.

CLASS, GENDER, PROMOTION ASPIRATIONS AND WORK–LIFE BALANCE

Work–life articulation strategies vary by occupational class. More educated women are more likely to be in employment (particularly full-time employment, see OECD, 2001; Rake et al., 2000), and are liable to be in partnerships with men in professional and managerial occupations. In the BSA–ISSP sample, there were significant variations by occupational class in household employment combinations. For example, 47 per cent of partnered professional and managerial respondents were in households where both worked full-time, as compared to 32 per cent of partnered routine and manual respondents. These kinds of variations in the extent of employment between households will serve to deepen material class inequalities. However shorter (employment) working hours in routine and manual households will tend to reduce levels of work–life stress, and at an individual level, routine and manual respondents worked shorter hours, and reported lower levels of work–life stress, than professional and managerial respondents. However lower levels of work–life stress come at a price, and there were significant class differences in levels of household income (which will of course be liable to generate other kinds of stress).[6] One way in which individual incomes may be enhanced is to gain promotion, but as we shall see, aspirations for promotion may themselves be a source of work–life stress.

The BSA survey included a question on individual aspirations for promotion, as well as further questions relating to the respondent's direct experience of 'family-friendly' conditions in the workplace – whether immediate supervisors would be understanding in relation to the demands of family life, whether the individual would lose money if time was taken off work for family problems, and how 'lost' working time would be made up. Our interest in career aspirations was informed by research that has suggested that individuals who are seeking to develop careers may be more likely to feel a greater tension between home and family life, given that career development usually involves demonstrating a high level of workplace commitment (Moen, 2003; Blossfeld and Drobnic, 2001; Wajcman and Martin, 2001; Halford et al., 1997). Given that, by convention, women usually assume the major responsibility for domestic arrangements (particularly childcare), it was antici- pated that career development might present particular problems for women as far as work–life balance was concerned.

Our data suggests that women are in general less career-oriented than men. Over a half of male respondents (53 per cent), but only a third of the women, felt it was important for them to move up the career ladder at work. One factor that might affect career aspirations is age (other things being equal, we might expect that people towards the end of their working lives might be less concerned about career development than younger people). Other factors that might affect career aspirations are the presence or absence of children, occupational class[7] (in general, opportunities for upward career development are greater in higher- rather than lower-level occupations), and employment status (career development usually requires full-time employment). A logistic regression (Table 7.1) (which includes all these factors as potential predictors of career aspirations) suggests that men are more than twice as likely as women to think that moving up the career ladder is important, and people in the managerial and professional class grouping are nearly three times more likely to think that moving up the career ladder is important than people in routine and manual jobs (the three-category NS-SEC classification has been used to categorize respondents. See note 7). Table 7.1 suggests that career aspirations are lower in the 'intermediate' category, a consequence we suggest of the over-representation of female employees in this grouping (see note 7). People in full-time employment are more than twice as likely as people in part-time employment to think that moving up the career ladder is important. However the presence or absence of children in the household does not appear to have a statistically significant impact on career aspirations.

Table 7.1   Logistic regression: important to move up the job ladder at work

	Odds ratio
Respondent's sex: male	2.026***
Age	.920***
Child in household	.885
Occupational class (reference category: routine and manual)	2.756***
Professional/managerial	.556*
Intermediate	2.169***
Full-time employment	4.775
Constant	
	1084
N	

Notes:
* p <0.05   *** p <0.001
–2 Log likelihood 1253.712
Nagelkerke R .342

The findings in Table 7.1 are shaped by the continuing differences in the patterning of men's and women's employment, notwithstanding the increase in women's participation. Women are significantly more likely than men to be in part-time employment, and significantly more likely to be 'intermediate' employees. In our subsequent analyses therefore, we control for these factors by focusing on full-time employees only, and excluding the 'intermediate' class grouping from our analysis.

A work–life stress scale[8] was constructed using four items from the ISSP survey (respondents were asked to indicate for each item whether this occurred several times a week, several times a month, once or twice, or never). Higher scores indicate higher work–life stress.

- I have come home from work too tired to do the chores which need to be done.

- It has been difficult for me to fulfil my family responsibilities because of the amount of time I spent on my job.
- I have arrived at work too tired to function well because of the household work I had done.
- I have found it difficult to concentrate at work because of my family responsibilities.

Scores on the scale indicate that levels of work–life stress are higher for women (mean 7.9522) than men (mean = 7.5419; t = –2.416; df = 801; sig. (p) <0.05), and higher for managerial and professional (mean = 8.0339) than routine and manual (mean = 7.3151; t = 3.739; df = 634 sig (p) <0.001) employees. This occupational class variation however would appear to be largely a consequence of the average weekly hours worked within different occupational classes. A third of full-time managerial and professional employees reported working over 50 hours a week, as compared with 15 per cent of routine and manual full-time employees ($\chi 2$ = 46.305; df = 3; sig (p) <0.001). Thus a multiple regression analysis on work–life stress suggests that for the whole sample, occupational class differences are not significantly predictive (Table 7.2).

Table 7.2   Results of a regression analysis predicting work–life stress (full-time employees only)

	All		Men		Women	
	b	β	b	β	b	β
Sex	.889	.185***				
Occupational class	–.322	–.066	–.252	–.053	–.414	–.081
Weekly hours of work	.052	.233***	.051	.227***	.058	.248***
Child (under 16) in household	–.517	–.107**	–.318	–.066	–.846	–.176**
'very' or 'fairly' important to move up the job ladder	–.413	–.088*	–.508	–.109*	–.227	.048
Adjusted R square	.097		.066		.102	
N = 610						

Notes:
b = unstandardized, β = standardized regression coefficients.
*** p <0.001   ** p <0.01   * p <0.05

Hours of work, as has been established in previous studies, have a significant impact on work–life stress for both men and women (White et al., 2003; Berg et al., 2003). However Table 7.2 indicates that whereas the presence or absence of children has a significant impact on work–life stress for women, this is not the case for men. Given that most women take the main responsibility for childcare, this is perhaps not surprising. Conversely, promotion aspirations appear to increase stress for men, but not for women. However, as we shall see, these variations by sex are importantly cross-cut by occupational class differences. Before we address this question however, we will briefly examine the impact of other employment conditions that might contribute to work–life balance.

As noted above, the BSA survey included questions on employer 'family-friendliness', particularly in respect of immediate supervision and whether a respondent would lose money if they took time off work for family reasons. In general, managerial and professional men and women fare rather better than those in routine and manual occupations. Forty-six per cent of routine and manual men and 50 per cent of routine and manual women said they would lose money if they took time off work for family reasons, as compared to only 18 per cent and 24 per cent of professional and managerial men and women. A combined code measured 'good' working conditions as follows: a respondent does not lose money if they have to take time off, their supervisor is 'very understanding' if they do take time off, and they put in extra hours or extra effort to cover absence, rather than using holiday or banked flexi hours. Table 7.3 shows that men and women in professional and managerial jobs are significantly more likely to have 'family-friendly' working conditions than those in routine and manual jobs (men: $\chi2 = 33.42$; df = 1; p <0.001, women: $\chi2 = 23.00$; df = 1; p <0.001).

Table 7.3 Working conditions by occupational class and sex (full-time employees only)

			Managerial and professional %	Routine and manual %	Total
Men		Good	68	41	56
		Poor	32	59	44
	N		253	201	454
Women		Good	62	30	53
		Poor	38	70	47
	N		215	79	294

However, do 'good' or 'family-friendly' working conditions have a measurable impact on levels of work–life stress? A comparison of means of work–life stress scores for different levels of working conditions found there was no significant relationship between 'good' or 'poor' 'family-friendly' working conditions and levels of stress. Despite their more favourable conditions of employment, managerial and professional respondents still report higher levels of work–life stress. Indeed Table 7.4 (that employs the same work–life stress scale as in the regression in Table 7.3) indicates that it is professional and managerial women who experience by far the highest levels of work–life stress.

Table 7.4   Work–life stress by class and gender (full-time employees only)

	Men Mean (SD)	Women Mean (SD)
Managerial and professional	7.75	8.40
	(2.13)	(2.37)
Routine and manual	7.24	7.47
	(2.54)	(2.08)
t-value	2.04*	2.86**
Df	282.36	247

Note: * p <0.05

As we have seen in Table 7.1, wanting to move up the job ladder at work appeared to have an impact on work–life stress levels for men, but not for women – perhaps a rather surprising finding. However when we explored the impact of promotion aspirations on groups differentiated by occupational class and sex, an interesting pattern of variation emerged (Table 7.5).

Aspirations for promotion, it would seem, do have an impact on stress levels for professional and managerial women, but the trend for professional and managerial men is much less marked and the difference between means is not significant. Neither weekly hours of work, nor the presence of children in the household, varied significantly as between 'aspirant' and 'non-aspirant' professional and managerial women. However as we have seen in Table 7.2, the presence of children in the household has an impact on work–life stress for women, but not for men. If we make the assumption that the presence of children may be taken as an indicator of domestic responsibilities, then the major difference between aspirant professional and managerial women and similar men would seem to lie in the impact of

Table 7.5   Occupational class, sex and the impact of promotion aspirations on work–life stress

Work-life stress scores:	Managerial and professional men Mean (SD)	Managerial and professional women Mean (SD)	Routine and manual men** Mean (SD)
'very' or 'fairly' important to move up the job ladder	7.74 (2.11)	8.78 (2.4)	7.78 (2.45)
'not very' or 'not' important to move up the job ladder	7.59 (2.2)	8.03 (2.31)	6.80 (2.55)
t-value	.511	2.095*	2.371*
Df	217	170	149

Notes:
* $p < 0.05$
** Only under a half of routine and manual women worked full-time, and of full-time women, only 20 expressed an interest in moving up the career ladder. Non-responses on attitude questions reduced numbers to 15. These numbers, therefore, were simply too small to permit further analysis. Our analysis therefore focuses on men only. However, the small numbers of full-time routine and manual women who wished to move up the career ladder did not report higher levels of work–life stress than those who did not.

these responsibilities. Women still carry out a disproportionate amount of domestic work (Sullivan, 2000), and we would suggest that it is this factor that contributes to the significantly higher levels of work–life stress amongst professional and managerial women who aspire to move up the job ladder.

A similar argument cannot be developed in the case of routine and manual men, who will share with other men the general 'male advantage' in respect of domestic work. However a comparison of the characteristics of routine and manual men who wished to move up the job ladder with those who did not revealed no systematic differences between the two groups except in one important respect. Significantly more of the men who wished to move up the job ladder were service sector employees [9] as compared with those for whom promotion was not important. Indeed nearly two-thirds (63 per cent) of aspirant routine and manual men were service sector employees ($\chi 2 = 9.21$, df = 1, $p < 0.01$). We would suggest therefore that an explanation for the greater levels of work–life stress amongst aspirant routine and manual men might be sought in the nature of their employment and the career paths on offer.

SERVICE SECTOR CAREERS AND WORK–LIFE STRESS

The unravelling of the 'mid-twentieth century social compromise' has been accompanied by widespread economic difficulties. The impact on employees of recent employer policies such as business 'delayering' and 're-engineering' has received considerable attention (for example Sennett, 1998). Efforts toward economic regeneration have also included the introduction of 'high-commitment' (or 'high-performance') management strategies. These seek to obtain greater discretionary effort from employees via teamworking, training and career development, performance appraisals and performance-related pay. An influential US case-study (Hochschild, 1997) has argued that such practices generate negative job-to-home 'spillover', although Berg et al. (2003: 185) have argued that these arguments cannot 'be generalised to non-supervisory workers'. A recent British survey (White et al., 2003) has demonstrated that 'high-commitment' management practices do have a negative impact on job-to-home spillover, particularly insofar as they increase working hours and work intensity. The impact of 'family-friendly' policies has been similarly contested. Dex and Scheibl (1999) have argued that family-friendly policies have a positive impact on employee commitment, but others have emphasized that workplace pressures may make it difficult for employees to take advantage of family-friendly policies even if they are available (Eaton, 2003; see also Crompton et al., 2003; Still and Strang, 2003). Thus even though the professional and managerial employees in the BSA/ISSP surveys may have had 'better' employment conditions than other workers (Table 7.2 above), they may not have been able to take advantage of the policies on offer.[10]

We were not able to generate a rigorous classification of employer practices (that is, whether 'high commitment' or otherwise) on the basis of the questions asked in the BSA/ISSP survey. However we have been able to suggest that routine and manual men who wished to be promoted appear to suffer negative job-to-home spillover. Training and career development is an important element of 'high-commitment' managerial practices, and it has been suggested that the work–life consequences for routine and manual men who respond 'positively' to such policies might be negative. Fifty-six per cent of routine and manual men in service employment said that it was important for them to move up the job ladder, as compared to only a third of men in non-service routine and manual employment, and two-thirds of the aspirant routine and manual men were service employees. We feel justified therefore in focusing upon evidence from the service sector in our further discussion of contemporary working-class careers.

In the past working-class careers have been characteristically short-range, to foreman or supervisor level only. Indeed this was a major reason for the fact that whereas middle-class incomes increased with age, working-class incomes tended to flatten beyond the peak earning age groups of the twenties to mid-thirties (Westergaard and Resler, 1975: 90ff). Indeed the relative paucity of opportunities for promotion amongst routine and manual workers in the past was one of the reasons, as was argued in contemporary case-studies, for the fact that lower-level workers tended to favour and/or put their faith in collective (that is, trade union) or general rather than individual modes of social advancement (Goldthorpe et al., 1968: 130). This does not mean however that opportunities for promotion were non-existent for those in routine and manual occupations. Public service bureaucracies such as the railways, post office and fire service offered working-class occupational careers – for example from engine cleaner to engine driver. Skilled craft workers (for example electricians, setters, fitters and welders) experienced occupational progression, given their long on-the-job training, from apprentice, to craftsman, to senior craftsman. Trade unions played their part in protecting working-class careers via skill accreditation and the negotiation of seniority rules. These kinds of occupational protections played their part in the 'search for shelters' (Freedman, 1984) that were established during the period of the mid-twentieth-century social compromise.

However, de-industrialization and the shift to service employment, together with the reduction of the membership (and influence) of trade unions, have largely removed the kinds of career protections once found in 'traditional' working-class occupations. Case study evidence suggests that individualized career paths are increasingly becoming a feature of routine and manual service sector jobs. For example Grimshaw et al. (2001, 2002) have argued that a significant effect of recent changes in service sector organizations has been to open up the gap in the job ladder between lower-grade employees and the first step on the promotional ladder: 'the most direct effect of the flattened jobs hierarchy has been to remove the architecture necessary for career progression' (2001: 38). Grimshaw et al. studied four large service sector organizations.[11] In all of these organizations, the intermediate grades in the job hierarchy had disappeared. Making the transition to the first rung of the managerial ladder had become increasingly dependent on individual appraisals, and Grimshaw et al. argue that: 'staff with ambitions to "move up" the organisation … know that they face an "all-or-nothing" effort in time and energy to make the transition to a mid-level post. They also know that if they are successful they will be faced with an enormous increase in the responsibilities they face and associated pressures on their working time' (2002: 109).

Grimshaw et al.'s findings are repeated in recent research that included a case study of career development and work–life balance in a major super-market chain, a significant source of unskilled service sector employment.[12]

Shopwell is characterized by 'high-commitment' employee policies that include the active development of the company culture ('the Shopwell way of working'), teamworking, employee appraisal and the extensive availability of training and career development. At the shop floor level, work at Shopwell was extremely flexible: indeed for many interviewees this flexibility was an important reason for working there – even though rates of pay were relatively low (2000 rates were £4.35 for employees aged 18 and over). In Shopwell, recent changes had seen the erosion of organizational hierarchies and the 'delayering' of the organizational structure, and supervisor positions were downgraded. Thus the organizational structure was relatively flat, and only 6 per cent of store employees were managers.[13] Nevertheless individualized career development is enthusiastically promoted by the company and most of the employees interviewed considered that the career structure was genuinely open.[14]

However only a minority of lower-level employees wished to be promoted, despite the improvement in pay that would result. Three main reasons were given by the interviewees for a lack of interest in promotion: being too old, lack of interest (for these interviewees, work at Shopwell was 'just a job', but most particularly the fact that promotion to management (even relatively low-level management) would mean working longer hours:

James: I've had approaches and chances to move up here but I've never pursued it because of the kids. Before you can get up the ladder they keep you on small wages and working long hours and I can't afford to do it. [James shared childcare with his wife, and longer hours working would have meant purchasing childcare.]

Alice: The kids are too young for me to put myself forward like that. ... You can go all the way to store manager and higher. They don't hold you back at all. You can go as far as you want to go. They will develop you ... At the moment I can't physically do any more hours than I'm doing now ... they don't have part-time supervisors. You have to work full-time.

Even employees who worked full-time and who were interested in promotion recognized these limitations:

Megan: I want to go further in the company and become a manager. It's quite easy to be a manager but I won't do it straight away. The children are too young and you need to work long hours at work. In two or three years I will want to do it.

Indeed managers at Shopwell did work long hours. In part, as the extract from James's interview suggested, this was in order to demonstrate the level of commitment to ensure 'promotability':

Daniel (first-level manager): I used to work longer hours to get promotion, you have to show you're committed by putting the hours in. They don't stress that but you do it yourself.

However one of the main reasons for long hours working by managers was that in Shopwell's ultra-flexible working environment, one of the major responsibilities of management was to provide cover for absent staff:

> Grace (first-level manager): [You work] 45 (hours) contracted, but can do 50, 55, 60 depending on how bad your department is. Because, as a manager, you are responsible for your department. So if there is a lot of sick, like there is at the moment, you won't get your two days off.

> Barry (first-level manager): I have worked 70 hours in the past. I work at home. I put in the hours when I need to. That's part of being a manager but you're never really asked to.

Here a contrast may be drawn with the reasons given for negative attitudes to promotion amongst lower-level employees in the 1960s. A meticulous coding of the replies given by the 'affluent workers' of the Goldthorpe et al. study generated seven different categories of reason for not being interested in promotion, from 'too much responsibility' to 'does not want to leave work-mates' (Goldthorpe et al., 1968: 124). However none of the men interviewed in the 1960s mentioned hours of work as a disincentive to aiming for a promoted position. As we have seen, this is in some contrast to the lower-level service employees interviewed in 2002.

Case-study evidence therefore suggests that working your way up in contemporary service sector organizations requires considerable effort, including longer working hours, on the part of the employee. We would suggest that herein rests the explanation for the level of work–life stress expressed in the BSA/ISSP survey by routine and manual men who wished to gain promotion. Although our survey data does not enable us to demonstrate this conclusively, we would suggest that the level of work commitment men in routine and manual service occupations have to demonstrate in order to achieve promotion makes it more difficult for them to fulfil their family responsibilities, and they are more likely to express work–life stress as a consequence. Promotion to manager brings more stress with it:

> Craig (Shopwell store manager): It's supposed to be family-friendly but the hours are impossible ... part of the reason my marriage broke down ... I'm contracted 45 hours, I actually work 60 ... you have to, for the needs of the business ... but there are good career prospects ... Definitely, yes. As long as you are prepared to sacrifice other things such as family to move up.

DISCUSSION AND CONCLUSIONS

In this chapter we have suggested that the term 'work–life balance' might be critically reviewed, given that it implies a relatively harmonious combination of employment and family life. We have suggested the term 'work–life articulation' to describe the *de facto* strategies used by individuals and households in order to combine employment and family. In Britain, strategies of work–life articulation vary by occupational class.[15] Individuals in professional and managerial households are more likely to be in dual full-time earner partnerships; routine and manual employees are more likely to be in partnerships with only one full-time earner. Such variations in the manner of work–life articulation will serve to deepen material class inequalities. However as we have demonstrated above, the level of reported work–life stress is considerably lower amongst respondents in routine and manual occupations, who also report shorter working hours. It might be argued therefore that we have here a kind of trade-off between levels of material reward and levels of work–life stress.

However the situation is more complex than this. The significant differences in work–life stress between different occupational classes (particularly professional and managerial as compared to routine and manual employees) mask important intra-class and gender variations. Managerial and professional women who seek career success have particularly high levels of work–life stress – indeed they manifest the highest levels of stress of any of the groups we studied. Career aspirations amongst managerial and professional men do not have an impact on work–life stress. This is in some contrast to routine and manual men who, if they wished to move up the career ladder, reported significantly higher levels of work–life stress than non-aspirant routine and manual men. We have argued that an explanation for these greater levels of stress amongst aspirant routine and manual men might lie in the pressures of individualized career development in the 'high-commitment' employee environments that characterize much contemporary service employment. We are not of course suggesting that 'high-commitment' practices are peculiar to routine and manual employment. Such employee management strategies are also found in managerial and professional jobs, and indeed will contribute to the high levels of stress associated with them (White et al., 2003). Rather, we are making the point that (at least as far as career development is concerned), their impact varies significantly by both gender and class.

Continuing opportunities for career development are a feature contributing to continuing and deepening inequalities between middle-class and working-class jobs. This does not mean that career opportunities are absent from working-class jobs. However our evidence suggests that routine and manual men with career aspirations have levels of work–life stress similar to those of professional and managerial men. Working-class women more frequently withdraw (at least in part) from the labour force to carry out childcare than middle-class women, thus lowering the level of the family income.

Alternatively (as in the case of James, the Shopwell employee cited above), both parents may take low-level jobs and juggle childcare (La Valle et al., 2002). However this means that the other partner is not available to provide support for the time input required to pursue an individualized service career strategy.

Our discussion has demonstrated therefore that despite the recent 'official' recognition of the topic of work–life balance in recent policy developments in Britain, there remain important issues that have yet to be resolved. As many others have argued, these issues are located in the wider political economy. The problem of domestic work and unpaid caring was once resolved by the domestication of women and their exclusion from the labour force (Fraser, 1994). With women's entry into the labour force, they are less able to carry out these unpaid tasks. The increase in women's aspirations has resulted in their entry into occupations in which, as we have seen, it is even more difficult to achieve work–life balance because of the demands of the job. Changes in women's employment patterns and aspirations have run in parallel with the shift from manufacturing to service employment, together with the development of 'high-commitment' managerial practices that shift the responsibility for career development onto the individual.[16] All of these related trends are combining to render work–life balance more problematic.

Trends in work–life articulation are serving to deepen material class inequalities in Britain. Class inequalities however are psycho-social as well as material. Material inequalities are linked with other inequalities that vary systematically by social class (for example health and morbidity). Similarly, cultural degradations usually correlate with, and reinforce, material inequalities.[17] However as we have seen, work–life stress would appear to operate in the reverse direction, and professional and managerial respondents reported more work–life stress. The psycho-social implications of work–life balance, as indicated by work–life stress, would seem to bear most heavily on individuals in managerial and professional occupations, particularly women. Individual aspirations have an impact on work–life stress that cuts across class boundaries, although both of the sub-groups that we have identified in this chapter share the characteristic of being 'newly aspirant'. Professional and managerial women face the problems of building a career in organizational worlds that have, until recently, been dominated by men. In addition, they are likely to take the major responsibility for domestic arrangements. Routine and manual men face the problem of demonstrating organizational commitment in employment milieux lacking in traditional working-class protections.

It might be suggested therefore that the increasing tensions and widening class inequalities that have been brought about by the increase in women's employment and the growth of individualized career paths raise important questions as to the necessity for and possibilities of the re-regulation of market capitalism. There are many reasons to think that the collective shelters that once offered some partial protections to working-class employees are unlikely to be reconstructed, not least because of the widespread development of individualized systems of employee control. Thus a replication of collective, class-based resistance, of the kind that once generated 'market shelters', is unlikely to happen.

Nevertheless the negative impact of the individualization and 'marketization' of employee relations for work–life stress is being experienced across the class structure, and by men as well as women. As feminists have long argued (for example Lewis, 2002; Glucksmann, 1995; Sevenhuijsen, 2002), 'struggles around the regulation of labour' (Edwards, 2000) have to incorporate the recognition of the significance of the 'caring' dimension for market employment. Caring is a universal necessity in the absence of which human beings could not survive, and caring is work. Caring work has been identified as a peculiarly 'feminine' *métier*, but this is not the case. Centuries of ideological renditions of 'the feminine', to say nothing of gender socialization and normative expectations, render it extremely likely that in any given population, women will carry out more care work than men. Nevertheless men can care as well as women, and it is important to recognize that although caring may be gender coded, it is not gendered in any essentialist sense (Fraser, 1994). Indeed as Fraser argues, gender equity is only likely to be achieved if the gendered division of labour is 'deconstructed' – that is, if men become more 'like women', combining the work of both employment and caregiving in their day-to-day lives. Nevertheless as Moen has argued, there is a 'mismatch between outdated occupational, corporate, and public-policy regimes and the realities of life in dual-earner households' (2003: 7), and given this mismatch, women's continuing responsibility for domestic life contributes to the persistence of the broad contours of occupational segregation. 'Marketized' labour therefore has to be 're-regulated' in order to accommodate the caring dimension if we are to avoid increasing economic and social polarization and continuing gender inequality. Possibly, the pressures of work life and time in contemporary societies might lead to 'universalist' pressures to ameliorate some of the consequences of individualized employee management strategies and increasing pressures in the workplace.

ACKNOWLEDGEMENT

The authors would like to gratefully acknowledge Dr C. Lyonette's assistance with data analysis.

NOTES

1. Many other commentators (too many to list here) have addressed this topic, which is often characterized as the decline of 'Fordism'.
2. Thanks to Miriam Glucksmann for suggesting this term.
3. In 1999, of couple families in Britain with a child under six, in 38.4 per cent of them the man worked full-time and the woman worked part-time. This was the second highest (after the Netherlands) proportion amongst the countries reviewed by the OECD (2001). The comparable figure for other countries reviewed included 18.6 per cent in the United States, 26.3 per cent in Germany and 6.9 per cent in Spain.
4. See *Guardian* 2 December 2002 'The right to choose'.
5. A specially-designed module of questions focusing on 'employment and the family' were asked of the same two waves of respondents (version B and version C) in the BSA survey. The project was sponsored by the Economic and Social Research Council R000239727, 'Employment and the Family'. In this chapter, we will be drawing on responses to both the 'employment and the family' and ISSP questions. A full description (technical details, questionnaires and counts) of the BSA/ISSP survey may be found in Park et al. (2003), Appendices I, II and III. The project involves cooperation with colleagues in Portugal, France, Norway, Finland, the Czech Republic and Hungary.
6. Sixty-one per cent of employees in managerial and professional occupations reported an annual household income of £32000 and above, compared with 22 per cent of those in routine and manual occupations. Fifty-three per cent of managerial and professional respondents reported that they were living 'comfortably' on their household income, as compared to a third of routine and manual respondents.
7. There can be few sociological concepts that have been more endlessly contested than that of 'class', and a wide range of disagreement exists as to both its measurement and sociological significance (Crompton, 1993, 1998). In this chapter, we will use the three-category version of the NS-SEC (National Statistics Socio-Economic Classification; see Rose and O'Reilly, 1998), which is the first British class scheme to have an explicit conceptual grounding in 'employment relations'. The new scheme has been extensively validated, and there would be a measure of agreement that it constitutes an improvement on previous *ad hoc* classifications (but see Prandy, 1998). However the persistence of occupational segregation by sex is, not surprisingly, still reflected in the application of the NS-SEC. In the three-category version of the NS-SEC, categories 3 (Intermediate) and 4 (Employers in small organisations and own account workers) are collapsed into a single 'intermediate' category. The British Census of 2001 reveals that women comprise 72 per cent of the 'Intermediate' category 3 (largely clerical workers), but only 26 per cent of small employers and own-account workers (category 4; calculated from Table S043, census report for England and Wales). Some have argued that the concept of 'class' has lost its significance in contemporary societies (Clark and Lipset, 1991; Pakulski and Waters, 1996). This topic raises debates that cannot be properly addressed in this chapter. Nevertheless it may be argued that although it may be the case that class identities have become less significant (for example as motors of collective action) than they once were, nevertheless the occupational order is still comprehensively stratified by class processes (Crompton et al., 2000).
8. Cronbach alpha 0.73, eigenvalue 2.2, 56 per cent of variance.
9. This includes wholesale and retail trade, hotels and restaurants, transport, finance, real estate, public administration and defence, education, health and social work and other social and personal services. Non-service employees include agriculture, fishing, mining, manufacturing, gas, electricity and water and construction.
10. This may possibly explain the lack of association between 'good' employment conditions and work–life stress, but we do not have data on the take-up of work–life policies.
11. Community care provision, retail, telecommunications services and telebanking.
12. This research, Organisation Careers and Caring, was sponsored by the Joseph Rowntree Foundation. For a full description see Crompton et al. (2003).
13. If head office jobs are included, the proportion of managerial jobs in the organization as a whole will be more than 6 per cent.

14. Interviews were carried out with key informants including two store managers and two personnel managers, who also supplied details of employment conditions, including the 'So You Want to be a Manager' promotion scheme and 'family-friendly' workplace policies. Further interviews were carried out with 29 basic grade employees (including three 'key workers') and ten first-level managers. In total, 41 semi-structured interviews were completed. Interviews were tape recorded, transcribed and analysed using Nvivo. For details of the interview guide, see Crompton et al. (2003). Interviews were gathered by Jane Dennett, Andrea Wigfield and Rosemary Crompton.

15. Cross-national evidence on household employment strategies by women's educational levels (OECD, 2001) suggests that occupational class variations in work–life articulation will be found in most countries. However the precise manner of this articulation will vary as between different national employment and welfare regimes.

16. In sociological discussions, these trends may be linked to the supposed growth of 'individualization', associated with a decline in class-centred politics together with a focus on the self (Beck, 1992). This 'focus on the self' has a number of dimensions. These include the supposed emphasis on the 'reflexive self' in 'late modernity', as the individual seeks to construct his or her own 'identity' unencumbered by the constraints of more traditional class or family (gender) identities, as well as an increased emphasis on the individual's responsibility for this construction. The development of individualized, rather than bureaucratic, career progression within contemporary organizations may be seen as one example of this trend. As a number of commentators have noted, this increased emphasis on individual 'self-realization' in fact meshes well with neo-liberal prescriptions for economic and labour market regulation (Frank, 2000).

17. Skeggs (1997) has explored the negative perception of working-class identities (and their rejection) by working-class women.

PART III

Work, life and the household

The preceding sections of this volume have discussed the spread of flexible, unpredictable and demanding work schedules as a feature of the new economy, the insecurity and stress associated with many of these new work patterns, as well as highlighting the different situations of those in the 'knowledge-based' professional and managerial classes compared to the lowest-paid and least secure 'servicing jobs'. The increased involvement of women in waged work has also been addressed, while drawing attention to the continued gender inequalities and class inequalities between women in the labour market conditions which women engage in. Finally, the potential role of state policies in relation to improving the working patterns available to men and women – including better 'work–family reconciliation' measures – and the differences between states in this arena of social regulation, has been highlighted.

Part III develops these themes through a focus on the intersection of the household arena with the employment patterns of the new economy. More precisely, the emphasis is upon how the prevailing gender division of labour around parenting is both reproduced and reshaped by the decisions and practices of men and women in relation to making time to be with their children *vis-à-vis* the workplace demands of jobs and careers in the new economy.

The three chapters in this section draw on qualitative interview material concerning parents' employment decisions and their rationalities for these decisions. Together, they illustrate how the demands of long, unpredictable or insecure work schedules can impinge on family life, in particular by conflicting with notions of what 'good mothering' involves. The result is that some mothers disengage with employment, shifting from a 'career' to a 'job' or exiting completely, and the various patterns observed for mothers are not simply explained by different class resources. Fewer fathers experience such dilemmas for current constructions of 'good fathering' do not invoke the desirability of reducing work time for childrearing. Those fathers who do seek to reduce their work time face a different set of pressures, for by doing so they contradict the masculine norms and expectations of the workplace.

Much of the recent debate about the reasons for differences in women's employment patterns – and particularly between those mothers who pursue full-time employment and those who move into part-time employment or quit their jobs – has been framed in relation to Catherine Hakim's 'preference theory' (Hakim, 1991, 1998, 2000). This is taken up in Chapter 8, where Simon Duncan argues that preference theory connects to the individualization thesis, for both argue that people are now the 'reflexive authors of their own biographies, rather than following structurally determined pathways'. With regards to women's employment patterns this means that the structural influence of class and gender relations has been eroded in favour of greater individual choice and scope for women to fulfil their preferences concerning domestic and employment roles. Duncan notes that critics of this theoretical position have emphasized that choices remain constrained by social structures such as class and gender, including McRae (2003) who draws a distinction between normative constraints (identities, gender relations within the family) and structural ones (labour market prospects, access to childcare services and so forth) and the underlying social class differences in resources.

Duncan argues that mothers' decisions about paid work and caring emerge from 'gendered moral rationalities': gendered because they address notions of what it is to be a 'good mother', moral because they provide guidance about 'the right thing to do', and rationalities because this provides a framework for decision making. He finds some class differences, but also differences between mothers in similar class locations, and argues that this variation cannot be explained simply by invoking preference theory ('classless choices') or by reference to class-based differences in labour market opportunities and household resources (a structural reading of rational action theory). Rather, preferences and constraints shape mothers' rationalities and employment practices in a nuanced process. These different rationalities are rooted in biographical experiences and observations of the experiences of members of their family and social networks. This biography influences whether individual women question or accept the viability of dependency in the 'male breadwinner' model of family life, whether they experience employment positively as a 'career' and a salient source of identity rather than as a 'job' engaged in primarily for financial reasons, the practices and norms concerning the gender division of labour in their relationship with their partners, and the normative views which prevail in their (local) social networks as to what constitutes 'good mothering' and 'proper gender roles'.

Fathers are the focus of Chapter 9, by Brandth and Kvande. Like the other two chapters in this section, Brandth and Kvande's analysis shows how the social and cultural context influences the choices parents make. They explore fathers' understanding and use of two Norwegian care policies: the 'father's quota' introduced into the parental leave system and the 'cash-for-care' scheme for families that do not use public childcare services and which provides some financial support for parents who reduce their working hours.

Following Connell (1987), they argue that 'hegemonic masculine identity' is largely constructed in relation to success in working life, which can come into conflict with being a participating father due to competing time demands. Conversely, 'care-giving related to children continues to be a field where masculinity is put to the test because it is gendered as feminine'. Brandth and Kvande report that the father's quota has been 'a great success' in that very quickly it has become normal for most fathers in Norway to take parental leave. They argue that this illustrates the importance of individual rights for fathers as an important mechanism which legitimates their claims for working-time adjustments, even if it is clear from the study that many fathers still have to negotiate this in the face of resistance from their line managers. In contrast the 'cash-for-care' scheme has done little to challenge the gender division of care responsibilities. Brandth and Kvande deepen their analysis using qualitative interviews with fathers employed in knowledge-based work in the new economy. These fathers have jobs which are demanding and greedy of their time, yet also fulfilling. Here the fathers preferred to take a full-time block of parental leave rather than any form of part-time or reduced working hours arrangements because they understood that this provided a clearer boundary between employment and parenting. Further, that some fathers emphasized how they would have liked to take longer leave if the opportunity had been available. In contrast, reduced or part-time hours were perceived negatively, on the grounds that they would be difficult to combine with the flexible time culture of their jobs.

In Chapter 10, Irene Hardill and Joost van Loon take the individualization thesis as their starting point, but like Duncan, they emphasize that structural relations shape the biographies which individuals carve out. Through interviews with both members of dual-career managerial and professional couples they explore how the process of individualization permeates employment decisions made in relation to the prevailing work patterns in the new economy and reverberates with the internal processes and intimate relationships of home life. A key conceptual tool in their analysis is that of 'identification' and 'identity-risks', whereby a consequence of individualization is that it becomes the individual's responsibility to (reflexively) manage the potentially competing demands, needs and desires made on them by others and themselves. People face specific dilemmas or 'identity-risks' in their biographies when they have to make decisions about which aspects of life should be prioritized so as to try and manage tensions between their 'multiple identities' (wife, mother, professional, and so on). How they attempt to resolve this depends on what they perceive to be the imperatives involved in 'being good at' their mothering, professional work and so forth, which has parallels with Duncan's analysis of 'good mothering' in Chapter 8.

Hardill and van Loon emphasize how the distribution of identity risks is structured by gender and socio-economic position. In particular, they show how the identity risks which emerge from the tensions of pursuing parenthood in conjunction with a professional vocation place particular pressures on women, for the identity of 'mother' invokes a form of presence and involvement in childrearing that is absent from current prevailing social constructions of what constitutes 'good fathering'. The identity risks for mothers are compounded by features of many professional and managerial jobs in the new economy, such as where long or unsocial working hours are the norm or where they are in precarious positions. The outcome is that many of the women in these dual-career couples had adjusted their working patterns in response to the demands of parenting – some as a conscious choice to 'being there' with their children, others due largely to the stresses and tensions of trying to manage the competing demands of professional and maternal roles. In contrast, the minority of fathers who made such an adjustment had done so as a positive response – to 'be there' with their children as a meaningful alternative to their unsatisfactory professional careers.

Together these three chapters demonstrate the persistent salience of gender and social class in understanding men and women's employment decisions and preferences. They also demonstrate how norms and obligations about what constitutes 'good' behaviour as mothers, fathers and as workers infuse the behaviour and rationalities of men and women. These norms, like behaviour, are open to change. That maternal employment is becoming more widespread in many countries where the stay-at-home mother used to be the typical pattern may contribute to this renegotiation, but norms do not simply adapt to fit with prevailing material conditions. If state policies press mothers to take employment in the absence of adequate social infrastructure, then the contradiction with mothers' normative understandings of what they should be doing as 'good mothers' produces emotional strain, stress and dilemma (McDowell et al., 2005). Clearly reconciliation measures (access to better childcare, more options for working-time adjustments and so on) help to reshape notions of how it is possible to provide 'good mothering' while employed, but the emphasis is largely upon women in most policies. Reconciliation measures which are designed to help reshape notions of 'good fathering' are less developed, yet as the Norwegian example discussed shows, they have the potential to start changing fathering practices as a basis for developing a more gender-equitable form of society premised on care work being undertaken by both sexes.

8. Mothers' work–life balance: individualized preferences or cultural construction?

Simon Duncan

INTRODUCTION: STRUCTURE, PREFERENCE AND THE WORK–LIFE BALANCE[1]

For individualization theorists, structural concepts like class and gender are 'shell institutions' (Giddens, 1999) or – more colourfully – 'zombie categories', which are 'dead and still alive' (Beck, 2002: 203). The form of such structures still exists, but the content has changed where people are now the reflexive authors of their own biographies, rather than following structurally determined pathways. True enough, these reflexive individuals are still subject to inequalities and constraints of various kinds, but structures of class and gender are dead classifications from the past, given a sort of shadow life by the individualized processes through which people construct their lives. While the 'grand theorists' of this position remain infuriatingly over-abstract, Catherine Hakim (1996, 2000, 2002) has operationalized this view as 'preference theory', dealing with women's employment behaviour and based on detailed empirical work. According to Hakim, 'affluent and liberal modern societies provide opportunities for diverse lifestyle preferences to be fully realized [so that] women [have] genuine choices as to what to do with their lives' (Hakim, 2000: 273). Social structures of class and gender are at best marginal for social explanation. This response fits well with a long period in Britain during which social structure – especially class – has been unfashionable in social science both as a concept and as an empirical tool. In turn this coincided with politically dominant notions of a 'classless society' promulgated by British governments in the 1980s and 1990s, and chimes in well with the current high political profile of 'choice'. While the political emphasis on individual choice and preferences is perhaps greatest in liberal welfare state regimes such as Britain and the USA, notions of choice and preference also emerge in most European societies with other forms of welfare state regimes in relation to the issue of maternal employment and 'work–family reconciliation'.

In this model of society with its emphasis upon liberalism, individualization and preferences it is apparent that 'work–life balance' will be seen as a matter of individual choice as constrained by the practical constraints of cost, time and accessibility. This indeed is the approach taken by the work–life balance campaign in Britain, as championed by the Department of Trade and Industry and supported by various think tanks such as the Work Foundation and some large employers like the supermarket chain Sainsbury's (Shorthose, 2004). The provision of childcare is a good example. Because this can be too costly, or does not cover work hours, or is simply not available, it is seen as a barrier to mothers' preferences in taking up employment. A solution then is to provide more childcare. That parents, particularly mothers, see themselves as having – and desiring – a social obligation to care for their children themselves, and that subsequently the nature of childcare provision is crucial to them, is not taken into account (Duncan et al., 2004). In addition, employment may not be particularly fulfilling especially for working-class mothers who do not possess sufficient human capital to establish a career. At the same time, the long-hours culture prevalent in many British workplaces is seen by some (but not apparently the government) as stopping parents (which again really means mothers) developing their careers, or even continuing in paid work at all, because then they would be unable to care properly for their children (Bunting, 2004). Again, this neglects issues about gendered identities and obligations that surround both paid work and caring, while for many a simple 'job' – without access to a 'career' – is a necessity rather than an opportunity. In other words the work–life balance campaign does not consider structures of gender and class, which can enable, or constrain, individual choice.

Melissa Benn has memorably suggested that 'being against work–life balance is like being against summer or good sex' (Benn, 2002; quoted in Shorthose, 2004). Like Shorthose, I am not against the work–life balance campaign; providing more childcare and eliminating the long-hours culture in Britain would have many beneficial effects (Bunting, 2004). Rather, the campaign is self-limiting because it takes for granted the idea of free choice within practical constraints. Work–life balance is seen simply as a balance of time and money. My contention is that while it does include these things – and these are important – it is more fundamentally a balance of everyday, practical morality. Parents, especially mothers, have to navigate within strongly held social normatives about what is the proper thing to do in combining employment and mothering. And these normatives, or gendered moral rationalities, will vary both socially and spatially (Duncan et al., 2003, 2004). In this way mothers do not have free choice to simply take up their individual life-style preferences as conceptualized by Hakim. Rather, they negotiate with others about what is the proper thing to do in their particular situation.

In this chapter I follow up this contention by examining how mothers in different class groups understand the relation between mothering and paid work. The following section describes the methodology used, and the third section simply describes the class differences found. The next section then goes on to assess how Hakim's preference theory can explain these differences. Finding that this approach is limited, the fifth section returns to the interview data in order to examine how mothers socially construct their understanding of how employment and mothering should be combined. In the final section I can then draw out some more general conclusions about individualized preference versus the cultural construction of choice.

METHODOLOGY

Sampling Strategy

The chapter is based on the results of 50 semi-structured interviews conducted with white mothers, with dependent children under 11, who were in an exclusive heterosexual couple relationship, and carried out during 1998–2000 in four English towns. Eleven is the age at which most parents see children as old enough to be on their own at times (Ford, 1996)[2]. These were taken from a total sample of 108 interviews covering social variations in ethnicity, sexuality and 'alternative lifestyles' as well as class. Interviews with eight male partners, and the records of three focus groups, were also available. The concern was not to produce a statistically representative sample, but to purposively sample amongst contrasting social groups of partnered mothers.

Interviewees' social class positions were assessed using a multidimensional 'objectivist' method. This included interviewees' own occupation (current or recent) and educational or vocational qualifications, the occupations of their parents and current partner, housing tenure and neighbourhood, and current social networks. For most of the sample, all these characteristics coincided, enabling an unambiguous class allocation. Five respondents showed more transitional class positions and were not allocated to any group. Three different class groups were defined on this basis, using the National Statistics Socio-Economic Classification (NS-SEC) as a guide (Rose and Pevalin, 2002). These were: (1) 16 'peripheral working-class' respondents (NS-SEC groups 12–14), living in Barnsley in South Yorkshire, Burnley in east Lancashire and Hebden Bridge in West Yorkshire; (2) 11 'central working class/intermediate' class respondents (NS-SCE groups 4–11), living in Barnsley and Burnley; (3) 18 professional and managerial respondents

(NS-SCE groups 1–3) mostly living in Hebden Bridge and in Headingley, Leeds.

The different sample locations allowed further distinction between these groups, where the geography of partnering and parenting is variable (Duncan and Smith 2002). Barnsley typifies areas dominated by a male breadwinner/ female homemaker family formation, although the economic basis for this has substantially decayed. Burnley, also a working-class industrial town, is in contrast typical of a 'dual-worker' area, where wives and mothers have traditionally been in employment. Hebden Bridge shares this history, but is now heavily gentrified by middle-class incomers seeking alternative lifestyles, while Headingley is a high-status inner suburb where middle-class professionals live alongside 'post-student' and student middle-class apprentices. It was striking that while nearly all of the working/intermediate class respondents in groups 1 and 2 and their partners had been brought up in their local areas, and most had lived there continuously, all the middle-class respondents were incomers, with many beginning their occupational and partnership careers in London.

Analytical Strategy

Analysis of the interviews used the Grounded Interview Rationality Diagram (GIRD) procedure (Duncan and Edwards, 1999; Duncan et al., 2003). All statements in the interviewees' accounts (including seemingly contradictory statements) about (1) combining employment and paid work, (2) allocating tasks with partners, and (3) choosing childcare were identified. Similar statements were grouped together, and from this grouping the main ways of accounting for these issues were inducted. These understandings were conceptualized as different 'gendered moral rationalities'. They were gendered because they dealt with notions of mothering, they were moral in providing answers about the right thing to do, and they were rationalities in providing a framework for taking decisions.

Identification of these rationales allowed the construction of summary diagrams showing the position held by individual interviewees, and the interviewee groups, in relation to the gendered moral rationalities. Thus for motherhood and paid work, the position of each interviewee with respect to three main accounts was plotted on the triangular model in Figure 8.1, and then further generalised into the shaded areas. The size of the different shaded areas thereby indicates the range and number of interviewees' statements.

It soon became apparent from the GIRD analysis that there were considerable differences within the group of professional and managerial mothers. These were marked off by geographical location and I further distinguished a 'gentrifying partners ' sub-group in Hebden Bridge compared

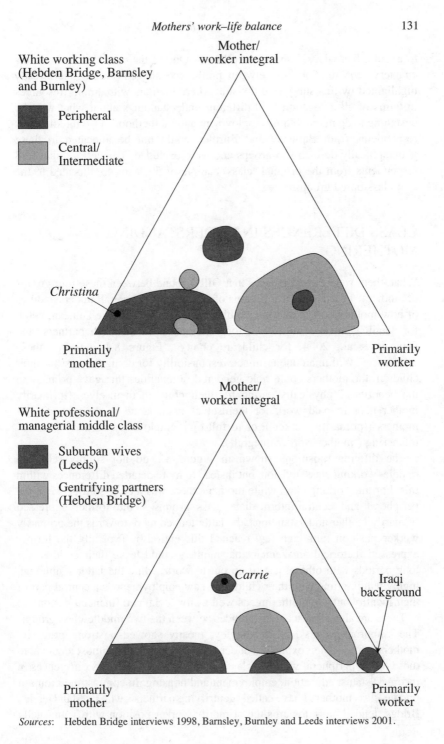

White working class
(Hebden Bridge, Barnsley
and Burnley)

Peripheral

Central/
Intermediate

Mother/
worker integral

Christina

Primarily
mother

Primarily
worker

White professional/
managerial middle class

Suburban wives
(Leeds)

Gentrifying partners
(Hebden Bridge)

Mother/
worker integral

Carrie

Iraqi
background

Primarily
mother

Primarily
worker

Sources: Hebden Bridge interviews 1998, Barnsley, Burnley and Leeds interviews 2001.

Figure 8.1   Combining motherhood and paid work

to a 'suburban wives' sub-group in Leeds. One of the central themes of this chapter – the relationship between preference and constraint – is already highlighted by this sub-group division where mothers with similar resources in terms of class location held different understandings about what was the best thing to do in combining employment and motherhood. Two middle-class respondents from Barnsley and Burnley could not be allocated to these geographically defined sub-groups and were excluded. This left a total of 48 respondents from the original 'class' sample of 50, with 43 allocated to the four class-based groups.

CLASS DIFFERENCES IN UNDERSTANDING MOTHERING

What, then, were the differences that GIRD found between these four groups of mothers? I focus here, for reasons of space, on their overall understandings of how motherhood should be combined with paid work (see Duncan, 2003, for detail, Duncan et al., 2003, for divisions of labour with partners, and Duncan et al., 2004, for childcare choice). Figure 8.1 indicates these differences. Within an unquestioned responsibility for doing the best for their children, the mothers could hold gendered rationalities that gave primacy to the benefits of physically caring for their children themselves ('primarily mother'), or to paid work for themselves as separate to their identity as mothers ('primarily worker'), or to full-time employment as part of 'good' mothering ('mother/worker integral').

The different positions shown in Figure 8.1 do not simply relate to middle–working class division, but instead to more detailed differences within this. For the working class white mothers, there was a clear split between the peripheral and central/intermediate class groups – the former expressed primarily mother understandings, the latter tended more towards the primarily worker position (although few reached this entirely). Typically the former expressed rhetorical amazement that mothers could leave their children for long periods with others, just to go out to work, while the latter – although highly valuing time with their children – saw employment as a central part of their identity outside mothering, as well as for social and financial reasons.

There are also significant differences between the two middle-class groups. The 'suburban wives', in Headingley, mostly showed a strong primarily mother identity. Their expressed understandings were often almost identical to those of the peripheral working-class group, despite huge class differences in incomes, status, education, employment and housing. In contrast the group of middle-class mothers I have called 'gentrifying partners', who lived in Hebden Bridge, tended more towards the primarily worker position with – unusually for white mothers – some mother – worker integral understandings (see Duncan et al., 2003 for black mothers). Typically they valued the worker role highly. In addition, for many, not only would staying at home restrict this role – it would also be bad for children to be around their parents too much.

Our results accord well other qualitative studies, and with representative surveys, which show that mothers usually see paid work in opposition to good mothering, that gender divisions of responsibility and labour in caring and providing are often taken for granted, and that most mothers prefer informal care by relatives if they are not able to provide this themselves (see for example Fenton et al., 2003; Irwin, 2003; Wheelock and Jones, 2002; Vincent and Ball, 2001). While there are changes – for example some mothers separate out and value a worker identity, gender divisions of labour are increasingly negotiated rather then prescribed, and a minority of mothers highly value formal childcare – such change is 'slow a-coming' as Jane Pilcher puts it (2000: 771). Class difference, if noted at all, is usually limited to a broad middle–working class division, or implied through the level of education. Mothers with few educational qualifications and who particularly value local networks of friends and relatives are more likely to hold 'traditional' views of motherhood (Fenton et al., 2003).

My analysis allows a restatement of the explanatory problem. First, why do different class groups of mothers show different understandings of motherhood (notably the peripheral working-class group compared with the gentrifying partner middle-class group, or the suburban wives middle-class group compared with the central working–intermediate class group)? Is this because of class differences in the ability to take up employment, or do without it? But, second, why do different class groups show similar understandings (notably the suburban wives and peripheral working-class groups)? And third, similarly, why do similar class groups show different understandings (the suburban wives compared to the gentrifying partner middle-class groups, or the two working-class groups)? Is this because women can express their individual preferences? The next section will assess the utility of two current operational frameworks in answering these questions – preference theory and rational action class theory.

EXPLAINING THE DIFFERENCES I: PREFERENCE VERSUS STRUCTURE

According to Catherine Hakim, 'there are no major constraints limiting choice or forcing choice in particular directions' for women's employment choice (2000: 18). In this way women's heterogeneous employment patterns are explained by heterogeneity in their lifestyle preferences, hence the appellation 'preference theory'. Although Hakim admits that the social and economic context can have some influence, lifestyle preferences are certainly 'the principal determinant' on women's employment choices (Hakim, 2003: 343). In any case, as Susan McRae (2003) points out in a critical article, any contextual constraints are in practice ignored by preference theory.

In this way preference theory neatly operationalizes the individualization view of late modern society for women's choice between employment behaviour. Indeed each uses the other for support. Thus Anthony Giddens, in his approving preface to *Work-Lifestyle Choices in the 21st Century* (Hakim, 2000) sees the book's demonstration that 'modern women [have] real choices between a life centred on family work and/or on paid work' as showing that 'we can no longer learn from history', where 'individualisation has been the main driving force for change in late modern society' (Giddens, 2000: vii). Later, Hakim quotes directly from this preface to defend preference theory:

> Some sociologists now accept that agency is becoming more important than the social structure as a determinant of behaviour. People do not only gain the freedom to choose their own biography, values and lifestyle, they are *forced* to make their own decisions because there are no universal certainties and norms about the good life, as in early modern industrial societies. (Hakim, 2003: 341)

In short, preference theory takes a resolutely structureless view of women's employment behaviour.

Preference theory has been heavily criticized on a number of grounds (Ginn et al., 1996; Crompton and Harris, 1998; McRae, 2003). Most of these collapse into the general charges that choice is always constrained, not least by social structures like class and gender that create a set of available choices, and that preference theory is tautological. Equally Hakim (1995, 1998, 2003) has robustly defended her position, where a general theme is that critics are 'so wedded to old theories prioritising social structural factors that they are unable to perceive the new scenario now emerging in modern societies' (2003: 343).

How far can preference theory account for the group differences described in section 2? It seems most applicable to the intra-class differences. The 'suburban wives' and 'gentrifying partners', despite similar class positions, levels of human capital, and biography before motherhood, would simply take different life-style choices. Similarly, although here there was more structural and biographical difference, the central/intermediate group preferred longer working hours, while the peripheral working-class mothers preferred shorter hours and to stay at home. Extending the logic, the conclusion would be that class in itself had little effect. Looking at the data more closely reveals some problems with this matching however. Firstly, some of the suburban wives and the peripheral working class were employed for longer hours than they thought right – to 'pay the mortgage' (suburban wives) or simply to 'get some money' (peripheral working class). They could not properly exercise their preferences. Secondly are the inter-class differences in how these preferences were put into practice. The gentrifying improvers took professional and managerial jobs; the central/intermediate group – with a similar preference towards paid work – took lower-status jobs. Similarly, the suburban wives had far greater choice of employment than the peripheral working class. The former were able to take higher-paid, higher-status jobs with better conditions – which often included greater ability to reconcile employment with caring. They could much more have their cake and eat it. Finally, where did these alternative preferences come from, and why are they socially patterned? Hakim (2000) appeals to a mix of varying testosterone levels, feminine and masculine personalities, and biographical influences, although she remains unconvinced and unconvincing and in the end simply returns to the fact that women have various preferences available, therefore they make them in seeking 'causal pleasure' (Hakim, 2000: 189). Preference remains primary – and tautological.

Writing in reaction to Hakim's preference theory, McRae (2003) conceptualizes two kinds of constraint facing women in their balance of employment and family – the normative and structural. The former includes women's own identities – their 'inner voices' – as well as gender relations in the family. This is something considered through the concept of gendered moral rationalities and I will return to this below. McRae largely ignores this type of constraint however, and instead focuses on the structural constraints of job availability, the cost and availability of childcare, and – underlying these immediate factors – social class. It is class that explains why some women have greater choice and can more easily overcome constraints.

Hakim rejects the relevance of this class-based explanation for women's employment behaviour on the grounds that they derive from 'male centred stratification theory' (2000: 2). She claims male practice is not relevant to women's choices between a life centred on private, family work and one centred on market or public work. There seems little conceptual logic in this corralling of class to the employment sphere alone and, as section 3 shows, mothers' choices between motherhood and employment do seem to be patterned by social class. So how might class differences contribute to explaining these patterns? We would expect middle-class mothers, with their greater ability to obtain higher paid and more satisfying jobs in better conditions, to be more likely to understand mothering as a role which could be combined with substantial employment. Thus the gentrifying partner group, primarily employed in higher education and public sector management, were oriented towards the primarily worker role. In contrast the peripheral working-class group, with much lower paid employment in unskilled and routinized jobs, were clustered towards the primarily mother pole (Figure 8.1). This overall middle–working class difference is also reflected in survey evidence of mothers' attitudes towards paid work. So far, so good for a class-based analysis emphasizing constrained possibilities.

Deviations from this explanation are equally obvious however. How do we explain the 'primarily mother' value position of the suburban wives group, and their orientation towards part-time employment – similar to the peripheral working class group – despite their high human capital and professional and managerial employment? And why does the intermediate/central group hold a value position more like the middle-class gentrifying improvers group, and take up full-time jobs, despite their relatively inferior labour market position? Are these groups of mothers acting 'irrationally'?

McRae (2003) points to the cost of childcare as an additional class constraint. Indeed the lower-paid peripheral group, and many mothers in the less well-paid intermediate/central group, were particularly concerned about questions of cost. They tended to use informal childcare if not their own care at home. The gentrifying improvers, less concerned with costs, favoured more expensive nursery options with child development as a key concern. But the same objection applies; mothers in the high-income suburban wives group still valued one-to-one care that placed the mother as the ideal. Arrangements in dividing work with partners – mentioned by McRae as another possible constraint – are similarly patterned. Suburban and peripheral groups tended to stress pre-given gender roles as opposed to the negotiation values favoured by the other two groups. The class patterning of values and choices do not always follow the class patterning of resources. Particular social groups appear to be acting 'irrationally' in terms of class and constraint.

Hakim's preference theory and a class-based constraint approach appear as mirror images of each other in explaining the mothering position of the four class groups of mothers as summarized in section 3. Each is most convincing where the other is least convincing. This seems to suggest combining the two approaches. Understandings and practices of mothering, and how they combine with employment and gender divisions of labour, are a mixture of choice (classless preference) and constraint (rational action in a class structure). But this is surely to state the obvious. We need to go further in asking how mothers develop these alternative preferences and rationalities. This is the subject of the next section.

EXPLAINING THE DIFFERENCES II: CULTURES OF CLASS AND MOTHERHOOD

This section asks how preferences, or rational action in response to class constraints, are produced and expressed. When we ask this question, the answer becomes more complicated than the simple 'choice versus constraint' dichotomy. And this complication turns out to be the cultural construction of choice and constraint. For example rationality in response to class constraints and opportunities is more complicated than simply maximizing individual economic returns. Thus the suburban wives group could be seen as using their superior labour market position to 'buy' more time with their children, in line with their primarily mothering values and pre-given gender roles. Some of these mothers implied that this withdrawal from the labour market was necessary not only for themselves as good mothers, but also as a means of maintaining social advantage for their children. As Betty put it:

> I think that children, growing children, is really a very important thing to be doing and really – on some level, I know it's economic ...

This is 'rational' economic action in a wider sense. There is some evidence for this behaviour in Figure 8.2, which plots employment time against the mother–worker continuum. Thus we find the very shortest employment hours – or complete withdrawal from the labour market – in the peripheral working-class group while the longest hours are worked by those from the gentrifying partner and intermediate/central working class groups. Suburban wives were mostly employed for fewer hours (those exceptions who did work full-time cited financial pressure as their reason, and usually expressed a desire for shorter hours). In a striking reversal, mothers employed as an OU tutor and as a fine art consultant (in the suburban wives group) worked for fewer hours than a cleaner and a blanket packer (in the peripheral group).

In like manner half the mothers in the intermediate/central group were the main or equal breadwinner (rare in the other groups). It was presumably less possible for them to buy caring time at home, especially when their wage rates were lower than the suburban wives – who in addition all had high-earning partners. Some even expressed a desire for longer hours. Mothers in the peripheral group, where many had few or no hours of paid work, and who also expressed strong preferences for one-to-one care – ideally the mother – could be seen as simply making this purchase by default. Their likely labour market returns would not allow them to buy an adequate work–life balance, so many 'bought' this through not working long hours. This qualification to a simple economic rationality begs the question however. For the qualification is 'cultural' in that moral values about proper childcare, and concerns about their children's outcomes, qualify mothers' 'rational' labour market behaviour. Relations with partners are also crucial. Working times do not seem simply to reflect economic necessity or possibility. Rationality is at least partly constructed culturally.

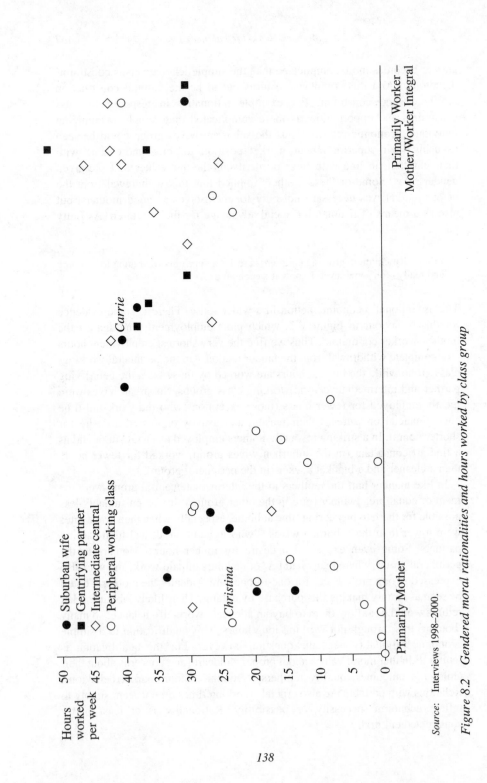

Hours
worked
per week

● Suburban wife
■ Gentrifying partner
◇ Intermediate central
○ Peripheral working class

Carrie

Christina

Primarily Mother

Primarily Worker –
Mother/Worker Integral

Source: Interviews 1998–2000.

Figure 8.2 Gendered moral rationalities and hours worked by class group

Some mothers explained their involvement with their children in strong, emotional terms. For example Sasha, who was a part-time community project worker in the transitional class group, spoke of:

> This thing comes into your life that is more precious than anything else that you own or have or want in the world and they become ... they become the first thing that you pay attention to rather than it be your career or your salary or your car or the house that you live in or whatever, they are the most important thing ye know – husband, whatever, they don't come into it really, they are the most important thing in your life and it changes your whole view on everything.

Similarly, Claudia from the suburban group described how:

> The first time it was a real shock because you know I'd had this really quite high powered job ... and I had a lot of status and I had money and all of a sudden I had nothing ... but at the same time I was absolutely bowled over by Jerry [oldest son], I just thought he was the best thing since sliced bread ... and that shocked me really, I didn't expect to feel like that. Prior to having him I just thought oh well ye know, it's a baby and then since I sort of had him it was like falling in love you know oh and I felt the same with Raymond [younger son].

This, she explained, was why she took on part-time work around school hours rather than work full-time in a career. Heather, also a 'suburban wife', called herself a feminist and had even thought, 'having a baby was almost a sign of weakness'. But after the birth and its unexpectedly strong emotions she found herself putting her baby first and her career second, and this meant part-time work despite financial dependence on her husband.

This emotional experience might seem simple enough as a basis for preference-based explanations – some mothers experience intense maternal feelings and they will prefer to be mothers at home despite significant human capital in terms of education and employment experience. There are a number of problems with this conclusion however. Firstly, most mothers in the sample expressed similar feelings, if not always so strongly. (Indeed to do otherwise would constitute 'bad mothering'.) Secondly, feeling these emotions does not mean moving into mothering at home. It was rather that being a mother was a constant social and emotional position. As Rita, also from the suburban wives group, put it, 'they sort of occupy so much of your sort of psyche all the time' and while emotionally upsetting at times, this was compatible with employment for 30 hours a week as a senior IT consultant:

> Yeah, it's not so much thinking, they just ... they just become part of life really you know, I wouldn't think ... oh is he happy, is he crying, is he alright sort of thing, I don't think of them in those terms like when I go to work now, I don't, I don't worry about them ye know, I know they're happy, I know they're looked after and

everything'll be fine, it's just that they're just there like a cloud, they're just part of life ...

McCarthy and Edwards (2002) summarize, this involvement is a significant social experience centred on emotion, moral identity and a particularistic relationship with children. It is much more than a simple individual preference for time allocation. It is part of life as a mother. It was also expressed by most mothers in the sample – including those with substantial hours of paid work. Experiencing motherhood as a significant social experience does not mean therefore some automatic translation into a 'primarily mother' identity. To understand how this involvement links into ideas about how best to combine mothering and paid work, and how this varies among different groups of mothers, we again need to consider how it is socially and culturally interpreted. In this sample two factors stand out – understandings of 'career' and relations with partners.

Li et al. (2002) have drawn attention to the importance of career to divisions in the working class. This division is not simply related to divisions in relative power and security in the labour market, whereby skilled workers are placed in a more advantageous position, although it is associated with it. In addition, Li et al. claim, the idea of career is linked to 'some socio-cultural aspect' of individual's lives (Li et al., 2002: 629) that gives value to job progress, job skills and satisfaction, and forward planning. This career/non-career division was replicated among our respondents – but with the important extension that this was just as marked for middle-class respondents as it was for those defined as working class.

Table 8.1 summarizes career orientation for the all four class groups. As can be seen, there are significant contrasts. Divisions within the working class resemble those found by Li et al. Mothers in the central/intermediate group were oriented towards career, sometimes highly so. They often expressed fulfilment in their employment in 'associate professional' or 'lower technical' social care occupations, and many aspired to career development and promotion. Similarly, most tended toward the primarily worker position, combining this employment with mothering. As in the research by Li et al., this association was however not a simple response to labour market opportunities, but was expressed in identity terms. Thus for Gabrielle, a full-time nurse, her career gave her:

A feeling of worth. I enjoy having friends and colleagues, I enjoy the job. It gives you more of a purpose really, it's like ye know I'm not just a mum or just a wife, I'm a nurse as well and I'm me ye know. It gives you another dimension.

This career identity was separated from just obtaining an income through employment. Gail described how her satisfaction in career outweighed the possibility of better pay for its own sake:

> This is more than earning money. Yeah I could perhaps move on to bigger things with more money but I enjoy helping people, I enjoy interacting with other people, as I say, I enjoy using me head in different ways to try and get round a problem ... I have moved up from general assistant, care assistant, assistant care manager, care manager ... I've just come back from a secondment at the hospital where there perhaps was scope to do a combined role but I chose to come back, I didn't want that, combining the role of care management plus the supervising systems, to me the supervising systems weren't working to be honest.

In contrast those mothers who merely had 'jobs' (or were unemployed) were members of the peripheral working-class group, and tended to a primarily mother position. Many of these respondents considered that career was not something for them, or even took a negative view that career was detrimental to mothering – despite the fact that their parental background and earlier biographies were little different to some of the central working-class respondents. As Lisa, who worked part-time as a bakery machine operator, said:

> I don't think a career and children go together 'cos I think at the end of the day something's got to give, I think summat has to be neglected and I think at the end of the day it's children who are neglected. I don't mean neglected by being ill treated neglected, I mean like with time and time with their mother, time with their father and they're like putting these, and I think mothers try to overcompensate that by buying them these ridiculous computers.

Table 8.1   Career orientation by social group

Number of attributes	Four	Three	Two	One	None	None and negative	Total
Gentrifying improvers	5		1				6
Central working class/intermediate		4	2	5			11
Suburban wives		2	4	3	1		10
Peripheral working class		1	2	4	4	5	16

Notes: Attributes are: 1. states has a career 2. has career plans, goals, and aspirations 3. takes a long-term employment perspective 4. gains intrinsic fulfilment from the job.

Source: Interviews 1998–2001; Li et al. (2002).

Fulfilment, for these mothers, was more to be gained from being a mother at home, in contrast to just getting money with a job. For Emily, who was unemployed:

> I could earn a lot more than him [husband] ... but I'm showing the children that I'm happy to sit here baking, sewing, I love being here when they come in whatever time it is.

This division was not simply a working-class phenomenon; there were similar divisions among middle-class respondents. Many of the suburban wives had deliberately placed their career to one side, while the gentrifying improver group had brought their career to the fore.

This is all the more striking given the equally high human capital possessed by the both groups – aspirations and identity are in this way autonomous from access to the labour market. Typically the suburban wives looked for fulfilment in part-time employment, sometimes conceptualized as a career – albeit on hold or abandoned – but did not identify with their career and were not aspirational within it. For example Jackie, a fine art consultant, had given up a high-powered career in the arts in London in order to make a conventional family life in Leeds. Working part-time as a freelance she valued her work for its fulfilment, but still felt guilty about even this commitment to career:

> I would always need something I think to keep my mind ticking over ... just for my own self-achievement, my own satisfaction, I mean that probably sounds awful ...'

Betty, a part-time university lecturer, had strategically separated these two roles in creating her biography:

> It was like there were two choices, either I get a job and pursue my career or I get married and decide to have a family and put my energies into that ...What I thought was that because I was twenty-seven when we got married, I thought about pursuing a career, I'd only just graduated remember so I would have to start at the beginning ... and I thought – I can see myself not wanting to stop work to have children and ... I was just afraid that if I went for the career first, when I came to me mid-thirties and I really had to think about whether to have children or not – because of the biological clock.

Consequently, Betty had:

> Difficulties ... with other women who put their careers first even when they've got children, it seems to me they value their career or their jobs more.

The gentrifying improvers group were most career oriented. The only respondent in this group expressing low career orientation was married to a traditionally minded working-class local. With this exception, members of this group saw their careers in both fulfilment and aspirational terms. In terms of career orientation then, the traditional class hierarchy was disrupted. The central/intermediate group had a higher career orientation than the suburban wives group. This matches the class distributions in gendered moral rationalities about combining paid work with mothering as described earlier in this chapter.

It was the cultural understanding of divisions of labour with male partners that seemed to underlie these group differences in orientation to career. Respondents in the two middle-class groups were overwhelmingly composed of graduates, often with extensive postgraduate training and recent and current experience of working in high-status professional and managerial jobs. All, in the recent past, had careers. Most respondents had met their partners in London or other university cities, where as young professionals they lived together and some had their first child. None were local to where they lived, but had moved to Headingley or Hebden Bridge respectively for the opportunities these areas provided. But the definition of these opportunities differed.

The gentrifying improvers seemed to see Hebden Bridge as a site where they could more easily combine the less gendered role of independent worker with partnered (but often unmarried) mother. Hence the group appellation of 'gentrifying partners'. In contrast, for the primarily mother group in Headingley the move was part and parcel of conventional – that is, strongly gendered – family building. Marriage and motherhood was part and parcel of the move. Leeds was somewhere where they could buy a bigger, better house with a garden, more suitable for children, usually premised on a good job offer for the husband, and properly become a family. Wives would concentrate on mothering at home, combined with part-time employment as appropriate for personal fulfilment, or as compelled where some worked longer hours than they thought best for financial reasons – to 'pay the mortgage'. Hence the group appellation 'suburban wives'.

We can investigate further how preference and constraint are socially constructed by examining two cases in more detail – those of Carrie and Christina who were chosen for their (a) typicality in their social groups. See Figures 8.1 and 8.2. Carrie was atypical in the suburban wives group: she followed a full-time professional career (although she would also like less hours) and earned more than her husband. She was also exceptional among this group in holding elements of a 'mother–worker integral' understanding – mothers needed to be stimulated by life outside mothering in order to be a good mother. Christina was typical for the peripheral group – she had a part-time unskilled job and earned less than her breadwinning husband. In terms of 'constraint' versus 'preference', both Carrie and Christina appear to act rationally in using their relative levels of human capital for appropriate employment/childcare mixes. Carrie's job as deputy school head was based on a higher degree followed by professional qualifications and experience in education, while Christina, who was a factory cleaner, had only low-level school-leaving qualifications and her employment experience was all in unskilled work. But asking why Carrie was exceptional in the suburban wives group, and Christina typical in the peripheral working-class group, can tell us much about how these preferences and constraints are socially and culturally constructed.

Firstly, Carrie was one of the few respondents showing class mobility, but while her northern working-class family had no career expectations for their daughter, she did identify with an aunt who was a primary school head. Secondly, this background had given her a horror of economic dependence on a man. Her mother, bright but working in a mill by age 14, was left after a divorce without a home of her own, earning poor wages in unskilled retail work. Not only that, but her father:

> Who's had a career ... has been able to afford himself a nice house with a garden and ... so I, I just thought that's never going to happen to me, hah! And you see it happen to so many women.

This object lesson in the value of career was reinforced by the experience of her sister–in-law, who gave up a 'powerful job' to look after her child and following an acrimonious divorce was left 'with absolutely nothing' living on '£90 a week benefit'. Thirdly, this object lesson taken from her class and family background had been extended into a worked-out feminist position, which had been practised in communal living and feminist politics in London. But despite all this, Carrie held elements of a primarily mother view:

> I'm a feminist I suppose but I still I can't shake off the idea that, you know, the good mother should always be there ... 'cos it's so ingrained isn't it in the cultural thinking I suppose. So I do think – a good mother is one who can be there for them.

So how did Carrie resolve this contradiction between her feminist views, the object lessons from her family background on the value of economic independence and career, and the need for good mothers to be there with their children? Squaring this circle largely depended on relations with her partner, Pete. He was heavily involved in both housework and childcare, so much so that:

> Our children have had two mothers, if you like and they've had two fathers 'cos I work so I'm like the traditional father.

This resolution depended on Pete's shared feminist-inspired gendered politics of family life (confirmed by a separate interview with him), worked through during the London experience of communal and political life. When they decided to move to Leeds to bring up children, they both held an agenda in which childcare, domestic work and access to career were shared.

So for Carrie bucking the group trend and taking on full-time work depended on particular biographical experiences, a contradictory class background, a feminist personal politics that had been practically developed, and above all a partner who shared and acted upon these politics. Carrie's comparative example also points to the cultural construction of the other suburban wives in the sample, with middle-class backgrounds, less developed feminism, and partners who saw themselves – and were seen by their wives – as providers more than carers.

On first sight, acting as homemaker, unpaid carer (she also looked after her aged father) and part-time unskilled worker appears to be a rational solution to Christina's class-based lack of human capital. But this rationality was also arrived at through a cultural and social journey. For Christina was not content with this 'rational choice within constraint' in combining employment and care, her employment preference lay with 'career':

> I'm still deciding what to do with my life at this age … all I've done I've had babies and done menial jobs … 'cos I'm quite a caring person and I feel like I could do summat useful and more than being a cleaner.

What was more, she was doing something about this, and had just started a course that would qualify her to be a nursery nurse. This preference for career could then, potentially, take Christina on the same employment path as many respondents in the central/intermediate' group. How then, despite this preference, did Christina end up as 'typical' for the peripheral group?

First Christina expressed a strong identification with her own mother, who had died when was in her twenties. Her own household divisions of labour and identity closely followed her mother's traditional breadwinner/homemaker model. In one important respect she differed from her mother however. Christina was an only child, and saw that as 'rubbish' which gave her no 'social upbringing'; she wanted to improve upon this and saw this as the explanation for her own large family of five children. Secondly, her husband Arthur strongly advocated a breadwinner/homemaker arrangement, even to the extent of undermining Christina's part-time job:

> He sees hissen as breadwinner, he says you leave your job, you don't need to work, you stay at home and I'll support yer.

He even believed that his wife was shortly to give up employment, whereas in fact she was planning to leave her factory-cleaning job for a better job – with possible prospects – assisting in a nature reserve. However although Christina wanted some financial independence and job fulfilment, she also agreed with the view that 'the mum should be with the kids' and take on the domestic work – it was striking that her sons did not 'even pick up their own clothes'. She even regretted that she had not been a full-time mother:

> If I'd just been a bit more braver and I wish I'd have stayed at home with the kids.

Thirdly, these traditional views of gender roles and responsibilities were consistent with normative views among these working-class interviewees, reflecting Barnsley as a type-case 'breadwinner area' on an aggregate statistical level. Most male partners had been miners or, if younger, had expected to be so like their fathers and grandfathers. Interviewees' mothers had been carers and at most part-time workers. The economic basis for these roles had weakened or even disintegrated as mining jobs disappeared, with fathers now in low-wage unskilled or casual work and mothers thrown into a more active wage-earning role. But the social definition of proper gender roles still referred to this more settled past (it was disturbing that several male partners were said to be depressed or ill because of this disjuncture in their expected biographies). Christina and Arthur had both been brought up in the same village area and made their social lives around this ex-mining community.

This social experience of local gender culture helps explain why working-class mothers from Burnley showed greater preference for career than their Barnsley counterparts. For a similar economic decline, as the cotton industry disappeared, did not appear to be so disturbing. For in this traditionally dual worker area, interviewees already had family experience of working mothers and fathers taking on domestic work. Although demonstration of this preference for career was sometimes required (for example several respondents had gone on cleaning, washing or cooking strike) mothers seemed more comfortable with a breadwinning role and fathers with domestic work. Certainly, as the demonstrations themselves show, mothers saw a career as a way forward for them. In this way class divisions in mothering are bound up with the (re)production of regionally specific gender cultures which maintain alternative concepts of the normal and ideal family, and of what is 'the proper thing to do' as far as women and men, and in particular mothers and fathers, are concerned (Duncan and Smith, 2002; Glucksmann, 2000). We can also add however that these gender cultures are also classed cultures.

CONCLUSIONS

In this chapter I have shown that, firstly, there appear to be class-based differences in how mothers combine employment and caring for their children.

These are not simple structural divisions between working class and middle class, but instead refer to more nuanced social identities. These class-based differences in mothering present different mixes of preference and constraint in choosing alternative courses of action. Secondly, the chapter shows that theories focusing on such preference or constraint do not go far beyond a tautological description of these alternatives. Rather – thirdly – preference and constraint are socially and culturally created through the development of career as an identity, through biographical experience, through relations with partners, and through the development of normative views in social networks. In this way preference and constraint become social moralities. In turn, the work–life balance campaign needs to pay attention to moral balance, as well as time and money. This moral balance consists of both the moral supply – as in the quality of childcare that is available – and to moral demand – as in the nature of the jobs that are on offer. Mothers need to be able to see that the needs of their children, as they define them, are indeed coming first, and that the jobs they are undertaking instead of childcare are both compatible and worthwhile. Making work pay, to quote one of New Labour's policy reform slogans, also means making work pay in moral terms.

NOTES

1. Thanks to Rosalind Edwards for comments, and to Wendy Holloway for her analysis of the interviews with 'Carrie' and 'Christina'.
2. Semi-structured interviews of around 1.5 hours were used. Interviewees were accessed using informal and formal contacts as starting points, and then snowballed within the contacted mothers' social networks.

9. Care politics for fathers in a flexible time culture

Berit Brandth and Elin Kvande

The many current claims about transformations in working life have made scholars of the welfare state area pronounce that the main challenges today are tied to finding the appropriate responses to these changes (Carnoy, 2002; Esping-Andersen, 1999). The old models do not seem to fit any more because the social policy programmes we are familiar with were based on another work system. Flexible work and flexible employment may find it difficult to function together with rigid social rights. Not even the conservative models based on free-market thinking are working any longer, Carnoy claims, because they are based on a family model whose 'best before' date has expired, and which ironically depends on the welfare state to function today. Bearing in mind changes both in work and family structures, and the diversity that welfare state measures have to deal with, in this chapter we are concerned with the type of care schemes that work and the reasons why they work.

In the 1990s Norway introduced two comprehensive reforms of care policy, the fathers' quota in 1993 and the cash-for-care scheme in 1998. One of the intentions behind these reforms was to give parents of small children more time to care for their children. 'Giving back time to the family' was one of the slogans used in the debates preceding the extension of the parental leave and the introduction of the cash-for-care scheme. Another important topic for discussion in today's debate on welfare policy is the freedom to choose for mothers and fathers, and flexibility when it comes to childcare arrangements. This was a central issue during the debate on cash-for-care and one of the important rationales for this reform, while one of the objections to the fathers' quota was that the parents were being given too little freedom to choose. This discussion focused on the 'mild coercion' the fathers' quota was claimed to represent.

Research comparing the fathers' quota and cash-for-care schemes has described how the basic ideas underlying these schemes are fundamentally different, and that they support different ideas about gender and family life (Leira, 1998, 2002b; Ellingsæter, 2003a, 2003b). The parental leave including the fathers' quota builds on the idea that the mother and father should be able to combine care for small children with a working career. It is a policy that supports the dual-earner family model. The criteria for entitlement to paid parental leave, the work contract, represent a strong encouragement for both parents to establish themselves in the labour market before having a baby as it is through paid work that parents earn the right to take paid leave without losing their jobs. The cash-for-care scheme is based on another care philosophy, the so-called 'family model', where the idea is to strengthen the family as a care producer by providing cash benefits irrespective of the parents' work activities. This type of policy supports the male breadwinner family model. More freedom of choice has been a crucial argument for cash measures in general, and in this case it refers to cash given particularly to facilitate one of the parents staying home. Both models have been expected to influence the work–family balance, but in different ways. While previous research comparing these two models has had a primary focus on mothers' use of the schemes, this chapter shall have an explicit focus on fathers' understanding and use of these schemes.

Both the cash-for-care and leave schemes have been introduced at a time where working life is undergoing major changes, generating conflicts and tensions. Recent research on the new economy reports both a greater degree of empowerment and more interesting jobs for many, but also intensification and longer working days for a growing number of people (Kvande, 2003; Rasmussen, 2002). This development may mean that it encroaches on family life and recreational time, and that the intentions of the schemes aimed at giving parents more time for their children are clashing with the developments in working life (Brandth and Kvande, 2002, 2003). In this chapter we focus on the importance of one work context: that of knowledge-based work, for the fathers' priorities and choices. Also, since research on men and masculinity has shown that working life is an important arena for shaping men's identity (Morgan, 1992; Collinson and Hearn, 1994) we will include a gender perspective in the analysis of fathers' time priorities. Childcare is traditionally a field with strong gender divisions, and it is therefore particularly interesting to study the power of change these schemes have. We will in this chapter examine how the various schemes cater to the needs of working life and social gender structures and influence fathers' negotiations, choices and use of the schemes.

THE FATHER-FRIENDLY WELFARE STATE?

Over the years leave associated with the birth of a child has had a shifting focus. During the nascent years of leave schemes the focus was on motherhood. Typically, such leaves were called maternity leaves. The idea was that the woman needed protection from the demands of work, and that this was in her and the child's best interests. In the 1970s equality between mothers and fathers was the underlying motivation for the expansion of the leave scheme. Mothers were to be ensured the opportunity to combine participation in the labour market with giving birth to a child and providing care. What was entirely new with the leave reform in the 1970s was that some of the leave could be shared between the parents, which meant abandoning the idea that leave was only an individual right for women. By granting fathers the right to leave, legislation in the 1970s signalled a new political view on men's responsibilities and participation in childcare. Both parents were given rights and obligations in relation to their home and their workplace.

In the 1980s and 1990s the leave scheme was gradually expanded. The idea of equality continued to be a strong objective. However the vision of a more equal sharing of childcare achieved through an optional parental leave did not yield noticeable results when it came to fathers' use of the leave. To further stimulate fathers into taking leave, an individual right for fathers modelled on the early maternity leave was introduced in 1993 together with a general expansion of the parental leave period. In addition to the explicit political aim to change the gendered division of work in relation to care for infants and toddlers, the fathers' quota brought another strong rationale into the mix, namely to strengthen the father–child relationship. Four weeks of the leave were thus reserved for the father, weeks that are generally not transferable to the mother. This has been called a development toward a father-friendly welfare state (Brandth and Kvande, 2003). The schemes are now aimed at promoting not only equality, but also fatherhood.

The Norwegian parental leave scheme is complex and consists of several elements. As seen from Table 9.1, both mothers and fathers have their individual rights (maternity leave and fathers' quota) in addition to joint rights (parental leave). The 'daddy days' are two additional weeks of welfare leave for fathers that are not paid by national insurance and not included into the total length of the leave. The total parental leave length is 52 weeks with 80 per cent pay. From these, nine weeks are for mothers and four weeks for fathers.[1] This leaves 39 weeks to be optionally shared. These 39 weeks are flexible also because they can be taken on a part-time basis until the child is two years old, the so-called time account scheme.

Parental leave is paid by national insurance and covers 100 per cent or 80 per cent of wages, depending on what length of the leave the family chooses. It is most common to choose 80 per cent wage compensation and longer leave. There is a ceiling for what is compensated by national insurance of approximately 42 500 euros (2005).

The four weeks reserved for fathers (the fathers' quota) amounts to 7.7 per cent of the total leave available. This represents about the average share of the

Table 9.1   The Norwegian parental leave rights

Maternity leave	Paid leave reserved for the mother 3 weeks before parturition 6 weeks after
'Daddy days'	Welfare leave for father in connection with birth Negotiated pay 2 weeks
Fathers' quota	Paid leave reserved for father 4 weeks
Parental leave	Paid leave that may be shared by the parents Either 29 weeks with 100 per cent pay or 39 weeks with 80 per cent

leave that fathers actually use, that is, 8.3 per cent. Mothers still mostly use the optional part of the paid parental leave period. The Norwegian leave scheme has thus from its inception been a gendered scheme as first mothers and then fathers received individual rights. Individual rights imply that the parents themselves cannot decide which of them is to stay home and mind the child. Thus the choice of who would take leave is taken out of the family's hands. The fathers' quota can be seen as a right that has been pre-negotiated by the state for men as fathers and employees.

The fathers' quota has been a great success; about 90 per cent of fathers eligible for leave take it (2004). Before the quota was introduced and fathers had to share a relatively short optional leave with the mother, only 4 per cent of fathers took leave. But, in the course of four years, taking leave changed from a minority to a majority practice for fathers in Norway. This instant take-up among fathers tells us that the existence of an individual right for fathers may have been important.

Cash-for-care was introduced in Norway in the autumn of 1998, and in brief means that parents with children from one to three years of age may receive public benefits amounting to a cash payment of around 400 euros a month, provided they do not use a full-time place in a public daycare centre. This payment is far below earnings from even a low-paid job. The cash-for-care scheme is not dependent on whether parents are working or not. It is not considered as wages and thus does not constitute the basis for earning other social and/or welfare benefits.

The idea of parental time squeeze was one of the underpinning factors for the introduction of cash-for-care, and it may therefore be considered as one of the welfare state schemes intended to balance family and work. Cash-for-care aims to encourage parents to spend more time with their children, and to use fewer public care alternatives. Therefore we can say that an intention behind this scheme is that it should lead to a reassignment of priorities for parental time, from working for a wage to providing care for one's own children. The other important rationale of this scheme is the promotion of it as a means of increasing parental choice with respect to childcare. These two aims may conflict. When using the cash transfer as they please, some parents may use private daycare while continuing working. Cash-for-care is also optional in the sense that it is designed to be gender neutral. As opposed to individual leave schemes, it is not intended as an instrument that can change the gendered division of work. It leaves it up to the family to choose whether the mother or father, or either of them at all, should stay home with the child.

The expectation that this reform would lead to a reduction in mothers' working hours was one important reason for the controversial character of this reform. However research evaluating the reform in the years after (Baklien et al., 2001) has shown that although many parents of one- and two-year-old children receive the payment, mothers have reduced their employment only to a very limited extent, while there has been no impact on fathers' employment or working hours (Baklien et al., 2001; Sletvold, 2000).

To summarize, there are a number of important differences between the fathers' quota and cash-for-care as care schemes. The fathers' quota is an individual right based on activity in working life. This genders it from the very start and makes choice very limited. Cash-for-care has been defined as a payment given to the family. It strongly emphasizes choice with respect to childcare and which of the parents should stay home. Its design is thus gender neutral. In this chapter we aim to understand how this dimension inhibits fathers from taking up the schemes.

WORKING LIFE AND MASCULINITY

'Choice' is a term that gives many positive associations, such as 'the competent choosing individual' and 'the rational actor'. As freedom to choose may give associations to individualism and detachment from social structures, a central question in the analysis concerns one of the basic issues in sociology – how the social and cultural context influence the choices made by the actors, that is, the fathers.

As pointed out, these two welfare state schemes, aiming to allow parents of small children greater opportunities to be with their children by working less, have been introduced during the same period of time that major restructuring is taking place in working life, causing families today to contend with competing claims on their time. Ellingsæter (1999) uses the concept 'time regime' to describe the changes in the use of time. In most Western societies the changes during the last ten to 20 years both in families and the labour market have led to a decline in the 'industrial time regime' (Ellingsæter 1999). In this time regime the reward and career structure has been connected to the standardized working-hour culture: the formal work contract regulates working hours in the industrial society. An example is how overtime is strictly regulated. Standardized working hours means that employees work during regular hours with a defined boundary between work and recreational time.

What is happening in many branches is a shift from standardization to increasing differentiation of working hours, toward what is called the 'flexible time regime' (Kvande, 2003). General work intensification and longer work-ing hours may be the consequences of this structuring of time (Rasmussen, 2002; Kvande, 1999). Hewitt (1993) shows how what she calls 'the new working-hour model' means that success in working life is contingent on spending very many hours at work. An employee is assessed according to the number of hours she or he has been willing to work, and to what extent work is given top priority. This includes the willingness to work weekends, participation in social events arranged by the company, how early one arrives in the morning and so on. American researchers (Bailyn, 1993; Epstein, et al., 1999) have found that parents who would like to work part-time are subjected to exclusion mechanisms in the new working-hour model. The time norms contribute to a 'labelling' or stigmatization of those who do not live up to them.

Many employees in the new time regime find that work is becoming more boundless (Sennett, 1998). This results in their spending increasingly less time with their families and applies in particular to knowledge companies where the new time norms demand total dedication, as opposed to the general principle in the industrial time regime of the normal working day. Within the flexible time regime there is a growing gap between the formal regulation of working hours and the actual practice. According to Ellingsæter (1999), this erodes the industrial time regime, as for example the scope of unpaid overtime is increasing. It is bearing this in mind that we must understand why an increasing number of fathers of young children are working overtime even though large groups purport that they prefer to work less. This may be explained by the strong 'pull' forces found in the time cultures of working life (Epstein et al., 1999).

Above we have established working life as an important structural context for the use and understanding of the welfare state policies. Moreover the gender structures of society are important contexts. In spite of substantial changes in the last three decades, the prevalent gender division of work continues to be the familiar pattern where most women have the main responsibility for childcare and also spend most time with the children (Kitterød, 2002). One of the results of this is that a large proportion of today's Norwegian women are working part-time. Even if two-provider families have become most common, men spend the most time in working life, which also can be seen as working overtime while the children are small (Kitterød and Kjelstad, 2003; Sheridan, 2004). Even if most of today's Norwegian mothers of young children are employed outside their homes, we may regard these as significant structural forces that will influence how the schemes are understood and used by fathers.

On the individual level it may also be claimed that work is important for men's construction of their masculine identity and thus for their time priorities. Being successful in working life is a cultural ideal. Connell (1987) uses the term 'hegemonic masculinity' for the dominating cultural ideals of men. There is competition between the dominating and subordinate masculinity practices. They are in mutual conflict, and one will try to dominate. Since hegemonic masculine identity for the most part is constructed in relation to participation in working life, it may conflict with being a participating father (Brandth and Kvande, 2003). Care-giving related to children continues to be a field where masculinity is put to the test because it is gendered as feminine. How have the schemes been able to challenge the dominating masculinity construction?

Since it is paid employment that qualifies for paid parental leave, women have used leave schemes to promote the political aim of increased participation in working life. The leave scheme complied with the dominating gender system, with the aim of influencing it in one direction. One issue to be examined in this article will be how care schemes, where eligibility is based on employment, influence the fathers' care practices.

DATA

To analyse these issues we use data from two projects where fathers in knowledge-based work were interviewed. The primary aim of one project was to study the consequences different uses of the cash-for-care scheme will have for equality between the genders in family and working life. Cash-for-care as a welfare scheme was here considered in relation to the employee situation in various companies. We were particularly interested in how different types of paid work influenced the experiences of parents of small children on the cash-for-care scheme. Our programme called for qualitative case-studies in companies. For the purpose of this chapter we have selected one company where the employees were researchers – primarily graduate engineers. In this company a sample of employees who were parents of young children and their partners were interviewed, a total of 18 persons. Moreover three representatives of management and employee representatives were also interviewed.

For this chapter we also use data from a study on parental leave. As a stage in this project questionnaire material was collected and couple interviews were conducted with parents of small children. The sample for the questionnaire study comprised all men in two municipalities who became fathers during a 12-month period in the middle of the 1990s. We interviewed 30 fathers and their partners from this sample. The fathers were employed in a number of types of company. For this analysis we have selected those who were employed in knowledge-based work who we thus assume come under the flexible time regime, a total of 12 fathers. All in all, we draw on 21 fathers in this chapter. We want to examine whether the flexible time culture influences how the schemes are understood and used. This material does not contain the same thorough information about the companies, but many questions asked the interviewees about their work, working hours and the relationship between work and family.

The structure of the analysis is that we initially describe the flexible time culture in our data material. Then we examine the understanding the fathers in this culture have of the fathers' quota and cash-for-care as schemes and how they use them.

KNOWLEDGE WORK AND THE FLEXIBLE TIME REGIME

In these 'knowledge-work' companies employees have a large degree of autonomy and responsibility in their work. A large portion of them worked with research and development for the oil and ICT industry, and had the possibility to work at home and juggle working hours. The essential thing is that the job is performed within the deadlines and that it is of good quality. Many employees work beyond normal working hours. Self-initiated and unregistered overtime is common. The fathers describe how they are strongly involved in their work and feel commitment to both their work tasks and their colleagues. Their efforts mean something, so they perceive the job as both demanding and fulfilling at the same time. It may be difficult to avoid getting carried away by the interesting work tasks and managing one's use of time. If they are unable to do so, the consequence is working long hours without compensation, they say. They are not ordered to work extra, but the nature of the work tasks means that this is exactly what happens. It is therefore often necessary to learn to draw the line within this type of work.

The Need for Setting Boundaries

Although the take-up rate of the fathers' quota is very high generally speaking, fathers with higher education have through the years been the most likely to use it (Brandth and Kvande, 2003). However among the highly educated, fathers who often work overtime, have high wages, a management position or are self-employed, use it less. The managers and the self-employed use it even less compared with the less-educated fathers. Considering the pressures that the flexible time regime put on fathers in this category, this is not surprising, and the interview material tells us how the fathers struggle to fence off work in order to use the fathers' quota.

One of them is Axel, who at the time of his interview was employed in a small computer business with ten employees. He was the manager of a small project organization, and responsible for customer contacts and developing a software product which the company placed much faith in. The company no doubt felt that they would lose an important cog in the wheel if he was away too long. When his daughter was born, Axel used the fathers' quota and in addition shared the parental leave with the child's mother so that each of them had a total of six months of leave.

When reflecting on how his work situation would influence his time with his child, he decided that cutting out work completely for six months would be best. His reasons were that it would be difficult to set limits in relation to the job if they were to choose, for example, a flexible time account scheme and return to work on a part-time basis, as he states 'from experience you know that you'll get full-time tasks anyway'. For Axel, consideration of his leave and the time he was to spend with his child came first and the job needed to be cut to fit. This caused him to challenge the nature of his job. He kept pressing and negotiated a leave arrangement that satisfied his wishes. He states:

> When a woman gets pregnant, it's completely natural that she should stay home for a year, and everybody seems to accept that. But if a man says that he wants to stay home for six months, reactions are like 'Oh, yeah', 'Why should you?' and this is the basis for negotiations. You have to ask your employer for permission, while the ladies aren't even questioned.

His employer was not exactly happy when he chose to take his leave, and Axel was forced to give his employer reasons for his choice. However this attitude made him even more certain that he wanted his leave:

> They proposed various counter solutions, including paying for day care and asking whether ... I could spend some time at work, not every day, only some days, or perhaps half days or such ... really, I understand them, you know. However, I never felt their thinking was 'Sure, Axel, we really think you should do this, this'll be

good for you!' I got no support from my boss. I had support from colleagues, but not from the boss.

This demonstrates that even if fathers have been granted rights, they encounter resistance in their company. Axel is working in a small knowledge-based company where his skills are in demand, and this company will easily become a greedy organization where his skills are a resource that must be exploited continuously. It is reasonable to assume that the negotiations became extra hard because they concerned a substantially longer leave than the fathers' quota of one month. However what this example clearly illustrates is the need for and importance of establishing boundaries within this type of job. With the right to leave it is possible to set limits within a boundless work situation. This negotiation situation would probably have been even more difficult if Axel did not have the fathers' quota as a good point of departure for his negotiations.

To have an individual right to leave which is earned through work activity is considered important by the fathers in general, and is a reason that received 67 per cent of the answers to why the fathers in our sample used the fathers' quota. It provides a legitimate reason for leave, and in the flexible time regime such a right seems particularly important in order to get the fathers home despite all odds. 'Most employers want you there all the time', one of the fathers who was a researcher said, but the fathers' quota is a right you have to use for the kids.

A Gendered Boundary

In the context of knowledge work with flexible working hours and where the flow of work is rather unpredictable, it is interesting to ask how cash-for-care works as a boundary setter. As mentioned before, cash-for-care is optional in the sense that it is not based on a requirement or a right to reduce work or take time off. But it gives the parents the choice, through an economic incentive, to work less in order to have more time with their children. As pointed out by Ellingsæter (2003b), the relevant choice of today's Norwegian parents is between different strategies to combine work and children, and not between being employed or at home. This means that in practice the choice is between either working full-time or part-time. In this section we analyse how this possibility for working part-time functions as a boundary-setter for fathers in knowledge work.

An important problem for parents of small children in knowledge-based work is the unpaid additional working hours they perform on private time. The employees are in a wage category where additional working hours are part of their pay, and thus their working hours are not covered by collective agreements and schemes as under a standardized time regime. One of the fathers in an ICT company states that he works between 50 and 60 hours some weeks, and that he is away from home for a good part of the week. In such a situation, cash for care has little importance for their sense of choice when it comes to working hours. The demands of this work for long hours are high, and the answer to the question of how the fathers are to have more time for their children is, according to the fathers, not found in the freedom of choice represented by the cash-for-care scheme. 'Cash-for-care does not fit the job I have, because I can't put the job away for a couple of days a week', one of the fathers said. Instead these fathers of young children need help to limit their overwork. A number of them mention how the leave schemes have this quality of setting boundaries and that they would rather have taken longer leave if they had had the opportunity to do so. As one of those we interviewed stated:

> I don't feel that we have any more freedom to choose from the cash-for-care scheme. We use it to pay a childminder, and then we don't get any more time together with the children. No, I really would have preferred that the money was used for longer leave.

A flexible time culture is difficult to combine with part-time work. Working part-time would in any case demand a great deal of each individual in the form of self-discipline.

While part-time work generally is difficult, using the cash-for-care scheme to reduce working hours is also difficult for additional reasons. It is not common for any of the fathers of small children (nor the mothers) in this type of company to use the cash-for-care scheme to reduce their working hours. One of our informants who has tried, puts it this way:

> I'm unable to do everything I need to do at work, and it also takes time to make my colleagues understand that I'm working part-time. You really end up like you're doing the same work as on a full-time job, only the pay is less.

Part-time work in this context basically means doing the same as working full-time, only for lower wages. For the company, part-time work may thus become very advantageous. The responsibility for getting the job done is each individual's, and if you are absent from work, no one else performs your tasks. Hence the best thing is to get the job done even if this means 'invisible additional time'.

That the male knowledge workers in our material never work part-time may be seen in terms of part-time work being understood as a female phenomenon. Part-time work is gendered; it is something 'women do'. It is how women reconcile work and family, and it is often connected to low pay and marginal connections to working life. Therefore part-time work is not relevant for male knowledge workers. It would increase the risk for stigmatization and not be compatible with a masculine work orientation. The cash-for-care scheme appears to be 'infected' by the same gendering, and understood as something some women might use; it is defined as a 'gendered boundary'.

This is also expressed in parental negotiations on time issues. We found that the parents have seldom openly discussed reducing working hours through the cash-for-care scheme. In many ways this is surprising. One would believe that freedom of choice in itself generates a need to negotiate different solutions. However in our interviews cash-for-care never appears as an explicit negotiation issue or as something parents have disagreed about. As put by one of them: 'Our thinking is quite similar when it comes to cash for care, both in relation to what we have chosen and what we otherwise think about it.' This suggests that cash-for-care falls into the gender pattern that is taken for granted, and that as a policy it has no independent power to change the practice in this area.

That the cash-for-care scheme only offers a limited income stream also makes it unlikely to have a major impact on decisions among these high-income employers. The impact is somewhat greater among lower-income households where the cash-for-care amounts to a higher proportion of earnings. However neither in these households does it have any effect on fathers' working hours. Mothers who have reduced their working hours are employed mostly in public health and care work (Rønsen, 2004).

Even though cash-for-care is designed as a gender-neutral scheme, it is understood and practiced as a gendered one. If one of the parents is to stay home, the answer of who is usually given in advance. We find this traditional division of work between women and men not only with couples where the mother and father have different incomes and status in working life. It is also found with couples where the parents generally have equal incomes. If the parents of small children have chosen to use the cash to reduce their working hours, it is the mothers who have done so.

What we see is that even if cash-for-care was not designed as an individual right for any of the parents, and even if it is purportedly 'optional', it is well adapted to a particular gender scheme where some mothers reduce their working hours and the fathers keep working as before. The fathers' quota is an important contrast to this because it is an individual right for fathers designed with the explicit aim to break with the traditional gender pattern in this field. It is not an optional scheme to be decided on by the mother and father, but a right given to fathers as employees. Arvid, a graduate engineer, illustrates this when he states: 'This thing with the four weeks was a matter of course. We saw it as only positive. It's an opportunity for the man too to have time at home.'

CONCLUSION AND DISCUSSION

In this chapter we have been interested in understanding the fathers' use of care policies in view of time norms at their place of work. The questions have particularly focused on the potential of the care schemes as boundary-setters against work demands. In comparing the two schemes the various processes in a flexible time culture that contribute to the fathers' use of the quota and not the cash-for-care scheme, becomes particularly evident.

By serving as a pre-negotiated right, the fathers' quota functions as a boundary against boundless work and time requirements. The high take-up rate of the quota shows the positive consequences of basing its eligibility in employment. Connecting care policy to employment means that it builds on the same thinking as many other welfare benefits and schemes regulating conditions in working life in Norway that are defined as a part of the work contract. Thus male employees who have become fathers in principle do not have to negotiate individually with their employers about using the right to the fathers' quota, although such negotiations are more likely to happen in a flexible time culture. Being a right that applies to male employees as a group makes it easier to avoid the stress and strain of being one among a minority, or being the only one to take leave to provide care for children. Precisely because the fathers' quota functions as an employee right, it appears to fit into men's and fathers' norms with respect to what are acceptable reasons for absence from work. This has probably contributed to the development of it as a majority practice in the course of a few years.

By representing an individual right for fathers, the fathers' quota breaks with the dominating gender scheme in this area, and is understood as masculine gendered. This is therefore something that is different in principle from the optional and gender-neutral thinking that is the basis of the cash-for-care scheme and which has proved to not have the same power to change. In spite of its gender-neutral design, cash for care is understood as gendered, but as feminine gendered. Choice makes cash for care a scheme for mothers. It does not challenge existing social structures, but allows family life to be marked by gender inequality and the demands of work.

Thus we see that care schemes that comply with the time demands of working life and the traditional gender norms, are not able to give fathers more time with their children. Consequently in the flexible time regime there is much to suggest that standard, non-flexible schemes are the ones that will be important. In short, schemes building on ideas of individual choice maintain the status quo, which in this case means that fathers do not spend more time with their children.

It is an interesting question whether today's welfare state regimes are adapted to post-industrial society, and what the transition from industry to service-providing activities and knowledge production means for the design of the welfare state. According to Esping-Andersen (1999), the welfare state was designed for the industrial society, that is, an earlier social order where ideals such as universalism and equality were prevalent. This approach to social policy has been challenged as greater uncertainty in working life, increased demands for flexible adaptation, major changes in family relationships and not least female participation in working life have led to other types of needs. The multiplicity of the post-modern society thus leads to more heterogeneous needs and expectations. Many have become dissatisfied by the inability of the welfare state to respond appropriately to these new needs. Asking whether the welfare state thus is incompatible with the post-industrial society, Esping-Andersen's reply is a clear 'no'. The paradox is nevertheless that the more difficult it is to maintain the welfare state schemes, the greater the need for them. If a flexible working life makes it difficult for parents of young children to use the state care schemes, could it not be that it is precisely because of this that such schemes are necessary? The issue thus is the types of scheme that are necessary to satisfy heterogeneous needs.

NOTE

1.   In July 2005 the fathers' quota was extended to five weeks, making the total leave 53 weeks.

10. Individualization and 'identity-risks' in dual-career households

Irene Hardill and Joost van Loon

INTRODUCTION

Individualization is now a widely used concept in social theory to describe the changing nature of prevailing social relations in late-modern Western societies (Bauman, 2001; Beck, 1992; Beck and Beck-Gernsheim, 2002; Giddens, 1991; Sennett, 1998). In general terms, individualization is the process by which the primary unit of social and political action is no longer an aggregate or collective entity, but becomes increasingly restricted to individual persons (a shift from 'we' to 'I'). However as Beck and Beck-Gernsheim (2002) point out, the concept itself is still too often misunderstood as a simple equivalent of neo-liberal individualism, which ascended to prominence during the era of Thatcherism and Reaganomics in the 1980s. Individualism is an ideology that positions the subject as in essence a unique, autonomous, self-standing and free-being, whose sense of self is only additionally influenced by social forces, but only because the subject grants this an active and conscious permission. As an ideology, it gives meaning and value to a specific relationship of the subject to his or her real conditions of existence (Althusser, 1971). In the case of individualism, this value is that of self-determination. In contrast, Beck and Beck-Gernsheim stress that individualization is a deeply social process and institutionally anchored: 'it is a structural characteristic of highly differentiated societies' and 'does not endanger their integration but actually makes it possible' (Beck and Beck-Gernsheim, 2002, p. xxi). The process of individualization effectively undermines the value of self-determination, because it is a consequence of socio-cultural conditions that are beyond the realm of the individual.

In this chapter, we seek to map some particular consequences of this process on the social organization of households. More specifically, we seek to link the concept of individualization with that of the flexibilization of the labour market, by arguing that the consequences of the latter are not simply restricted to the world of work, but spill over into other areas of the social, in particular those of the organization of households and the meaning of intimate relationships.

We shall use the case of 'dual career households' as a primary example of how the process of individualization affects the everyday lives of men and women.[1] These consist of co-habiting and married couples, who both have a deep commitment to the labour market through holding managerial or professional posts. Dual career-households are a primary example of the individualization thesis because they exist as a 'unit' of two individuals, each with their own career. A career is more than a job, as it requires a form of commitment that is not exclusively instrumental but deeply personal. Yet, although separated as professionals with (desired) careers, dual career households are also bound by intimacy and love in a committed relationship, which can be seen as a response to human needs. This bond may be further extended by the presence of children, who may or may not be dependent on their parents.

The leading question of this analysis is: how do people in dual career households organize their lives and what does this tell us about individualization? Central aspects in this analysis are gender, having children, intimacy and social emotional needs that arise from living as a couple. It also includes some aspects of the changing nature of work such as the rise of 'atypical' work (fixed term contracts, complex and disjointed careers and social and geographical mobility). We aim to describe and analyse dual career households, as an illustration of the individualization thesis, which corresponds with the flexibilization of the labour market. Flexibilization is not the same as individualization, but instead is a particular manifestation of the way in which individualization affects the labour process and labour market. It is through the mediated forms of relations of production such as contracts and projects, that the labour market becomes increasingly fragmented and subject to a profound temporal destabilization. It is the disjuncture between biographical time and work time that constitutes the essence of flexible labour, and the 'experience' of this disjuncture is seen through increased job-insecurity, work-related stress and the rise of short-term thinking, alongside the erosion of collective forms of work-organisation (Sennett, 1998). In turn, governments that seek to expand the integration of families into the national economy by promoting working parenthood and extending the institutionalization of childcare, further reinforce the mutual reinforcement of individualization and flexibilization.

A third concept deployed to enable us to reflect more critically on this spill over of individualization and the flexibilization of labour markets is that of 'identification' and identity risks. The centrality of 'identification' in contemporary life is linked to this shift of burden to the individual. It is now up to him or her to decide what action should be undertaken; he or she alone is responsible for the consequences. As Lash (2000) has argued (also see Beck et al., 1994), this entails a process of reflexivity[2] in which the person has to externalise part of him or herself to provide an appropriate basis for decision-making. The manifestation of this self-externalization often takes the form of 'identity', or better, multiple identities, which are not always compatible (for example, wife, mother, professional worker, citizen, ethnicity, sexual orientation, religion and so on). These identifications are expressions of needs, desires and interests. Identity-risks are thus the effects of the incompatibility of different manifest needs, desires and interests. They manifest themselves as decisions over what aspect of life should be prioritised, with unforeseen consequences for the person and his or her immediate social environment. The incompatibility of needs, desires, structural and moral imperatives and strategic decisions manifest itself in specific dilemmas which people face as part of their biography. At these potential turning points, their identities are 'at stake' and how they respond is likely to depend to a large extent on how they ultimately perceive their identity risks.

Identity-risks can be linked to what Beck and Beck-Gernsheim see as the key consequence of individualization in Western societies: the imperative 'to seek biographical solutions to systemic contradictions' (Beck and Beck-Gernsheim, 2002: xxii). As the primary unit of action and social integration becomes the individual person, systemic incompatibilities, which were previously addressed at the level of collectivities, will now manifest themselves as incompatible demands, interests or needs for the person him or herself.

In this chapter, we analyse the disjuncture between career-needs (that is, the demands of the job or workplace that are such that this often means putting the job first) and personal socio-emotional needs, in particular those related to family life (committed relationships, marriage and parenthood, which are constitutive of an appeal to and valuation of meaningful existence; Charlesworth, 2000). We focus on those households with children and in associating identity-risks with the increasingly strained commitments to both paid employment and intimate relationships, we ask in what ways people resolve the tensions between work-based and family-based imperatives. As both are being reconfigured by individualization, to what extent are people able to articulate a sense of value in terms of commitment to both work and intimate relationships?

Finally, a criticism that could be levelled at some notions of individualiza-tion is that they tend to foreground rational, cognitive and instrumental orientations at the expense of socio-emotional needs and desires, including those linked to intimacy and life. Reflexivity always entails non-rational aspects, and these are clearly manifest in a range of identifications with which people position themselves in relation to prevailing moral, ethical and political discourses. Therefore we will ask what the place of 'sacrifice' and 'vocation' might be within the process of individualization. If Beck and Beck-Gernsheim's individualization thesis is correct, then we assume that the non-instrumental aspects of personal lives will become increasingly entangled with risk assessments (Breen, 1997), and subject to rationalization, commodification and the rendering of accountability (including the allocation of blame and resentment).

DUAL-CAREER HOUSEHOLDS

In dual-career households, both partners have a deep commitment to the labour market through holding managerial or professional posts. They receive two salaries sometimes boosted by such things as company cars, private health insurance and performance-related pay. Both partners therefore have made considerable investments in the labour market and seek jobs with a high degree of commitment, and an intrinsically demanding character (Rapoport and Rapoport, 1978). Moreover female partners, who are mothers, have a stronger attachment to the labour market after childbirth than do mothers in other households.[3] Although accounting for only 8 per cent of households (head aged 20–59 years), their numbers seem set to increase (Hardill et al., 1997: 314). Clearly, in socio-economic terms, dual-career households form a privileged group, better able to compete economically, and exercise their influence in achieving priorities, than many other population groups. As we shall see in the following section, for dual-career households the intertwining of home and work is likely to be particularly complicated. Moreover they have been described as the 'optimum survival kit' household (Forrest and Murie, 1987) for the late twentieth century (and twenty-first century). Indeed as work is central to most governmental social welfare strategies, the two-wage household, but especially the dual-career household, is their preferred model of economic unit.

Dual-career households have a rather different dynamic than those in which one person is responsible for the family income and the other manages the domestic front (single-income households) or simply has another paid job (dual-earner households). In dual-career households, individualization is most pervasive because here two individuals are actively engaged in the process of constructing complex risk-biographies. Although individualization also affects other household types, such as dual-earner or single-earner ones, it is the highly individual choice that point to 'the self' (the need to be valued for one's professional being) to voluntarily pursue a career that exerts additional pressure on decision-making beyond its association with necessity such as the need for income, the care-needs of children and so on. Opting out by not pursuing a career is a far greater identity-risk for someone who has had a career than for someone who has not. In dual-career households, both partners face decisions that may have implications not just for their own careers but for those of their partners as well, but in dual-earner households, priority is given to one career only. However in all cases the range of possible outcomes exponentially increases with the number of actively participating individuals (for example, the educational needs of children are also distributed rather unequally in geographical terms).

Partners in dual-career households may not share economic resources, nor may they share the same house or apartment seven days a week. But often they are bound together emotionally; they care for each other. They want to commit to each other in the form of a loving relationship but individually they both want to commit to paid work. This single-minded pursuit of two careers or 'individualization' can result in some couples adopting complex living arrangements, such as:

- Being 'shift parents' juggling childcare and new working patterns (Daycare Trust, 2000).
- 'Living together apart' as 'commuter/weekend couples' (Green et al., 1999; Winfield, 1985), or in so-called 'transnational astronaut' families with 'parachute' children (Pe-Pua et al., 1996).
- For a growing proportion of couples, living together may not be for a lifetime.

By examining how members of dual-career households live with identity-risks, we seek to understand some of the consequences of individualization for the way in which people are able to 'make a living', which is more than merely an economic process. Specifically we focus on one key aspect of this lived experience: how are children accommodated in dual career households? Identity-risks can be defined as the anticipation of undesirable consequences of specific decisions taken by people as part of 'making a living' in everyday life settings. These include decisions about career moves, promotions, geographical location, housing, education, insurance, social security, personal security and so on, but also more emotional aspects of making a living such that are involved in being parents, spouses, lovers and so on. The undesirable consequences are anticipated (as risk-perceptions) but inherently unknowable, including the probability of whether they would occur at all. The link to identity is primarily in terms of establishing answers to the question: 'who am I'? And – subsequently – 'what does it take to be that'? Identity-risks are a tangible consequence of individualization, and the questions they bring into being provoke multiple and potentially incompatible answers, which manifest themselves as dilemmas. In a nutshell, life in an individualized society centrally evolves around the accommodation of identity-risks into an ordinary everydayness and the (continuing) failures thereof.

Identity-risks emerge out of the imperative of 'being a good x', and 'x' stands for a range of labels under which the person socially and symbolically organizes his or her everyday life. In the modern world, 'being a good x' is generally associated with the performativity of 'doing a good job'. For example, 'being a good mother' is generally associated with being able to do the things that good mothers do: provide loving care for her children (giving them time and attention), creating a loving, homely environment for the family, organizing (which could mean outsourcing) the meals, the cleaning, the relationships with external institutions (school, GP, dentist and so on). Different ranges of imperatives are associated with being 'a good wife', or being 'a good professional'. Individualization has resulted in a shift of burden or responsibility and decision making from the social to the individual. However the imperatives cannot be simply renegotiated at an individual level because the person still operates in a social network, which not only includes the expectations, needs and demands of other people, but also structural impositions of, for example, the state as well as economic forces. What defines 'good' is not simply a matter of personal opinions, norms or private conscience (see also Duncan, this volume).

It is vital to stress that individualization and identity-risks are not only theoretical issues. Whereas social theory can give a logical account of the ways in which such transformations will affect social processes, empirical research has not unequivocally supported these predictions. That is to say, the concept of individualization has by and large remained an abstraction. Empirical research is required to see in what ways its consequences can be made visible, and we begin this process in a modest way in the remaining part of this chapter.

METHODS

We draw on the personal and household biographies of dual-career households augmented by published statistics. Our investigation of the individualization process on people's everyday lives involved approaching the personnel directors of five large organizations based in Nottingham to help in the identification of dual-career households. The five organizations consisted of a National Health Service hospital, a higher education establishment, a major bank, and two large market-oriented private sector manufacturing companies (one engaged in the food and drink industry and the other in pharmaceuticals). In this way we gained access to staff in a relatively comprehensive range of managerial, professional and associated occupations. In each of the dual-career households identified, at least one partner is employed at a Nottingham base by one of the five employers. The other partner could work for any employer (or indeed work in a self-employed capacity) in any location. A semi-structured self-completion questionnaire survey (which was completed by 130 households; for a fuller discussion of the methods see Hardill, 2002) was followed by in-depth face-to-face interviews with a sub-set (30 households) of those who completed the survey element of the research. The sub-set is an indicative sample of the 130 who participated in Phase One, and was drawn in roughly equal numbers from the five organizations. Each partner was interviewed separately (Pahl, 1989; Valentine, 1999). We draw on the qualitative interview material in this chapter.

EMPIRICAL RESULTS

Most households in this study have commodified some of the tasks of home (cleaning and so on), and use is also made of labour-saving devices, so juggling two careers involved off-loading some tasks onto another person (childcare, cleaning and gardening). However one partner (usually the woman) tends to take responsibility and manages the domestic front as well as a career, as happens in dual-earner and single-income couple households.

Managing the work–home interface can cause stress and trigger identity-risk. Ginn and Sandell (1997) have reviewed studies of stress arising from the home–work interface (Lewis and Cooper, 1983, 1988; Cooper et al., 1996; Ginn and Sandell, 1997). Such stress arises not only from pressures in the work and home environments but also from gender role attitudes internalized by individuals (also see Dumelow et al., 2000).

In their study of stress amongst British social workers, Ginn and Sandell (1997: 428) found that stress levels were related to home (their family caring responsibilities) and to work (paid employment). This source of stress was found to impact early in women's biographies, for a number of single women highlighted that they had had to make choices between their relationships and their career during their training years, which signals the actual traumatic nature of identity risks. Those who did have children faced increased stress levels, which were related to the age of the youngest child. To a lesser extent informal care-giving also raised stress levels. This source of stress is likely to increase with the ageing of the populations of advanced capitalist economies. Stress is a strong indicator of identity-risks. What presents itself as a psychological dysfunction of maladaptation is in fact socially produced and structured. Individualization has led to a transfer of causal association (blame) from the social organization of everyday life to the person who is afflicted by it.

In this study there were some stark examples of the impact of the stress involved in the home–work interface. Four of the interviewees mentioned that they had failed marriages, and two felt that work had been partly to blame. They had prioritized their careers to the detriment of the relationship; they had invested too much time in the career rather than time 'being there' for the relationship. Joanne for example talked about her career and a failed marriage. She had been working very long hours in a hospital and then, 'my [first] son died and about 3 months after my [first] husband went off with his secretary, I had to review what I was doing'. She then decided to switch to general practice to try and 'have a life'.

Joanne's account resonates with the identity-risks that emerge out of tensions between a professional vocation and the vocation of parenthood. Such tensions however are not equally distributed between men and women. For the latter, the vocation of motherhood (for example 'being a good mother') cannot be brushed aside (because of both cultural and institutional imperatives) as easily as by men, who appear to be more able to have 'sacrificed' the responsibilities associated with fatherhood when they clashed with the demands of the job. The key difference is that 'good mothering' involves being present with the children in a way that the construction of 'good fathering' (currently) does not.

This example suggests that the distribution of identity-risks is skewed and the bias is along gender lines. In this sense, individualization too is a different matter for (most) men and women, with the latter being repositioned in a far less enviable situation. However the socio-economic position of women is an equally important differentiating factor. Research for example suggests that in the UK a rapid return to full-time employment after childbirth is confined to an elite of highly educated professional and managerial women (Ginn and Arber, 1995). These women are in households which are more likely to be able to commodify a number of the tasks of social reproduction (childcare, cleaning and so on) (Mattingly, 1999; Momsen, 1999). On the face of it, their employment is little affected by motherhood, conforming closely to the pattern conventionally associated with men's employment. This group most closely fits Beck and Beck-Gernsheim's individualization thesis, as they have been able to organize their lives through increasing their arsenal of options. However some women in this group have reported paying a high price for this in terms of stress, which if sustained over a long period is likely to entail risks to physical health as well. Both uncertainty as to when the working day will end and the sheer quantity of hours demanded are too much for some women as was illustrated by Joanne and Jane (Box 10.1). The identity risks they face are both related to proving that they can do a man's job, whilst also maintaining that they can be still 'good mothers'.

BOX 10.1   THE CASE-STUDY HOUSEHOLDS

1. Pete (manager with a large manufacturing organization) and Helen (nurse) both in their mid-forties with two grown-up children, met when they were students. Pete's career has always led and they have made five inter-regional moves. Since the birth of their first child she has also had to work nights all the time to fit in round his job.

2. James (self-employed consultant) and Sarah (university researcher) are both in their early fifties, have two grown-up children, and have lived together for over 30 years. They met at school, they went to the same university (he was a couple of years ahead of her) and his job has always led, and as a result they have moved inter-regionally four times.

3. Joanne (doctor) and Ken (regional sales manager) are in their early forties and met about a decade ago when they both had established careers. Joanne has been married before. They have a five-year-old son at a private school and they employ a nanny.

4. Nigel (a part-time lecturer with contracts with three employers) and Anne (a school teacher) are both in their early forties, and have been together for ten years. This is Anne's second marriage. Anne's two children from her first marriage live with them along with their eight-year-old daughter. Anne has the 'lead' career, and Nigel has been a house husband.

5. Simon (a sales executive) and Samantha (a senior analyst programmer) are in their early thirties, and work full-time for the same manufacturing company. They have been together for just over a decade, and met at work when they were both 'on a fast-track general management scheme', but have had two spells as a commuter couple.

6. Diana (mid-thirties, university lecturer) and Bob (mid-forties, further education lecturer) met when Diana was a student. They have a baby son and while they prioritize her career, they are very much equal partners. They employ a nanny to care for their son. Diana has held a series of fixed-term contracts but now has a tenured lectureship.

7. Becky (software consultant) and Gary (accountant) are in their early thirties and met at university. They have a baby

> son and while they prioritize his career, until her maternity leave they both worked very long hours.
> 8. Jane (food technologist) and Mark (sales representative) are in their mid-thirties and have been together for a decade. They have a young child who attends a private nursery.
>
> Source: Hardill (2002).

Childbirth greatly increases the unpaid caring work associated with home as our in-depth interviews demonstrates. Nineteen (of the 30) households had children, and in 14 the female partner took either a career break or adjusted her working hours by working part-time. Some of the older women (in their fifties at the time of the interview) did indicate that when they were pregnant their employer had no maternity scheme; one was just expected to 'disappear'. Sarah for example resigned her post when she was pregnant:

> You have to think back to 1969 /70 [when] the whole attitude to women with children working was very different. When I think back, women who graduated with me, quite a few of them got married and went [straight] into part-time jobs and never had full-time jobs. That was the social attitude you had in the Sixties.

In stark contrast, only one male partner had ever taken a career break, and another was planning to. Nigel and Anne have both taken time out to care for their daughter. Anne was prime carer for one year:

> When I was pregnant with Becky, it was Nigel's first child. He hated his job [social work] and I wanted to get back to work and it was an obvious solution. He really wanted to look after Becky.

Nigel said:

> We actually role reversed as they call it ... for me it was my first child, I felt that by going out to work I was missing out on something important.

He went on to say:

> We don't particularly want both of us to be working full-time ... the pressures attendant on two full-time careers would be enormous.

Both partners in another household are planning career adjustments for a child they hope to have. Samantha indicated that, 'we will probably try and have children next year. I will take maternity leave ... at the end of those six months Simon will apply for a career break [5 years]. He can't wait – seriously

– he cannot wait to give up work.' Simon is feeling disillusioned with his current job.

Both Nigel and Simon orient themselves towards fatherhood as a meaningful alternative to their 'failing' professional careers. Both disliked their jobs and this served to legitimate a change in prioritization. However they are still quite exceptional. Although a number of other male partners took a few days of their holiday entitlement around the time of their child's birth, most made no adjustment to their working pattern at the time of the birth and afterwards. Sarah said, 'James still pursues his career as if we had no children, indeed as if he was still single, all the give has been on my part.'

Thus identity risks show themselves in this context of combining parenting with professional work quite differently, and as gendered. Professional work is not merely instrumental as a means of earning an income; it has to be meaningful and enjoyable. Individualization is not merely a process by which the burden of responsibility is shifted from institutions and collectivities to private persons; it also entails a new set of imperatives and obligations of how to live one's life: making a living has to be enjoyed. Whereas for women identity-risks can emerge as an incompatibility of demands between parenting and professional careers, for men the individualization process is more geared towards maximizing personal satisfaction.

The identity-risks faced by women in relation to motherhood are compounded by precarious labour market situations. For example some women were employed on fixed-term contracts when they were pregnant, like university researcher Diana:

> A year into my three year contract I became pregnant. I know that [the Head of Department] was most displeased. When he found out that I was entitled to maternity leave I think that upset him even more. He took the view that women are either a mother or a professional woman and you can't be both. He just felt that things were likely to become complicated where a woman had to juggle the responsibilities of a profession as well as looking after young children. He felt that the Department would be short-changed.

For Diana, the identity risks were made present by her line manager's attitude. She faced the prospect of being identified as an incompetent professional, who was unable to sufficiently devote herself to her professional vocation. She went on to say:

> Whilst I was pregnant I was doing more [work] than I should have done. I was taken into hospital for an emergency C-section because I developed hypertension. I'm sure it was all work-related, [due to] the stress that was on me really. I think words fail me when it comes to describing the pressures that were placed on me, not necessarily verbal. I suppose, like many women do who are pregnant or otherwise,

we tend to overcompensate and really work flat out. I suppose I was working flat out at a time in my life I shouldn't have been.

Diana has since moved to another university and has secured a tenured lectureship.

Diana's experience illustrates how identify risks can trigger health risks. Another such example is Sarah. Sarah explained that, 'I didn't apply for maternity leave when I had my son because the previous pregnancy had miscarried.' Health worries therefore prompted Sarah to resign her post and leave work before she was entitled to maternity leave, to try and avoid another miscarriage. Here identity risks spill over into socio-somatic health risks. Health risks manifest themselves as embodied limits to individualization and expose the fallacy of individualism. The ideology of individualism still seeks to maintain a notion of the body as 'whole', complete and self-sufficient. The individual self has to take responsibility for his or her own well-being. Hence stress-related health problems are an individual problem.

However the process of individualization actually shows the body to be 'open' and 'dependent'. The demands of having a career and a meaningful intimate relationship are often not compatible. When they are stretched to the point of rupture, something has to give. For some it will be their career, for others their relationships and for others their bodies and health. However it is only with the physical breakdown of the body that individualism is truly exposed as incompatible with individualization. Individualism generates a sense of 'lack' that particularly affects women. This is because being 'a good woman' (mother/wife/daughter) entails culturally and structurally enforced imperatives of being 'open' and 'dependent' (for example responsiveness and care). This lack in turn often manifests itself as guilt, blame or in some cases resentment. In other words, it is because of the pervasiveness of individualism that especially women experience identity-risks in such an acute and self-destructive fashion. Individualism always backfires onto the individual – it is her responsibility, her inability, her lack, her deficiency, her fault and she alone is to blame. This suggests that without individualism, individualization would be a lot more bearable.

One particular example where this becomes clear is the experience of maternity leave itself, which can heighten identity-risks. One interviewee, Becky, was on maternity leave when she was interviewed, and while she intended to return to work she did express concern as to how she would cope. Prior to their child's arrival, Becky had done most of the unpaid work in the home, but Gary also helped, 'a lot'. On maternity leave she had slipped into a routine of having sole responsibility for childcare, acknowledging that she was making 'a rod for my own back'. Like a number of other women interviewed, Becky commented that it was during a period of maternity leave that she started doing more and more household tasks and assumed responsibility for most childcare duties. When she does go back to work she thought it would be hard to break the pattern and share the household work more equitably. Moreover her job as a software consultant involves business trips away from home and she didn't think she would be able to do this. Becky acknowledged that, 'while Gary is a supportive partner no way would he care for [their son] if I was away overnight on a business trip'.

For some of the women interviewees, committing to children through a career break or working part-time for a spell was a conscious choice to enjoy motherhood. This group emphasized that they could not see the point in having a child and then not 'being there' for them (see Duncan, this volume). Responsibility to family was stressed by Sarah: 'it's a family and you have a responsibility to keep a home and your children need a base'. Thus for Sarah it was important that she invested time in the home. However the nature of this investment changes over the life course. Sarah is now in an 'empty nest' household, and is committed to her job, and deriving a great deal of personal satisfaction. Thus her partner James commented that now their children have left home, 'Sarah's job is probably more important now than it's ever been in our relationship.'

For other couples a coping strategy is exploiting the working patterns of the 24/7 economy, by using the shift system and becoming 'shift parents'. It is estimated that 61 per cent of working families contain parents employed outside regular 9–5 hours, managing shifts, and working during early mornings, evenings, nights and weekends (Daycare Trust, 2000: 1).[4] Round-the-clock work particularly affects workers in service, plant and machinery operation and managerial and professional jobs (Daycare Trust, 2000: 1). To the extent to which these work patterns are chosen rather than imposed by the lack of alternatives in the flexible labour market, these work patterns enabling couples to commit to two careers but at a personal cost, this coping strategy means that they have sacrificed their time together and thus may reduce the means for developing and maintaining their intimate personal relationship. However there are virtually no formal childcare services open to match late or extended hours, except nannies, so their choices are limited (Statham and Mooney, 2003). Pete and Helen have been 'shift parents', with Helen, a qualified nurse working nights. Pete said that, 'Helen would work nights and I would work days.'

CONCLUSION

In this chapter we have drawn on empirical research: case-studies of personal and household biographies of dual-career households living and working in the East Midlands. We have focused on the practices of living as a collective unit, especially coping strategies adopted against a background of individualization and careers. In this chapter we have shown that for many dual-career households, 'making a living' in the context of labour market flexibilization as well as individualization is a daily struggle over scarce resources, especially time and energy. In contrast, money is not often cited as an issue. The individualization thesis suggests that the burden of decision-making and thus responsibility (and potential blame) is increasingly shifting from institutions and collectivities to private persons. The dual-career households in our sample reflect this as both partners seek to develop a personal career, responding to a professional vocation. Married life, and having children, does not always fit well with this vocation; choices have to be made and this is reflected in the interviews when partners speak of 'giving' and 'sacrificing'.

Vocations, gifts and sacrifices are all part of 'identifications'. 'Being', which is the core of identification, is intrinsically linked to a desire to 'being good' as a professional, a spouse, a parent, a sibling, a child and so on. The individualization process however has led to a differentiated sense of 'being'. No longer able to call on the social authority of a collective being, the individual being has to negotiate his or her own trajectory through life. Thrown back on him or herself, the individual being is solely responsible for making decisions as well as for their consequences.

Our case-studies also show that Beck and Beck-Gernsheim are right in differentiating between individualization and individualism. The latter is basically a particular ideological response to the former – one that seeks to re-establish the integrity of the individual in the face of its differentiation and disintegration. Morally speaking, individualism prioritizes private conscience over a social one. It may seem that conflicts are more easily resolved if the repertoire of considerations is singular; however within married life for example all actions have potential repercussions for others. In other words, individualism is a form of denial and inherently unsustainable within married life. Individualism is disrupted by feelings of guilt or resentment, which function as a reminder that we are not alone; and our private conscience is not sufficient on its own.

In contrast to individualism, individualization is not an ideology but a social condition. Instead of stressing the uniqueness and integrity of the individual, it points towards its fragile, fragmented, open and dependent state. The couples in our interviews all experienced their dependence on each other, on structural and institutional conditions, and this was reconstructed in terms of 'contingencies'. Yet the desire for stability, for roots, for the ability to anticipate and even predict the consequences of one's actions has not disappeared. This is the crux of identity-risks; they are experienced as lack of integrity, stability, continuity and so on. This lack manifests itself as the incompatibility of needs, desires and interests that constitute the basis of 'making a living'. In particular the women in our interviews experienced this lack, some as a deficiency, others as a fact of life. We suggest that this is because their identity-risks are more manifest as anticipated undesirable outcomes. Being 'a good professional', being 'a good wife' and being 'a good mother' (leaving aside being a good daughter or sister) are not easily reconciled, especially because what defines 'goodness' is intensively subjected to social engineering, public scrutiny, cultural impositions and moral imperatives (far more than say being a good husband or father). The privatist solution of individualism is hardly available for women, only because it is (still) deemed socially unacceptable (and irreconcilable with being 'a good woman'). One factor that makes that abundantly clear is having children.

The experience of identity-risks among couples with children is intensely more complicated than among those without. Even those 'empty nest' couples are still strongly affected by the conditions of parenthood. In all but a few exceptions, having children has affected women more then men. For many, it has impeded their career prospects. However for most women, having children was also seen as an inalienable part of their being; the vocation of motherhood and the sacrifices it demands are not solely constructed as negative. This is largely because most women did not construct their identities in an individualist fashion. Whereas they were individualized in arranging how to make a living, their existence was still highly social. A number of women experienced problems in trying to cope with the incompatible demands; they reported anxiety, stress and health problems. In all of these cases, children were involved. In contrast, only two men linked a lack of job satisfaction with a (possible) shift to prioritizing parenting. The contrast with the women is stark in that they are both only privileged in being able to make such a decision, but also still felt the need to legitimate this by referring to a disillusionment at work. For most men, it seems that identity-risks are less related to incompatible demands, but instead to a lack of ability of satisfying a meaningful vocation.

Finally, in our study it is predominantly women who have sacrificed personal careers for the household. Especially having children shifted the burden of this sacrifice towards them. Whereas for some this was reflected on with resentment, for others it was seen as a necessary part of making a living. The place of sacrifice in the role of vocation is often ignored. Men who single-mindedly pursue a career also sacrifice, not just their time and energy, but more importantly some of their socio-emotional needs. Sacrifice is not something one has to do consciously. The fact that their spouses may be unhappy or even resentful is the price they must pay for their individualism.

NOTES

* This chapter draws on research funded by the Leverhulme Trust (grant F/740), the Ministère de l'Equipement, des Transports et du Logement, France (F 00-62) and The Canadian Faculty Research programme (2001). The research was undertaken in partnership with Anne E. Green, David W. Owen, Robert Watson and Anna C. Dudleston. We are grateful to the dual-career households who participated in the study, to Olwyn Ince for her research assistance. The views expressed here are those of the authors alone.

1. In this chapter, we have restricted our analysis to heterosexual couples.
2. Reflexivity is defined differently by Beck et al., 1994. Whereas Giddens sees it as a process of self-externalization and thus bound by consciousness, the former understands reflexivity as self-confrontation, the primary origins of which are not consciousness but a precognitive experience of oneself as 'being-in-the-world' (see Beck et al., 1994). Scott Lash (2000) creates a third term of 'aesthetic reflexivity', which mediates between the two. It is a process by which a particular experience is being valorized by invoking a sense of subliminal revelation. Through aesthetic reflexivity, we subject our being-in-the-world to a judgement regarding its 'appeal' to a higher sense of purpose than that of 'mere being'.
3. Employment among mothers with a degree has risen the most rapidly (from 57 per cent in 1981 to 78 per cent in 1989; see Brannen, 1998: 79).
4. Using data analysed by the Daycare Trust, 34 per cent of working families contain a parent who worked weekends, 30 per cent of working families contain a parent who worked long hours, and 18 per cent of women with children in two-parent households regularly work evenings (Daycare Trust, 2000: 1–3).

PART IV
Work, time and urban services

The juggling of paid work with the other demands on our time is not an easy act to perform. It is a 'precarious accomplishment' (Fagan et al., 2004), one that is always open to being undermined by the unpredictable events of everyday life that disrupt the most organized of schedules. The chapters so far in this book have revealed in all manner of ways how, whether well or poorly paid, the coordinating of tasks necessary to ensure both the social reproduction of the household and to remain in paid employment is becoming harder to achieve. The emergence of the 'new economy', the range of ways in which national welfare states have sought to address issues of 'work–life balance', and the responses of different types of households have simply reaffirmed how getting by demands high levels of emotional and physical energy.

In the city, where the stresses and strains of everyday life are felt most intensely, where the pace of life is quickest, and yet perhaps ironically the obstacles to movement are greatest, this accomplishment takes a particularly acute form, different in nature from the challenges facing those who live in places disconnected from services, and where also getting about can be hard. As Jarvis (2004: 1) argues, drawing on her work in London, '[i]n most advanced economies there is a worrying tendency for housing, jobs, shopping, schools, transport and leisure to be spatially fragmented. These amenities (some public, some private) form a geographically specific "infrastructure of everyday life"'. In the US the Census Bureau now has a category entitled 'extreme commuting' for those workers who travel 90 minutes or more each way. Last year 3.5 million Americans were in this category. Perhaps not surprisingly New York has the highest proportion of its workers performing extreme commuting (Howlett and Overberg, 2004). And it is not just that people are now travelling further to work – moving between the different nodes in the social reproductive network – home, work, school and so on – is becoming harder, not easier and slower, not faster. For example in London over the period 1977 to 1982 the average traffic speed in the morning rush hour was 12.2 miles per hour: by the end of 2003 this had dropped to 9.9 miles per hour. Getting out of London at the end of the working day is no easier: for the same periods the figures were 12.1 and 9.6 miles per hour (Transport for

London, 2003). Expanding travel-to-work areas, longer and more intense rush-hours, the growing congestion associated with school runs and so on speak to the current challenges facing individuals, households and governments as they seek to reach compromises that meet the expectations and needs of individuals, households, firms and states.

It is in this context that the chapters in Part IV examine the organization and delivery of urban public services. They perform this from the vantage point of users, planners and employees of public services. Together the chapters present a further layer of complexity on those already put in place in previous parts of the book. They examine the different ways in which governments are restructuring what they do and how they do it, with important implications for the terms under which individuals, particularly women, perform paid and unpaid work. What the studies reveal is how categories and terms such as 'time' and 'space' are not pre-given, closed, but can be opened up for contestation, dispute, negotiation in the making of a case for a more just and equitable society.

In the first chapter of Part IV Sarah Walsh, Susan Baines and James Cornford examine the UK government's self-titled 'modernization' of public service delivery. They focus on one strand of the reforms: on the introduction of e-government, by which is meant both the quantitative automation of services and their qualitative redesign. It is about '24/7 government' (Kraemer and King, 2003), about better meeting the demands of public service users. In light of this agenda, which would appear to be sympathetic to the balancing of work–life issues, the authors use interviews with those involved in a particular project, one to promote information-sharing among public sector agencies working with children with disabilities and their families. The study reveals some of the issues bound up in empowering so-called 'users', for their involvement in the design and delivery of services appears to come at a cost. Often already overstretched individuals, who might be balancing unpaid caring with paid work, found it hard to do what was expected of them, particularly when they felt that their interventions and opinions were often ignored. On the face of it an unquestionably progressive development, the involvement of those using services in their design and delivery actually imposed extra demands on those least able to manage. The study acts as a cautionary warning. Although the involvement of users takes different forms in different states, nevertheless the increased use in industrialized economies of the language of marketing or 'customer services' appears to require further thinking through if it is not to make matters worse for some groups.

The second chapter by Jean-Yves Boulin widens the geographical focus to Europe, to examine the ways in which local governments in a number of countries are seeking to restructure their services as a means of better coordinating their delivery. He provides an overview of the rationale for what he calls 'urban time policies'. With striking parallels with Walsh et al.'s contribution, Boulin sets out how governments are changing how they organize the when and the where of service delivery. However rather than focus on one particular project, Boulin instead documents the different areas of policy, such as childcare, education, social services and transport, in which the organization and delivery of policies is being rethought in an effort to make them easier to access. Drawing attention to examples from Germany, Italy, the Netherlands, Spain and the UK, to which we turn in the last chapter of Part IV, this chapter highlights the challenges facing local governments when they begin to take seriously not just where they deliver services but when. In Italy time agencies or time offices (*ufficio di tempi*) have been established, an example of the leading-edge institutional reform that might be necessary elsewhere if the returns to better coordinating public services are to be fully realized. This takes us to the third chapter in this fourth part, that by Jo Morris and Jane Pillinger, which takes the themes already examined in this section, those of government restructuring and the time–space coordination of public services, and examines the case of Bristol in south west England.

The Time of Our Lives was an ambitious work–life balance project that the authors argue delivered positive results for both staff and managers in a range of service areas in Bristol City Council. Funded through the UK government's Department of Trade and Industry's (DTI) Work–Life Balance Challenge Fund, which has given over 400 organizations almost £12 million to pay for consultancy services on flexible working practices, unions and local government managers worked together to find new ways of organizing when services were delivered, striving to meet the work and non-work aspirations, needs and preferences of staff. The project formed part of the UK's Trade Union Congress's (TUC) wider approach to work-life balance, with the organisation arguing that 'one of the most essential ingredients in the organisation of work is time: when we work; for how long; how we balance working time with time outside of work' (http://www.tuc.org.uk/theme/index.cfm?theme=changingtimes). The authors move on to situate their study in the context of wider international trends in how labour unions are devising new policies to address the needs and wants of public sector managers and employees, understood both as workers and also as carers of one sort or another (Boessenkool and Hegewisch, 2004). What the chapter reveals is both the possibilities of new initiatives such as those developed not just in Bristol, but as Boulin outlines, elsewhere in Europe, and also their limits. Despite their differences, the three chapters reveal the challenges ahead, for individuals and for households, for unions and for governments, if we are to achieve a more time-just society.

11. E-enabled active welfare: creating the context for work–life balance

Sarah Walsh, Susan Baines and James Cornford

INTRODUCTION

Much research has been devoted to providing a better understanding of the strategies and stratagems of individuals, households and employers as they seek to negotiate the issue of balancing the demands of work against those of other aspects of life. This chapter, in contrast, touches upon the wider context within which such work–life calculations and decisions can be made. Our particular concern here is with the specific configurations of public services, including health, education and social care, which form an important part of the wider environment within which such decisions are made. We explore some of the ways in which this public service environment – the publicly funded and coordinated part of what we might term the 'servicescape' – is being reconfigured under the UK government's current programme for implementing electronic government.

The present period provides a particularly rich moment for exploration of the changing servicescape in the UK. The prime minister's announcement in March 2000 that all public services would be 'e-enabled' by 2005 has led to a major programme of change across the public sector. E-enabling services, we are told, is not just about automating existing processes; it is about 'transformation' (ODPM, 2002). Services will be transformed to become more accessible, cost-effective, convenient, responsive and joined-up. The redesign of services has led to the adoption of not just new technologies but also new rhetoric, processes and practices, even a new culture of public service (Hudson, 2003). Public services, it is argued, can be coordinated and delivered in a seamless or joined up manner. Through such joining up, it is suggested, services can be re-cast as 'customer-focused'.

Yet the 'customers', 'users' or even 'e-citizens' in whose name reforms to welfare services are being undertaken tend to remain only a shadowy presence in the rhetoric of the reformers. The confusion about nomenclature –

consumer? customer? user? citizen? – is symptomatic of wider ambiguities about the relationship between individuals and households, on one hand, and the organs of the (welfare) state on the other. E-government in the UK exists alongside, but not necessarily in harmony with, an increasingly urgent expectation on the part of government that service users will become active participants in decisions about services, taking on some role in the planning and governance of services. Moreover welfare states have always depended upon the unpaid provision of services from within the family and household (Esping-Andersen, 1999). Thus many service users, or at least their households, are in reality active providers of welfare services. It remains to be seen if e-government reforms will bring benefits to – or make new demands upon – the unpaid workforce of carers.

In seeking to shed some light on these questions, we draw on our long-running research with local service redesign and implementation teams in a number of locations in the UK. We examine one site in which tensions around e-services, participation and work–life balance are being played out with particular poignancy – a project to promote information sharing among agencies working with disabled children and their families.

E-GOVERNMENT: REFASHIONING OF THE CONTEMPORARY SERVICESCAPE

At the heart of the wider 'modernization' of public services is the notion of customer focus. The Blair government's Modernising Government White Paper of 1999 makes this clear, albeit couched in the more acceptable terms of a focus on 'public service users':

- Ensuring that policy making is more joined up and strategic
- Making sure that public service users, not providers, are the focus, by matching services more closely to people's lives
- Delivering public services that are high quality and efficient. (Cabinet Office, 1999: 6)

Subsequent policy documents have been less shy about conceiving that user as a 'customer' for public services. The 1999 White Paper makes clear the close links between the customer, or user, focus and the joining up of services. The emphasis on 'public service users' builds on a long-established critique of the public services as being particularly liable to 'producer capture' – that is, services that come to be designed and managed for the benefit of the professionals producing those services rather than their users. More sophisticated versions of this critique saw the problem as less one of services being organized directly for the benefit of producers, but rather that each group of producers perceived the user through their own professional lens, making it impossible to capture the wider picture.

Each group of professionals saw a part of the problem without seeing the whole. For example where a health service worker might see a medical problem susceptible to treatment by drugs, a social worker might see a problem of family breakdown in which any medical symptoms are merely epiphenomenal. From the point of view of the client or user, each service appears disconnected or uncoordinated, each having its own framing of the problem and offering its own putative solution, each demanding the client retell his or her story. Notions of multiple deprivation, and the idea of multiple and circular causation of 'wicked problems', have generated widespread support for such a view.

Through joining-up the producers of public services, it is claimed, services can be recast as 'customer-focused', no longer driven by the imperatives of their producers. Service providers who were isolated in their organizational and professional 'silos' – and able to see only one aspect of the individual citizen – can now be connected across 'silos' and, through technology, provided with the information to enable them to see a more holistic picture. A range of technologies, principally developed in the private sector, have promised the goal of improved integration through the sharing and consolidation of data and the opening up of new communication channels.

Of course the theme of 'joined-up' or 'holistic' government, in particular at the policy-making level, is not new (Pollitt, 2003; 6 et al., 2002). It has long been recognized that while the state is conceptually one and indivisible, it is institutionally in pieces, and that those pieces are not well coordinated. There is a long history of joint endeavour based on shared planning, co-location of services and other physical means of attempting to promote more coordinated public policy and policy delivery. What is new is the scale of ambition of the current attempts at joining-up and the shift from the level of policy making to the level of policy implementation and of service delivery. The new belief in the possibility of such joining-up is substantially based on the claimed powers, and in particular the integrating capacity, of information and communication technologies.

The history of technology-based service redesign might make us suspicious of such grandiose claims (Bellamy, 2002; Geoghegan et al., 2004). However it is clear that this kind of reasoning represents a strong thread in the current attempts to reshape public services and is one with the potential, at least, to reconfigure the context in which the dilemmas of work–life balance are worked out in a highly positive direction. Information, it is argued, will be electronic, ubiquitous and available anywhere, any time – so-called '24/7 government' (Kraemer and King, 2003: 1). However current e-government strategy in the UK is about more than electronic access to information and services. The objective is to use more readily available information to 'radically increase the speed and efficiency of the processes that underpin services' (ODPM, 2002: 8). E-government is therefore not simply about the automation or even informatization of processes, but rather about their radical redesign. The result of such redesign, British citizens have been told, will be that they can have services delivered when and where they need them, greatly easing the constraints of time and space and opening up new opportunities to rearrange the relationships between (paid and unpaid) work, rest and play (PIU, 2000).

REDESIGNING SERVICES AROUND THE SERVICE USER

Reorienting services around users is implicitly a multi-agency activity and there is a clear drive from government towards joining up through partnership and multi-agency working. Multi-agency environments demand collaboration across organizations and agencies with different cultures, aims, incentives, management structures and information systems. The literature on multi-agency working suggests that one of the main reasons why it is difficult to achieve in practice is the challenge of reconciling different professional groups' mindsets and terms of reference, including their understanding of the service user(s) (Green et al., 2001; Lupton et al., 2001). Within multi-agency teams providing children's services, commentators have observed various and sometimes conflicting perceptions of the client (for example as the individual child, the child's family or even the wider community), as well as different timescales of relationships with clients. Easen et al. (2000), for example report conflict within multi-agency community interventions because schools, with an eye on performance measures, focused upon the individual child and looked to 'quick-fix' solutions, while community workers thought in terms of engagement with children and their families over a longer period.

The case of services for homeless young people, as observed by one of the authors, provides a stark example of the different mindsets of service providers in a multi-agency environment. A group of statutory agencies (local authority-based social service and housing departments) and number of voluntary agencies, such as Barnardos, already well used to working together, sought to form a multi-agency initiative based on new technology to better underpin and extend their collaborative efforts. One of the first practical tasks that the representatives sought to undertake was the creation of a common, or joint (the term was never finally decided), assessment form that could be administered by any of the agencies. This was undertaken as a paper exercise to explore the shape of the form prior to its technical implementation.

Unsurprisingly the first item on the form was the name of the young person. At this point differences emerged in the ways in which the various agencies 'frame' the young person. For example for some of the voluntary agencies the relevant term was that proffered by the young person. If a young man chose to identify himself as 'Nosher' then it was important to respect his wish. By contrast, some local authority agencies (housing and social work) felt that to be unacceptable. They required a 'proper' name (for example in order to let housing).

Such conflicting approaches emerged at a range of levels. For example some of the agencies stressed capturing the young person's history because they had a strong causal model of homelessness, and so placed great stress on diagnosing the reasons for the young person becoming homeless. For other agencies, by contrast, diagnosis was less important, if not seen as positively to be avoided in favour of creating a viable prognosis for the client. These arguments, and others, continued throughout the design of the common assessment form.

In the process of design and implementation of new information systems, project managers, systems suppliers and frontline professionals are grappling with the problem of who the users of public services are, and how they should be imagined. The very process of modernizing public services by redesigning and reorienting services around the needs of users raises new questions about the identity of service users, revealing that such identities are frequently contingent and contested. Multi-agency service environments, with their multiple organizational traditions and cultures, render these dilemmas more acute. The literal nature of IT systems, with their need for constant disambiguation, renders them increasingly visible. The most significant of the tensions so laid bare concern the ways in which users are figured as discrete individuals or as embedded in relationships of family, kinship and community. This tension throws into relief the roles of service users – and their families – as co-producers of services and as such go to the heart of debates about the work–life balance.

We can distinguish two distinct but related aspects of co-production of welfare services that impact upon the life–work balance and which are ill recognized in e-government initiatives and reforms. These are:

- the continuing dependence in welfare states upon unpaid service provided within the household;
- the expectation that as active citizens service users will participate in service planning, coordination and evaluation.

The state cannot, and never could, answer all welfare needs. Welfare work undertaken within the household as part of family obligations – beyond the market and the welfare state – was embedded in the post-war model of the welfare recipient (Esping-Andersen, 1999; Lewis, 2000). Arguably such care became more, not less, significant in the UK in the 1980s and 1990s as a result of policies of marketization and with the transfer of more expectations onto the private realm of the family. An example of the latter was the success of the National Health Service (NHS) in treating more patients in hospitals; the length of time spent in hospitals by patients was successfully reduced as a result of the relocation of much recuperative care to the household (Clarke et al., 2001). 'Satellite' National Accounts, which attempt to include unmarketed sources of value such as care provided within the family, indicate that unpaid work has increased as a proportion of all work in most developed economies, including the UK (Williams, 2002). Further evidence of the scale of unpaid caring activity comes from the 2001 Census of Population. For the first time, the Census asked a question about whether people looked after a family member, neighbour or friend on account of long-term illness, disability or old age. Such unpaid caring tasks were reported by one in ten people in England and Wales (ONS/DoH, 2003).

Service users, and their families and wider social networks, are not only involved in the direct provision of care services. Central government has increasingly required local service providers and the NHS to involve users, and the public more generally, in the planning and development of services and in major decisions (DETR, 2000; DH, 2001; DH, 2004). Participation in the governance of local services is now a target for which local authorities and service providers must prepare, and numerous policy documents include guidelines and standards for its achievement (Newman et al., 2004). For example the forthcoming Children's National Service Framework (NSF) has been developing national standards along these principles. The NSF's External Working Group on Disabled Children[1] made participation one of its key themes. The document states that one area to be covered by the standards is the requirement that:

> ... disabled children and their parents are involved as active partners in making decisions about their treatment, care and services; and in shaping services.

One of the interventions relating to the above standard asserts that:

> ... agencies have a written user involvement strategy setting agreed quality standards and an action plan for involving as equal and active partners, disabled children and their parents. This includes mechanisms for resolving disagreements. Agencies publicise how they promote the involvement of children and parents.

This theme of increased participation is already being promoted by the agencies that audit and evaluate service provision (see for example the Audit Commission, 2003, report on *Services for Disabled Children*).

Despite this drive towards increased participation, particularly evident within recent government policy documents, involvement in shaping services is not without cost for citizens. Recent research on area-based initiatives to tackle social exclusion shows that demands on people who participate on behalf of their communities can be enormous. They are put under great pressure with insufficient support and may suffer overcommitment, overwork and burn-out (Anastacio et al., 2000; Osborne et al., 2002). An action research project, Shaping Our Lives, looked at participation by users of disability services in designing user-led outcomes. This study revealed that while regularly meeting together led to them growing in confidence both individually and collectively, many expressed a great deal of 'involvement fatigue' (Evans and Banton, 2001).

What does this mean on the ground? With the above aspects of the co-production of welfare services in mind, we now turn to a case-study highlighting such issues in services for disabled children and their families. We explore ways in which parents of disabled children negotiate their daily lives within the servicescape and how they respond to a new initiative under e-government designed to increase joining-up and user focus.

E-ENABLING SERVICES FOR CHILDREN WITH DISABILITIES AND THEIR FAMILIES

The modernization agenda of the UK Government forefronts investment in technology, putting the citizen at the centre, and making public services more joined-up, transparent, open and accountable (see for example DoH, 2004). These reforms are particularly evident within children's services where numerous national initiatives are being piloted at local level including Children's Trusts, Integrated Children's System (ICS), Information Sharing and Assessment (ISA) and Framework for Multi-agency Environments (FAME). An important aspect of each of these initiatives is reconfiguration of service delivery to disabled children and their families.

The social exclusion, disadvantage and discrimination many disabled children and their families face are well documented. Russell (2003) shows that households with a disabled child have a much greater likelihood of unemployment and poverty than other disadvantaged groups (for example lone parents and disabled adults) and that lack of appropriate flexible family support services can frequently lead to family breakdown. She argues that although government has begun to address their disadvantages through a new range of legislation and policies, 'the true and additional costs of caring for a disabled child are not necessarily fully acknowledged in public policy' (Russell, 2003: 217).

One pilot which we have studied,[2] part of the UK's local e-government programme, is developing an electronic multi-agency assessment tool. Its aim is to pilot the improvement of services to disabled children and their families in a local authority area by coordinating often fragmented information into a shared assessment that will be available to the numerous services with which disabled children and their carers interact. In this section we draw upon the experiences of professional workers and parents within this project in order to examine ways in which the process of e-enabling services can reveal new possibilities, and new conflicts, that impact upon the work–life balance. The information we report is drawn from close interaction between the researchers (including one of the authors) and the project team. The researchers were given unlimited access as observers to project board meetings and to numerous other meetings and events including workshop sessions with professional workers and with the IT company responsible for the system design. A series of recorded focus groups with parents of disabled children were also undertaken.

Within this project, one of the main strengths cited by the project board was the desire to involve service users in the creation of the new assessment process. Parents for example were encouraged to participate in workshop sessions that were facilitated to enable an active contribution to the shaping of services. However although many parents attended workshops, their views on being involved in such service redesign were divided. Some were enthusiastic:

> I want to be involved at every stage – high up not just as a tokenistic parent on a board where decisions are rubber-stamped – I want proper involvement in decision-making.

Others were reluctant for a number of reasons including lack of confidence and, very significantly, lack of time:

> What time for involvement – why should we have to get involved?

> What do we get in return?

> I don't want to get involved – I just want better services.

> Professionals are paid – parents are not – but we're expected to get involved.

Even where parents felt that they had something to contribute, their experience did not always suggest that participation would be effective: 'Parents know best but they often don't listen to us'.

Parents were invited, alongside professional workers, to comment upon the kinds of information that would be included in the new system. The project team wanted to develop a 'service user screen' where parents or children could access and input information. However some parents stated that they did not want to input on the system but preferred an equivalent of 'Ask Jeeves' which would enable them to log onto the system and ask questions which would be answered by a panel of professionals. Parents felt they could then ask questions pertinent to themselves and their families, receive answers, and have some control over their situation. They saw such a facility as much more pertinent to their needs than simply accessing information from, and adding information to, a system. By their own admission, the professionals had not anticipated these views.

The focus groups undertaken by the research team highlighted the intense pressures on time for parents of disabled children. Parents pointed out for example the difficulties in finding care and services for disabled children in the school holidays (whereas summer play schemes for non-disabled children were seen as being widely available). Mothers, and some fathers, described not being able to work because of the unrelenting demands of caring. Money worries, isolation, stress on relationships, and health problems were commonplace. Respite care, when it was available, was typically from the extended family:

> My husband works every other weekend and during that weekend I'm stuck in the house by myself – well with the kids – because I can't go anywhere with both of them and I think what can I do with Pippa when Carl is severely autistic. I can't go to soft play in town, it's far too busy, he'd have a tantrum, and it's just a nightmare. What you need is places to go where it's safe and maybe there's other disabled children there or you need social things that my daughter could also have fun [with]. Pippa can go to ballet, swimming lessons, this, that and the other. Carl *should* be able to go to soft play and football activities.

> My mum was the only one to look after the children because they are hard work. I am the one that works, Paul doesn't work. I work full-time, I am up during the night, I am the one that gets up in the morning and does the pack-lunches and gets them ready and gets them washed and then I go and do a full day at work and then I get in at night and then I do the homework and I do the bath time. I have been on Prozac for three years.

When asked to talk about their needs and wishes, parents focused on practical help. They called for improvements in relationships with professionals, for more control over their situations, for information specific to their individual circumstances, and for more social activities to take their children to (including those of their children who may not be disabled). Parents were overall positive about the principle of joint electronic assessment forms. They welcomed the promise of not having to repeat their stories to each new professional with whom they interacted. Indeed they often wondered why this joining-up had not already happened.

Although policy rhetoric outlines the greater use of ICT, multi-agency working and involving service users, it remains as yet uncertain whether all this will result in more joined-up, seamless services that are more efficient and effective for service users. Influence upon service delivery by service users was not evident within the ICT project under discussion despite good intentions and genuine efforts on the part of the project team. Moreover the requirement to involve service users may ultimately place more demands upon parents. As we have seen, some parents want to contribute in order to improve services; but they are already precariously juggling their work–life balance and they are disadvantaged due to the pressure, time and cost of caring for a child with a disability. This workforce of unpaid family carers remains hard-pressed, stressed and under-resourced.

CONCLUSION

The Modernising Government White Paper identified two roles that public service users might play in interaction with government: people as 'consumers' and people as 'citizens' (Cabinet Office, 1999). E-government reforms in general seem to promise benefits to people as consumers. Yet some of these promises, on closer examination, are built upon a narrow – and fiercely contested – concept of the user of public services as a customer analogous to the purchaser of private sector services. The consumer is imagined as an individual driven by preferences and disembodied from the contexts of family, kinship and community. In order to think through implications of modernization of the servicescape for work–life balance more clearly it is necessary to recall that users of public services play multiple, overlapping roles as customers, citizens, co-producers and co-designers of services within the household and community. Within e-government projects service users, as citizens, may be consulted – but this does not necessarily result in their views being incorporated into the new systems. Moreover involvement in service design makes demands on time and energy in ways that do not fit well with the realities of either paid work or unpaid caring.

NOTES

1. NSF External Working Group on disabled Children: 'work in progress' document. Draft 3 February 2003 (www.doh.gov.uk/nsf/children/consulationdraft3.pdf, accessed 30 May 2003).
2. The location and name of the pilot are not disclosed in this chapter in order to preserve the anonymity of the participants.

12. Local time policies in Europe

Jean-Yves Boulin

INTRODUCTION

In Poitiers, on the initiative of the so-called Time Agency (Agence des Temps), six evenings were organized in community centres from 26 August to 2 September 2002, between 17.30 and 19.30. These allowed children and their parents to accomplish everything they needed to do for the start of the new school year: purchase school-meal vouchers and bus passes, register at the Media Library (Médiathèque), the music conservatory, the art school, the sports department, and sign up for community centre activities. They also let them meet the various associations involved in organizing activities for young people. The experiment was repeated in 2003 and 2004, and will be continued. Other French cities have adopted this one-stop agency for the new school year. In Belfort, various different experiments were launched by the Time and Mobility Agency (Maison des Temps et de la Mobilité) in the course of 2002. These included an administration system for car pools in the conurbation of Belfort-Montbéliard, a weekend transport project for young people, and the development of a 'digital street' project. This last – known as *rue numérique* – consisted of distributing video images in the street, giving information about locations, opening hours and so on for public services offices, associations, shops and businesses. It also included a joint night transport system for young people at the weekend, a project establishing a childcare service for those working unusual hours in collaboration with the Centre d'Information des Droits des Femmes, and various other schemes.[1] Fifteen other cities or French local authorities are involved in projects aimed at improving the coordination of time and space for their inhabitants.

These initiatives join those launched in other countries. Italy has been something of a pioneer in this area, closely followed by Germany, Holland, Spain and even the UK (the city of Bristol). In France, this is a new level of interest on the part of the public authorities – at government level as well as at local authority level – in time issues and their territorial or local implementation. One sign of this new orientation with regard to time and space is DATAR (Délégation à l'Aménagement du Territoire et à l'Action Régionale), a spatial planning agency directly linked to the prime minister. Since 2000 it has helped structure and disseminate research and experiments in France, previously limited to a few cities or areas (St Denis, Poitiers, the Belfort area, the Gironde *département*) whose inclusion in this project resulted from their participation in a European programme supported by the European Social Fund.[2]

Shifting attention to other European countries reveals widely shared objectives. In countries such as Italy, Germany and the Netherlands, there is a significant gender dimension. The Italian 'times of the city' model tries to balance social time through a more equal distribution of the different activities of everyday life between women and men.[3] Wherever this type of policy has been developed (by imitation of the Italian example in Germany, France or Spain, or in the Netherlands with substantially different origins regarding the process, but not the nature of the problems), the question of the combination of the multiple tasks of everyday life constitutes one of its central issues. Greater sensitivity to time, at the public level, and particularly the fact that the value attached to free time is increasing, makes social inequalities with regard to time more visible. These are more discernible – or immediately felt – with regard to spare time, supposedly free, than they are with regard to constrained time – working time.[4] Local actors will therefore be increasingly confronted by a new territorial governance problem: to prevent social, gender and generational inequalities in the usages of time and space from getting worse.

Local time policies are new. They testify to a new interest in time-oriented issues. These policies are focused upon a variety of matters. These include urban congestion, mobility and transport; school and childcare; working time and service opening hours; and revitalization of urban spaces. They appeal to many planners, consultants, academics, politicians, trade unionists and advisers, on the grounds of their innovativeness, creativity and 'reflexive modernization'. Taking them seriously implies concrete and utopian thinking, theoretical and practical expertise, and a capacity and preparedness for transversal cooperation, as well as a willingness to participate. They require an open mind on the part of both individuals and organizations about their physical, social and cultural environment. They also require a new consensus-based political approach.

THE FOUNDATIONS OF URBAN TIME POLICIES

Local time policies acknowledge new time relations, new forms of time usage, and new values attached to both social times and different time sequences. They encompass new relations to space, raising problems of time and the relationship between time and space and new behaviours on the part of citizens in relation to the state. This brings into relief the time needed for getting involved in co-decision making. It even requires a new relationship with the environment, which equally raises time-related problems. These new attitudes with regard to different social times, their interlinkage and interaction, just like those regarding the relationship between time and space, are the result of social and societal changes situated as much in the sphere of non-work as in that of work.

Profound Changes in the World of Work that Blur the Boundaries between Work and Non-Work

The changes observable in the field of work refer to the nature and content of work as much as to the periods and rhythms of working time. Work is becoming effectively less and less tangible, while undergoing a double process of intensification and densification. This induces a mobilization of the cognitive capacities of individuals, the tendency of which is to establish a continuum between work and non-work. Equally, the utilization of mobile devices reinforces the blurring of boundaries between work and non-work. This confusion is heightened by the flexibilization of working time, one of the results of which is a tendency towards making time devoted to work and time outside work less distinct. Add to that the increasing discontinuity of working careers resulting from the deterioration of working conditions and from the continuing high rate of unemployment.

This blurring of boundaries between work and non-work occurs in the context of changed representation of social times, as well as changes in the way in which interaction between the two spheres is viewed. Many factors come together in this development of perceptions and values attached to different social times. In the forefront one might put the increasing involvement of women in the labour market. Equally there is the transformation of family structures – the growth in the number of double-earner and single-parent families – and changes in life styles.

Women are regarded as actors or agents in a transformation of the interlinkage and interaction between working time and non-working time, of a new equilibrium between different social times. Because of the very slow evolution of the gender social division of labour (Brousse, 1999), their lives are subject to a temporal complexity. This results from the accumulation of several constrained times (working time, domestic time, educational time), whilst women continue to suffer from a lack of time in comparison with men (Gershuny, 2000; Méda, 2001).

Women's participation in the labour market indicates the significance of the value of work as a constitutive element in collective and individual identities. At the same time, it strongly underlines the existence of other social times, notably those of care (maintenance of domestic space, bringing up children, care for dependents), and this has contributed to undermining the domination of working time over other social times. Italian women, who have played a central role in the dynamic of the *Tempi della città* policies, through their activities in trade unions, political parties and associations, have contributed to eradicating this time of unpaid activity from the private sphere – and therefore from negotiation by individual couples. They confer on it the status of a social time, which is relational, as well as an element of personal identity. This time is becoming the object of public policies, as is free time, which is regarded as a form of time that is not only legitimate, but also valued. It is also constitutive of social identities.

Greater Sensitivity to Different Social Times

Time is the object of strong expectations (Chronopost, 2001; Viard, 2002). These are a symptom of a shortage of time, of an increase in temporal pressure which has been revealed by numerous European surveys which report that Europeans consider that they do not have enough time for their family and their social life and take the view that their temporal structures are determined by their working time over which they have no, or insufficient, control.

In the world of work these expectations demand two things:

1. A reduction in working time, revealed by the above-mentioned surveys, but also by the large-scale survey conducted by the Dublin Foundation involving 30 000 persons in 16 European countries (Bielinski et al., 2002). In general, Europeans would like working hours of between 30 and 35 hours instead of the current 35–40 hours.
2. Greater autonomy in determining their working hours and work schedules. Satisfaction with regard to work schedules is greatest in the Netherlands, which also seems to be the country in which employees have the most latitude in this respect.[5] The Dublin Foundation's survey shows that – for the 16 European countries analysed – one-third of part-time employees, primarily women, would like different working hours and work organization. It shows that precarious forms of employment (fixed-term contract – *contrat à durée déterminée* or CDD – and temporary contracts) are fairly unanimously rejected; 14 per cent of full-time employees would like to be able to work part-time for one or more periods of their life; 20 per cent of employees would like to be able to take a sabbatical (see Bielinski et al., 2002).

At the beginning of the 1980s, a certain behavioural homogeneity could be observed, which unified life rhythms, including those of non-working time.

Since, however, one has observed a generalized acculturation to different usages of free time and therefore a new freedom of usage and of choice. Cultural norms seem to be sliding towards the individual appropriation of free time (the 'right to one's own time', Ost, 1999).

The valorization of social times[6] – outside paid work – calls into question the system that regards it as directly determined by working time, whether it is spillover (employees reproducing positive and negative experiences undergone during working time outside their work) or compensation (free time has a corrective function in relation to constraints encountered at work) (Parker, 1983). Today this analysis would imply that time outside work – that is to say, family time, the time of associative and social life, the time of political participation and free time – facilitates the construction of individual and collective identities, together with working time, in a balance constructed by each individual and by society as a whole. Here we touch on the representations and values attached to each of those social times that vary from one epoch to another, and from one society to another. The construction of this balanced relationship presupposes control, simultaneously individual and collective, over the interlinkage and interaction between social times. This control operates, on the one hand, through the implementation of working time policies which take account of the constraints and aspirations of employees with regard to non-work (work–life balance policies), leading us back to ask whether non-work could be included in working time negotiations in the same way as employment flexibility was in the past. On the other hand, constructing this balanced relationship could be achieved through negotiations relating to the social organization of time based on new forms of synchronization and the harmonization of different timetable systems.

The Destabilization of the Social Organization of Time

Historical analysis of the rationalization of our societies and working time (Boulin and Mückenberger, 2002) shows that we are passing progressively away from a coherent temporal and spatial organization, one congruent with a system of representation and values that made work central to the construction of collective and individual identities. We are moving towards an organization that is becoming progressively incoherent in its spatio-temporal dimension. It is becoming less and less adequate for the values attached to different social times. The trends emphasized call into question the three structuring principles of the social organization of time that were created as a result of the Industrial Revolution and the Fordist compromise of the 1920s (Cross, 1993):

1. Time discipline based on the centrality of work is no longer valid, due to

the observable individualization of modes of life and by the emergence of
non-working time as a constitutive element of social identity.

2. Synchronization through the sequence of activities (sedimentation of a
    standardized working time at the margins of which are situated segments
    of time – the evening, the weekend, paid holidays – assigned to non-work)
    is becoming less prevalent with the development of flexible working time.
    More and more individuals work 'atypical' hours – previously devoted to
    non-work activities – and others rest on weekdays. This typically leads to
    a shift in the representations attached to different days and hours:
    weekends and nights undergo changes in their cultural and social
    dimensions which may result in a weakening or, conversely, a
    strengthening of their symbolic significance.

3. Synchronization through the gender division of labour or the
    specialization of sex roles is called into question by the presence of
    women in the labour market, and by the fact that they remain there even
    when they have children. The Dublin survey shows that the traditional
    'male breadwinner' model has been rejected by European populations,
    but time-use studies indicate that the consequences of this rejection
    have yet to be realized, as far as the gender division of labour is
    concerned.

PRINCIPLES, STAKES AND METHODS OF LOCAL TIME POLICIES

All these trends show that lived time and space cannot be reduced to working
time and space alone. They are interwoven. This interrelationship generates a
spatio-temporal complexity, not determined by external temporal and spatial
structures alone, but equally dependent on the behaviour of individuals and
communities, and shaped by them. That is to say, by social and cultural
diversity. This interweaving is the context for the principles, stakes, contents
and methods of time policies.

Rethinking Collective Operations

Urban time policies are a way of rethinking collective operations, as much in
their temporal as in their spatial dimension. Their context is the transformation
of the relationship between work and non-work and of the structuring
principles of the social organization of time. The way in which the temporal
regimes of productive (material and immaterial) activities are regulated and
interlinked in a given territory impacts dramatically upon the use of time and
space.

Transformations of the length and organization of working time call into question the current operation of services, owing to the great variety of uses made of the different components of a territory. These include urban transport, public and administrative services, leisure and socio-cultural services, public spaces, and so on. This indicates that actors other than workplace negotiators should also be involved in decisions over working times as other time schedules are affected by new working time arrangements, for example school timetables, crèches, socio-cultural and sports activities, but also commercial services.[7] The legislator integrated this systematic and territorial dynamic in the second 'Aubry law' (19 January 2000).[8]

Anticipate the Local Level when Thinking Globally

Urban time policies developed in Italy since the beginning of the 1990s, those developed more recently in Germany and France, and policies for planning daily time in the Netherlands, all follow this logic. They broaden the field of analysis and action beyond the enterprise and working time alone. They include places where temporalities are experienced. They cover the improvement of the quality of life, equality between the sexes, age groups and social categories, the reconstruction of social bonds and even urban renovation as equal objectives. They are based on an approach to daily life that is related to real problems of individual and collective organization. These problems include the increasing difficulties in combining different daily activities, principally those relating to paid work on the one hand and those located in the family and social sphere – that is, unpaid work – on the other. This may be a matter of care for children and other dependent persons, social activity (associative, friendly or relational), or leisure. These policies also result from the multiplication and diversification of time use, as well as from an increasing sensitivity with regard to temporal questions understood as much in quantitative terms, for example the reduction of working time, as in qualitative ones such as the control that each person has over their own temporal structures.

These policies cannot be developed outside their territorial contextualization. They are therefore conducted at the local level but linked to a process which associates local initiatives with higher-level authorities at the regional, national and supranational scales.[9] The interest in such an approach is that it makes it possible to think about the dynamics of time use and temporal patterns alongside international, national and regional developments such as globalization and decentralization processes, whose effect in reconstituting time and reconfiguring space is potentially important.

Inherent to these policies is a dilemma for social actors between adaptation to existing structures on the one hand and anticipation, or taking control of development on the other – by constructing interlinkages and interaction between time and territory. A territory, taking into account changes in working time and life styles, may be compelled to adapt itself – for example by changing opening hours in order to meet 'demand', moving towards a 24-hour society. Or the territory, on the basis of its economic, social and cultural characteristics, may construct its own time project and the interlinkage or interaction of time and space (especially integrating the question of places and activities which would be induced to operate 24 hours a day).

Control of Time, Accessibility and New Forms of Regulation

Time policies aim to enable people to control their temporal structures, and the interlinkage and interaction between their different temporalities, especially through the concept of accessibility. Behind these notions of control and accessibility there is a distinction between available time and the availability of time – between the quantities of time you have on your hands and your scope of action in using it. In effect, what good is it to have free time if for economic reasons one cannot use it, or if one loses it in waiting and travelling time, lengthening everywhere? Accessibility linked to cost affects the unemployed, those in precarious employment, and the socially excluded while working single parents or two-earner families may lack available time given the different locations and temporalities of different activities.

Urban time policies, without claiming to provide a solution to the entire question, are one of the elements of a response, along with social policies such as transfer revenues, and working time policies developed in enterprises.

The central problem that arises from this point of view is the construction of new forms of regulation or temporal regimes aiming at re-synchronizing (in a different way) economic, social and cultural activities. One of the central ideas is the dialectical relationship between different timetabling systems: enterprises, administrative services, transport and communications, health and educational services, leisure services, and so on. These policies emphasize the need to reconcile diversified modes of operation for individuals who are sometimes producers, sometimes consumers; sometimes parents, sometimes preoccupied with their own needs; sometimes solitary (or even isolated), sometimes immersed in social relations.

By simultaneously reflecting on working time, the unequal gender division of labour, harmonization of timetabling systems, and the better functioning of public services, the Italians have incorporated temporal policies into many issues. Temporal regulation cannot remain confined to a single object. It must enter into harmony with its context. In other words, urban time policies reveal a passage from societies in which time (of work, of schools, of commerce, and so on) was endogenously regulated, to societies in which the point of regulation becomes the interlinkage and interaction of social time.[10]

TRANSVERSALITY AND SOCIETAL DIALOGUE: TOWARDS A NEW FORM OF GOVERNANCE

Examination of time policies implemented in Europe (Boulin and Mückenberger, 2002) brings to light the multiplicity of their points of application:

- School timetables and rhythms (Cremona, Bolzano, Bremen, Poitiers, Rennes, St Denis, and so on) (Bonfiglioli, 2004; Mückenberger, 2004).
- Opening hours of childcare facilities (Paris, Poitiers, Dordrecht) (Boulin et al., 2002).
- The timetables of public and private services and their coordination (for example Sunday opening of libraries in the Netherlands or in Bristol, and citizens' day in several Italian cities, such as Rome, Cremona or Bolzano, and also in Bremen) (Bonfiglioli, 2004; Mückenberger, 2004; Boulin et al., 2002).
- The interlinkage and interaction between working time and other social times (Rennes and many examples in the Netherlands) (Ministry of Social Affairs and Employment, 2002).
- Provision for new services or new ways to deliver services such as the one-stop agencies in Poitiers, Bremen, Modena and other cities in Italy. (Mückenberger, 2004; Boulin et al., 2002).
- Safety and security in public spaces (Bremen and Milan) (Bonfiglioli, 2004; Mückenberger, 2004).
- The transformation of transport services and the right to mobility, including revised time schedules of public transportation facilities and mobility pacts in Italy and Germany, with examples such as Modena, Bolzano, Bremen and Belfort in France. (Bonfiglioli, 2004; Mückenberger, 2004; Boulin et al., 2002).
- Urban renovation and urban revitalization including mixed land uses, with the shift from monochronic to polychronic spaces as in the cases of Pesaro – the renovation of Piazza Redi – or the revitalization of Via Claudia Augusta in Bolzano, and the museum tour in Cremona (Bonfiglioli, 2004).

This diversity, and the multiplicity of objectives, together emphasize the challenges confronting local authorities. These include the development of a diagnostic of general strategies relating to mobility and traffic congestion, as well as specific policies that recognize the needs of particular population categories or areas, such as working parents, or isolated districts. Additionally there are temporal strategies to deal with time conflicts, which involve the harmonization of timetable systems and the innovation of services in a variety of ways.

From the point of view of initiative and methods, the Italians, imitated by the Germans and the French, have made radical innovations, at the institutional and the procedural level. In order to coordinate within local authorities they invented 'time agencies' or 'time offices' (*ufficio di tempi*). This is a municipal body, or at least one that strongly links and interacts with local authorities.[11] This ensures cooperation between different public administration services, while being tuned in to the inhabitants and the users of the territory in question. This time office has the task of identifying problems, launching studies to assess temporal diagnosis, and making different stakeholders sensitive to the time dimension of social, economic and cultural problems. Several examples of such initiatives can be quoted: civil forums (Bremen), public meetings (*mardi du temps* in Poitiers; *forum du temps* in Belfort). They aim to enhance the time consciousness of the local population and various stakeholders such as firms and the public administration.

In order to extricate itself from a purely sectoral social dialogue, only involving employers and trade unions in internal and functional negotiations, the Italians have created 'roundtables of quadrangular negotiations', that is, negotiation processes which in addition to the municipality bring together enterprises and trade union organizations, users and/or their associations. These groups are then involved in the formulation of problems and solutions through decision-making roundtables (so-called *tables de co-projection*, involving social actors such as women's associations and consumer associations). It is within the framework of this dialogue, helped by the time agencies, that compromises must be constructed to resolve temporal conflicts – those inherent in our individualized and diversified societies. This process, in an ideal-typical manner, brings together top-down and bottom-up initiatives.

This is a new type of governance, combining formal political representation at the local level in Germany, the UK or Spain, and/or the national level as in Italy and France with direct citizen participation through forums and surveys which allow them to express their expectations, constraints and problems. This wide and direct representation makes it possible to take account of the different dimensions of time in a particular area and question the time management of different actors, public and private, whether they are service recipients, employers, users, clients, employees or citizens.

NEW METHODS OF ANALYSING AND REPRESENTING TIME–SPACE PATTERNS: CHRONOTOPIC ANALYSIS

Investigation of the spatio-temporal dimension of everyday life is nothing new, but it has taken a new turn with 'times of the city' policies. The school of time geography, set up by Hägerstrand at the University of Lund in the 1950s and 1960s (Hägerstrand, 1985), proposed a methodology for mapping the spatio-temporal dimension of individuals' everyday life. The graphic formalization of their sequence of activities across time and space represented the complexity of everyday itineraries, but this was never fully exploited (Carlstein et al., 1978). Nevertheless the embryo of a spatio-temporal approach was created, one whose limitations undoubtedly lay in the very individualized nature of the analysis of movements and their low-level articulation by means of a system of interpretation based on social differentiation and social relations.

Chronotopic analysis, developed by the Politecnico in Milan (Bonfiglioli and Mareggi, 1997), makes it possible to better characterize the spatio-temporal dimension of a particular area by analysing the different flows and levels of occupation of space, through different temporal sequences. A given space is used differently at different times – of the day, week, month or year – and contains different populations that contribute to these flows and levels of occupation. The 'chronotope' is therefore defined as a physical zone, characterized by modes of use by different populations, but also by the same population using it in different ways at different times. This analysis integrates the findings of urban sociology which divide city-users into four categories: (1) residents, (2) commuters, (3) tourists, and (4) business(wo)men (Martinotti, 1997). On that basis, chronotopic analysis is characterized by two basic features: (1) physical structures in a given area are linked to the rhythms of life and modes of utilization of different populations, and (2) description is undertaken in terms of the point of view of these populations, integrating their constraints and their expectations.

CONCLUSION

If the development trends and problematics underlying time policies are common to most European countries, these policies are being developed, in a conscious fashion – that is, as a transversal and interlinked, interactive process – only in four countries: Germany, Italy, France and the Netherlands.[12] They are characterized by different developments and make sense only in the socio-cultural, economic and political contexts of each of these societies. In Italy, Germany and France one may see a territorial anchoring of these policies which tend to spread by means of the networking of the cities and territories concerned, and the exchange of tools and methods of analysis and representation (chronotopical or chronographic maps). In this regard one can speak of local time policies. In the Netherlands, integrated local authority policies are rare:[13] public and/or private actors and/or institutions, through the development of micro-projects, carry out most projects.

Comparative analyses conducted in Europe (Boulin and Mückenberger, 2002) reveal that the use of time is today at the centre of research, discourse, planning processes and actions which touch on urban questions. The content of this new politics is centred on questions of time, while a new strategy accompanies urban time policy. These rest on the one hand on new forms of participation – such as citizens' forums and surveys within the community – and on the other hand, on cooperation between different local services. The development and maturity of time policies (14 years in Italy, nine in Germany, four in France) attests to the passing from public timetabling policies to those that try to grasp the spatio-temporal dimension of everyday life. This is a sign that what is at stake in these policies is not just the improvement of social functions, but also the encapsulation of a more profound transformation of the relationship between individuals and communities and time, and that between different social times and values and representations attached to these different times.

They therefore have an undeniable cultural dimension. They participate at the very minimum through their content, their implementation process and the actors associated with them, in a triple evolution:

- Helping represent the interlinkage and interaction between working time and other social times, to integrate the lifestyle and time-use pattern changes in the social construction of time and of territory. New behaviours are fostered by these policies which take into account the changing values attached to the different social times: the main examples are library Sunday opening and citizens' day, which are ways of creating new collective times and of reinforcing social cohesion in a context of increasing individualization.
- Helping create different relations between men and women, between different age groups and social categories.
- Encouraging enterprises to get involved and take responsibility for their local area (corporate social and sustainable environmental responsibility).

These policies each lead to an 'urbanistics of time'. Urban science and architecture must integrate the dual dimensions of lived space and time. This includes spatial areas: a city of small distances that brings together slow spaces – 'zigzagging' mobility – with routes characterized by rapid mobility. A mixture of uses that make it possible for the sleeping city, the working city and the city to have fun living together. It also includes buildings. It covers infrastructures that make mixed uses possible, according to the hour of the day, week or year. In other words, it allows a shift from monochronic spaces towards polychronic spaces.

Finally, in our view, urban time policies must be integrated into the development of a European Social Model whose temporal dimension has so far been largely ignored.[14] The guidelines of the European Union, as formulated at the Lisbon Summit – which committed Europe to developing as a knowledge society and to expanding male and female employment rates – presuppose that European citizens can manage their temporal structures. The guidelines treat these as having synchronic dimensions through the management of working schedules and the temporal organization of the territory, and diachronic dimensions, namely the possibility of controlling the sequence of different phases of the life course.

The crucial question is to measure not just objective changes related to everyday time, acceleration, fragmentation, inequalities, but also the representations and values attached to different social times. 'Temporal prosperity' (Garhammer, 1999) or 'temporal well-being', understood as the capacity to control one's own temporal structures, are achieved among other things by means of a harmonization between the social organization of time and the arrangement or structure of lived times and spaces.

NOTES

1. Gwiazdzinski and Klein (2002).
2. This European Programme for Territorial Excellence, launched by two partners in the European social dialogue (the European Trade Union Congress, ETUC, and the European Centre of Enterprises with Public Participation and of Enterprises of General Economic Interest, CEEP) was aimed at promoting the development possibilities of local social dialogue, as well as its relevance and potential points of application. Three countries have initially been associated with this project: Germany, France and Italy, subsequently joined by Spain and Ireland. The urban time policies that have been the object of examination and experimentation for about ten years in Italy and Germany constituted the initial basis of this network's action and study.
3. The motivation of the *Tempi della Città* can be attributed to a bill developed in the mid-1980s by female PCI members of parliament, which played a major role in awareness raising and later policy orientation. This bill contained 27 articles whose object was to influence working time, the sharing of tasks between men and women and times in the city (PCI, 1990).
4. It should be noted that not all working time categories are equal and that some benefit from greater autonomy in their working time and in the determination of their work schedules.
5. The law of February 2000 in effect permits every Dutch employee to reduce or increase his or her working time. Moreover provisions governed by the principle of 'flexicurity' make it possible to constrain production flexibility, instituting guarantees for employees as regards

the course of their career, as well as their level of social protection (Wilthagen and Tros, 2004).

6. One might stress here the apparent paradox that resides in the fact that while work remains a cardinal value for Europeans (Futuribles, 2002), at the same time they seek a reduction in working time.

7. This gives rise to questions of competence: in Italy, the catalyst with regard to urban time policies was the law on decentralization no. 142 (1990) which gave mayors the power to organize negotiations in order to modify the timetables of public and private services.

8. Paragraph 7 of Article 1 reads as follows: 'In towns of more than 50 000 inhabitants, the president of the inter-municipal body, in liaison, shall, if need be with the mayors of bordering communes, facilitate the harmonisation of public service schedules with those needs arising, notably from the point of view of the reconciliation of working life and family life, from the evolution of work organisation in activities located on the territory of the commune or nearby. To this end he shall bring together, according to need, the representatives of bodies or administrative authorities of the services concerned and put them, if need be, in touch with the social partners of enterprises and of communities in order to promote understanding of needs and to facilitate the pursuit of local adaptations suitable for satisfying them.'

9. As one can see in the French case (supported by DATAR and with the involvement of several ministries; recognition by the second 'Aubry law'), the Dutch case (financing of more than 200 projects by the Ministry of Social Affairs), and the Italian case (law 142 followed by 10 years of experiments which inspired law 53 (2000), the so-called Turco law, which generalizes the measure to all towns of more than 30 000 inhabitants and encourages the development of regional laws).

10. That does not exempt the social partners and/or governments from the question of the regulation of work schedules or of the functioning of different institutions, but brings to the fore the fact that endogenous regulation in each of these social fields cannot take place independently of the transformations affecting the other fields.

11. At Belfort for example the Time and Mobility Agency has taken the form of an association.

12. However one can see the implementation of similar measures in Spain (in Asturias principally around the problematic of activities for young people at night, but also in Andalusia around the question of women's work and in Barcelona), and in the UK in relation to the night economy, but also the opening hours of public and administrative services (in Bristol for example).

13. With the exception of the town of Amersfort, which was preparing to establish a time agency. But this project eventually failed. From 2004 onwards some cities like Rotterdam intended to develop such local initiatives.

14. Again, it is worth emphasizing a number of developments from this point of view: in the report on the future of social protection in Europe written at the request of the Belgian presidency of the European Union, Esping-Andersen and co-authors underline the importance of taking into account temporal questions (Esping-Andersen et al., 2001), while the Commission has integrated this dimension of time policies in its sixth framework programme.

13. Developing positive flexibility for employees: the British trade union approach

Jo Morris and Jane Pillinger

INTRODUCTION

Working time has become a central feature of national and European policy and this has resulted in radical thinking about the nature and organization of work and working time patterns. The European Commission's prediction that the linear career concept of the twentieth century (education, work, retirement) will increasingly be replaced by the 'norm of the varied working life' is increasingly being realized in practice (Naegele, 2003).

Significant change in working time in recent years has been marked by a slowing down of the long-term trend towards reduced working hours, a greater intensity of work and an increased incidence of long working hours, particularly in the UK, Denmark, Finland and Belgium (OECD, 2003). The increasing complexity of people's lives brought about by societal, family, demographic and household change, resulting from the growth of women's participation in the labour market, longer periods of time spent in full- and part-time education and early retirement, means that more workers are seeking flexible working hours and work–life balance. Trade unions have been advocating shorter working hours (35-hour week), an end to the long hours culture and greater opportunities for employees to work flexibly. Employers are increasingly placing an emphasis on flexible work for the recruitment and retention of staff, competitiveness, growth and improved services. In this context the perspective of the life course (Anxo and Boulin, 2005) and of lifetime hours (Boulin and Hoffman, 1999) has helped to foster a better understanding of how workers' differential working time preferences, patterns, demands and pressures vary across their working lives. Rethinking the organization of time in relation to work and personal lives throughout working life is central to new thinking on work and time (Pillinger, 2002).

This chapter examines some of these tensions and shows how trade unions in the UK are developing new worker-friendly definitions of flexibility in response. The synchronization of employer and employee time needs in the workplace lies at the heart of positive workplace flexibility, contributing to sustainable work–life balance policies for employees as well as a high-performance workplace. We will argue that innovative working time arrangements that benefit employees and employers are a result of economic, labour market and social pressures, as well as the European Union's Social Market model. Unions have signed up for the high-performance workplace and have used the European model of social partnership to adapt working arrangements to the needs of a feminized workforce and to develop a work–life balance approach. In exploring these issues the chapter provides an overview of some innovative pilot projects to develop work–life balance.

EUROPEAN AND NATIONAL POLICY CHALLENGES

EU member states share similar policy challenges generated by long-term economic, structural, societal and demographic changes. The EU's response has focused on the implications of the changing nature of employment, work organization and working conditions, the modernization of social protection, and enhancing employment rates, particularly through the inclusion in the labour market of women, people with disabilities and older workers.

Two key policy developments helped the direction of flexible labour markets and employment policy in the EU. The Commission's 1993 White Paper on Growth, Competitiveness and Employment (EC, 1993) set the benchmark at the European policy level for a flexible and competitive labour market that subsequently influenced the wording of the Directives on parental leave and atypical work, agreed through the social dialogue at the European level between employer and union organizations. These Directives were positioned as instruments to create a flexible and competitive European economy at the same time as ensuring employee security and facilitating the reconciliation of professional and family life. In a similar way the March 2000 Lisbon Economic Council set the challenge to create sustainable, technology-intensive growth, with social cohesion and with more and better jobs (EC, 2004b).

In this context, European Employment Guidelines have stressed that competitiveness increasingly requires companies to be more flexible and that modernizing work organization is a core task for companies if they are to survive growing international competition (EC, 2003a). These issues are increasingly being addressed by the EU's Employment Taskforce Report through the setting of priorities for the development of the European labour market (European Commission, 2004). New working-time patterns are seen as necessary to meet both the new demands of technological change as well as social change. Employee motivation and adaptability is viewed as a core component of productivity in modern methods of work organization. As a result the taskforce consistently stresses that there needs to be reconciliation between the needs of the company and the expectations of the employees, who want to manage their working hours in a flexible manner. In addition the European Employment Guidelines underline the need to promote employability and participation in lifelong learning in order to create a competitive and dynamic knowledge-based society (EC, 2004b).

EU policy stresses the importance of social partnership and the social dialogue to find effective solutions to work organization and working time. The social partners have been encouraged to negotiate agreements to modernize the organization of work through new working time arrangements such as reducing working hours, reducing overtime, developing part-time work, lifelong learning and career breaks, 'with the aim of making undertakings productive and competitive and achieving the right balance between flexibility and security' (TUC, 1998: 5). Social partnership is also seen as integral to equal opportunities in the workplace, including the reconciliation of family and work time.

EQUAL OPPORTUNITIES AND THE RECONCILIATION OF FAMILY AND WORK LIFE

Gender is central to any analysis of working time, particularly because women's time falls outside of the commodified time systems that operate in the paid workplace. Policies that aim to reconcile family and working life have had to recognize that work needs to be organized within different time frames for carers, disproportionately women. In this respect some experiments in making working time more flexible have had the consequence of legitimizing women's exit from the labour market, and therefore have further undermined women's position in the labour market. Working time experiments in Finnish municipalities and health services to introduce a six-hour day, part-time pensions, part-time benefits and work rotation, the bulk of which have been taken up by women, have had this negative consequence associated with them (Pillinger, 2000). Similarly the impact of the 'right to request' flexible working for parents and carers established under the 2002 Employment Act in the UK, discussed below, could also adversely affect women. The Maternity Alliance (2004) found that while 25 per cent of parents said that their working conditions had improved, 27 per cent said that their situation had worsened. Likewise according to Rubery et al.'s (2004) analysis of the Nation Action Plans on Employment, gender mainstreaming has had a limited impact in that 'The adjustment to work and family life is seen for the most part as an issue for women, through the choice of part-time work and not an issue of changing the behaviour of men in the labour market' (2004: 25).

THE CHALLENGE OF FLEXIBILITY AND WORK–LIFE BALANCE FOR A DIVERSE LABOUR MARKET

The impacts of societal change compound the pressures of work intensification, a long-hours work culture, and the unpredictability of changing shift patterns or 'non-standard' working hours. The feminization of the UK labour market, whereby women now make up more than half the workforce, has resulted in a variety of atypical work contracts and arrangements as women adopt strategies to deal with the dual demands of parenting and work. An aging population, together with the move away from state welfare care, places an increased care burden on families, particularly women; and the rise in younger women who are working in turn creates new pressures for grandparents who are relied upon to perform regular or emergency childcare duties. Additional pressures on working lives, such as traffic congestion and public transport overcrowding for commuters, can also be pressure points for change in working patterns. Avoiding the rush-hour has become an important reason for many people to change their working hours, and may be a critical issue for people with disabilities using public transport.

Demand for working conditions which balance work and personal lives are no longer restricted to parents and carers. The intensification of work, the long-hours culture and the move of jobs from manufacturing to a customer-facing service sector make demands on all workers of all ages. British workers work the longest hours in Europe, with the longest hours worked by male employees, especially fathers, managers and professionals and employees with supervisory responsibilities (DTI, 2004). One in ten of the workers putting in 48 hours a week or more had suffered some form of physical problem as a result of working long hours.[1] Besides an unqualified 48-hour limit on working hours per week, the TUC argues that better-managed workplaces and cultural change are needed so that people can get their jobs done in the time available and are rewarded for working smartly, not for putting in long hours (TUC, 2002a).

From an employer's perspective the business case for work–life balance can be seen from the results of a Department of Trade and Industry's survey (DTI, 2003) which found that the majority of employers (92 per cent) agreed that people will work best when they have a work–life balance; a similar number of employers did not consider that there were major cost implications involved in implementing flexible working options. Of those employers that have already implemented work–life balance practices, 81 per cent believed that they had had a positive effect on employment relations, with 75 per cent stating that the workforce had become more motivated and committed, and 60 per cent reporting a better retention of staff. However employees believe that working flexibly would impact negatively on their careers (DTI, 2004b). This data also showed that work–life balance had positively contributed to increased productivity (49 per cent of companies), improved recruitment and retention of staff, reduced rates of absenteeism, reduced overheads, improved the customer experience and created a more motivated, satisfied and equitable workforce (DTI, 2003b).

Recruiting and retaining staff means that employers have to pay attention to work–life balance issues and to social, community and environmental concerns. With 70 per cent of employees wanting to work more flexibly, the business case appears clear with 46 per cent of employees choosing flexible working as the most important factor impacting on the choice of their next job (DTI, 2004). Similarly, supporting parents at work has also become important to recruitment and retention of staff. The survey Working and Caring in London (2002) found that parents did not think employers provided enough practical support to enable them to combine work and caring, whilst 92 per cent of non-working mothers stated that flexible working hours would be essential in returning to work. The quality of working life has overtaken pay as the prime workplace concern for many employees. The DTI employees survey (2004) found that 33 per cent of those polled would prefer to work flexible hours rather than receive an additional £1000 in pay.

IMPLEMENTING WORK–LIFE BALANCE

The legacy of the Thatcher years meant that for the trade union movement flexibility was synonymous with a deregulated, casualized, low-paid and low-status workforce. In 1997 many trade unionists were deeply sceptical at best, and often hostile, to the concept of partnership. European and national policy has since then encouraged unions and employers to build on the foundations of equality legislation and workplace equal opportunities policies to develop sustainable models of positive flexibility and work–life balance. The model often enables new approaches to be taken, finding new solutions to old problems. The hallmark of success is creative thinking 'outside the box' through joint problem solving, within a framework of established employee rights and entitlements (TUC, 2002a).

Inspired by the unions and the TUC, innovative thinking and positive examples of flexible working have been developed through the Time of Our Lives and Changing Times initiatives[2], which have operated alongside the

TUC's campaign to end long working hours. The need for a change in the culture of work has been highlighted in the TUC's guide to work–life balance *Changing Times* which argues that work–life balance requires a reorganization of work, the development of trust, partnership approaches, and joint problem solving. This marks a clear change in the way that industrial relations is organized and the move towards more consensual, joint and partnership working is regarded as a key instrument of the process of change. The TUC Changing Times process consists of an eight-stage model based on successful joint union– management initiatives. The process puts an emphasis on the need to ask employees about their preferred working patterns, and to involve staff in identifying problems and finding solutions.

Alongside this has been a drive by government to change the culture of work and identify the business benefits of work–life balance. Employers for Work–Life Balance was initiated as part of the Government's Work–Life Balance Campaign for England and Scotland, launched in 2000, to encourage employers to introduce flexible working practices that would improve the working lives of employees and contribute to improving service delivery. The best-practice guide to work–life balance, *The Essential Guide to Work–Life Balance*, argues: 'Working longer and longer hours is not good for business – or for you ... Work–life balance isn't only about families and childcare. It's about working "smart" ... And it's a necessity for everyone, at whatever stage you are in your life' (DTI, 2001: 5).

More recently, in 2003, the implementation of the 2002 Employment Act gave workers with young and disabled children the right to request flexible work. Employers have a duty to give serious consideration requests from employees wanting to work flexibly and these requests can only be refused if there is a clear business reason for doing so. In February 2005 the government consulted on proposals to extend maternity and adoption pay from six to nine months; give a right to mothers to transfer a proportion of their maternity leave and pay to fathers; and to extend the right to request flexible working hours to carers of adults and parents of older children.[3] Legislation impacting on work–life balance includes the Sex Discrimination Act, which applies to employees who are refused part-time work when they return from maternity leave if indirect discrimination is established, and the Part-time Workers (Prevention of Less Favourable Treatment) Regulations 2000, which establishes rights for part-time workers not dependant on proving sex discrimination. The Disability Discrimination Act also requires employers to make reasonable adjustments in the workplace for disabled employees. Refusing a disabled person the flexible working arrangements would constitute discrimination under the Act.

In supporting these developments there have been a range of governmental and institutional mechanisms to support and encourage flexible working time arrangements and some practical illustrations are provided in the remainder of this chapter.

CHANGING TIME: EXAMPLES OF INNOVATIVE TRADE UNION-LED WORK–LIFE BALANCE INITIATIVES IN THE PUBLIC SECTOR

The following three examples have been inspired by the TUC's campaign on work–life balance through the Time of Our Lives and the TUC Changing Times process. All three projects were in the public sector and used a partnership approach.

Time of Our Lives Project: Reclaiming Flexibility for Workers

In 1996, before the new Labour government came to power, the TUC and the Dutch confederation the FNV set up a joint EU-funded project to examine what positive flexibility might look like. To some extent the idea for the project had been inspired by the Italian *Il Tempa della Citta* Time in the City projects (see Boulin, this volume) which involved unions and other stakeholders in experiments to link working time to city time schedules, including the opening times of public services and times of public transport (TUC, 2001). To the TUC and FNV this inclusive approach by stakeholders to deliver a better quality of life was attractive and prompted thought about how there could be better organization of working time in the UK and Netherlands, both of which have a high incidence of female part-time working. The FNV had already adopted a policy, in contrast to many European unions, to promote high-quality part-time work and encourage men to work part-time in order to address the inequitable division of domestic labour, which led to many women working part-time.

In the UK it was impossible for many unions to imagine flexibility positively in the context of a deregulated labour market where rights at work had been systematically reduced. But at the same time the TUC was part of the European negotiating team for the new EU social partner Directives, which committed employers and unions to contribute to establishing 'flexibility with security' to promote a competitive economy, as well as assist work–life balance. The joint project aimed to explore new possibilities and raise awareness of different working time options and innovative solutions (TUC, 1998). It was agreed that in the second stage both the TUC and FNV would run employer–union pilots to see what positive flexibility might look like in practice. A change of government in 1997 – Labour's landmark victory - made the Bristol City Council pilot in the UK all the more pertinent.

Bristol City Council Time of Our Lives

The Time of Our Lives project in Bristol City Council (BCC) was led by the TUC and the Employers' Organisation for Local Government. It was agreed that the council and unions would:

- Explore the potential for innovative working patterns that would improve both the quality of council services and employees' ability to balance their paid work with the rest of their lives.
- Develop models of partnership between trade unions and employers to enable them jointly to identify better ways to organize work and time.
- Develop a positive model of flexibility that was 'win–win' for employees, employers and customers.
- Share experiences of different ways of reconciling work, personal responsibilities and aspirations and access to council services.
- Widely disseminate lessons learnt.

The Bristol pilot set out to find working patterns that would enable people to secure their preferred balance between paid work and personal life and improve service delivery. The survey was sent to 700 staff with a response rate of just under 28 per cent. It showed that nearly 80 per cent of the respondents wanted some form of flexible working. Three findings are particularly interesting:

- A higher proportion of women (35 per cent) than men (25 per cent) wanted opportunities for education and training.
- Men (34 per cent) were more likely than women (26 per cent) to say they wanted more family time.
- The most common reason for wanting change was the desire to work more effectively in an 'uninterrupted, focused' way.[4]

The focus groups found that staff were initially cautious of new ways of working, but as a consequence of discussion both men and women were prepared to try out new working patterns. Indeed the focus groups themselves were instrumental in helping staff to think 'outside the box' and come up with solutions. A further key to success was the council's commitment to implement solutions that reflected the views of staff and trade unions.

A pilot flexible working project was initiated in the Library Service on the request of UNISON, the trade union.[5] The branch secretary recognized that the proposed national pilot in Bristol for flexible working could simultaneously meet the public's request for extended opening hours and by maximizing library use, resist the threatened cuts in the libraries' budget. Furthermore she was able to convince the membership of the potential benefits.

Sunday working was introduced but was voluntary and accompanied by the usual additional payments. Additional staff were recruited to work alongside volunteers, many of whom were part-time workers who wanted to increase their hours while avoiding childcare costs. The popularity of voluntary Sunday working came as a surprise to management and the union.

The scheme was judged a success. Sunday opening resulted in a marked increase in library use – for the central library visits increased from 305 in May 1999 to a peak of 1062 at the end of February 2000, and hourly issues regularly outperformed mid-week averages. The libraries also attracted a wider range of users, especially families who used the computing facilities and children's library (Cressey, 2001, quoted TUC, 2001).[6]

A further staff initiative suggested by the union was the introduction of team-based self-rostering. This enabled staff to organize work more effectively and control their working times. They were particularly keen to avoid the severe traffic congestion at the start and end of the conventional working day, which made childcare arrangements difficult owing to the unpredictability of their overall time away from home.

Similar projects were carried out in Health and Environmental Services, though a number of predominantly male work groups, such as pest control, were initially reluctant to move from their 8 a.m. to 4.30 p.m. day. However, following the success of flexible working in other parts of the council the men asked to test out flexible hours in order to avoid the chronic rush-hour traffic congestion in Bristol. This resulted in the service being open for longer periods each day, with staff agreeing their hours on a team basis.

Following the success in Bristol a number of other major projects in the public sector followed; the two below illustrate approaches in a government department and the National Health Service.

Our Time: a Partnership Work–Life Balance Project in the Inland Revenue

A Modernisation Agreement between the government and civil service unions, reached in 2000, committed the unions and government departments to find ways of working together to deliver better public services, whilst safeguarding jobs.[7] The Inland Revenue wanted to extend the opening hours of its enquiry centre so that each area had one evening (up to 8 p.m.) and a Saturday morning enquiry service for customers. The customer base of the Inland Revenue was changing, with more people needing face-to-face advice about tax credits and self-employed tax. The working time culture in the Inland Revenue was largely 8 a.m. to 4 p.m., with 85 per cent of staff leaving at 4 p.m. under the terms of their flexitime agreement. Changes in working arrangements were resisted by staff in local offices but the national union understood that if new opening hours were not implemented, there might be job losses, either through moving the work to call centres, a greater reliance on electronic forms of communicating with customers or by outsourcing the enquiry work. The national union was able to help local members establish new advantages for staff in changed working time arrangements, despite the fact that they would be implemented on a no-cost basis and so without premium rates.

The Our Time project (PCS, 2002) was first proposed by the union and aimed to:

- Improve working time arrangements to maximize work–life balance over the duration of an individual's working life.
- Extend access to the service and improve the quality of service provided.
- Develop partnership working and identify how this could practically be applied.
- Provide opportunities to upskill staff and deliver lifelong learning in the workplace.
- Spread the use of the expensive technology in Inland Revenue offices, currently insufficient for the peak core flexi hours.

These aims were agreed at a planning meeting where managers and union representatives developed a shared understanding of both the problems and solutions. The project team established staff preferences through a survey and focus groups examined ways to match staff and business needs. The focus groups were particularly important in giving staff new ideas about working time options, for example taking time off during the middle of the day to care for the elderly or taking longer holidays through the time bank scheme.

Three pilots tested the central aim of the Our Time project – to match business need with improved work–life balance for staff. The enquiry centre and telephone teams tested the scope for extended opening using staff volunteers and the risk, intelligence and analysis team piloted the mutual benefit of increased staff flexibility where there was no external customer interface. The success of the pilots can partly be attributed to the willingness and ability of line managers to manage a team flexibly even though initially they perceived that flexible working would undermine their ability to meet the required business targets.

Extended opening became more popular with staff as they saw how the volunteers were using the system to their own advantage. A number of men, including line managers, opted to work a compressed week over four days; the most usual reasons being to look after children one day a week (and often save a significant amount on childcare costs for preschool children) or participate in sporting activities. Individual arrangements were tailored to need; for instance one person returned to university but with an agreement that he would work for the Inland Revenue during the vacations, the time when most staff wanted to take holiday leave. Another, whose wife was on dialysis, provided remote technical back-up for the extended opening hours and so did not have to reduce his hours in the period immediately before his retirement (and therefore affecting his pension).

Extended opening in the Enquiry Centre (IREC) was most difficult to manage because the centre was small and initial demand did not justify more than two staff members. This raised health and safety concerns, for example for staff leaving work at 8 p.m., especially on dark winter nights. However customer attendance at IRECs steadily increased during the pilot, with both Thursday evenings and Saturday mornings proving popular. Overall staff used the volunteer rotas to bank holiday time for later use, to qualify for car parking places (at a premium as the office was very near the shopping centre) for Saturday mornings, after which they could go shopping, and improve career opportunities. Staff also combined flexible working with the opportunity to develop their own learning needs, from computer skills to learning a new language. Thus a further achievement of the Our Time project was the development of lifelong learning.[8]

The Our Time project was set up as a pilot to help the wider Inland Revenue and other government departments develop creative solutions to time organization. New ways to deliver the service were established which met both employee and business needs. There was a genuine commitment and enthusiasm from both sides to build a new trust and it showed that despite a major reorganization and prolonged industrial action, it was possible to maintain an initiative that included staff as partners.

Changing Times in Health Services

Croydon Primary Care Trust (PCT) has piloted the development of partnership working to improve staff working lives and is supported by the National Health Service (NHS).[9] The NHS Improving Working Lives Practice assessment had already given the Trust a high rating for its practices on work–life balance but current schemes tended to be rather ad hoc and there were concerns about the management of flexible working. Key issues were the need to recruit and retain staff at a time of significant labour shortages, and the need to continuously improve and extend service delivery by providing services at times and locations that were requested by customers. The aims of the project were to:

- Explore different options for working time in order to contribute to improving working lives and work–life balance for staff and improve service delivery.
- Embed and implement work–life balance across the PCT through partnership working.
- Improve the capacity of managers to effectively manage new working time options.

A resource kit 'Changing Times in Health: A practical guide to work–life balance'[10] has been developed from the work carried out in the PCT, providing guidance and practical examples to assist with the development of work–life balance initiatives across the NHS. Three pilots were established, two of which relating to health visitors and district nurses are discussed below. The third scheme relating to general practice (GP) centres had to be abandoned owing to a merger between centres.

Health Visitors Pilot[11]

A local health clinic piloted a compressed hours scheme for health visitors to enable them to extend their service into the evenings. A survey of service users found that working parents were often unable to access the current health visiting service but 56 per cent of clients stated that they would make use of early evening home visits and 69 per cent an evening clinic. The revised hours would give working parents access to the service, and potentially encourage greater participation of fathers in family life. The team benefited through more effective planning of workloads that improved their working lives and job satisfaction and gave them more personal time, which enhanced their quality of life. The organization correspondingly benefited from a highly motivated staff, who were more committed and empowered to delivery a better quality of service, and who reduced their rates of sickness and absenteeism. Staff were very positive about the new working arrangements that also received a very positive responses from clients. The results and learning from this pilot is being disseminated through the Trust.

District Nurses Pilot[12]

A three-month pilot was developed by district nurses working in the PCT who identified a gap in service provision between 7.30 and 8 a.m. and 5 and 6 p.m. This gap existed alongside a need to improve the continuity and flexibility of palliative care, increase the capacity to manage insulin-dependent diabetic patients and provide an improved service to intravenous (IV) therapy patients.[13] In addition to improving care the project also sought to improve staff work–life balance.

By moving onto a compressed hours model the district nurses were able to cover the gap and provide a better quality of service at times patients preferred. Given the range of skills involved, it was essential to ensure that the correct mix of staff was on duty at any one time, and this may have been one of the reasons why this project was less successful than others discussed above. Because of staff shortages (sickness and turnover) this skill requirement could not be guaranteed so the pilot had to end two weeks early to the disappointment of patients. The district nursing team was clear that the flexible hours depend on sufficient staff being in place to provide cover. This learning has been passed on to the trust.

The Partnership Forum through which the pilots discussed above and other working time initiatives were developed, gave meaning to staff involvement, where staff, union representatives and managers from a cross-section of services across the Trust met regularly over a period of 18 months to progress new ideas and to joint problem-solve in relation to flexible working. The Partnership Forum championed work–life balance and provided a space for the exchange of creative ideas and good practice. Two issues emerge as particularly critical to successful implementation of flexible working: commitment of senior management, and ensuring the minimum skill mix and staffing ratios to provide an extended service. Even more crucial is the need to involve staff, to identify their working time preferences and to involve them in finding solutions. As the pilots discussed above indicate, through open discussion between unions, employees and management it is possible to design working patterns that give employees greater control over their working times, provide clients with extended hours and better service delivery, and remain within budget constraints.

WORK–LIFE BALANCE AND TIME ORGANIZATION IN THE PRIVATE SECTOR

In the private sector proposals for the 'win–win' organization of working time tend to be less complex schemes designed to meet specific business needs. In some sectors flexible work arrangements can suit employees with young children but can perpetuate the gender pay gap. Examples of a range of private sector flexible working time initiatives are documented widely (TUC, 2001, www.tuc/changingtimes; DTI, 2003a, 2004). One example is the development of a shorter working week at Playtex, the bra manufacturer, in response to a survey carried out jointly between the union and management. The survey indicated staff preferences for a compressed four-day week, with earlier starting times and a 30-minute lunch break. There was a positive impact on flexibility and productivity, and the negotiated scheme was popular amongst staff (TUC, 2001).

Other examples can be found in the female-dominated finance sector, which has spawned a range of work–life balance initiatives, mainly in response to the high labour (17.9 per cent) turnover in the sector. Flexible working time initiatives targeted at and taken up by women workers, who form the majority of employees, by LloydsTSB, the Royal Bank of Scotland, the Cooperative Bank and the Nationwide Building Society are claimed by employers to have helped to recruit and retain staff (Employers for Work–Life Balance, 2004). For example 86 per cent of mothers at Nationwide return to work after maternity leave, half on a part-time basis.[14] The menu of flexible options, including compressed and annualized hours and term-time only working, won Nationwide the Parents at Work organization Best Boss competition.

On the whole, traditional equal opportunity policies in the UK have mainly benefited mothers rather than fathers. The working time organizational model is more likely to provide benefits for men as well, albeit sometimes with unanticipated benefits. Solaglas, a UK subsidiary of a French multinational glassmaker, employed glaziers and installation workers. Its Moving Forward Agreement with the unions provided improved terms and conditions of employment together with flexible working designed to increase efficiency and improve customer service. The agreement provided permanent status, annual salaries and a pension, as well as training for career opportunities. In addition it introduced flexible working with starting times between 7 and 11 a.m. Monday to Saturday, and computerized working for home-based glaziers using palm tops for job allocation, progress reports and factory contact. The company boosted its productivity and profitability so effectively that the French parent company made significant reinvestment. Staff benefited from the enhanced terms and conditions of employment and the flexible working gave greater choice in working time, which benefited employees with caring responsibilities. (TUC, various)[15] Private sector firms have also introduced new working practices to encourage older workers to remain in employment.[16]

DISCUSSION AND CONCLUSIONS

The modernization of public services, including extended opening, has been high on the agenda of the Labour government in the UK. Similarly private sector employers concerned about recruitment and retention have realized the business benefits from flexible working patterns, especially given the record low unemployment rates in the UK and the corresponding need to widen the labour force.

Whilst both TUC (2001 and subsequent years, see Bibliography) and CIPD (2004) research shows the long-hours culture continues unabated, a DTI (2003b) survey showed that 70 per cent of job seekers want to work more flexibly and almost half would look for flexible working over any other benefit offered by employers. Firms offering flexibility claim that staff retention and morale are significantly improved and productivity is increased.

The broad range of working time patterns now being used include options about how many hours are worked, when people work and where people work. In particular work–life balance arrangements have been developed within organizations to widen the choices available to workers including support with childcare and eldercare, extended holidays and leave schemes, access to sports and leisure facilities during the working day, lifelong learning, personal development and training.

So is the emphasis on work–life balance simply a corporate response to a tight UK labour market? There is a clear business drive to introduce flexible work policies, particularly in the customer-orientated service and public sectors, where there is a desire to recruit and retain especially female employees. In the private sector flexible working policies have largely been directed to assist women, and to lesser extent older workers, adapt to their employment needs. But choice is constrained in a society where childcare is expensive and inadequate. Flexible working policies can enable a parent to meet the dual needs of family and work during childrearing years, but without a range of other positive equality policies, including equal pay, flexibility can turn into the glue of the sticky floor that holds women back and keeps them unequally paid. Not only does this reinforce occupational segregation, but it also restricts women's choices and limits their potential in the labour market.

Unions have agreed to confront the inherent tension between the needs of customers and employees (many of whom are customers when not at work) through finding creative ways to maximize employee choice and maintain quality employment whilst improving service. In all of the pilot projects discussed above it was partnership working and an approach based on joint problem solving that helped staff to understand the implications and opportunities posed by different working time arrangements, in areas such as annualized hours, compressed hours, flexible hours, including part-time work, job-sharing, term-time working and time banking. Partnership and team working helped staff to think more creatively about the benefits of flexible working hours to themselves and to the delivery of services. The TUC's Changing Times process raised awareness of the need for effective project planning and giving enough time to plan, discuss and implement a new working time arrangement through team and partnership working.

Achieving change rests on the recognition that the organization of working time could give more choice to a diverse workforce with varying working time preferences. On occasions national union policies conflicted with local working time culture. Initiatives in Bristol City Council and the Inland Revenue showed, not surprisingly, that unions at national level had a longer-term perspective on the implications of resisting change than union activists. National and local union representatives were important change agents, interpreting the implications of social and economic circumstances to their members, steering through new approaches to bring new work–life benefits to employees. At Bristol and in the Our Time project, local unions moved from scepticism or hostility to proactive problem solving, demonstrating commitment to delivering high-quality public services whilst giving members more choice and control over working arrangements.

The working time initiatives, experiments and innovations discussed in this chapter reflect a major change in the way that work is organized and particularly how work organization and working time is adapting to changing economic and social circumstances. As a political issue the reorganization of time in relation to work and personal lives is central to new thinking about balancing working time with improving the quality of services and business competitiveness. As a whole the examples demonstrate that working time issues are being considered within a framework of people's differential needs and preferences over the life course. This does however raise the question about how different needs, aspirations, preferences and interests over the life course can be reconciled with a good-quality working life, whilst also contributing to improved quality of services.

Flexible working time initiatives have often resulted in an unanticipated enthusiasm for, as union and management participants in the Inland Revenue Our Time project put it, 'a completely new way of working' (PCS, 2002). In the Changing Times in Health project the establishment of a Partnership Forum that was both endorsed and positively supported by local unions became the source of new union members and new enthusiasm for workplace representation. Key successes from the examples are related to the development of joint working and partnership approaches, which addressed flexibility within a broad framework of work organization, and work location alongside improved and extended service delivery.

The debate about work–life balance and working time flexibility has shifted from one of family-friendly working arrangements, part-time work and equal opportunities to a wider notion of workplace flexibility that addresses issues ranging from lifelong learning to recognition of workers' personal, social, political or leisure-time interests. In this respect work–life balance has shifted into the core of organizational development strategies and work organization and has become firmly embedded into social partner decision-making processes at European, national and company and local workplace levels. Core to this development has been the approach inspired by the European Union and implemented by the TUC on partnership working, resulting in a systematic approach to the development of partnership agreements and joint approaches to positive forms of flexibility and work–life balance. Working time projects have also required there to be a better management of time on a team basis in order that equal opportunities and equity between team members can be guaranteed. This is particularly important in ensuring that non-carers have access to flexible hours. Key issues are raised about how these processes can be managed and linked into organizational development and management competencies that reflect the changing workplace.

Diversity of time-need in the workforce, as well as changing needs over an employee's working life, mean that it is no longer sustainable for unions only to pursue family-friendly policies, which meet the needs of one section of the workforce, albeit an important group who require special consideration. Reducing the long-hours culture in the UK is the first step to giving men and women more options about the organization of their working hours; men need more time to participate in the family and in civil society more generally, while mothers need to escape the penalties of enforced short-hour working, necessitated by time demands of other family members. Government, employers and unions need to confront the division of labour at work and at home – the two are inextricably linked.

As social partners signed up to Social Europe, UK trade unions are going beyond a strong regulatory approach, necessary though that is, to engage with workers and employers organizing time to suit the demands of a modern economy and needs of a diverse workforce. In the public sector, where trade union organization and social partner relationships are strongest, it has been shown that imagination and creativity can produce models of work organization that recognize the individual needs of the worker and business. If this creativity and potential is to be further developed, and not viewed as a set of one-off examples that are inspired by innovative relationship developed between unions and employers, there is clearly a need to create and further embed these new working relationships between employers, unions and the government in ways that are underpinned by a more systematic approach to partnership and a regulatory framework.

NOTES

1. The TUC's About Time campaign has shown that UK workers put in more than £23 billion of unpaid overtime in 2004; the TUC calculates that around 5 million people work an average of seven hours and 24 minutes without pay every week, worth an average of £4500 per year for each worker. The research showed that 150 000 craft workers were averaging an extra six hours a week and 70 000 plant and machine operatives were doing an additional five hours 36 minutes of unpaid work (2004).
2. The process has been widely used in both the public and private sector and is outlined in the

TUC Changing Times website www.tuc.org.uk/changingtimes and in the publication Changing Times.

3. Government consultation paper 'Work and families: choice and flexibility', DTI (2005).

4. The Time of Our Lives in Bristol: developing positive flexibility for employees and services; TUC (various).

5. UNISON is Britain's biggest trade union with over 1.3 million members. It covers frontline staff and managers working in public services and for private contractors who provide public services and the utilities and the voluntary sector.

6. Evaluation of the Bristol City Council/Working Time Flexibility Projects; Peter Cressey, University of Bath, 2001.

7. The 2000 Modernisation Agreement committed civil service unions and government departments to finding ways of working together to deliver better public services whilst safeguarding jobs. In recent years the Inland Revenue has encouraged staff to be involved in the change process but creating a genuine partnership at both national and local level was a challenge.

8. Following a local learning needs analysis new union learning reps were able to set up learning access points with computers provided by the union and the employer in each of the three offices in the pilot area. PCS Learning Services in London provided free remote access to Learn Direct courses to all members of staff (including non-members). This was the first time that the union had brought its learning services provision into a government department as a partnership project, providing a model for other parts of the civil service. Union learning reps were enthusiastic in promoting the service with the result that 85 people registered with Learn Direct in the pilot offices, approximately two out of ten staff. The union produced a new guide to bringing learning into the workplace (TUC, various).

9. The Croydon initiative is run through the programme through the South West London Strategic Health Authority. See Department of Health (2005), 'Improving working lives'.

10. http://www.swlha.nhs.uk/context.aspx?id_Content=7022.

11. Health visitors are persons employed to give advice to people, especially older people and the parents of very young children, about healthcare, sometimes by visiting them in their own homes.

12. A nurse who, employed in a particular area to care for people who are ill or injured, often visits them in their homes.

13. Intravenous (IV) therapy delivers drugs and fluids to patients. It can be delivered to patients in hospitals, long-term care and outpatient facilities, physicians' offices and homes.

14. At the Nationwide Building Society more than seven out of ten of its 15 000 employees were women. Between 1999 and 2003 Nationwide doubled the number of home workers to 148 and employed 71 term-time workers. Eighty-three per cent of employees with annualized hours contracts were female.

15. *The Time of Our Lives* (TUC, 1998) and TUC Changing Times website www.tuc.org.uk/changingtimes.

16. Sainsbury's supermarket has a Personal Retirement Plan through which employees can draw partially on their company pension to make up reduced salary; the company pays the administration costs and contributes to the pension scheme to age 75 years and members have a say in how the plan is run. Sainsbury's benefits from reliable employees that help match the customer profile, especially during the daytime.

PART V

Equality policies in the new economy

As the contributions to this book in the preceding parts have shown, the new economy, as shorthand for a range of economic and social changes, has variable and uneven impacts for different social groups in different spatial contexts. Neither the wholly optimistic nor the straightforwardly pessimistic predictions for the new economy seem satisfactory. Class and gendered inequalities remain, as several chapters have made clear, and are both being reinforced and also assuming new shapes and patterns in the new economies of Europe and the US. The topic of this final part of the book is the nature and adequacy of current policies for addressing these inequalities.

In recent years, policies promoting gender equality have assumed a greater prominence at various levels of governance, from the international to the local. For example the UN's Millennium Development Goals include the promotion of gender equality and the empowerment of women, whilst the EU has adopted a Framework Strategy for Gender Equality which 'aims at coordinating all the different initiatives and programmes under a single umbrella built around clear assessment criteria, monitoring tools, the setting of benchmarks, gender proofing and evaluation' (EC, 2000b). This strategy includes the introduction of 'gender mainstreaming' in policy design and evaluation, and this principle has been formally taken up in EU employment and social inclusion policy. The high profile of gender issues is reflected in the range of policy reforms across the individual EU member states directed at raising women's employment rates (Rubery et al., 2004). So, for example, in the UK, policies promoting gender equality have included the implementation of a National Childcare Strategy to improve childcare provision, the creation of a Women and Work Commission to examine solutions to the persistent gender pay gap, the introduction of tax credits to 'make work pay' for families on low wages, the improvement of parental leave entitlements, and the promotion of the 'business case' for work–life balance policies amongst employers.

In contrast to developments in the EU, gender equality issues do not have the same prominence in public policy debates in the US, despite evidence that some of the progress made towards gender equality in the 1960s and 1970s has been undone in the subsequent decades (National Committee on Pay Equity, 2005; Institute for Women's Policy Research, 2004). There have been some positive developments in the US however. For example state provision for family leave and childcare is still extremely limited, but there has been an increase in workplace provision of work–family policies since the mid-1990s and the Child Care Bureau of the Department of Health and Human Services has promoted public–private partnerships at state and community levels to improve the quality, supply and access to care for working families. Provision in the US remains highly skewed to employees in large firms and the better-paid occupations, making life very difficult for low-income parents (Heymann, 2000; Families and Work Institute, 1998).

Whilst gender equality now occupies a more prominent role in policy discourse at different levels, these policies often stem from concerns about economic competitiveness and sustainability in the more competitive global economic climate, especially in the face of declining fertility rates and an ageing workforce in the advanced industrial world. The OECD for example maintains that investment in family-friendly policies is needed since strong economies and manageable pensions systems depend on both higher fertility rates and higher employment rates (OECD, 2004). Thus women should be facilitated to combine paid employment with their continued responsibility for childrearing, to both contribute to the economy directly and to produce the next generation of workers. In the UK, the government's slogan of 'work for those who can, security for those who can't', which has accompanied the introduction of 'active' labour market policies requiring those out of the work and claiming benefits to take more active steps to move into work, has been espoused as both a necessity for strong economic performance and as a route out of poverty for individuals.

Promoting gender equality as part of a policy for economic productivity and growth however raises a number of issues and tensions, because of both the multifaceted nature of gender relations and also the entwining of gender relations with other aspects of inequality and disadvantage. Work–life balance policies, as discussed in Part II, may enable women to better compete with men in particular workplaces, but are less able to challenge the overall segregation of jobs by gender or the gendered domestic division of labour. Still less are they likely to challenge class and other inequalities between women. This is important in the context of the new economy where, as we have seen, inequalities between women are growing due to the reorganization of work, which has increased the lowest-paying servicing jobs dominated by women.

The two chapters in Part V address some of the tensions and uncertainties, as well as opportunities, in current gender equality policies in different contemporary contexts. In the first chapter, Teresa Rees compares and contrasts equality policies emanating from, on the one hand, a group of major global corporations who are addressing the shortfall in science, engineering and technology personnel in the EU, facilitated by the Women and Science Unit of the European Commission, and on the other, public sector bodies in the UK, in particular the Welsh Assembly which has a statutory obligation to pay 'due regard' to equality of opportunity for all in all that it does. Rees' examination suggests that while the rationales for equality policies may be very different in each case – for the former it is 'the business case' for diversity that holds sway, while in the latter it is the European model of social justice – in both cases, the tools of 'gender mainstreaming' are being used. Thus Rees' chapter gives cause for cautious optimism regarding the growing prevalence of gender mainstreaming, a long-term strategic approach to promoting gender equality, in both the private and public sectors.

The second chapter in this part turns to policy interventions in the social democratic Nordic states, where the notion and principles of gender mainstreaming took root earlier than in most other countries. Lena Gonäs, Ann Bergman and Kerstin Rosenberg discuss the revision of the Swedish Equal Opportunity Act in 2000, which required employers to conduct an annual review of policies and practices concerning working conditions and pay differences between men and women, and to prepare an action plan for eliminating unwarranted pay differences. They explore the impact that this legislation has had in the academic sector. Their case study of Karlstad University shows that despite the introduction of a pay review following the legislation, and the raising of the salaries of some female employees, there is still widespread gender disparity in salary levels across the university. Their findings suggest that there is a considerable gulf between the official rhetoric of gender equality and the reality of daily practice in the university, with few employees having much knowledge of the Act or indeed of the pay-setting process in their workplace.

These case-studies suggest that evaluation of current equality polices must be focused on their outcomes for particular social groups within particular contexts and settings. A rhetoric of gender equality, these studies reveal, is not sufficient (and perhaps not essential) to the implementation of policies that facilitate greater equality between men and women in the workplace. Equality policies in the new economy must be sensitive to the multidimensional nature of gender relations and the uneven effects of policies across different areas, as well as to the potentially diverse gendered interests of different groups of women and men.

14. Promoting equality in the private and public sectors

Teresa Rees

INTRODUCTION

In two very different working environments, growing attention is being paid to equality policies and more specifically, to the idea of 'promoting equality'. Large, multinational, private sector global corporations, whose businesses include a major research and development (R&D) function, use the language of 'managing diversity'. They are especially concerned about making the most of qualified women scientists. The European Commission has launched a major initiative to work with such companies in developing effective policies. At the same time, public sector bodies in Europe are increasingly being driven by a legislative framework that imposes a duty to 'promote equality' in employment and service delivery. The framework derives from the European Union's Amsterdam Treaty that commits member states to equal treatment for all in employment and vocational training, on the grounds of gender, disability, race and ethnic origin, religious and political belief, sexual orientation and age. It also commits member state governments to a policy of mainstreaming gender equality. What common issues are faced by these very different sets of employers, one driven by the business case, the other more by social reform, to promote equality? What are the similarities and differences in approach? These are the questions addressed in this chapter.

This chapter consists of two halves. The first half describes some initiatives being taken by a group of significant European and North American companies, facilitated by the Women and Science Unit in the European Commission's Research Directorate-General, to address the projected shortfall in qualified science, engineering and technology researchers.[1] These initiatives are designed to ensure a better record in recruiting, retaining and promoting, in particular, women industrial researchers. The policies that are being developed include paying much better attention to work–life balance issues. A number of these companies have been working on such policies for some years and they describe how they achieved a 'critical mass' of women at middle levels but then reached a plateau. They report that they then had to introduce new policies, addressing broader issues of organizational and cultural change, to continue to increase the proportion of women in middle and senior grades. Some of these companies have made a public statement of their commitment to work on this agenda and will be reporting on their progress on a regular basis, again facilitated by the European Commission (see below).

The second half of the chapter looks at pressure on the public sector to implement equality policies more actively. In the UK, during 2005 legislation to establish a new equalities and human rights body – the Commission for Equality and Human Rights (EHR) – was passing through Parliament. The Commission for Equality and Human Rights is designed to replace the three existing statutory equality agencies (the Equal Opportunities Commission, the Commission for Racial Equality and the Disability Rights Commission). It will have responsibility, in addition, for the three new equality strands identified in the Amsterdam Treaty (faith and other belief, sexual orientation and age), as well as human rights. This same legislation includes a commitment by the Government to legislation to require public bodies to 'promote' gender equality. Public bodies already have such a duty in relation to race, and one is going through the statute books in relation to disability. What will it mean? How will it work? What can we learn from existing duties, such as that in Wales where the National Assembly is obliged to pay 'due regard' to equality of opportunity for all, in all that it does? Can such duties make a difference to work–life balance and the employment experiences of women?

WOMEN IN INDUSTRIAL RESEARCH: MANAGING DIVERSITY

At the Lisbon Summit held in 2000, heads of state and government of the European Union (EU) expressed concern about the economic competitiveness of the EU *vis-à-vis* other global regions. They made a commitment to enhance the EU as a knowledge-based economy. Following this, at the Barcelona Council of Ministers in 2002, a target was set to increase the investment of EU gross domestic product in R&D from the level of 1.9 per cent in 2000 to 3 per cent by 2010. This compares with Japan where 3 per cent of GDP is already spent on R&D, and the US where the figure is 2.7 per cent. About two-thirds of this new investment in R&D, it was calculated, would need to come from industry. Indeed it would entail the private sector doubling the number of industrial researchers that it employs by 2010.[2] This will entail finding an additional 700 000 qualified researchers in science, engineering and technology (European Commission, 2003a: 18).

However this target has been set in a context where the European labour supply is already both shrinking and ageing. More specifically, the projected numbers of new graduates entering the labour market with science, engineering and technology degrees are insufficient to meet this demand. So how will the target be met?[3] Women have been identified as the major supply source, both by EU commissioner for research, Philippe Busquin and his directorate-general and by major R&D companies (Blagojević et al., 2004; European Commission, 2005b; Rübsamen-Waigmann et al., 2003). Indeed the Commission had already set a target of 40 per cent participation of women at all levels in implementing and managing its own Framework Programme of research.

At present, women constitute about 15 per cent of 'industrial researchers' (defined as qualified people working in R&D in science, engineering and technology in the private sector) in the EU15.[4] However there are significant national differences. Women make up between 18 per cent and 28 per cent of industrial researchers in eight out of the ten member states that provide gender-disaggregated statistics; however in Germany and Austria the figure remains below 10 per cent. As Germany is one of the major players in EU R&D, its poor performance in employing women has a significant impact on the EU average. Women are now over 50 per cent of the graduates being produced in the EU15, but make up only 41 per cent of those with degrees in science, mathematics and computing and 20 per cent of those in engineering, manufacturing and construction courses. At PhD level, they comprised 40 per cent of all new completions in 2000, ranging from 50 per cent in life sciences, 30 per cent in mathematics, 27 per cent in physical sciences, 20 per cent in engineering and 19 per cent in computing (all figures from Rübsamen-Waigmann et al., 2003; see also EC, 2003b).

Such gender segregation by subject choice at university is of course well documented. So too is what has been described as the 'leaky pipeline', whereby women drop out of scientific careers at every stage in the career ladder, in both the private and the public sector (Etzkowitz et al., 2000; Glover, 2000; Osborn et al., 2000; Schiebinger, 1999). While women occupied 31 per cent of all academic positions in the EU15 in 2000, they comprised only 13.2 per cent of women in senior posts (EC, 2003b). The ETAN report on women and science showed how in universities and research institutes throughout the EU, men are selected for academic positions disproportionately to their numbers in the recruitment pool at every grade, in every subject and in every country. This is irrespective of the equality policies of the country and whether or not women constitute a majority of the undergraduates in that subject (Osborn et al., 2000). Many qualified women scientists drop out of academic careers at each level, in each discipline, in each country. As we have seen, they make up an even smaller proportion of scientists in the private

232   *Equality policies in the new economy*

sector than in the public sector. In the UK alone, it has been calculated that
there are 50 000 women with science, engineering and technology degrees not
using their scientific education (Greenfield et al., 2002).

It was against this backdrop of an increasing demand for industrial
researchers and knowledge about the 'leaky pipeline' in the public sector that
the EU's Research Directorate-General Women and Science Unit launched a
project on women in industrial research. An expert group was set up led by
two scientists, Prof. Dr Helga Rübsamen-Waigmann from Bayer AG (based in
Germany) and Dr Ragnhild Sohlberg, from Norsk Hydro ASA (based in
Norway). The 17 expert members included senior managers from the US as
well as Europe, representing companies such as Microsoft, Astra Zeneca,
Nike, L'Oréal and Schlumberger, as well as some small and medium-sized
enterprises. The expert group's report, *Women in Industrial Research: A Wake
Up Call for European Industry,* was launched by the European Commission in
Berlin, in October 2003 (Rübsamen-Waigmann et al., 2003). The high-profile
event included 70 presentations from companies and was attended by over 350
representatives of European industry from 40 countries with science,
engineering and technology R&D functions (see European Commission, 2005,
for the conference report).

Relatively little is known about the careers of women in industrial research
compared with those in the public sector. An analysis of European Labour
Force Survey data commissioned from Meulders et al. by the Women and
Science Unit showed however that between 1995 and 2000, the employment
of highly qualified women scientists and engineers in industry increased faster
than that of men in the EU15. This may partly explain why nearly 60 per cent
of all women scientists and engineers in industry and the Business Enterprise
Sector are under 34: younger than their male colleagues. They were also more
likely to have temporary contracts, and to be employed in small and medium-
sized enterprises. About 17 per cent of female scientists and engineers in the
business sector works part-time: a lower proportion than non-scientist women
employed in the same sector but a higher proportion than their male scientist
colleagues. The analysis also revealed that only 28 per cent of women who
work as scientists in the Business Enterprise Sector have one or more children
(fewer than other women working in the same industry). Significantly,
dropout rates of women from scientific careers are higher than those of men
(all figures from European Commission, 2003a). This has concentrated the
minds of members of some senior boards on issues of work–life balance.

What policies do companies initiate to seek to recruit, retain and promote
women in R&D? This was discussed by the expert members of the Women in
Industrial Research Group, and informed by reports from members of sub-
panels of industrial companies such as IBM and Siemens. In addition, an
analysis of a series of 29 case-studies in 11 member states was prepared for

the Women and Science Unit (European Commission, 2003a). The participants in the expert group, the sub-panels and the 29 case-studies presented and discussed accounts of practices in their companies, including what had worked and what had not before identifying recommendations for the sector (European Commission 2003a, 2005a, Rübsamen-Waigmann et al., 2003). In analysing these accounts of what companies have done to increase the number of women in industrial research, a number of themes emerge.

In the first instance, many of these companies report that they first became interested in seeking to promote a more nationally diverse workforce before turning their attention to the 'woman' question. As companies' markets became more global, it made sense to ensure that customers were able to interact with qualified people from their own countries and cultures, in order to establish better rapport and facilitate good communication. Schlumberger for example, a global engineering corporation, decided in the 1970s to 'recruit and develop people from the countries in which we work proportionally to the business perspectives and revenue' (Gould, 2004: 2). Hence the company wanted to field senior engineers and managers from non-Western countries in the Middle East and Latin America, preferably people of the same nationality as its customers. Their top management now comprises 23 people from 11 nationalities. For Schlumberger, wanting an international team of engineers was the entry route to wider diversity issues. In the early 1990s therefore, because of business reasons identified below, a similar approach was taken to the hiring of women. Now, 9 per cent of managers are women, in a highly male-dominated sector, a figure projected to grow to 23 per cent in the longer term.

Secondly, it is clear that it is the business case that motivates the companies to address the issue of women. However there may be one or more versions of the business case. For Schlumberger, it was the 'missing talent' argument:

> Once more, the reasoning was business-driven – why deprive the company of access to half of the world's intellectual potential? (Gould 2004: 3)

Some companies reported that they faced recruitment and retention challenges. Reducing attrition rates saves considerable resource. Moreover, women are playing an increasingly important role as purchasers, whether as domestic customers or as corporate buyers. To be able to offer senior women employees with whom customers can interface was regarded as important, just as in the case of non-Western engineers in Schlumberger in the 1980s. Finally, given that the specific focus here is on industrial research, companies wanted to create an innovative and creative work culture. Such a culture is more likely to generate scientific innovation – after all 'cloned people produce cloned ideas'. As Astra Zeneca say:

The vision of our diversity programme is to build an inspiring, innovative and creative culture that everyone wants to belong to and contribute to. (quoted in Rübsamen-Waigmann et al., 2003: 40)

The emphasis here is on common goals shared by people from different backgrounds. This means that experiences of varied out-of-work activities as well as ascribed characteristics may begin to be regarded as having a business value.

The policies these case-study companies employ to attract, retain and promote more women industrial researchers can be grouped under a number of headings:

- Work–life balance measures are most frequent: these are designed to appeal to men as well as women. They are deliberately presented as work–life balance policies rather than specifically as family-friendly measures. Some companies offer 'concierge' facilities, where employees can drop off dry cleaning or shopping requests at the entrance to the workplace and collect it on the way out. Others provide support if a child is unwell.
- Flexible work schedules are identified, including opportunities for working at home, hot-desking, exploring alternatives to the need for excessive travelling, re-examining work remits and uses of new technologies.
- Transparency in recruitment and promotion is mentioned by many of these companies, departing from previous practices of relying on personal networks. This includes open communication systems, monitoring of succession planning and fast-tracking for overcoming gender biases, staff review systems, and reviews of success criteria in promotion. These measures sometimes reveal how significantly patronage and nepotism have traditionally influenced promotion.
- Integrating equality into the company's way of driving business characterized those organizations that made the most serious commitment to the agenda. The tools used included target setting, statistical monitoring and evaluation, succession planning, dual-career policies, and integrating equality objectives into departmental goals, performance review and reporting mechanisms. The key element was 'growing ownership' of the agenda.
- Schemes aimed at women, such as fostering role models, mentoring and networking are also identified by case-study companies as important in challenging gender segregation in scientific positions.

Work–life balance measures appear to be the starting point for most of the companies, with other policies designed at more radical organizational and cultural change being implemented after reaching, but not being able to progress beyond, a critical mass of women in research positions. Of course it can be argued and sold to men that well-qualified men have nothing to fear from these policies. On the contrary, they may well benefit from them. Indeed by linking appointments and promotions more closely and transparently to merit-driven criteria, opportunities are opened up not simply to women, but potentially to a more diverse group of men.

Many of the policies are in effect good employment practices, with some positive action for women to compensate for their exclusion from male networks. However the more committed companies that are developing tools to integrate gender equality are using tools which have been identified, *inter alia*, as fundamental to 'promoting equality'; that is, the gender main-streaming approach towards gender equality (Rees, 1999). Vital institutional requirements for gender mainstreaming include commitment from the top, along with expertise, awareness-raising and training. These companies identified these too as important to organizational and cultural change. Gender mainstreaming is more usually associated with public sector and third-sector organizations, but when there is sufficient commitment, driven by the business case, to bringing about change then the private sector too will use these tools and ensure the appropriate institutional arrangements are made. However they are unlikely to be aware of or to use the term 'gender main-streaming'.

At the Berlin conference launching the expert group's report in November 2003, a group of chief executive officers (CEOs) that had already encountered recruitment and retention difficulties made a public commitment to action on women in industrial research (see Box 14.1).

So far the CEOs of the following companies have signed this commitment: Airbus, Air Liquide, Eads, Hewlett Packard, Rolls-Royce, Schlumberger and Siemens. Between them, these companies employ considerable numbers of people worldwide.

Again, these measures include a mixture of positive action (sponsoring a role model) and the use of gender mainstreaming tools (organizational and cultural change) and demonstrate one of the institutional prerequisites for gender mainstreaming (commitment from the top). The emphasis on developing women through universities is connected to the concern about labour supply. The existing programmes to be further exploited include European Commission-funded activities designed to foster women in science, engineering and technology, and engaging with women's networks. The analysis and dissemination of the business case is designed to encourage other companies in the sector, in particular small and medium-sized enterprises, to take the issue seriously. To ensure a vibrant sector, it is necessary for companies of all sizes in the supply chain to thrive: if some go under because

---

BOX 14.1   CEOs PUBLIC COMMITMENT (BERLIN 2003)

The CEO and top management of each signatory company will:

1. take a stand and demonstrate their company's approach at public events
2. sponsor a woman professor in science/engineering as a role model to promote strategic partnerships with the education sector to encourage women in science and engineering
3. promote change within their companies and through co-operation with other companies and universities
4. make use of existing national and inter-national programmes to support women in industrial research
5. analyse the business case to strengthen internal and public communications.

Source: European Commission, 2005b: 7

---

of recruitment or retention difficulties then it can impact upon the operation of larger players.

In the industrial research sector then in some large national and international companies involved in the WIR project, many gender-mainstreaming tools are being implemented, if not under that name, to bring about organizational and cultural change designed to enhance the qualitative and quantitative employment of women. The business case for diversity is by now well recognized by such large companies that need to develop the competitive edge of their R&D functions.[5] How does this compare with what is happening in the public sector?

THE PROPOSED UK COMMISSION FOR EQUALITY AND HUMAN RIGHTS

The Amsterdam Treaty of the European Union made a number of commitments on equality. In the first instance, gender mainstreaming would become the official EU policy approach towards gender equality, supplemented by equal treatment and positive action. Secondly (as mentioned above) there would be Directives to ensure that all member states enacted national legislation on equal treatment on the grounds of gender, race and ethnic origin, disability, sexual orientation, religious and other belief, and age. In Great Britain, a legislative framework for the first three equality dimensions was already in existence, on the grounds of employment and training and the delivery of goods and service. Legislation has since been enacted for the fourth and fifth, and is planned for the sixth – age – in 2006; in each case in relation to employment and training only. In Northern Ireland, legislation has existed on equality on the grounds of religion for many years and a single equality body has been set up. As discussed earlier the UK Government has also decided to set up a single equalities body – the CEHR that will take responsibility for each of the six dimensions, as well as human rights. At the time of writing, 2005, this legislation is currently passing through Parliament.[6]

Among members of the task force and the steering group set up to advise the DTI on the Commission, there was an almost unanimous call for a Single Equality Act to harmonize rights by equality strand. As it is, there is clearly an inequality among the equalities dimensions built into the proposed legislation. Proposals for some dimensions extend to goods and services as well as employment and training, those for others do not. There is a spatial set of inequalities too, with different legislation operating in each of the devolved administrations in relations to equality. The Department for Trade and Industry Women and Equality Unit announced in March 2005 that government intention is now to work towards a Single Equality Act.

The new Commission for Equality and Human Rights will only cover Britain. It is instructive to look at the experience of Northern Ireland, which has had a single equality body for some years. Section 75 of the Northern Ireland Act (1998) places an 'active duty of promotion' of equality on designated public authorities. Named public authorities are required to have due regard to the need to promote equality of opportunity:

- between persons of different religious belief, political opinion, racial group, age, marital status or sexual orientation;
- between men and women generally;
- between persons with a disability and persons without; and
- between persons with dependants and persons without.

Public authorities are also required to have regard to the desirability of promoting good relations between persons of different religious belief, political opinion or racial group. They must produce an equality scheme as a statement of commitment to the statutory duties and as a plan for performance on the duties. They must assess the equality impact of their policies and publish the outcome. Consultation with those affected by public policy decisions is at the heart of the new law. The duty to promote equality is carried out through the Equality Impact Assessment process (EQIA). If a public authority's assessment of the impact of a policy shows a possible 'adverse impact' on any group, it must consider how this might be reduced, and how an alternative policy might lessen any adverse impact. It must also show that it considered how any alternative policies might better achieve the promotion of equality of opportunity (Chaney and Rees, 2004).

In Scotland, nine equality dimensions are identified in the Act that set up the Scottish Parliament. The statutory obligation there is to 'encourage' equality of opportunity. Although this is weaker than the statutory framework in Northern Ireland, or indeed in Wales, the political culture is one where a mainstreaming approach has been taken to promoting equality (Chaney and Rees, 2004).

The Government of Wales Act that set up the National Assembly for Wales includes a clause that obliges it to pay 'due regard' to equality of opportunity for all in all that it does: no equality dimensions are specified, or excluded. The mainstreaming approach is embedded in the Government of Wales Act. The Act makes provision for a Cabinet minister to take responsibility for the equalities agenda, a cross-cutting Equalities of Opportunities Committee and annual reporting on the equality agenda taking place in plenary.

In an evaluation of the Assembly's first term of office, it was judged that this statutory obligation was in effect an 'absolute duty' to promote equality. It was described as enabling, for example in allowing attention to be focused on groups (such as travellers and asylum seekers) that cut across the standard equality dimensions (Chaney, 2004; Chaney and Fevre, 2002). The 'due regard clause' has been used to 'promote equality' in various ways, for example introducing an equal pay review into the civil service of the Assembly.

The nearest we have to understanding what a statutory duty to promote gender equality might look like in Britain, following the proposed legislation, is the experience of the race duty and the experiences of the devolved administrations, in particular in Northern Ireland and Wales. While it is early to judge, the race duty has focused on process, through Race Equality Schemes. In Northern Ireland too, the focus has been on employers producing equality schemes (Chaney and Rees, 2004).

In Wales, in terms of promoting gender equality, gender mainstreaming has informed the approach to governance (Chaney and Fevre, 2002). This has been partly because of the commitment of individual Assembly members. The Assembly now boasts 50/50 men and women members and five out of the nine Cabinet members are women. Even in the Assembly's first term, women made up 42 per cent of Assembly members, a higher figure than that in the Scottish Parliament, the Northern Ireland Assembly and indeed the Westminster Parliament. Significantly, the Assembly members include gender equality experts. The Assembly funds the vast majority of the public sector in Wales and has integrated some mainstreaming tools in the way it allocates resource. For example, it has reinstated contract compliance to ensure supplier companies have equality policies.

The National Assembly has conducted a gender mainstreaming review (National Assembly for Wales Equality of Opportunity Committee, 2004). The term is used openly and frequently in debates, it is part of the culture. It has introduced family-friendly working hours, its proceedings (including committee meetings) are open to the public, televised live and published in English and Welsh. It has reformed its own recruitment system, opening up senior appointments to open competition. It has modernized the public appointments system, making procedures of appointment more transparent and merit-based, and ensured independent assessors are trained in equality. It has conducted annual audits of departments' awareness of equality and provided equality and training. Staff are required to develop equality objectives as part of their performance review. Indeed equality is an issue actively discussed during staff review and appraisal. The equality dimensions of new policies are routinely assessed. The Assembly funds the all-Wales National Coalition of Women's Organisations and Stonewall Cymru (Wales) to provide a communication channel through which women's voices and the lesbian–gay–bisexual community can be heard.

Much of Wales has European Union (EU) Objective 1 and/or Objective 3 status, and those involved in EU Structural Funds from both the public, private and voluntary sectors are familiar with and have to adhere to the European Commission's strictures on gender mainstreaming in projects and programmes. The concept of gender balance in committees for example is a familiar concept because of the requirements of Structural Funds.

Gender mainstreaming is a long-term strategic approach to promoting gender equality and it is early days to assess the impact of the 'absolute duty' in Wales. The reasons for adopting gender mainstreaming in Wales and other devolved administrations have been driven largely by the European model of social justice. It is about 'doing the right thing'. However in some cases gender mainstreaming has been seen as a way of delivering on other agendas. For example in Ireland it is linked to the combating poverty agenda. In the European Commission Research Directorate-General, it is about fostering excellence in science (Osborn et al., 2000) and addressing skills shortages (as discussed above). In the UK, at central and local government level, it has been linked to social cohesion, best value, democracy and community participation and enhancing effectiveness and efficiency. These constitute, for argument's sake, the public sector's 'business case' for promoting gender equality. However in Wales the mainstreaming agenda is seen as being about promoting equality in its own right.

CONCLUSION

The global corporations operating in industrial research have sound business reasons for wanting to make more of women as employees. Public sector bodies in Britain will in future have a duty to promote gender equality. In the devolved administrations, and in particular in Wales, this is already on the agenda. While the rationales may be very different, in both cases similar tools identifiable with the gender mainstreaming approach to promoting equality are being used. Gender mainstreaming is a long-term strategy that requires the use of a range of tools and a set of institutional requirements. It needs to be supplemented by positive action and equal treatment measures to be effective. So far, industrial research companies and public sector bodies are picking and mixing their tools: there is little evidence of comprehensive adoption of gender mainstreaming as an approach. However some of these industrial research companies and the National Assembly for Wales are adopting a more comprehensive approach. The differences in motivation and indeed discourse – from managing diversity to promoting equality – could not be starker. It remains to be seen whether gender mainstreaming, under whatever guise, will in effect become the new equality policy for the new economy.

NOTES

* The author was the rapporteur for the European Commission's *Women in Industrial Research* report (Rübsamen-Waigmann et al., 2003b) and the report on women and science in the public sector (the ETAN report) (Osborn et al., 2000). She was a member of the DTI's task force, and then steering group, on the Commission for Equality and Human Rights. However none of the views expressed in this chapter necessarily represent those of contributors to any of these reports, the European Commission, the DTI, the task force or the steering group.

1. See the European Commission Research Directorate-General Women and Science Unit website section on women in industrial research: http://europa.eu.int/comm/research/wir.
2. This was before the accession of new member states in 2004.
3. The European Commission's report on women scientists in Central, Eastern European and Baltic states found that women accounted for 38 per cent of the scientific workforce, but were often faced with inadequate resources and poor scientific infrastructure (Blagojević et al., 2004). Indeed there is a concern that the EU15, and other parts of the world, will denude the Eastern European countries, including some of the new EU member states, of their scientists.
4. This applies to the 15 EU member states only. See Rees (2002) for a review of national policies on women and science in the 33 countries associated with the EU Framework Programmes on R&D, which includes the new member states.
5. Interestingly enough however, Smith-Doerr has found that in the US, in the new biotech sector which is dominated by small, flexible companies, 'female scientists working in dedicated biotech firms have a much higher probability of being in a position to lead research teams than do their female colleagues in more hierarchical life sciences organisations' (Smith-Doerr, 2004: 6).
6. See the DTI website for emerging documents: equality.project@dti.gsi.gov.uk.

15. Equal opportunity and unwarranted pay differences: a case study of gender-related pay differences in a knowledge-based society

Lena Gonäs, Ann Bergman and Kerstin Rosenberg

INTRODUCTION

This chapter focuses on gender-related pay differences, and on the legal and institutional framework for equal opportunity that has been developed in Sweden. In connection with yearly pay reviews, Swedish employers are required by law to analyse the pay of men and women, and to identify unwarranted differences. The empirical data on which this chapter is based are from a study of unwarranted pay differences at Karlstad University, one of several new universities in Sweden. The methodology included multivariate statistical analysis, a job evaluation, and a qualitative analysis of individual work and pay histories. The concluding section of this chapter discusses the results of the study in relation to strategies for reducing gender-related pay gaps.

HISTORICAL BACKGROUND

The Swedish system of labour relations was based on collective agreements negotiated within a loose legislative framework. What came to be known as the 'Swedish model' consisted of high-level negotiations and agreements between the two main parties, business and labour, based on their common interest in a peaceful labour market and the benefits of economic growth (Meidner, 1994). Both parties had an interest in avoiding the involvement of government and legislature in setting wages and salaries or specifying working conditions.

But this arrangement began to change in the 1970s, with the passing of the

Employment Security and Co-determination Act, and further with the Equal Opportunities Act in the early 1980s; a new era in labour relations was clearly established (Nycander, 2002).

Collective Agreement on Gender Equality in Working Life

In 1972, a special task force on equal opportunity was set up in the office of the prime minister. Its purpose was to investigate and monitor equal opportunity issues. After repeated calls by various members of the Swedish parliament for legal regulation of these matters, a parliamentary commission was appointed in 1976 to formulate a law against discrimination based on gender.

However this initiative was met with solid resistance from the main actors in the labour market: the Swedish Employers' Confederation (SAF) and the two principal labour confederations, LO which is comprised of unions representing primarily blue-collar workers and TCO, the confederation of white-collar unions (Baude, 1992). Both business and labour argued that a law on equal opportunity in working life would be an unacceptable intrusion into areas that should be regulated by labour agreements.

To demonstrate their point, SAF and LO in 1977 devised an agreement on 'action for equality between women and men'. This agreement came about for political reasons – not, as would normally be the case, after lengthy discussion in the workplace on the issues involved. The central agreement was formulated in very general terms, as it was meant to serve as a framework for more precise local agreements. It included references to ILO's Convention 100 on equal pay for equal work or work of equal value, and to Convention 111 on discrimination in connection with employment and training. All forms of discrimination were to be prohibited; the agreement also called for the implementation of measures for achieving equality between men and women to be implemented at the workplace level (Baude, 1992; Nycander, 2002).

In form and content, this agreement served as a model for the Equal Opportunity Act adopted some years later, even though goals and measures are more precisely defined in the Act.

EQUAL OPPORTUNITY LEGISLATION

In 1979, the Swedish parliament passed the first law on gender equality in working life, which went into effect on 1 July 1980. The new law allowed for equal opportunity measures to be regulated by collective agreements; this would eliminate any need for state intervention, thereby meeting a principal objection of the central organizations of both labour and business.

As a consequence, the law's provisions for governmental control of equal opportunity measures were applicable only to the small minority of businesses that were not covered by collective agreements. The law had two main objectives: one was to protect individual workers against discrimination based on gender; the other was to end the gender-based division of labour. It was the latter objective that formed the basis of a policy for integrating women and men in the same kinds of work (Baude, 1992). But no guidelines were provided as to how this should be done, how to deal with obstacles to fair competition between women and men for desirable and well-paid jobs, or how to improve the situation of women at male-dominated workplaces (Dahlberg, 1984, 1998).

The Equal Opportunity Act (EOA) underwent a major revision in 2000. The Act (2000: 773) included amendments that provided better correspondence with the new Article 141 EC (European Commission) and the European Court of Justice's case law concerning rules on pay discrimination. The objective of the revised Act is to promote the equal rights of men and women in working life; it also states specifically that its primary intent is to improve the conditions of women in working life.

The second paragraph (2 § Act 2000: 773) stipulates that employers and employees shall cooperate in the implementation of active measures for achieving equality between men and women. Specifically, they shall strive for the equalization of pay and working conditions between women and men who are doing work that is equal or of equal value.[1]

The criteria specified in paragraph two have been included in job evaluation guidelines developed and published by the Equal Opportunity Ombudsman (Jämo, 2000). Responsibility for measures to promote gender equality is placed squarely on the employer, who shall:

- within the framework of existing resources and opportunities, create working conditions that are suitable for both men and women;
- make it easier for both men and women to combine employment and parenthood;
- take measures to prevent sexual or any other type of harassment resulting from a complaint of gender discrimination.

The new rules regarding measures to eliminate pay discrimination require all employers to conduct an annual review of policies and practices concerning pay, working conditions, and pay differences between men and women performing work that is equal or of equal value (§ 10). Employers with ten or more employees must prepare an action plan for eliminating unwarranted pay differences, the plan to cover a period no longer than three years.

Also new in the revised EOA of 2000 is the requirement that the employer provide the employee's organizations with any resources it may need in order to participate in the survey, analysis and formulation of the action plan for pay equality. A collective agreement does not relieve the employer from the obligation to implement appropriate measures and develop action plans.

Pay discrimination due to gender is prohibited by the Equal Opportunity Act. This differs from other bans on other types of discrimination in that women do not comprise a minority group in the labour market or a homogeneous group with regard to class, race or ethnicity (Fransson, 2000). Fransson also poses the question as to why the gap between ideology and reality is so great in the case of pay discrimination. The labour market parties have agreed that pay discrimination is unacceptable. Yet despite the above-noted legislation, very little has occurred during the intervening years to reduce the pay gap between men and women (Gonäs and Spånt, 2004).

Fransson argues that the current legislation on equal opportunity has served to conceal the gender conflict. It is only in comparison with men that women can claim pay discrimination, and they must demonstrate that their work is equal in value to that of men. In several cases, judgments of the Swedish Labour Court ('AD') have explained the higher pay of men on the basis of individual skills and market conditions.

Private and public employers were united in their resistance to the governmental proposal concerning revision of the EOA, especially the requirements to conduct systematic pay comparisons and job evaluations. The requirement to fully inform the employee's union about pay and other conditions was also strongly opposed. Such information had not previously been divulged, especially by private companies. This was perhaps the most controversial change in the law on such matters that has taken place during the mid 1990s until the present (2005), as it touches upon a fundamental conflict between the interests of employers and the state. Employers regard government regulation as an intrusion into their domains and prerogatives.

Employers also questioned the use of job evaluation in the pay-setting process. Labour unions, on the other hand, had begun to discuss job evaluation long before. They were already advocating job evaluation in the late 1940s; but it was too difficult and complicated to use at that time, and the issue was set aside (Meidner, 1973).

The transition from collective to individual pay negotiations places new kinds of demands on the individual employee. The role of the union's central organization has changed, and negotiations nowadays are coordinated on a branch basis (Egerö, 2003). A Mediation Institute has been established to help the main parties conduct a well-functioning pay-setting process. Negotiations between the National Agency for Government Employers and the relevant unions have resulted in multi-year agreements that provide a basis for the pay-setting process at Swedish institutions of higher education.

GENDER RELATIONS AND THE EDUCATION SECTOR

There has been a sustained increase in women's personal investment in education. In terms of both student numbers and academic degrees obtained, women have surpassed men. Thirty-nine per cent of Swedish women aged 25–44 during year 2002 had obtained a higher education; the corresponding figure for men in the same age-group was 32 per cent. It is difficult to estimate the pace of this trend; but the proportion of women with a higher education became greater than that of men in 1985, and the gap has increased since then. Correspondingly the female proportion of enrolments has increased from 37 per cent in 1971–72 to 59 per cent during 1999–2000, female graduates from 42 per cent to 61 per cent and female doctorates from 11 to 37 per cent over the same period. The sex distribution of higher education personnel is shown in Table 15.1.

Table 15.1   Number and sex distribution (%) of teachers in higher education, by category, 1998

Category	Number		Sex distribution	
	Women	Men	Women	Men
Postgraduate studentship	2840	4320	40	60
Research appointment	990	1600	38	62
Junior lecturer	2960	3030	49	51
Senior lecturer	1320	4290	24	76
Postdoctoral fellow	430	750	36	64
Professor	240	1920	11	89

Source: Statistics Sweden (SCB, 2002).

While women accounted for 60 per cent of the undergraduate degrees awarded in 1998, only 40 per cent of postgraduate students in that year were women. Research appointments displayed the same pattern, and males also predominated among senior lecturers, research fellows and professors. The only exception was the position of junior lecturer, where the gender ratio was more equitable.

UNWARRANTED PAY DIFFERENCES — THE CASE OF KARLSTAD UNIVERSITY

In connection with the annual pay review at Karlstad University in 2000, union and employer representatives studied the salaries of junior and senior lecturers. The results indicated that the salaries of 37 women in various university departments needed to be reconsidered. The 2001 review found 47 women whose salaries appeared to deviate from stated policy on gender equality.

The director of the university initiated the project described in this chapter. The main objectives were to study the causes of unwarranted pay differences and to provide suggestions on measures for change. The project consisted of four components:

- a multivariate statistical analysis of the gender pay gap;
- a job evaluation survey;
- an interview survey based on a twinning approach;
- change-oriented development activities.

Work on the project began in 2002, and the results of the first three components were reported in 2005 (Gonäs, Rosenberg and Bergman, 2005).

Karlstad University: Salaries of Junior and Senior Lecturers

The pay review conducted at Karlstad University in 2002 included 1167 individuals, of whom 630 (54 per cent) were women and 537 (46 per cent) were men. This ratio falls within the accepted limits of gender equality in Sweden.

Thus in general terms the university may be regarded as gender-equal. It may be noted however that there is a difference in the value of men's and women's work in terms of pay. The average monthly salary of men was over SEK 2500 (€275 or $360) higher than women's. Expressed differently: the average salary for women was 86 per cent of that of men. The study reported here focused on two different staff positions: junior lecturer and senior lecturer. Before taking a closer look at variables that can explain the pay differences between men and women in those two jobs, it will be useful to describe current gender patterns at the university.

The various fields of study at the university are organized within two sectors, the male-dominated nature and technology (N/T) sector and female-dominated humanities and social sciences (H/S) sector. With regard to the two positions on which the study focused, men in both sectors dominated the senior lecture category, with women dominating only the junior lecturer positions in the H/S sector (see Table 15.2).

The comparison of average monthly salaries in Table 15.3 shows that there was no difference between male and female lecturers in the female-dominated H/S sector in either 2000 or 2002. The figures for the male-dominated N/T

Table 15.2   Gender segregation in Karlstad University

	Female % share of jobs	
	Senior lecturer	Junior lecturer
Nature/technology (N/T)	21	33
Humanities/social science (H/S)	33	57

Source: Wages statistics, Karlstadt University.

sector, on the other hand, show that men's average salaries in both 2000 and 2002 were higher than women's in both the junior and senior positions. Concerning pay rises during 2002 (included in the monthly salary figures), it can be seen that they had no effect on gender-related salary differences in the N/T sector. In fact the difference increased from 2 to 4 per cent in the junior lecturer category.

Salaries of Junior and Senior Lecturers – a Multivariate Analysis

The following tables are based on multiple regression analysis, a statistical method for measuring the relationship between two or more independent

Table 15.3   Average monthly salaries for lecturers by gender, sector and seniority, 2000 and 2002

	Average monthly salary 2000		Women's salary as % of men's	Average monthly salary 2002		Women's salary as % of men's
	Women	Men		Women	Men	
N/T						
Senior lecturer	27 700	28 874	96	30 880	32 208	96
Junior lecturer	22 753	23 288	98	24 997	26 132	96
H/S						
Senior lecturer	28 700	28 672	100	31 066	31 032	100
Junior lecturer	22 349	22 372	100	24 749	24 702	100

Note: N/T = nature/technology; H/S = humanities/social sciences.

Source: Wages statistics, Karlstad University.

variables and one dependent variable. In this case, the dependent variable is the relationship between the average monthly salaries of senior and junior lecturers. The independent variables are age, length of employment, sector affiliation (N/T) or (H/T), gender and employment status, permanent or temporary. Since the data are based on the entire population of 522 junior and senior lecturers at the university – not a sample – no test of statistical significance has been applied.

The data yield a picture of conditions in year 2002. Table 15.4 shows how various factors affected the average monthly salaries of junior and senior lecturers in 2002. It can be seen that there is a very large difference in the model's explanatory power with regard to the two categories. The coefficient of multiple determination R^2 indicates that the model explains only 7 per cent of the variation in the average salary of senior lecturers, but 42 per cent of the variation at the junior level. This means that there must be factors, other than those included in the model, which influence senior lecturers' monthly salaries. We assume that the model's explanatory power might have been greater if it had included a variable of whether or not the senior lecturers had completed their doctoral studies. On the other hand the model can be seen as quite useful in explaining the salary gender gap among junior lecturers.

The values in Table 15.4 represent the earnings difference that can be attributed to the variable in question measured in SEK (approximately 10 SEK is equivalent to €1 or $1.5). Thus it is evident that sex has an effect on salary size; men earn at least SEK 200 more than women every month in both the junior (SEK 242) and senior categories (SEK 204) and in both cases this effect

Table 15.4   Factors affecting average monthly salaries of senior lecturer and junior lecturers, 2002

	Senior lecturer	Junior lecturers
Age	77	113
Years employed	–20	12
Sector (N/T)	980	1770
Sex (male)	204	242
Employment (permanently employed)	908	1341
	R^2 0.069	R^2 0.425
	n 180	n 342

Note: N/T = nature technology.

Source: Authors analysis and wages statistics, Karlstad University.

is larger than length of employment or age. It can also be seen that belonging to the N/T sector has a larger effect on the junior than on the senior lecturer category. Employment status has an evident effect on salaries in both categories, but especially on those of junior lecturers. In short, all the variables of the model have a larger effect on the junior than on the senior lecturer category.

Table 15.5 describes the situation for senior lecturers when sex is not included as an independent variable. Instead, the table shows the extent to which factors such as age, length of employment, university sector and type of employment influence the salaries of male and female senior lecturer.

Table 15.5 indicates that the model does not have very much explanatory power with regard to senior lecturers. The value of R^2 is very low for both genders. The variables of the model explain only 2 per cent of the salary variation among women, and only 9 per cent for men. Once again, the salaries of senior lecturers must be influenced by factors other than those that can be measured with these particular variables.

Nevertheless we can see that age has a greater effect on women's salaries than on men's. For every additional year of life, female senior lecturers receive 156 SEK more per month, while men receive SEK 44 more. Length of employment has no positive effect for either men or women. Sector affiliation, on the other hand, influences the salary of both sexes, but the effect is greater for men. Men in the N/T sector receive an average of SEK 1149 more per month than H/S men. Women in the N/T sector receive SEK 926 more per month than H/S women. Employment status is also more important for men than women. A permanently employed male senior lecturer receives SEK 1093 more per month than one who is temporarily employed. The corresponding figure for female senior lecturers is only SEK 100.

Table 15.5   Factors affecting average monthly salaries of female and male senior lecturers (excluding sex)

	Women	Men
Age	156	44
Years employed	−12	−14
Sector (N/T)	926	1149
Employment (permanently employed)	100	1093
	R^2 0.02	R^2 0.09
	n 50	n 129

Note: N/T = nature/technology.

Source: Authors analysis and wages statistics, Karlstad University.

Table 15.6 indicates that the model for junior lecturers has significantly greater explanatory power than the model for senior lecturer. The model's variables 'explain' 32 per cent of the variation in the monthly salaries of the female junior lecturers, and 49 per cent of the males. Comparing the two sexes, it can be seen that age, length of employment and sector affiliation has a larger effect on the average monthly salary of male junior lecturers than on the females in that category. In other words, the males benefit more from their age and length of employment, and from their association with the N/T sector, than do female junior lecturers. But women derive greater benefit than men from permanent employment.

Table 15.6 *Factors affecting average monthly salaries of female and male junior lecturers, 2002 (excluding sex)*

	Women	Men
Age	93	121
Years employed	−16	48
Sector (N/T)	1234	1981
Employment (permanently employed)	1464	1254
	R^2 0.321	R^2 0.494
	n 168	n 172

Note: N/T = nature/technology.

Source: Authors analysis and wages statistics, Karlstad University.

The average monthly salaries of both categories, junior and senior lecturer, display a gender gap which cannot be explained by age, sector or length of employment and thus can only be attributed to gender. Age also has a larger effect on female than on male senior lecturers while the reverse is found for the junior category. Moreover belonging to the N/T sector is financially more advantageous to both women and men but more so for men.

It should be kept in mind that the variables included in the quantitative section of the study do not by any means provide a complete basis for explanation. The statistical models employed are limited to a number of variables whose explanatory power can and should be discussed. However the data do provide a basis for the conclusion that factors such as age and length of employment definitely have significance, but not very much. Sector affiliation and, to some extent, employment status have a greater effect on the average monthly salary of both sexes.

JOB EVALUATION

A job evaluation was carried of the positions of junior lecturer and senior lecturer in accordance with a well-established system based on a comprehensive review of the demands placed on the individual who performs the work. The factors used in this study are: knowledge and proficiency, skill, responsibility, and effort. The job evaluation is concerned only with the formal description of job-related tasks. Other components included when determining compensation are evaluation of merit, results and, in some cases, market value.

The sample consisted of 40 people including one male and one female junior lecturer, and one male and one female senior lecturer from each of ten university departments chosen by the head who was asked to ensure that all subjects were covered: nature and technology, humanities and social sciences, healthcare, and music and arts. Based on the interview data, job descriptions were formulated and assessments and evaluations of individual jobs made resulting in eight prototypes (see Table 15.7).

Evaluation Results

Table 15.7 compares the evaluation scores for the eight prototypes with the

Table 15.7   The evaluation scores compared to average monthly salary of female and male junior and senior lecturers

Prototype position and sector	Evaluation scores	Average monthly salary (SEK)		
		Women	Men	All
Junior lecturer, N/T	702	23 829	24 692	24 415
Junior lecturer, H/S	708	23 075	23 575	23 283
Junior lecturer, Music and arts	722	24 467	22 902	23 338
Junior lecturer, Healthcare	734	23 766	—	23 766
Senior lecturer, H/S	774	28 681	29 960	29 668
Senior lecturer, Healthcare	774	30 650	48 300	33 171
Senior lecturer, N/T	788	29 250	30 550	30 290
Senior lecturer, Music and arts	792	25 000	26 067	25 800

Source: Authors analysis and wages statistics, Karlstad University.

average monthly salaries of males and females. The results summarized in Table 15.7 show a larger range of values (32 points) for the four junior lecturer prototypes than for the senior lecturer prototypes (18 points). There is also a difference of 40 points between the highest-ranked junior lecturer prototype and the lowest-ranked senior lecturer prototype. This difference between the two main categories is greater than that within each of them.

The role played by job evaluation in determining salaries is specified by current personnel policy. The relationship between the evaluated and the average salary is illustrated in Figure 15.1, which is based on the data in Table 15.7.[2]

The evaluation results also show that men receive higher salaries than women, except for the position of junior lecturer in the music and arts sector, where the average salary of women is greater than men's. A comparison of the job evaluation results with average salaries indicates that if the salaries of N/T junior lecturers are at the proper level, those of the other three categories of junior lecturer are too low. Likewise the salaries of all senior lecturers are too

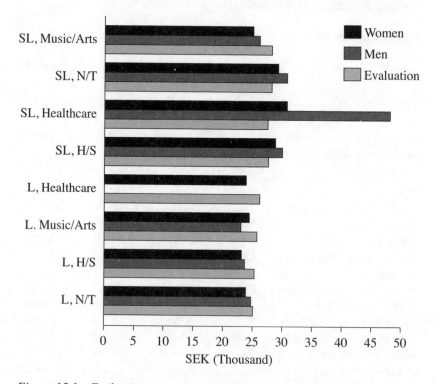

Figure 15.1   Evaluation scores compared with average monthly salaries of junior and senior lecturers, by sector for year 2001

high in relation to their job requirements, except for those in the music and arts sector.

The main conclusion of the job evaluation is that the junior lecturer prototypes may be regarded as of equal value on the basis of the Equal Opportunity Ombudsman's definition (50-point equality index), and the same is true of the senior lecturer prototypes. Inasmuch as the range of values for the senior lecturer positions is smaller, they may be regarded as 'more equal' than the junior lecturer positions.

The results also show that the values for the senior lecturer prototypes partly overlap; these may therefore be regarded as of more equal in value. Within the scope of the 50-point equality index, it is possible to add another category consisting of the junior lecturer positions in the healthcare sector and the senior lecturer positions in both the H/S and healthcare sectors. This possibility suggests that the demands placed on senior lecturers are not significantly greater than those on junior lecturers.

The differences between the reference job descriptions relate to factors such as research responsibilities.

From Table 15.7 it becomes clear that there is no simple relationship between the rankings on pay and the job evaluation. For male junior lecturers there is an inverse relationship between pay and the evaluation results. For women it is the same tendency, but not quite so clear. Nevertheless the healthcare sector has the highest job evaluation score combined with the second-lowest pay level. For senior lecturers, the picture is similarly complex with both women and men in the healthcare sector having the highest pay but not the highest job evaluation scores. Indeed senior men in this sector have much higher salaries than both their job evaluation warrants and women in similar positions.

RHETORIC VERSUS REALITY

Overall, 18 qualitative interviews were carried out with twinned or matched pairs of women and men. The women were selected from a list of individuals, all female, with low salaries that were unwarranted by objective criteria and matched by men who were otherwise fairly similar. Interviews covered topics ranging from their general thoughts about salaries, including the basis on which they should be determined, their thoughts on collective bargaining to more specific questions concerning the employees' knowledge of equal opportunity legislation, job evaluation and the concept of unwarranted wage differences. Other topics included personal background and work history, as well as when – and under what circumstances – salary level had played a decisive role in their career choices. The data was analysed following the grounded theory approach (Strauss and Corbin, 1998).

Few of the interviewees were familiar with job evaluation. One, who had a background in business and had worked with personnel matters, had experience with job evaluation as a tool used in the placement of new employees within an existing pay structure. But none of the respondents had any experience with the use of job evaluation to eliminate unwarranted pay differences in accordance with the intentions of the Equal Opportunity Act.

Indeed overall there was inadequate knowledge about existing regulations and how they might be applied, indicated by the following typical remarks:

> Should know about it ... haven't read up on it ... not very well informed. (Female junior lecturer)

> I have glanced through the equal opportunity plan, but I have not been required to follow it in any respect. (Male junior lecturer)

It is clear that these two individuals are aware of the Act's existence, but equally clear that they are not certain about the contents of the legislation. The only respondents who unequivocally stated that they were familiar with the contents and purpose of the Act had worked with it in various capacities, for example equal opportunity liaison in a department of the university.

Several respondents commented on the need for active measures to end gender segregation although not all of them were familiar with the legal definition of the term. The woman in one of the interview pairs said that one must dare to try new approaches. The man argued that the compulsory element of the Act, that is, that any workplace with ten or more employees must prepare an EOP, ensured that any such plan would be filed and forgotten. He felt that the Act had no practical effect, and that the requirement to prepare a plan was an obstacle to incorporating gender equality concerns into daily routines. 'It is no longer enough to count heads', argued this man. He felt that it was necessary to specify objectives and the means for attaining them. It is necessary to try new methods, for example to say outright: 'You will get no funding if you do not appoint a female research assistant or, in the [female-dominated] healthcare sector, take on a man as a doctoral student or research assistant' (see SOU, 1998: 6).

There was also a clear sense of imbalance between public rhetoric and daily practice. While the Act provides a context for individuals' conceptualization of gender equality, and helps to increase awareness gender inequality, and that this is a problem, the respondees highlighted its inadequacies: for example that it is quite possible to conduct one's life without applying the provisions of the Act at work or at home. At the workplace, it is necessary to use the rhetoric of equality and observe the letter of the law by preparing an EOP. However by giving lip service to the principle of gender equality, it is possible that this simply contributes to establishing a conception of gender equality that does not exist in practice (see also Bekkengen, 2002). Nevertheless the requirement that pay has to be monitored and unwarranted pay differences addressed has led to some pay awards, even this concept is not necessarily clearly understood or explained.

Indeed in terms of understanding the idea of 'unwarranted' pay differences there was a broad range of interpretations. Unwarranted pay differences are related to both the competence and the experience of the individuals in question, as well as their market value and opportunities for taking advantage of their market positions.

All of the women selected for inclusion in this study had salaries which were unjustifiably low, and all benefited from the legislation, indicating that it has had some impact even though with one exception, people were not informed that this was the reason. Neither their employer nor their union representative had informed them of the regulations and how to apply them.

Market Thinking – a Distinguishing Issue

The question of the market's significance for determining salary levels is a theme that constantly turned up in the interviews. Some respondents were annoyed that market thinking had made inroads within the university, while others asserted that it was entirely necessary in order for the university to develop a profile of high competence.

In general, the men underlined the significance of the market for determining salaries. The only woman who did so was one with a leading position – and she did so not for the sake of her own salary, but in reference to the need to recruit competent personnel.

Employment in the university has a generally positive effect on women's wages but a negative one for men. A nurse's salary might increase as the result of university employment, while a civil engineer is forced to accept a reduction. This can be partly explained by gender segregation in the labour market as a whole, and by pay differences between the traditional male and female segments of the labour market.

Fair Pay and the Role of Job Evaluation

The concept of fair pay can be defined in many different ways. One way is based on the question of self-support: a wage or salary must be adequate to cover the individual's living expenses. One should be able to support oneself under fairly reasonable conditions. As one respondent expressed it,

My salary, that is something for me to survive on and pay my bills – to have my daily bread, a roof over my head and all the rest of it. In other words, I don't see my salary as some sort of reward for doing a good job. For me, it has more to do with providing for my survival.

Another quotation expresses a different conception of fair pay:

So I am satisfied that I am adequately compensated for the work I do. That my salary matches my performance and the demands that are placed on me.

Here, it is job performance that provides the basis of the fair pay concept – and that the performance has been recognized and fairly evaluated.

A third definition of fair pay includes two elements. One is the basic amount, which is related to the job requirements. The other is market-based, in other words as much as the employer is prepared to pay in addition to the basic amount.

Pay Negotiations and Local Policy

All of the women thought that they would have difficulty in negotiating their own salaries directly with their immediate superiors. They stated that they disliked such encounters, and would feel uncomfortable negotiating to enhance their own interests. Jenny Säve-Söderbergh (2003) in her dissertation presents data suggesting that women are treated differently than men in individual wage negotiations and that they also have a lower economic outcome of these negotiation. She also comments the lack of studies concerning gender differences in individual wage setting processes.

Some of the men in our study, those with backgrounds in the private service sector, did not mind negotiating their own salary. They were more comfortable with such bargaining and negotiations with the boss on salaries and working conditions and it had been a natural process in their previous employment. But even these men expressed concern over having to link demands for pay directly to specific achievements and likened it to standing with 'cap in hand' in a pay-setting process that is a throwback to a bygone era.

Market demand plays an important role in determining salary level, according to the evaluation guidelines, while education and formal competence have significance for job description, level of difficulty, performance and work quality. Determining the individual's salary is conditional on discussions between employee and supervisor about career development and their role in the enterprise, as well as a salary dialogue, though employees are not made aware of these conditions. Once again, it appears that here we have an issue that no one has really been informed about – that is, wages policy and the criteria upon which it is based.

CONCLUSIONS

The results of our study demonstrate clear differences in the salaries of men and women doing work of equal value at Karlstad University. This applies to the positions of junior lecturer and senior lecturer, in both of which categories men receive higher salaries than women (all else being equal). Thus even when allowance is made for age, experience, sector and job complexity, gender differences remain.

Further, this gender difference has persisted, despite annual pay reviews in accordance with Sweden's Equal Opportunity Act. While the policy rhetoric is progressive, and has led to pay increases for women experiencing unwarranted gender pay gaps, problems with the legislation remain.

Efforts to establish a visible salary-setting process for equal pay for equal work or work of equal value can be problematic. Since the provisions of the Equal Opportunity Act apply only to individual employers, a salary survey can only be used for comparisons within the organization of a single employer.

Moreover few employees seem to know how the gender equality legislation is formulated, with its requirement that employers take measures to correct unwarranted pay differences. Also job evaluation and how wages and salaries are determined are areas where a lot of information is missing, from the point of view of the single individual. Individuals possess experience-based knowledge of workplace conditions and daily practice. Separate from that is a rhetorical sphere, and a set of regulations whose means and methods of application are seldom clear and simple. The law is formal and abstract, whereas working life – with its differences between social groups, and injustices including unwarranted pay differences – is something real and concrete. Not even when the law is applied to the well-defined category of individuals with unjustifiably low pay do they receive relevant information. In short, there is not only a lack of knowledge among affected individuals, but also a failure to convey information about the provisions and application of the law. Certain pay-setting principles and components can become increasingly invisible, while other parts become more and more clear. It is therefore important to make visible such components of the process as job evaluation, and assessment of credentials and the establishment of market value if the objectives of the legislation for greater equality are to be realized.

NOTES

1. Equal value is defined as follows: 'A job is regarded as being equal in value to another job if, based on an assessment of the nature and demands of the job, it can be regarded as having value equal to the other job. The assessment of the demands of the job shall be made with the use of various criteria relating to knowledge, skill, responsibility and strain.' It is further

specified that, when assessing the nature of the job, it is the working conditions that are to be considered.

2. It is important to note that the difference or agreement between average and evaluated salary is not a real phenomenon. A 'correct' level can be determined if the employer and the employee's union can agree that a given job is assigned the proper salary in relation to the requirements of the job. If such an agreement can be reached, other salaries can be determined by reference to that job, taking differences in job requirements into account.

16. Conclusion: work, life and time in the new economy

**Diane Perrons, Colette Fagan,
Linda McDowell, Kath Ray and Kevin Ward**

One of the primary aims of this book has been critically to assess some of the grand ideas that permeate social and economic theory about work, life and time in the new economy through detailed studies of different countries in Northern and Western Europe and the United States. The chapters have focused on different aspects of the relationships between changing working patterns and the complexities of organizing social reproduction as growing numbers of women move into or are obliged to look for waged work, while still taking primary responsibility for caring for dependants. Starting with the organization of work, each section has added a new layer of complexity, moving from the general issues raised by work–family coordination or reconciliation – what is often called work–life balance in the UK – to more specific questions about gender divisions of labour within households and the logistics of managing paid work and caring in particular places. The final substantive section of the book examined the development, application and limitations of equalities policies through specific examples. In different ways however all the chapters identified policy issues that need to be addressed if greater gender equity is to be achieved rather than undermined by the particular configurations of the new economy in different nation states.

The purpose of this concluding chapter is to draw out some of the theoretical and conceptual issues that have emerged in this collection with an emphasis on understanding the nationally differentiated picture of work, life and time found in Northern and Western Europe and the United States. The aim is to highlight and draw lessons from those national policies that are more progressive from the perspective of gender equity. We emphasize the key role played by the state and different regulatory regimes that shape current economic trajectories as they unfold in different countries and challenge claims that the prevailing global neo-liberal order is inevitable. Our arguments draw inspiration, in particular, from the feminist literature on comparative welfare and gender regimes that have explored the ways in which institutional

259

configurations shape national variations in gender relations and the extent of inequalities associated with women's care-providing roles (see for example Lewis, 1997a; Sainsbury, 1994).

The chapter begins by outlining a notion of gender equity. It then draws out some of the findings from the case studies and reflects on their contribution towards the achievement of greater gender equity and their success in meeting women's practical and strategic gender interests. Our concept of gender equity rests on the recognition that different groups of women (and men) potentially have different gender interests. The social relations of class and race may differentiate women's interests in particular circumstances. We utilize Maxine Molyneux's (1985) notion of the distinction between 'practical' and 'strategic' gender interests, recognizing that policies that may be in women's short-term interests ameliorating certain dimensions of difference or inequality may not in the longer term alter the structures of inequality. Here transformative policies that reshape the distribution of opportunities are necessary to address women's strategic gender needs. Further, we take a wider focus than that implied by a narrow 'sameness' model of equality, which implies essentially similar roles for men and women, and suggest that gender equality and gender difference have to be thought about separately for both men and women, allowing a wider range of criteria to be used for defining more equitable arrangements between the genders (see Fraser, 1997: 45–8).

GENDER EQUALITY, GENDER EQUITY AND THE STATE

Gender equality is an established part of the policy agenda in all the countries addressed in this volume. The profile of gender issues has been raised in the European Union by developments in the employment policy agenda since the adoption of the European Employment Strategy (EES) in 1997 and, in particular, since the target of raising the rate of women's employment participation in the EU to 60 per cent in 2010 was set by the Lisbon summit. The EES includes the introduction of a commitment to gender mainstreaming as a means to promote gender equality, in line with the EU Strategy for Gender Equality (EC, 2000) that followed from the Global Platform for Action adopted at the fourth conference on Women in Beijing in 1995. While the EU has had an explicit undertaking to promote equality between men and women since the original founding treaty[1] this new strategy has a dual-track approach, introducing gender mainstreaming alongside the existing approach of specific equal opportunities actions to address areas of particular concern. Gender mainstreaming requires that a gender perspective be adopted in the design and evaluation of all policies and programmes, so that 'before decisions are taken, an analysis is made of the effects on women and men respectively' (EC, n.d.).

Such policies require an understanding of gender equality. The following definition is taken from an EU document that provides a guide to gender impact assessment:

> By gender equality we mean that all human beings be free to develop their personal abilities and make choices without limitations set by strict gender roles; that the different behaviour, aspirations and needs of women and men are equally valued and favoured. Formal (de jure) equality is only a first step towards material (de facto) equality. Unequal treatment and incentive measures (positive action) may be necessary to compensate for past and present discrimination. Gender differences may be influenced by other structural differences, such as race/ethnicity and class. These dimensions (and others, such as age, disability, marital status and sexual orientation) may also be relevant to your assessment. (EC, n.d.: 3)

This broad understanding of gender equality proposed by the EU is an advance on earlier thinking which both tended to see women (and men) as an undifferentiated category and largely restricted interventions to the economic realm. New definitions to encompass a broader arena of daily activities, institutions and regulations that define gender relations are also now dominant in theoretical work on gender. Thus the US political theorist Nancy Fraser (1997: 45) has defined gender equality as a 'complex notion comprising a plurality of (seven) distinct normative principles'. These are: anti-poverty, anti-exploitation, income equality, leisure-time equality, equality of respect, anti-marginalization and anti-androcentrism.

The inclusion of anti-marginalization and anti-androcentrism as normative principles suggests that equality will not be attainable if the traditional version of a male breadwinner, female caregiver model persists and women remain isolated in the domestic sphere. Thus current definitions of equality, including that in the EU's Strategy for Gender Equality, must go beyond parity in employment participation rates or a narrowing of the gender pay gap. This is reflected in part in the EU's widening area of competencies, extending to social as well as economic policy issues. This extended scope is clearly apparent in five fields for action set out in the strategy document: promoting gender equality in economic life; promoting equal participation and representation; promoting equal access and full enjoyment of social rights for women; promoting gender equality in civil life; and changing gender roles and overcoming stereotypes (EC, 2000b). Such a commitment, together with the adoption of gender mainstreaming, indicates that at least in policy discourses, gender issues have moved from the margin to centre stage. In principle, gender equality is no longer just a remit for the Employment, Social Affairs and Equal Opportunities Directorate of the European Commission; other Directorates such as Information Society and Media and Regional Policy are now required to pay attention to the gender impact of their policies.

The reason for the strengthening of gender issues is not entirely clear given that there is little evidence of widespread feminist campaigning in Europe. It may simply mirror broader international tendencies following Beijing, although as we note below there is little evidence that gender mainstreaming has taken root in policy debates in the USA. This reveals the uneven global influence of such initiatives (Hafner-Burton and Pollack, 2002). It may reflect a growing Nordic influence on the EU Equality Strategy with the membership of Finland and Sweden since 1995, both of which have a longer history of progressive gender equality strategies. A more instrumental explanation is that parts of the gender equality strategy have been mobilized to help secure the target of expanding female employment as a necessary condition for meeting other identified EU policy objectives such as the development of a 'knowledge society' or to address the economic implications of ageing and fertility decline. Indeed evaluations of the evidence to date suggest that the commitment to gender mainstreaming remains fragile and has a problematic emphasis on employment numbers rather than quality of jobs (Rubery et al., 2004). Whatever the motivation, these developments in the EU policy agenda help to shape national policies, and in turn political and economic developments in the national arenas feed into the EU agenda. This articulation of different realms of governance contributes to the institutional context within which individuals and households make choices in relation to working patterns and care.

In the United States by contrast, gender mainstreaming has not taken root in policy discourse of either the government or feminist campaigning bodies and policy institutes.[2] The neo-liberal political agenda, which has hardened since 2001 under President Bush, clearly creates a more hostile environment than the generally more interventionist political frameworks of the EU (Hafner-Burton and Pollack, 2002). Thus in the US there have been a number of challenges to previous improvements in women's rights: the legality of affirmative action in university admissions policies for example has been called into question in court cases and attempts have been made to revoke abortion rights (American Association for Affirmative Action, 2003; National Organisation for Women, 2005). Further, although the 1996 welfare reform introduced by President Clinton has resulted in increased employment rates, poverty has also risen among low-waged workers and the impact of the reform has been particularly harsh on single mothers and black families (Institute for Women's Policy Research, 2003). There are other indicators that women are losing ground in the US: the long-term increase in women's labour force participation rates has stalled since the official end of the recession in November 2001, and the gender wage gap has widened (Institute for Women's Policy Research, 2004).

In the EU, despite potential contradictions between economic and social policies, what is clear is that gender inequality is taken seriously in policy thinking, reflecting continuing adherence to the distinctive European Social

Model in some spheres, including employment regulation. The degree of commitment however varies between member states, reinforced by the current political emphasis on using the 'soft' approach, the Open Method of Coordination (OMC), rather than the legal requirements of Directives. Nonetheless the structural indicators and targets of the OMC provide useful benchmarks against which to assess current policies and indicate a relatively distinct European position on gender equality in contrast to the United States.

The UK is perhaps the exception among the EU members, more similar in many aspects of policy to the USA than to European Social Model, especially in terms of the emphasis on economic competitiveness and labour market flexibility. However the UK differentiates its position from the US by seeking to combine 'flexibility and fairness' (Brown, 2003, para 277).[3] It might be argued then that the UK demonstrates partial commitment the European Social Model by, for example, extending maternity, paternity and parental leave and yet retaining its opt-out from the Working Time Directive. In practical terms this means that living standards for many people, especially low-income families in the UK, are higher than in the US (Ehrenreich, 2005; Toynbee, 2005) but lower than those of other EU countries with similar levels of GDP, in for example the longer hours worked and the greater incidence of child poverty in the UK.

CURRENT PATTERNS OF WORK IN THE NEW ECONOMY – A MEANS FOR PROMOTING GENDER EQUITY?

As we have documented in this volume, a marked shift in working patterns and a changing gender composition of employment is evident in Europe and the US. The temporal and spatial boundaries of paid work have widened and working patterns have become more varied and flexible. Employment is becoming more feminized and as a consequence social reproduction and ways of managing work and life have become more complex, generating growing interest in family-friendly or work–life balance policies. These general trends are evident in many countries in Northern and Western Europe and in the United States but are not uniform. They develop within different institutional settings which shape outcomes and choices within prevailing cultural traditions and welfare regimes. Thus it is important not to assume that similar terms capture the same changes or policy initiatives. First, there is considerable variation in working hours between different countries – the UK and the US have the most varied patterns (see Bishop, 2004; Fagan, 2004; Presser, this volume). Extending the boundaries of the conventional working day and week and widening the range of work schedules extends the scope for labour market participation. Thus the new working patterns may meet women's practical gender interests by providing greater opportunities for paid employment for those with continuing caring responsibilities. However some of these forms of work – the highly flexible short part-time hours worked in the UK or US in the evening or at the weekend for example – offer little more than this. The range of jobs is restricted, opportunities for career progression limited, and in the UK part-time work has a high pay penalty (Manning and Petrongolo, 2004). These forms of employment generally mean that the traditional patterns of responsibility for domestic labour and childcare remain untouched.

In countries where affordable childcare provision is limited these new working patterns tend to result in 'serial parenting' in dual-parent households. In the US for example it has been shown that when men work non-standard hours and their partners work a standard day, men are more likely to take on more household tasks (Presser, this volume). Similar findings have been reported from a six- country EU study (Perrons, 1999). In countries where the levels of formal childcare provision are higher, in France for example, a wider range of work schedules is feasible for parents looking after young children. However even here parents face coordination problems as the opening hours of crèches do not generally match flexible working times and so create problems for those who work non-standard hours. The mismatch between working hours and service provision was also addressed in the City Times studies in the chapters by Boulin and Morris and Pillinger (this volume). France has also introduced a reduced working time (RWT) law (the 'Aubry law') which may improve work–life balance for working parents. Its actual effect however depends on how the reduction is implemented. In some firms, the RWT seems to have resulted in a greater number of imposed and non-standard hours, although in the public sector it seems to have reduced working hours and allowed greater negotiation over scheduling. Despite new working patterns there seems to be little change in the domestic division of labour in France, apart from, as in the US, increased interactions between fathers and children (Fagnani and Letablier, this volume).

Several chapters in this book addressed the impact of more varied working hours on partnership stability and child welfare. In the US, Presser found that couples with children working non-standard hours, especially night work, experienced more stress and higher rates of marital instability. Flexible working allows women, typically the main carers, to combine paid work and domestic responsibilities rather than promote greater sharing of care between women and men, except for enforced periods when women are in the work-place and men are at home with the children. Equating flexible hours with family-friendly policies is therefore not necessarily appropriate as flexible working has ambiguous impacts and may do little to enhance gender equity in or out of the workplace. Flexible working under different policy regimes however may be more beneficial. Although in many European countries a higher proportion of the workforce work standard hours (between 35 and 40 a week) (Bishop, 2004), flexibility is achieved through reduced working days for example, or more generous leave arrangements in terms of time and in terms of being paid. These options initially were developed to assist parents but have now been extended to those responsible for caring for elderly dependants in some countries.

The Nordic countries, Sweden in particular, are positive models here, with generous leave arrangements (in terms of the time allocated and flexibility in how it is taken as well as good financial support) plus extensive childcare services. Here the 'care conundrum' is largely resolved by the state, rather than relying on market mechanisms as the UK has so far chosen to do.[4] Even so, rather than a fundamental restructuring of the gender divisions, employment remains highly gender-segregated, especially in care work, and women still do most of the domestic labour, as well as making time adjustments to do so. Nonetheless the Nordic model has delivered better services and conditions than many other nation states, meeting several of the criteria that measure gender equity. In these countries there is a relatively small gender gap in terms of employment participation rates and working hours, a relatively narrow wage structure, and so a relatively narrow gender pay gap. A large proportion of the continuing gender pay gap is accounted for by employment segregation. There have also been improvements in measures introduced to increase fathers' involvement in parenting (see Brandth and Kvande, this volume).

Other aspects of changing work patterns relate to intensity and insecurity. Quantitative and qualitative data indicate that life has become more pressured both in work and across the work–life divide. Workplace data show that work has become more intense, especially in the UK. In comparison with the EU12, UK workers experienced the highest increase in work intensity with workers in the restructured public sector expressing the greatest overall increase (Burchell, this volume). These changes however were most pronounced in the early 1990s and future trends are not clear. Crompton and Brockmann (this volume) also examined work intensity and showed that women with career aspirations working in managerial and professional occupations experienced higher levels of work–life stress compared to men in similar positions and to women and men in routine and manual forms of work. However men with career aspirations in these routine and manual occupations also reported high levels of stress, in part because the long hours required prior to and following promotion reduced their capacity to meet caring obligations.

These trends in the restructuring of work patterns and increasing work pressures and insecurities have occurred in the context of changing industrial relations. In the UK trade union membership has declined sharply: less than half the workforce is now represented by a union. In the past, trade unions played an important role in ensuring and protecting career progression in traditional, especially male working-class occupations and their decline leaves this group of workers with reduced bargaining power. The extent of trade union decline is less marked in continental Europe and the positions of many regularly employed people are protected by stronger collective bargaining arrangements than in the UK or the US. The scope and coverage of trade union protection however is often less well developed in the service sector than in traditional male-dominated manufacturing industries, leaving many female-dominated occupations underprotected (Rubery and Fagan, 1995).

Further, while the individualization of wage settlements is less common in continental Europe it is not unknown, even in the Nordic States. In Sweden for example, where a requirement to monitor gender inequality in pay is enshrined within the Equal Opportunities Act, a pay gap is still evident, even within the public sector, in part a consequence of the introduction of individualized performance payments, made on top of collectively negotiated rates. Gonas et al. (this volume) showed that within the university sector in Sweden unwarranted pay differences between men and women arose from these merit awards, a practice that disadvantaged women, in part because men bargained more forcefully on their own behalf. Similarly in Denmark, an individualized component in public sector pay acts to widen the gender pay gap (PEP, 2003).

New forms of work, shaped by national and supranational contexts, provide the context within which individuals and households negotiate the division of their time between childcare and waged work, with long, unpredictable or insecure work schedules of jobs and careers for many in the new economy. These decisions are shaped both by structural factors – class and race – which affect access to childcare, and by normative ideas about gender roles and identity which are shaped by local circumstances as well as national ideologies and policies (see Duncan, this volume). Long-standing and persistent normative ideas about what constitutes good mothering mean that despite the demise of other traditional values in increasingly individualized societies (Beck, 1992), men rarely face the same complex dilemmas and choices as women (Hardill and van Loon; Brandth and Kvande, this volume). It seems that households where both parents work on a full-time basis have higher levels of reported stress than in one-and-a-half earner parent households. This latter group however has correspondingly lower earnings (Crompton and Brockman, this volume). While some people may decide that working long hours is not fulfilling and others may be able to afford the luxury of walking away from a pressurized lifestyle (Fisher, this volume), many low-income workers, single parents among them, have little choice and often have to work non-standard hours irrespective of their preferences.

As we noted, new working times may extend the temporal and spatial boundaries of paid employment opening up new possibilities for all parents to join the labour market, but at the same time lead to complex and time-pressured lives, sometimes involving complicated scheduling arrangements and serial parenting. These pressures are often aggravated in large cities where distance between services and activities may mean that the simple tasks of daily life – going to work, taking children to childcare and shopping – takes longer than in smaller places (Jarvis, 2005). The findings from the studies on 'City times' and e-governance offer some possible solutions but also highlight limitations (Walsh et al., this volume). Studies from Italy, France (Jean-Yves Boulin, this volume) and the UK (Morris and Pillinger, this volume) show that local initiatives, especially new working schedules for employees and longer opening hours for public services, may be developed in ways that widen access to these services and activities necessary for individual and collective reproduction and at the same time meet their own employees wishes for more flexible hours.

Harmonization policies to match the interests of employees, employers and consumers require imaginative thinking however as well as cooperation between unions, employers and workers. And the demand for expanded opening hours to accommodate the consumption preferences of these flexible workers might exacerbate class inequalities in working patterns as low-paid workers in retail and other consumer services are asked to work longer or more fragmented and antisocial hours. Such policy initiatives possibly may meet both economic objectives for greater productivity and practical gender interests (in the sense of allowing those with caring responsibilities, still disproportionately women, to manage their work–life balance) but further research is needed to establish whether such policies might also meet strategic gender interests. Here greater equity in the total working times undertaken by women and men is an essential criterion.

STATE POLICIES, GENDER EQUITY IN EMPLOYMENT AND THE GENDERED DIVISION OF DOMESTIC LABOUR

By adopting a comparative perspective, this collection has highlighted the significance of the regulatory frameworks within which people make their decisions. Statutory workplace regulations play an important role in shaping individual and household choices. In general terms Social Democratic welfare regimes provide a more coordinated set of policy measures to promote gender equity and so have a positive impact on work–life balance policies and gender equity. Thus they contribute towards the realization of women's strategic gender interests more effectively than policies adopted in other welfare regimes. Relying on employment measures is more common in for example conser-vative 'male breadwinner' regimes such as Germany or in neo-liberal regimes. This may promote increases in female employment but tends to leave gender inequalities largely unchanged. While the UK government falls into this last group of regimes and broadly adopts a 'light' regulatory touch, the devolved administrations of Wales, Scotland and Northern Ireland have different approaches. In Wales for example the National Assembly has accepted a 'duty to promote equality', adopting gender mainstreaming as its mechanism. This has begun to have an impact on the running of the Assembly and on public appointments (Rees, this volume). Elsewhere in Europe, a range of other schemes is now showing results. In Norway for example, the 'take it or lose it' scheme in relation to 'Daddy leave', which has been in place for a number of years, is now producing almost 100 per cent take-up rates, while the previous more flexible arrangements allowing couples to arrange leave between themselves reinforced the status quo (Brandth and Kvande, this volume).

Whilst a strict regulatory environment is no guarantee of gender equity in the economic sphere it is more likely to have positive effects than an appeal to employers' business interests. Despite this, in the UK the DTI (2003a) has emphasized the business case for labour market flexibility as part of its work–life balance campaign, launched to encourage employers to adopt such measures on a voluntary basis. As Rees (this volume) has showed, the business case inclusion of women can have purchase. It has been accepted by a number of major global organizations that are introducing new measures for women in science, technology and engineering, facilitated by the Women and Science Unit of the European Commission. However similar commitments made by corporations in the past have proved somewhat transitory, as support tends to fluctuates with the state of the economy (Bruegel and Perrons, 1995). It is also a strategy that is more likely to be seen as appropriate for increasing women's participation in highly skilled occupations and professional employment. More research is needed to determine the extent to which strategies for widening employment access are simply rhetorical, whether they are pragmatic responses to specific shortages, and to what extent their scope might be extended to include women in lower-skilled jobs within their remit if the European Union is to achieve its goal of real gender equity.

Several important questions raised by the contributors to this volume have not yet been fully answered. They are for future research to address. Key areas needing more work include explorations of why gender inequalities persist or are reshaped in new forms and patterns of working, and why so little change seems to have taken place in the domestic division of labour. Further, more research is necessary to identify the processes driving inequality, particularly continuing employment segregation and the lower monetary rewards in jobs where women are overrepresented.

It is clear that many of the broad patterns of gender inequity are common, at least across the countries included in this volume, although as we have noted, different policy instruments have different degrees of success. Although women are overrepresented in low-paying forms of work in all these nation-states, the extent of their well-being also depends on the level of overall inequality in the countries concerned. But as we showed in Chapter 1, in the new economy there is a general tendency for inequality and social divisions to widen. Earnings inequalities have been widening in many countries in Northern and Western Europe including in the Nordic states (Esping-Andersen, 2004), although the extent of inequality and the duration of poverty is moderated by state policies and so varies considerably between states.

Persistent poverty and inequality is most marked in the UK and the US where 'welfare to work' programmes based on the implicit assumption that unemployment and poverty are attributable to individual failings have been introduced. But here too there is a distinction between the US and the UK. The 1996 welfare reform in the US ended all entitlements to cash support for single mothers and their children, replacing cash aid with limited assistance to mothers to find a job and for childcare, but only a small proportion of women are eligible. Further, entering low-wage employment is not a solution to poverty: the average wage of women leaving welfare is far less than a living wage (Ehrenreich, 2005). Although the UK has modelled its own welfare to work policies on the US programme, it also combines elements of the European Social Model. Tax credits are paid to all low-income workers, with additional tax credits and some support for childcare for parents. Thus those in low-wage work in the UK remain poor, but seldom face destitution as in the US. In addition, at present lone parents are not compelled to take employment until their youngest child is of school age. Furthermore in accordance with the European Social Model maternity, paternity and parental leave are statutory rights, although in terms of paid leave they are ungenerous in comparison to elsewhere in the EU (although more generous than in the US).[5]

The UK has an additional number of problems from the perspective of gender equity. There is a high incidence of low-wage jobs in which women are over-represented and although a minimum wage now exists it is only 30 per cent of average wages. Apart from Spain (28 per cent) this is the lowest proportion in the European Union (Stewart, 2005). Further, the tax credits outlined above support rather than challenge the payment of poverty wages. The UK government does not want to 'interfere' directly with the 'market' determination of earnings despite rising earnings inequalities since the late 1970s. In this respect, paradoxically, it is actually following the European Employment Strategy that refers to the progressive elimination of gender gaps in the labour market but argues that:

> The underlying factors of the gender gaps in unemployment and in pay should be addressed and targets on the reduction of such gaps should be achieved as a result, *without calling into question the principle of wage differentiation according to*

productivity and labour market situation. (paragraph 16 of the revised employment guidelines 2003; EC, 2003a: L197/15; emphasis added)[6]

This statement shows that when market and social objectives conflict, it is usually market goals that are paramount. This statement and policies based upon it fail to recognize that the market is not independent from social influences. Wage determination itself is a gendered process: the jobs in which women are disproportionately concentrated are underpaid for the very reason that it is women who do them. Thus although in parts of EU discourse the market is represented as natural and inalienable, it is hardly neutral in its effects. Challenging the low pay of women's jobs is essential if gender inequality is to be addressed, especially as segregation in waged work remains endemic. Commodified care work for example, an expanding sector in the new economy, remains almost entirely feminized. In some Nordic countries such work has been professionalized and is better paid as it is recognized here that care work is an essential social investment rather than a social cost in direct response to employment needs (see Nyberg, this volume). If gender mainstreaming is taken seriously in broader economic debates about budgets and macroeconomic investment policies, then it may become a lever for a wider acknowledgement that care is productive work, creating the potential for its re-evaluation.[7] But caring is not only 'work'. The powerful moral belief in the value of caring for others 'for love' must also be recognized. A re-evaluation of care and employment and a reorganization of their gendered allocation and the associated financial rewards is an essential element of a strategy to achieve gender equity.

NOTES

1. The 1957 Treaty of Rome and the subsequent Treaty of Amsterdam (Articles 2 and 3).
2. A search for the mention of 'gender mainstreaming' or an equivalent term found that this concept does not feature in the policy statements and objectives and associated resources posted on the following websites: the US government's Department of Labor (www.dol.gov), the department's Women's Bureau (www.dol.gov/wb) and the Equal Employment Opportunities Commission (www.eeoc.gov/); the National Organization for Women (www.now.org) which is the largest organization of feminist activists in the US, or the Institute for Women's Policy Research (www.iwpr.org) which is a major US public policy research institute on gender equality.
3. Thus Gordon Brown, the Chancellor of the Exchequer, in the Budget Speech argued that 'the modern route – indeed, I believe, the only route – to full employment for all regions and nations is to combine flexibility with fairness' (Brown, 2003, Para. 281) having pointed out that the UK has 'now agreed to submit to the EU jobs review our employment strategy that could help Europe's 15 million unemployed. Britain does lead in job creation, in tax credits that make work pay, and this week – learning from Europe – we have introduced new maternity rights and the first ever paternity pay; and in striking the balance between dynamism and social standards, our position is that no change to European regulations, like the working time directive, should risk British job creation' (Brown, 2003, Para. 277).

4. The revised National Childcare Strategy (PBR, 2004) and the proposals for increasing care provision before and after school in the 2005 Budget may have a positive impact in this respect but at the time of writing (2005) these commitments and their consequences remain to be seen.
5. Only about 60 per cent of American workers are eligible for maternity leave, small firms being free to make their own policies. Women manage by using a combination of sick leave, vacation or personal days, and short-term disability, which is paid at a fraction of the original salary (Burgess, 2005).
6. This paragraph has been dropped from the new draft of the revised employment guidelines (September 2005) but the tension between flexibility and gender equity nevertheless remains.
7. See Diane Elson (1998) for an account of this perspective.

Bibliography

Afsa, C., P. Biscourp and P. Pollet (2003), 'La baisse de la durée du travail entre 1995 et 2001', *INSEE Première*, 881, Janvier.

AKU, *Arbetskraftsundersökningarna* (Labor Force Surveys), (1990, 1993, 2000), Stockholm: SCB (Statistics Sweden).

Althusser, L. (1971), *Lenin and Philosophy and Other Essays*, New York: New Left Books.

American Association for Affirmative Action (2003), 'AAAA Statement on the University of Michigan cases', www.affirmativeaction.org/UofM-Cases-2003.html

Anastacio, J., B. Gidley, L. Hart, M. Keith, M. Mayo and U. Kowarziki (2000), *Reflecting Realities: Participants' Perspectives on Integrated Communities and Sustainable Development*, Bristol: Policy Press.

Anker, R. (1998), *Gender and Jobs: Sex Segregation of Occupations in the World*, Geneva: International Labour Organization.

Anxo, D. and J.-Y. Boulin (2005), *A New Organisation of Working Time throughout Working Life*, Dublin: European Foundation.

Arnuad, J. (2003), 'Are the stability pact and the Lisbon Strategy compatible?' Notre Europe Seminar on Budgetary Discipline and Macro-Economic Policy in Europe, 8 March, http://www.notre-europe.asso.fr/IMG/pdf/Semi18-en.pdf.

Audit Commission (2003), *A Review of Services for Disabled Children and their Families*, London: Audit Commission.

Baklien, Bergljot, AnneLise Ellingsæter and Lars Gulbrandsen (2001), *Evaluering av kontantstøttereformen (Evaluation of the cash-for-care reform)*, Oslo: Research Council of Norway.

Bailly, J.P. (rapporteur) (2002), *Le temps des villes. Pour une concordance des temps dans la cité.*, Avis et rapports du CES, Ed. Journeaux Officiels.

Bailly, J.P. and E. Heurgon (2001), *Nouveaux rythmes urbains: quels transports?* Datar: Editions de l'Aube.

Bailyn, Lotte (1993), *Breaking the Mold*, New York: Free Press.

Batstone, E. and S. Gourlay (1986), *Unions, Unemployment and Innovation*, Oxford: Blackwell.

Baude, A. (1992), *Kvinnans plats på jobbet (A Women's Place at Work)*, Stockholm: SNS förlag.

Bauman, Z. (2001), *The Individualized Society*, Cambridge: Polity.

Beck, U. (1992), *Risk Society: Towards a New Modernity*, London: Sage.

Beck, U. (2000), *The Brave New World of Work*, Cambridge: Polity Press.

Beck, U. (2002), 'Zombie categories; interview with Ulrich Beck', in U. Beck and E. Beck-Gernsheim, *Individualisation*, London: Sage.

Beck, U. and E. Beck-Gernsheim (2002), *Individualization: Institutionalized Individualism and its Social and Political Consequences*, London: Sage.

Beck, U., A. Giddens and S. Lash (1994), *Reflexive Modernization: Politics, Tradition and Aesthetics in the Modern Social Order*, Cambridge: Polity Press.

Becker, P.E. and P. Moen (1999), 'Scaling back: dual-earner couples' work–family strategies', *Journal of Marriage and the Family*, 61, 995–1007.

Beers, T. (2000), 'Flexible schedules and shift work: replacing the "9-to-5" workday?', *Monthly Labor Review*, 123 (6), 33–9.

Bekkengen, L. (2002), *Man får välja. – om föräldraskap och föräldraledighet i arbetsliv och familjeliv*, Malmö: Liber Förlag.

Bellamy, C. (2002), 'From automation to knowledge management: modernizing British government with ICTs', *International Review of Administrative Sciences*, 68 (2), 213–30.

Bennett, A. and S. Smith-Gavine (1987), 'The Percentage Utilisation of Labour Index: (PUL)', in D. Bosworth and D. Heathfield (eds), *Working Below Capacity*, London: Macmillan.

Berg, P., A.L. Kalleberg and E. Appelbaum (2003), 'Balancing work and family: the role of high-commitment environments', *Industrial Relations*, 42 (2), 168–87.

Bergqvist, C., A. Borchorst, A.-D. Christensen, V. Ramstedt-Silén, N. Raaum and A. Styrkásdóttir (eds) (1999), *Equal Democracies? Gender Policies in the Nordic Countries*, Oslo: Scandinavian University Press.

Bergqvist, C. and A. Nyberg (2001), 'Den svenska barnomsorgsmodellen – kontinuitet och förändring under 1990-talet', in Marta Szebehely (ed.), *Välfärdstjänster i omvandling*, SOU 2001:52, Stockholm: Fritzes.

Bergqvist, C. and A. Nyberg (2002), 'Welfare state restructuring and childcare in Sweden', in Sonya Michel and Rianne Mahon (eds), *Child Care Policy at the Crossroads: Gender and Welfare State Restructuring*, New York: Routledge.

Bhavnani, K., J. Foran and P. Kurian (2003), *Feminist Futures: Re-imagining Women, Culture and Development*, London: Zed Books.

Bielinski, H., G. Bosch and A. Wagner (2002), *Working Time Preferences in Sixteen European Countries*, Dublin: European Foundation for the Improvement of Living and Working Conditions.

Bishop, K. (2004), 'Working time patterns in the UK, France, Denmark and Sweden: analysis of usual hours reported in four European countries with different institutional arrangements', *Labour Market Trends*, 112 (3), 112–22.

Blagojević, M., M. Bundele, A. Burkhardt, M. Calloni, E. Ergma, J. Glover, D. Groó, H. Havelková, D. Mladenič, E.H. Olesky, N. Srettenova, M.F. Tripsa, D. Velichová and A. Zvinkliene (2004), *Waste of Talents: Turning Private Struggles into a Public Issue. Women and Science in the Enwise Countries*, Brussels: Directorate General for Research, European Commission, and http://europa.eu.int/comm/research/science-society/pdf/02_enwise_report_intro-140704.pdf.

Blair, S. (1993), 'Employment, family, and perceptions of marital quality among husbands and wives', *Journal of Family Issues*, 14 (2), 189–212.

Blossfeld, H.-P. and S. Drobnic (eds) (2001), *Careers of Couples in Contemporary Societies*, Oxford: Oxford University Press.

Boessenkool, A. and A. Hegewisch (2004), *Working Time for Working Families: Europe and the United States Report*, Washington, DC: American University Washington College of Law, the Washington Office of the Friedrich Ebert Foundation and the Hans Böckler Foundation and at http://www.wcl.american.edu/gender/worklifelaw/publications/Working%20Time%20conference%20report.pdf].

Bonfiglioli, S. (2004), 'L'Italie met en place des politiques de temps urbains pour un rapprochement entre vie privée et vie professionnelle', in E. Istace, M. Laffut, R. Plasman and C. Ruyters (eds), *Sphères privée et professionnelle: vers une recomposition des actions*, Paris: De Boeck.

Bonfiglioli, S., M. Mareggi (a cura di), (1997), *Il tempo e la città fra natura e storia. Atlante di progetti sui tempo della città*, Rome: Urbanistica Quaderni, n°12, Inu Edizioni.

Bogen, K. and P. Joshi (2001), 'Bad work or good move: the relationship of part-time and nonstandard work schedules to parenting and child behavior in working poor families', paper presented at the Conference on Working Poor Families: Coping as Parents and Workers, held at NIH, Bethesda, MD, 13–14 November.

Boisard, P., D. Cartron, M. Gollac and A. Valeyre (2003), *Time and Work: Work Intensity*, Dublin: European Foundation for the Improvement of Living and Working Conditions.

Boulin, J.-Y. (1999), *New Paths to Working Time Policy*, ETUI: Brussels.

Boulin, J.-Y., F. Godard and P. Dommergues (eds) (2002), *La nouvelle aire du temps*, Datar: Editions Aube.

Boulin, J.-Y. and R. Hoffman (1999), 'The conceptualisation of working time over the whole life cycle', in J.-Y. Boulin and R. Hoffmans (eds), *New Paths in Working Time Policy*, Brussels: European Trade Union Institute.

Boulin, J.-Y. and U. Mückenberger (2002), *La ville à mille temps*, Datar: Editions Aube.

Bourdieu, P. (1984), *Distinction: A Social Critique of the Judgement of Taste*, Cambridge: Harvard University Press.

Bourdieu, P. (1998), 'Utopia of endless exploitation: the essence of neoliberalism', *Le Monde Diplomatique*, December, translated by Jeremy J. Shapiro http://www.forum-global.de/soc/bibliot/b/bessenceneolib.htmlast.

Boyer, D., L. Crompagne and C. Vérité (2004), 'Les 35 heures dans les CAF', *L'Essentiel*, 25, Paris: CNAF,

Brandth, B. and E. Kvande (2002), 'Reflexive fathers: negotiating parental leave and working life', *Gender, Work and Organization*, 9 (2), 186–203.

Brandth, B. and E. Kvande (2003), *Fleksible fedre* (Flexible Fathers), Oslo: Universitetsforlaget.

Brannen, J. (1998), 'Employment and family lives', in E. Drew, R. Emerek and E. Mahon (eds), *Women, Work and the Family in Europe*, London: Routledge.

Brannen, J. (2005), 'Time and the Negotiation of work–family boundaries: autonomy or illusion?', *Time and Society*, 14 (1), 113–31.

Brayfield, April A. (1995), 'Juggling jobs and kids: the impact of employment schedules on fathers' caring for children', *Journal of Marriage and the Family*, 57, 321–32.

Breen, R. (1997), 'Risk, recommodification and stratification', *Sociology*, 31 (3), 473–89.

Brooks, J. (1973), *The Go-Go Years*, New York: Weybright and Talley.

Brousse, C. (1999), 'La répartition du travail domestique entre conjoints reste largement spécialisée et inégale', *France, portrait social, 1999–2000*, Paris: INSEE.

Brown, G. (2003), Hansard Column 277, and 281 9 April http://www.publications.parliament.uk/pa/cm200203/cmhansrd/vo030409/debtext/30409-04.htm#30409-04_spmin1.

Bruegel, I. and D. Perrons (1995), 'The economics of equal opportunities', *Gender, Work and Organisation*, 2 (3), 113–24.

Bunting, M. (2004), *Willing Slaves: How the Overwork Culture is Ruling our Lives*, London: HarperCollins.

Burchell, B.J. and C. Fagan (2004), 'Gender and the intensification of work: evidence from the European Working Conditions Survey', *Eastern Economic Journal*, 30 (4), 627–42.

Burchell, B.J., D. Ladipo and F. Wilkinson (eds) (2002), *Job Insecurity and Work Intensification*, London: Routledge.

Burgess, K. (2005), 'Agitating for change: maternity leave is important for everyone', http://preconception.com/resources/articles/agitating.htm, last accessed 19 June 2005.

Büttner, O., M.-T. Letablier and S. Pennec (2002), 'L'action publique face aux transformations de la famille en France', Rapport de recherche 02, Paris: Centre d'études de l'emploi.

Cabinet Office (1999), *Modernising Government*, London: HMSO.

Carlstein, T., D. Parkes and N. Thrift (eds) (1978), *Timing Space and Spacing Time*, London: Edward Arnold Publishers.

Carnoy, M. (2000), *Sustaining the New Economy: Work, Family, and Community in the Information Age*, New York: Russell Sage Foundation.

Carnoy, M. (2002), *Sustaining the New Economy*, Cambridge, MA: Harvard University Press.

Casper, L.M. (1997), 'My Daddy takes care of me! Fathers as care providers', *Current Population Reports* P70-59 (September), Washington, DC: Census Bureau, US Department of Commerce.

Castells, M. (2000), 'Information and global capitalism', in W. Hutton and A. Giddens (eds), *On the Edge: Living with Global Capitalism*, London: Jonathan Cape.

CFDT (1999), *Le travail en questions*, Paris: CFDT.

Chaney, P. (2004), 'The post-devolution equality agenda: the case of Welsh Assembly's statutory duty to promote equality of opportunity', *Policy and Politics*, 32 (1), 63–77.

Chaney, P. and R. Fevre (2002), *An Absolute Duty: The Equality Policies of the Government of the National Assembly for Wales and their Implementation: July 1999 to January 2002, A Report for the Equal Opportunities Commission, the Disability Rights Commission and the Commission for Racial Equality*, Cardiff: Institute of Welsh Affairs, wales@iwa.org.uk.

Chaney, P. and T. Rees (2004), 'The Northern Ireland Section 75 equality duty: an international perspective', Vol. 2 of E. McLaughlin and N. Faris, *Section 75 Review: The Section 75 Equality Duty – An Operational Review*, London: Northern Ireland Office.

Charlesworth, S. (2000), *A Phenomenology of Working Class Experience*, Cambridge: Cambridge University Press.

Chatriot, A., P. Fridenson and E. Pezet (2003), 'La réduction du temps de travail en France entre réglementation tutélaire et négociation encadrée (1814–1978)', *La Revue de l'IRES*, 42, 9–40.

Chronopost (2001), *Le temps des uns, le temps des autres*, Paris: Chronopost International.

CIPD (2004), *Calling Time on Working Time?* London: Chartered Institute Personnel and Development, <http://www.cipd.co.uk/NR/rdonlyres/4FF9B072-6B03-465F-9C65-8AC3CA5E0247/0/3029worktimeregs.pdf.

Clark, T. and S.M. Lipset (1991), 'Are social classes dying? *International Sociology*, 6 (4), 397–410.

Clarke, J., M. Langan and F. Williams (2001), 'Remaking welfare: the British welfare regime in the 1980s and 1990s', in A. Cochrane, J. Clarke and S. Gewirtz (eds), *Comparing Welfare States*, London: Sage.

Collinson, D. and J. Hearn (1994), 'Naming men as men: implications for work, organisation and management', *Gender, Work and Organization*, 1 (1), 2–22.

Connell, R. (1987), *Gender and Power: Society, the Person and Sexual Politics*, Cambridge: Polity Press.

Cooper, C., P. Liukkonen and S. Cartwright (1996), *Stress Prevention in the Workplace: Assessing the Costs and Benefits to Organisations*, Dublin: European Fund for the Improvement of Living and Working Conditions.

Corbin, A. (1995), *L'avénement des loisirs: 1850–1960*, Paris: Aubier.

Coyle, D. and D. Quah (2002), *Getting the Measure of the New Economy*, London: Isociety, The Work Foundation.

Cressey, P. (2001), 'Evaluation of the Bristol City Council/working time flexibility projects', internal paper, University of Bath.

Crompton, R. (1993, 1998), *Class and Stratification*, Cambridge: Polity Press.

Crompton, R., J. Dennett and A. Wigfield (2003), *Organisations, Careers and Caring*, Bristol: Policy Press.

Crompton, R., F. Devine, M. Savage and J. Scott (eds) (2000), *Renewing Class Analysis*, Blackwell: Oxford.

Crompton, R. and F. Harris (1998), 'Explaining women's employment patterns: orientations to work revisited', *British Journal of Sociology*, 49 (1), 118–36.

Cross, G. (1993), *Time and Money: The Making of Consumer Culture*, New York: Routledge.

Crouch, C. (1999), *Social Change in Western Europe*, Oxford: Oxford University Press.

Czarniawska, Barbara (2004), 'Women in financial services: fiction and more fiction', in K. Knorr Cetina and A. Preda (eds), *The Sociology of Financial Markets*, New York: Oxford Press.

Dahlberg, A. (1984), *Jämställdhetslagens tillämpning. En studie av en kommunal sektor: In Den könsuppdelade arbetsmarknaden. Exempel från kvinnoforskningen vid Arbetslivscentrum*. Stockholm: Arbetslivscentrum.

Dahlberg, A. (1998), *Från ord till handling: Uppfattningar om jämställdhet och kön i tre gotlandsorganisationer*, Gotland: Länsstyrelsen.

Daly, M. and K. Rake (2003), *Gender and the Welfare State. Care, Work and Welfare in Europe and the USA*, Cambridge, UK and Malden, MA, US: Polity Press in association with Blackwell.

Daycare Trust (2000), 'Shift parents left without childcare', *No more Nine to Five: Childcare in a Changing World*, London: Daycare Trust and http://www.daycaretrust.org.uk/NewsNewsDetail.cfm?NewsID=37.

Department of Health (DH) (2001), *Shifting the Balance of Power within the NHS: Securing Delivery*, London: DH.

Department of Health (DH) (2004), *The NHS Improvement Plan: Putting People at the Heart of Public Services*, London: DH.

Department of Health (DH) (2005), 'Improving working lives', http://www.dh.gov.uk/PolicyAndGuidance/HumanResourcesAndTraining/ModelEmployer/ImprovingWorkingLives/fs/en, last accessed June 2005.

Department of Trade and Industry (DTI) (2000), *Work and Parents: Competitiveness and Choice*, Green Paper, London: Stationery Office and http://www2.dti.gov.uk/er/g_paper/index.htm.

Department of Trade and Industry (DTI) (2001), *Work–Life Balance: The Essential Guide to Work–Life Balance*, DTI: London.

Department of Trade and Industry (DTI) (2003a), Worklife Balance website – for information about publications, conferences and case studies, http://www.dti.gov.uk/work-lifebalance/.

Department of Trade and Industry (DTI) (2003b), *The Second DTI Work–Life Balance Study: Employers Attitudes*, DTI: London.

Department of Trade and Industry (DTI)/HM Treasury (2003c), *Balancing Work and Family Life: Enhancing Choice and Support for Parents*, London: Stationery Office.

Department of Trade and Industry (DTI) (2004), 'The Second Work–Life Balance Study: results from employees' survey', DTI Employment Relations Research series No. 27.

Department of Trade and Industry (DTI) in association with the Department for Constitutional Affairs, the Department for Education and Skills and Department for Work and Pensions (2004), *Fairness for All: A New Commission for Equality and Human Rights*, White Paper, London: Stationery Office.

DETR (2000), *Preparing Community Strategies: Government Guidance to Local Authorities*, London: DETR.

Deutsch, F.M. (1999), *Halving It All: How Equally Shared Parenting Works*, Cambridge, MA: Harvard University Press.

Dex, S. and F. Scheibl (1999), 'Business performance and family-friendly policies', *Journal of General Management*, 24 (4), 22–37.

Doogan, K. (2005), 'Long-term employment and the restructuring of the labour market in Europe', *Time and Society*, 14 (1), 65–87.

Downey, G. and M. Fisher (2004), 'The anthropology of capital and the frontiers of ethnography', *Frontiers of Capital: Ethnographic Reflections on the New Economy*, under consideration at Duke University Press.

du Gay, P. (1996), *Consumption and Identity at Work*, London: Sage.

Dumelow, C., P. Littlejohns and S. Griffiths (2000), 'Relation between a career and family life for English hospital consultants: qualitative, semi-structured interview study', *British Medical Journal*, 320 (27), 1437–40.

Duncan, S. (1996), 'The diverse worlds of European patriarchy', in Maria Dolors Garcia-Ramon and Janice Monk (eds), *The Politics of Work and Daily Life*, London and New York: Routledge.

Duncan, S. (2003), 'Mothers, care and employment', CAVA Working Paper, 1, Leeds: University of Leeds, and www.leeds.ac.uk/cava.

Duncan, S. and R. Edwards (1999), *Lone Mothers, Paid Work and Gendered Moral Rationalities*, London: Macmillan.

Duncan, S., R. Edwards, P. Alldred and T. Reynolds (2003), 'Motherhood, paid work, and partnering: values and theories', *Work, Employment and Society*, 17 (2), 309–30.

Duncan, S., R. Edwards, P. Alldred and T. Reynolds (2004), 'Mothers and childcare: policies, values and theories', *Children and Society*, 18 (4), 245–65.

Duncan, S. and D. Smith (2002), 'Geographies of family formations: spatial differences and gender cultures in Britain', *Transactions Institute of British Geographers*, 27 (4), 471–93.

Easen, P., M. Atkins and A. Dyson (2000), 'Inter-professional collaboration and conceptualisations of practice', *Children and Society*, 14, 355–67.

Eaton, S.C. (2003), 'If you can use them: flexibility policies, organisational commitment, and perceived performance', *Industrial Relations*, 42 (2), 145–67.

Eccles, R. and D. Crane (1988), *Doing Deals: Investment Banks at Work*, Cambridge, MA: Harvard Business School Press.

Edwards, P. (2000), 'Late twentieth century workplace relations: class struggle without classes', in R. Crompton, F. Devine, M. Savage and J. Scott (eds), *Renewing Class Analysis*, Oxford: Blackwell.

Egerö, A.-M. (2003), *Tretton perspektiv på lönebildningen. Antologi*, Stockholm: Medlingsinstitutet.

Ehrenreich, B. (1989), *Fear of Falling: The Inner Life of the Middle Class*, New York: Pantheon Books.

Ehrenreich, B. (2005), 'Gender inequality: old patterns, new challenges', Ralph Miliband Lectures on Inequalities: Dimensions and Challenges, LSE, 3 February.

Ehrenreich, B. and A. Hochschild (2003), *Global Women*, London: Granta Books.

Ekberg, J., R. Eriksson and G. Friebel (2004), 'Sharing responsibility? Short- and long-term effects of Sweden's "Daddy-month" reform', Working paper 3/2004, Stockholm: Swedish Institute for Social Research (SOFI), Stockholm University.

Eklund, Klas (2001), *Var ekonomi: en introduction till samhällsekonomi*, Stockholm: Prisma.

Ellingsæter, A.-L. (1999), 'Time and the transformation of work: the industrial time regime in flux', in G. Birkelund (ed.), *Kjønn and arbeid. Nye former for arbeidsliv* (*Gender and Work: New Forms of Working Life*), Rapport 1. Oslo: NFR.

Ellingsæter, A.-L. (2003a), 'The complexity of family policy reform: the case of Norway', *European Societies*, 5 (4), 419–43.

Ellingsæter, A.-L. (2003b), 'Når familiepolitikk ikke virker ... Om kontantstøttereformen and mødres lønnsarbeid' (When family policy does not work ... On the cash for care reform and mothers' paid work), *Tidsskrift for samfunnsforskning*, 44 (4), 499–527.

Elson, D. (1998), 'The economic, the political and the domestic: business, states and households in the organisation of production', *New Political Economy*, 3 (2), 189–208.

Emerek, R. (1998), 'Atypical working time – examples from Denmark', in E. Drew, R. Emerek and E. Mahon (eds), *Women, Work and the Family in Europe*, London: Routledge.

EPF (2004), 'The balancing act: shifting household structure at the root of work life balance issues', newsletter 28 October Washington: Employment Policy Foundation, and http://www.workandfamily.org/newsletters/2004/ba20041028.pdf.

Epstein, C.F., C. Seron, B. Oglensky and R. Sauté (1999), *The Part-time Paradox, Time Norms, Professional Lives, Family and Gender*, New York: Routledge.

Employers for work–life balance (2004), http://www.employersforwork–lifebalance.org.uk/, last accessed June 2005.

Esping-Andersen, G. (1999), *Social Foundations of Post-industrial Economies*, Oxford: Oxford University Press.

Esping-Andersen, G. (2002), *Why We Need a New Welfare State*, Oxford: Oxford University Press.

Esping-Andersen, G. (2004), 'Inequality and the Welfare State in Europe', Ralph Miliband Lectures on Inequalities: Dimensions and Challenges, LSE, December.

Esping-Andersen, G., D. Gallie, A. Hemerijck and J. Myles (2001), 'A new welfare architecture for Europe?' Report submitted to the Belgian Presidency of the European Union, mimeo.

Estrade, M.-A. and V. Ulrich (2003), 'Réduction du temps de travail et réorganisation des rythmes de travail', *Données sociales*, Paris: INSEE.

Etzkowitz, H., C. Kemelgor and B. Uzzi (2000), *Athena Unbound: The Advancement of Women in Science and Technology*, Cambridge: Cambridge University Press.

European Commission (1993), *Growth, Competitiveness, Employment, the Challenges and Ways Forward into the 21st Century*, Luxembourg: Office for the Official Publications of the European Union.

European Commission (2000a), 'Towards a Community Framework Strategy on Gender Equality 2001–2005', Brussels, Communication from the Commission to the Council, the European Parliament, the Economic and Social Committee and the Committee of the Regions.

European Commission (2000b), 'Community Framework Strategy on Gender Equality (2001–2005)', http://europa.eu.int/comm/employment_social/equ_opp/strategy/2_en.html#1.

European Commission (2003a), 'Council Decision on Guidelines for Employment in member States', Official Journal of the European Union, http://europa.eu.int/eur-lex/pri/en/oj/dat/2003/l_197/l_19720030805en00130021.pdf.

European Commission (2003b), *Women in Industrial Research: Analysis of Statistical Data and Good Practices of Companies*, Luxembourg: Office for Official Publications of the European Communities.

European Commission (2003c), *She Figures 2003: Women and Science: Statistics and Indicators*, Luxembourg: Office for Official Publications of the European Communities.

European Commission (2004a), 'Joint Employment Report', Document 7069/04, http://europa.eu.int/comm/employment_social/employment_strategy/report_2003/jer20034_en.pdf.

European Commission (2004b), 'Towards a more dynamic approach to implementing the Lisbon Strategy', http://www.esc.eu.int/publications/pdf/booklets/EESC-2004-001-EN.pdf.

European Commission (2005a), 'Gender Mainstreaming', http://europa.eu.int/comm/employment_social/equ_opp/gms_en.html

European Commission (2005b), *Women in Industrial Research: Speeding up Changes in Europe*, Luxembourg: Office for Official Publications of the European Communities.

European Commission (n.d.), 'A guide to gender impact assessment', http://europa.eu.int/comm/employment_social/equ_opp/gender/gender_en.pdf.

European Parliament (2000), 'Presidency Conclusions', Lisbon European Council, 23 and 24 March, http://www.europarl.en.int/summits/lis1_en.htm.

Eurostat (2002), 'Women and men reconciling work and family life', *Statistics in Focus Population and Social Conditions Theme 3 9/2002*, Luxembourg: Eurostat European Commission.

Eurostat (2004), *How Europeans Spend their Time: Everyday Life of Women and Men 1998–2002*, Luxembourg: Office for Official Publications of the European Communities.

Evans, R. and M. Banton (2001), *Learning from Experience: Involving Black Disabled People in Shaping Services*, Leamington Spa: Council of Disabled People, Warwickshire.

Fagan, C. (2001), 'Time, money and the gender order: work orientations and working-time preferences in Britain', *Gender, Work and Organization*, 8 (3), 239.

Fagan, C. (2004), 'Gender and working-time in industrialized countries: practices and preferences', in J. Messenger (ed.), *Working-time and Workers' Needs and Preferences in Industrialized countries: Finding the Balance*, London: Routledge.

Fagan, C. and B. Burchell (2002), *Gender, Jobs and Working Conditions in the European Union, European Foundation for the Improvement of Living and Working Conditions*, Luxembourg: Office for Official Publications of the European Communities.

Fagan, C., K. Ward, L. McDowell, D. Perrons and K. Ray (2004), 'Schedules of work and family life in Britain: towards a typology', paper presented at the Work, Employment and Society conference, Manchester, 1–3 September.

Fagnani, J. and M.T. Letablier (2004), 'Work and family life balance: the impact of the 35 hour laws in France', *Work, Employment and Society*, 18 (3), 551–72.

Fairris, D. (2004), 'Towards a theory of work intensity', *Eastern Economic Journal*, 30 (4), 587–602.

Families and Work Institute (1998), 'Business work–life study: a sourcebook', www.familiesandwork.org.

Fenton C., H. Bradley and J. West (2003), 'Winners and losers in labour markets: young adults' employment trajectories', Research Report, Swindon: Economic and Research Council, and http://www.regard.ac.uk.

Financial Women's Association (FWA) http://www.fwa.org.

Financial Women's Association Archives (FWA) (1957), *The New Yorker*, 'Talk of the town', FWA clipping.

Financial Women's Association Archives (FWA) (1980s), 'FWA award recipient guidelines', New York City.

Financial Women's Association Archives (FWA) (1981), 'FWA board minutes', New York City, 2 September.

Financial Women's Association Archives (FWA) (1981), 'FWA board minutes', New York City, 4 November.

Financial Women's Association Archives (FWA) (2003), 'FWA Newsletter', New York City, March.

Fisher, Melissa (2003), *Wall Street Women: Gender, Culture and History in Global Finance*, PhD dissertation, Columbia University Department of Anthropology.

Fisher, Melissa (2004), 'Wall Street women's "herstories"', in K. Lipartito and D. Sicilia (eds), *Constructing Corporate America: History, Politics, Culture*, New York: Oxford Press.

Folbre, N. (1994), *Who Pays for the Kids?*, London: Routledge.

Ford, R. (1996), *Childcare in the Balance: How Lone Parents Make Decisions about Paid Work*, London: Policy Studies Institute.

Forrest, R. and A. Murie (1987) ,'The affluent home owner – labour market position and the shaping of housing history', *Sociological Review*, 35 (2), 370–403.

Franco, A. and K. Winqvist (2002), 'Les homes et les femmes concilient travail et vie familiale', Luxembourg: *Statistiques en bref*, Eurostat, theme 3, 9/2002.

Frank, T. (2000), *One Market under God*, New York: Doubleday.

Fransson, S. (2000), *Lönediskriminering*, Uppsala: Iustus Förlag.

Fraser, N. (1994), 'After the family wage', *Political Theory*, 22, 591–618.

Fraser, N. (1997), *Justice Interruptus: Critical Reflections on the Postsocialist Condition*, London: Routledge.

Freedman, M. (1984), 'The search for shelters', in K. Thompson (ed.), *Work Employment and Unemployment*, Buckingham: Open University Press.

Fridenson, P. and B. Reynaud (eds) (2004), *La France et le temps de travail (1814–2004)*, Paris: Odile Jacob.

Fuchs-Epstein, C., C. Seron, B. Oglensky and R. Sauté (1998), *The Part-Time Paradox: Time Norms, Professional Lives, Family and Gender*, New York: Routledge.

Furedi, F. (2004), *Therapy Culture: Cultivating Vulnerability in an Uncertain Age*, London: Routledge.

Futuribles (2002), *L'évolution des valeurs des européens*. No. 200 (July–August).

Gallie, D. (2002), 'The quality of working life in welfare strategy', in G. Esping-Andersen, D. Gallie, A. Hemerijck and J. Myles, *Why We Need a New Welfare State*, Oxford: Oxford University Press.

Gallie, D. (2004), 'Work pressure in Europe 1996–2001: trends and determinants', paper presented to the British Journal of Industrial Relations workshop on The Quality of Working Life, LSE, 17 September.

Gandel, S. (2002), 'Women losing out in Wall St. downsizing: 20% job drop, top execs disappearing', *Crain's New York Business*, 14 October.

Garey, A. (1999), *Weaving Work and Motherhood*, Philadelphia, PA: Temple University Press.

Garhammer, M. (1995), 'Changes in working hours in Germany: the resulting impact on everyday life', *Time and Society*, 4 (2), 167–203.

Garhammer, M. (1999), 'Time structures in the European Union: a comparison of West Germany, UK, Spain and Sweden', in J. Merz and M. Ehling (eds), *Time Use – Research, Data and Policy*, Baden-Baden: Nomos.

Geisst, C. (1997), *Wall Street: A History*, New York: Oxford University Press.

Geoghegan, L., J. Lever, I. McGimpsey (2004), *ICT for Social Welfare: A Toolkit for Managers, Labour Markets and Training*, Bristol: Policy Press.

Gershuny, J. (2000), *Changing Times: Work and Leisure in Postindustrial Society*, Oxford: Oxford University Press.

Giddens, A. (1991), *Modernity and Self Identity*, Cambridge: Polity Press.

Giddens, A. (1999), *Runaway World: How Globalisation is Shaping Our Lives*, London: Profile.

Giddens, A. (2000), 'Preface' in C. Hakim, *Work–Lifestyle Choices in the 21st Century: Preference Theory*, Oxford: Oxford University Press.

Gillies, V. (2005), 'Raising the "meritocracy": parenting and the individualisation of social class', discussion paper, Families and Social Capital ESRC Research Group, London Southbank University.

Ginn, J. and S. Arber (1995), 'Moving the goalposts: the impact on British women of raising their state pension age to 65', in J. Baldock and M. May (eds), *Social Policy Review*, 7, London: Social Policy Association.

Ginn, J., S. Arber, J. Brannen, A. Dale, S. Dex, P. Moss, J. Pahl, C. Roberts and J. Rubery (1996), 'Feminist fallacies: a reply to Hakim on women's employment', *The British Journal of Sociology*, 47 (1), 167–74.

Ginn, J. and J. Sandell (1997), 'Balancing home and employment: stress reported by social services staff', *Work, Employment and Society*, 11 (3), 413–34.

Glover, J. (2000), *Women and Scientific Employment*, Basingstoke: Macmillan.

Glucksmann, M. (1995), 'Why "work"? Gender and the "total social organisation of labour"', *Gender, Work and Organisation*, 2 (2), 63–75.

Glucksmann, M. (2000), *Cottons and Casuals: the Gendered Organisation of Labour in Space and Time*, Durham: Sociology Press.

Golden, L. (2001), 'Flexible work schedules', *American Behavioral Scientist*, 44 (7), 1157–78.

Goldthorpe, J.H. (1996), 'Class analysis and the reorientation of class theory: the case of persisting differentials in educational attainment', *British Journal of Sociology*, 47 (3), 481–505.

Goldthorpe, J.H. (2000), *On Sociology: Numbers, Narrative and the Integration of Research and Theory*, Oxford: OUP.

Goldthorpe, J., H.D. Lockwood, F. Bechhofer and J. Platt (1968), *The Affluent Worker in the Class Structure*, Cambridge: Cambridge University Press.

Gonäs L. and S. Spånt (2004), 'The gender pay gap in Sweden: a national report', *Karlstad University Studies 2004: 55*, Karlstad: Karlstad University.

Gonäs, L. (ed.) (2005), Pä Gränsen till Sammanbrott, Stockholm: Agora.

Gonäs L., A. Bergman and K. Rosenberg (2005), *Osakliga löneskillnader mellan kvinnor och män. En studie vid Karlstads universitet*, Karlstad: Karlstad University Press.

Gould, A. (2004), 'Waking up to the need for women in science and technology', keynote presentation by Andrew Gould, CEO and president of Schlumberger, Berlin, Germany, 10–11 October 2003, http://www.oilfield.slb.com/media/about/speech_womenscitech.pdf.

Green, A., M. Maguire and A. Canny (2001), *Keeping Track: Mapping and Tracking Vulnerable Young People*, Bristol: Policy Press.

Green, A.E., T. Hogarth and R.E. Shackleton (1999), *Long Distance Living: Dual Location Households*, Bristol: Policy Press.

Green, F. (1999), 'It's been a hard day's night: The concentration and intensification of work in late 20th Century Britain', University of Kent at Canterbury: Department of Economics, discussion paper 99/13.

Green, F. (2000), 'Why has work effort become more intense? Conjectures and evidence about effort-biased technical change and other stories', Department of Economics discussion paper 00/03, University of Kent at Canterbury.

Green, F. (2003), 'The rise and decline of job insecurity', paper presented at the ESRC seminar series Work, Life and Time in the New Economy, Manchester, http://www.lse.ac.uk/worklife.

Green, F. and S. McIntosh (2001), 'The intensification of work in Europe', *Labour Economics*, 8 (2), 291–308.

Greenfield, The Baroness Susan, J. Peters, N. Lane, T. Rees and G. Samuels (2002), *Set Fair: A Report on Women in Science, Engineering and Technology from The Baroness Susan Greenfield to the Secretary of State for Trade and Industry*, London: Department for Trade and Industry http://www2.set4women.gov.uk/set4women/research/the_greenfield_rev.htm.

Greenspan, A. (1998), 'Is there a new economy?' *California Management Review*, 41 (1), 74–85.

Grimshaw, D., H. Beynon, J. Rubery and K. Ward (2002), 'The restructuring of career paths in large service sector organisations: "delayering" upskilling and polarisation', *Sociological Review*, 50 (1), 89–115.

Grimshaw, D., K.G. Ward, J. Rubery and H. Beynon (2001), 'Organisations and the transformation of the internal labour market in the UK', *Work, Employment and Society*, 15 (1), 25–54.

Guest, D.E. (1990), 'Have British workers been working harder in Thatcher's

Britain? A re-consideration of the concept of effort', *British Journal of Industrial Relations*, 28 (3), 293–313.

Guthey, E. (2004), 'New economy romanticism: narratives of corporate personhood, and the antimanagerial impulse', in K. Lipartito and D. Sicilia (eds), *Constructing Corporate America: History, Politics, Culture*, New York: Oxford Press.

Gwiazdzinski, L. and O. Klein (2002), 'Maison du temps et de la Mobilité', presentation/press kit, Maison des temps et de la mobilité, mimeo.

Hafner-Burton, E. and M. Pollack (2002), 'Mainstreaming gender in global governance', *European Journal of International Relations*, 8 (3), 339–73.

Hägerstrand, T. (1985), 'Time geography: focus on corporeality of Man, Society and Environment', in S. Aida et al. (eds), *The Science of Praxis and Complexity*, Tokyo: United Nations University.

Hakim, C. (1991), 'Grateful slaves and self-made women: fact and fantasy in women's work orientations', *European Sociological Review*, 7 (2), 101–21.

Hakim, C. (1995), 'Five feminist myths about women's employment', *British Journal of Sociology*, 46, 435–54.

Hakim, C. (1996), *Key Issues in Women's Work: Female Heterogeneity and the Polarisation of Women's Employment*, London: Continuum.

Hakim, C. (1998), 'Developing a sociology for the twenty-first century: preference theory', *British Journal of Sociology*, 49 (1), 137–43.

Hakim, C. (2000), *Work–Lifestyle Choices in the 21st Century: Preference Theory*, Oxford: Oxford University Press.

Hakim, C. (2002), *Models of the Family in Modern Societies: Ideals and Realities*, Aldershot: Ashgate.

Hakim, C. (2003), 'Public morality versus personal choice: the failure of social attitude surveys', *British Journal of Sociology*, 54 (3), 339–45.

Halford, S., M. Savage and A. Witz (1997), *Gender, Careers and Organisations*, Basingstoke and London: Macmillan.

Hamermesh, D.S. (1999), 'The timing of work over time', *Economic Journal*, 109 (452), 37–66.

Hanson, J.T. (2000), 'Broad's-eye view', in *Working Woman*, September.

Hanson, J.T. and R. John (n.d.), 'Cyberspace mentors', in *Women Working 2000 + Beyond*, http://www.womenworking2000.com/feature/index. php?id=42.

Hardill, I. (2002), *Gender, Migration and the Dual Career Household*, London: Routledge.

Hardill, I., A.E. Green, A.C. Dudleston and D.W. Owen (1997), 'Who decides what? Decision making in dual career households', *Work, Employment and Society*, 11 (2), 313–26.

Hatch, J. and A. Clinton (2000), 'Job growth in the 1990s: a retrospect', *Monthly Labor Review*, 123 (12), 3–18.

Hattery, A. (2001a), 'Tag-team parenting: costs and benefits of utilizing nonoverlapping shift work in families with young children', *Families in Society: The Journal of Contemporary Human Services*, **82** (4), 419–27.

Hattery, A. (2001b), *Women, Work, and Family*, London: Sage Publications.

Hecker, D.E. (2001), 'Occupational employment projections to 2010', *Monthly Labor Review*, 124 (11), 57–84.

Hedges, J.N. and E.S. Sekscenski (1979), 'Workers on late shifts in a changing economy', *Monthly Labor Review*, 102 (9), 14–22.

Heelas, P. (2002), 'Work ethics, soft capitalism and the "turn to life"', in Paul du Gay and Michael Pryke (eds), *Cultural Economy*, London: SAGE Publications.

Hervé, E. (2001), 'Temps des villes', Ministry responsible for Cities and the Office of the Secretary of State for the Rights of Women and of Vocational Training, mimeo.

Hertz, R. and J. Charlton (1989), 'Making family under a shiftwork schedule: Air Force security guards and their wives', *Social Problems*, 36 (5), 491–507.

Heymann, J. (ed.) (2000), *The Widening Gap: Why American Working Families are in Jeopardy and What Can be Done About It*, New York: Basic Books, summary available from www.iwpr.org/pdf/heymann.prf.

Hewitt, P. (1993), *About Time: The Revolution in Work and Family Life*, London: Rivers Oram Press.

Himmelweit, S. (2005), 'Can we afford (not) to care: prospects and policy', Gender Institute Working Paper 15.

Himmelweit, S. and D. Perrons (2005), 'Can society afford the costs of care', paper presented to the ESRC Gender Equality Network, London School of Economics, June.

Hochschild, A. (1997), *The Time Bind*, New York: Metropolitan Books.

Hodgkinson, T. (2004), 'How to be idle', London: Hamish Hamilton.

Hoffman-Zehner, J. (2001), 'Happenings at 85 Broads', speech presented at 85 Broads', 16 May, 2001 event – 'What's your destiny?'.

Hörning, K.H., A. Gerhard and M. Michailow (1995), *Time Pioneers: Flexible Working Time and New Lifestyles*, Cambridge: Polity Press.

Howlett, D. and P. Overberg (2004), 'Think your commute is tough?' *USA Today*, 29 November, http://www.usatoday.com/news/nation/2004-11-29-commute_x.htm.

Hudson, J. (2003), 'E-galitarianism? The information society and New Labour's repositioning of welfare', *Critical Social Policy*, 23 (2), 268–90.

INSEE (2002), *Employment Survey*, Paris: INSEE, http://www.insee.fv/en/home/home_page.asp.

INSEE (2004), *Femmes et hommes. Regards sur la parité*, Paris: INSEE: Références (Edition 2004).

Institute for Women's Policy Research (2003), 'Before and after welfare reform: the work and well-being of low-income single parent families', report downloaded from www.iwpr.org.

Institute for Women's Policy Research (2004), 'Women and the economy: recent trends in job loss, labour force participation and wages', report downloaded from www.iwpr.org.

Irwin, S. (2003), 'The changing shape of values, care and commitment', paper presented to the ESPAnet conference, Danish National Institute of Social Research, Copenhagen, November, http://www.sfi.dk/graphics/ESPAnet/papers/Irwin.pdf.

Jämo Rapport 2000:1, 'Att arbeta med arbetsvärdering'. Stockholm: Jämo.

Jackall, R. (1988), *Moral Mazes: The World of Corporate Managers*, New York: Oxford University Press.

Jacobs, J.A. and K. Gerson (1998), 'Who Are the Overworked Americans?', *Review of Social Economy*, 56 (4), 442–59.

Jansson, F., E. Pylkkänen and L. Valck (2003), *En jämställd försäkring?: bilaga 12 till Långtidsutredningen 2003*, SOU 2003:36, Stockholm: Fritzes offentliga publikationer.

Jarvis, H. (2004), 'City time: managing the infrastructure of everyday life', paper presented at the *ESRC Work, Life and Time in the New Economy series, Seminar 5: Social, Spatial and Temporal Frameworks for Everyday Work and Life*, London, 27 February.

Jarvis, H. (2005), 'Moving to London Time: household co-ordination and the infrastructure of everyday life', *Time and Society*, 14 (1), 133–54.

JPMorgan Chase Community Programme Report (2003), http://www.jpmorganchase.com/community/diversity/workplace.

Kamerman, S.B. and A.J. Kahn (eds) (1991), *Childcare, Parental Leave, and the Under 3s: Policy Innovation in Europe*, New York and London: Auburn House.

Kanter, R.M. (1977), *Men and Women of the Corporation*, New York: Basic Books.

Kaufman, H. (2000), *On Money and Markets: A Wall Street Memoir*, New York: McGraw Hill.

Kautto, M. (2000), *A Balance Sheet for Welfare of the 1990s*, SOU 2000:83, Stockholm: Fritzes.

Kitterød, R.H. (2002), Store endringer i småbarnsforeldres dagligliv (Major changes in the daily life of parents of small children). Stockholm: Statistisk sentralbyrå, 16 (4–5), 14–22.

Kitterød, R.H. and R. Kjeldstad (2003), 'A new father's role? Employment patterns among Norwegian fathers 1991–2001', *Economic Survey*, 1, 39–51.

Kok, W. (2004), 'Facing the challenge: the Lisbon Strategy for Growth and Employment', report from the high-level group chaired by Wim Kok, http://europa.eu.int/comm/lisbon_strategy/pdf/2004-1866-EN-complet.pdf.

Kolker, R. (2003), 'Down and out on Wall Street', in *New York Magazine*, 17 March.

Korpi, W. (1999), 'Ojämlikhetens ansikten: Genus, klass och ojämlikhet i olika typer av välfärdsstater', *Sociologisk Forskning: Supplement 1999*, 40–92.

Kraemer, K. and J.L. King (2003), *Information Technology and Administrative Reform: Will the Time after E-government be Different?* Irvine: Centre for Research on Information Technology and Organisations, University of California.

Kvande, E. (1999), *Paradoxes of Gender and Organizations*, Trondheim: NTNU.

Kvande, E. (2003), 'Kvinnelige mellomledere i grådige organisasjoner' (Female middle managers in greedy organizations), in A.L. Ellingsæter and J. Solheim (eds), *Den usynlige hånd. Kjønnsmakt og moderne arbeidsliv*, Oslo: Gyldendal akademisk.

Ladipo, D., R. Mankelow and B.J. Burchell (2003), 'Working like a dog, sick as a dog: job intensification in the late 20th Century', in B.J. Burchell, S. Deakin, J. Michie and J. Rubery (eds), *Systems of Production: Markets, Organisations and Performance*, London: Routledge.

Lallement, M. (2003), *Temps, travail et modes de vie*, Paris: Puf.

Lash, S. (2000), 'Risk Culture', in B. Adam, U. Beck and J. van Loon (eds), *The Risk Society and Beyond: Critical Perspectives in Social Theory*, London: Sage.

La Valle, I., S. Arthur, C. Millward and J. Scott with M. Clayden (2002), *Happy Families? Atypical Work and its Influence on Family Life*, Final report, York: Joseph Rowntree Foundation.

Leat, D., K. Steltzer and G. Stoker (2002), *Toward Holistic Governance: The New Reform Agenda*, Basingstoke: Palgrave Macmillan.

Leira, A. (1998), 'Perspectives. Caring as social right: cash for child care and Daddy leave', *Social Politics*, 5 (3), 362–78.

Leira, A. (2002a), *Working Parents and the Welfare State: Family Change and Policy Reform in Scandinavia*, Cambridge: Cambridge University Press.

Leira, A. (2002b), 'Updating the "gender contract"? Childcare reforms in the Nordic countries in the 1990s', *NORA*, 10 (2), 81–9.

Lepetit, B. and D. Pumain (eds) (1993), *Temporalités urbaines*, Paris: Economica.

Letablier, M.-T. (2004), 'Work and family balance: a new challenge for policies in France', in J. Zollinger Giele and E. Holst (eds), *Changing Life*

Patterns in Western Industrial Societies, Advances in Life Course Research, Vol. 8, Oxford: Elsevier.

Lewis, J. (1992), 'Gender and the development of welfare regimes', *Journal of European Social Policy*, 2 (3), 159–73.

Lewis, J. (1993), 'Introduction: women, work, family and social policies in Europe', in Jane Lewis (ed.), *Women and Social Policies in Europe, Work Family and the State*, Aldershot, UK and Brookfield, US: Edward Elgar.

Lewis, J. (ed.) (1997a), *Lone Parents in European Welfare Regimes*, London: Jessica Kingsley.

Lewis, J. (1997b), 'Gender and welfare regimes: further thoughts', *Social Politics*, Summer, 160–77.

Lewis, J. (2000), 'Gender and welfare regimes', in G. Lewis, S. Gewirtx and J. Clarke (eds), *Rethinking Social Policy*, London: Sage.

Lewis, J. (2001), 'The decline of the male breadwinner model: implications for work and care', *Social Politics*, 8 (2), 152–69.

Lewis, J. (2002), 'Gender and welfare state change', *European Societies*, 4 (4), 331–57.

Lewis, S. and C. Cooper (1983), 'The stress of combining occupational and parental roles: a review of the literature', *Bulletin of the British Psychological Society*, 36, 341–5.

Lewis, S. and C. Cooper (1988), 'Stress in dual earner families', *Women and Work*, 3, 139–68.

Lewis, S. and J. Lewis (1996), *The Work–Family Challenge*, London: Sage.

Leyshon, A. and N. Thrift (1997), *Money Space: Geographies of Monetary Transformation*, London: Routledge.

Li, Y., F. Bechofer, R. Stewart, D. McCrone, M. Anderson and L. Jamieson (2002), 'A divided working class? Planning and career perception in the service and working classes', *Work, Employment and Society*, 16 (4), 617–36.

Lupton, C., N. North and P. Khan (2001), *Working Together or Pulling Apart? The National Health Service and Child Protection Networks*, Bristol: Policy Press.

Manning, A. and B. Petrongolo (2004), *The Part Time Pay Penalty*, London: DTI Women and Employment Unit.

Martinotti, G. (1997) 'La nuova morfologia sociale della metropolis', in Politecnico di Milano (eds), *Il tempo e la città fra natura et storia. Atlante di progetti sui tempi della città*, Rome: Urbanistica Quaderni, no. 12; Inu edizioni.

Maternity Alliance (2004), *Happy Anniversary. The Right to Request One Year On*, London: Maternity Alliance.

Mattingly, D.J. (1999), 'Job search, social networks, and local labor market dynamics: the case of paid household work in San Diego, California', *Urban Geography*, 20 (1), 46–74.

McCarthy, H. (2004), *Girlfriends in High Places: How Women's Networks are Changing the Workplace*, London: Demos.

McCarthy, J. and R. Edwards (2002), 'The individual in public and private: the significance of mothers and children', in A. Carling, S. Duncan and R. Edwards (eds), *Analysing Families: Morality and Rationality in Policy and Practice*, London: Routledge.

McDowell, L. (1997), *Capital Culture: Gender Divisions at Work in the City*, Oxford: Blackwell.

McDowell, L., D. Perrons, C. Fagan, K. Ray and K. Ward (2005), 'The contradictions and intersections of class and gender in a global city: placing working women's lives on the research agenda', *Environment and Planning A*, 37 (3), 441–61.

McDowell, L., K. Ray, D. Perrons, C. Fagan and K. Ward (forthcoming), 'Women's paid work and moral economies of care', *Social and Cultural Geography*.

McRae, S. (2003), 'Constraints and choices in mothers' employment careers: a consideration of Hakim's Preference Theory', *British Journal of Sociology*, 54 (3), 317–38.

McRobbie. A. (2002), 'From Holloway to Hollywood: happiness at work in the new cultural economy?' in Paul du Gay and Michael Pryke (eds), *Cultural Economy*, London: SAGE Publications.

Méda, D. (2001), *Le temps des femmes: pour un nouveau partage des rôles*, Paris: Flammarion.

Méda, D. and R. Orain (2002), 'Transformations du travail et du hors travail: le jugement des salariés', *Travail et Emploi*, 90, 23–38.

Meidner, R. (1973), 'Samordning och solidarisk lönepolitik under tre decennier', in Tvärsnitt. Sju forskningsrapporter utgivna till LO:s 75 års jubileum 1973' (Co-ordination and Solidarity Wages Policy. Seven research reports to LO's 75th Anniversary). Stockholm: Bokförlaget Prisma, LO.

Meidner, R. (1994), 'The rise and fall of the Swedish model', in W. Clement and R. Mahon (eds), *Swedish Social Democracy*, Toronto: Canadian Scholars Press.

Meisenheimer II, Joseph R. (1998), 'The services industry in the "good" versus "bad" jobs debate', *Monthly Labor Review*, 121 (2), 10–21.

Melbin, M. (1987), *Night as Frontier: Colonizing the World After Dark*, New York: Free Press.

Messenger, J. (ed.) (2004), *Finding the Balance: Working-time and Workers' Needs and Preferences in Industrialized Countries*, London: Routledge.

Milanovic, B. (2002), 'True world income distribution, 1988 and 1993: first calculation based on household surveys alone', *Economic Journal*, 112 (January), 51–92.

Miles, M.B. and A.M. Huberman (1994), *Qualitative Data Analysis*, London: SAGE.

Ministry of Social Affairs and Employment (Netherlands) (2002), *Daily Routine Arrangements*, The Hague: Ministry of Social Affairs and Employment.

Moen, P. (ed.) (2003), *It's about Time: Couples and Careers*, Ithaca, NY: Cornell University Press.

Molyneux, M. (1985), 'Mobilisation without emancipation? Women's interests, the state and revolution in Nicaragua', *Feminist Studies*, 11, 227–54.

Molyneux, M. (1998), 'Analysing women's movements', in C. Jackson and R. Pearson (eds), *Feminist Visions of Development*, London: Routledge.

Momsen, J.H. (1999), *Gender, Migration and Domestic Service,* London: Routledge.

Morgan, D. (1992), *Discovering Men*, London: Routledge.

Moss, P. and F. Deven (1999), 'Parental leave in context', in P. Moss and F. Deven (eds), *Parental Leave: Progress or Pitfall?*, Netherlands: Netherlands Interdisciplinary Demographic Institute.

Mott, P.E., F.C. Mann, G. McLoughlin and D.P. Warwick (1965), *Shift Work: The Social, Psychological, and Physical Consequences*, Ann Arbor, MI: University of Michigan Press.

Mückenberger, U. (2004), 'Des politiques du temps de travail aux politiques des temps des villes', in E. Istace, M. Laffut, R. Plasman and C. Ruyters (eds), *Sphères privée et professionnelle: vers une recomposition des actions*, Issy-les-Moulineaux: De Boeck Université.

National Assembly for Wales Equality of Opportunity Committee (2004), *Report on Mainstreaming Equality in the Work of the National Assembly*, Cardiff: National Assembly for Wales.

Naegele, G. (2003), A *New Organisation of Time over Working Life*, Dublin: European Foundation for the Improvement of Living and Working Conditions.

National Committee on Pay Equity (2005), 'The wage gap over time', www.pay-equity.org/info-time.html.

National Organisation for Women (2005), 'Key issues', www.now.org/issues.

National Statistics (2004), 'Marriage and divorce rates: EU comparison, 2002', *Social Trends*, 34, http://www.statistics.gov.uk/STATBASE/Expodata/Spreadsheets/D7265.xls.

Newman, J., M. Barnes, H. Sullivan and A. Knops (2004), 'Public participation and collaborative governance', *Journal of Social Policy*, 33 (2), 203–23.

Nock, S.L. and P.W. Kingston (1988), 'Time with children: the impact of couples' work time commitments', *Social Forces*, 67 (1), 59–85.

Nolan, J. (2002), 'The intensification of everyday life', in B.J. Burchell, D. Ladipo and F. Wilkinson (eds), *Job Insecurity and Work Intensification*, London: Routledge.

NVSS (2004), 'Births, marriages divorces and deaths, provisional data for June 2004', US Department of Health and Human Services, *National Vital Statistics Report* , 53 (11), http://www.cdc.gov/nchs/data/nvsr/nvsr53/ nvsr53_11.pdf.

Nyberg, A. (2000), 'From foster mothers to childcare centers: a history of working mothers and childcare in Sweden', *Feminist Economics*, 1, 5–20.

Nycander, S. (2002), *Makten över arbetsmarknaden. Ett perspektiv på Sveriges 1900-tal* (Controlling the Swedish Labour Market: A Perspective on the Swedish 20th century), Stockholm: SNS Förlag.

O'Connell, M. (1993), 'Where's Papa? Father's role in child care', *Population Trends and Public Policy Report # 20*, Washington, DC: Population Reference Bureau.

ODPM (2002), 'The national strategy for local e-government', http://www.localegov.gov.uk/Nimoi/sites/ODMP/resources/20021127%20 Final%20NS%20with%20cover.pdf.

OECD (1995), 'Long-term leave for parents in OECD countries', *Employment Outlook*, Paris: OECD.

OECD (2001), 'Balancing work and family life: helping parents into paid employment', *Employment Outlook*, Paris: OECD.

OECD (2002), *Babies and Bosses – Reconciling Work and Family Life, 1*, Australia, Denmark and the Netherlands, Paris: OECD, http:// www1.oecd.org/publications/e-book/8102111E.PDF.

OECD (2003), *Employment Outlook*, Paris: OECD.

OECD (2004), *Babies and Bosses – Reconciling Work and Family Life, 3*, New Zealand, Portugal and Switzerland, Paris: OECD.

ONS (Office of National Statistics)/DoH (Department of Health) (2003), 'Census 2001: informal care' (http://www.carers.gov.uk/census-carers.pdf).

Orloff, Ann (1993), 'Gender and the social rights of citizenship: the comparative analysis of gender relations and the welfare states', *American Sociological Review*, 58 (3), 303–28.

Ortner, S. (2003), *New Jersey Dreaming: Capital, Culture, and the Class of '58*, Durham and London: Duke University Press.

Osborn, M., T. Rees, M. Bosch, C. Hermann, J. Hilden, A. McLaren, R. Palomba, L. Peltonen, C. Vela, D. Weis, A. Wold, J. Mason and

C. Wennerås (2000), 'Science policies in the European Union: promoting excellence through mainstreaming gender equality', a report from the ETAN Network on Women and Science, Luxembourg: Office for Official Publications of the European Communities, http://www.cordis.lu/ improving/women/reports.htm.

Osborne, S., R. Beattie and A. Williamson (2002), *Community Involvement in Rural Regeneration Partnerships in the UK: Evidence from England, Northern Ireland and Scotland*, Bristol: Policy Press.

Ost, F. (1999), *Le temps du droit*, Paris: Editions Odile Jacob.

Ostrower, F. (1995), *Why the Wealthy Give: The Culture of Elite Philanthropy*, Princeton, NJ: Princeton University Press.

Outward Bound Organisation, http://www.outwardbound.com/.

Pahl, J. (1989), *Money and Marriage*, London: Macmillan.

Pakulski, J. and M. Waters (1996), 'The reshaping and dissolution of social class in advanced society', *Theory and Society*, 25, 667–91.

Parents at Work (2004), 'The Working and Caring in London 2002 survey – by Parents at Work, the City of London Early Years Development and the Childcare Partnership', www.parentsatwork.org.uk.

Park, A., J. Curtice, K. Thomson, L. Jarvis and C. Bromley (2003), *British Social Attitudes, the 20th Report*, London: Sage.

Parker, S. (1983), *Leisure and Work*, London: Allen & Unwin.

PBR (2004) 'Choice for parents, the best start for children: a ten year strategy for childcare', HMR Treasury, Pre Budget Reports, associated documents, http://www.hm-treasury.gov.uk/pre_budget_report/prebud_pbr04/ assoc_docs/prebud_pbr04_adchildcare.cfm.

PCI (1990), *Sezione Femmninile Nazionale PCI, Proposta di legge di iniziativa populare 'le donne cambiano i tempi'*, Roma (4 April).

PCS (2002), *Our Time*, Inland Revenue work–life balance resource pack, London: Public and Commercial Services Union.

Pelisse, J. (2002), 'A la recherche du temps gagné. Les 35 heures entre perceptions, régulations et intégration professionnelle', *Travail et Emploi*, 90, 7–22.

PEP (2003), European project on equal pay, http://www.equalpay.nu.

Pe-Pua, R., C. Mitchell, R. Iredale and S. Castles (1996), *Astronaut Families and Parachute Children: The Cycle of Migration between Hong Kong and Australia*, Canberra: Australian Government Publishing Service.

Perrons, D. (1999), 'Flexible working patterns and equal opportunities in the European Union: conflict or compatibility?' *European Journal of Women's Studies*, 6 (4), 391–418.

Perrons, D. (2004a), *Globalization and Social Change: People and Places in a Divided World*, London: Routledge.

Perrons, D. (2004b), 'Equity and representation in the new economy' in

J. Kelly and P. Willman (eds), *Union Organization and Activity*, Leverhulme Vol. 2, London: Routledge.

Perry-Jenkins, M. and H.-L. Haley (2000), 'Employment schedules and the transition to parenthood: implications for mental health and marriage', paper presented at the annual meeting of the National Council on Family Relations, Minneapolis, MN, November.

Pham, H. (2003), 'Les 35 heures dans les très petites entreprises', Dares: *Premières Synthèses/Informations* 46.1.

Phillips, K.R. (2002), 'Parent work and child well-being in low-income families', Occasional Paper Number 56, Washington, DC: Urban Institute.

Piketty, T. and E. Saez (2003), 'Income inequality in the United States, 1913 to 1998', *Quarterly Journal of Economics*, 118 (1) 1–39.

Pilcher, J. (2000), 'Domestic divisions of labour in the twentieth century: change slow a-coming', *Work, Employment and Society*, 14 (4), 771–80.

Pillinger, J. (2000), *Working Time in Europe: A European Working Time Policy in the Public Services*, Brussels: European Trade Union Institute.

Pillinger, J. (2002), 'The Politics of Time: Can Work–Life Balance Really Work?', in *Equality Opportunities Review*, 107, July, 18–21.

PIU (Performance and Innovation Unit) (2000), *E.gov: Electronic Government Services for the 21st Century London*, London: PIU/Cabinet Office.

Pollitt, C. (2003), 'Joined up government: a survey', *Political Studies Review*, 1 (1), 34–49.

Prandy, K. (1998), 'Deconstructing classes: critical comments on the revised social classification', *Work, Employment and Society*, 12 (4), 743–53.

Presser, H.B. (1986), 'Shift work among American women and child care', *Journal of Marriage and the Family*, 48 (3), 551–63.

Presser, H.B. (1994), 'Employment schedules among dual-earner spouses and the division of household labor by gender', *American Sociological Review*, 59 (3), 348–64.

Presser, H.B. (1995), 'Job, family, and gender: determinants of nonstandard work schedules among employed Americans in 1991', *Demography*, 32 (4), 577–98.

Presser, H.B. (1999). 'Toward a 24-hour economy', *Science*, 284 (11 June), 1778–9.

Presser, H.B. (2000), 'Nonstandard work schedules and marital instability', *Journal of Marriage and the Family*, 62 (1), 93–110.

Presser, H.B. (2001), 'Toward a 24-hour economy: implications for the temporal structure and functioning of family life', in *The Social Contract in the Face of Demographic Change: Proceedings*, 2nd Rencontres Sauvy International Seminar, Montreal, Quebec, 4–6 October, Paris: Institut National D'Éstudes Démographiques.

Presser, H.B. (2003), *Working in a 24/7 Economy: Challenges for American Families*, New York: Russell Sage Foundation.

Quah, D. (1996), 'The invisible hand and the weightless economy', occasional paper no. 12, Centre for Economic Performance, London School of Economics.

Rake, K., H. Davies, H. Joshi and R. Alami (2000), *Women's Incomes over the Lifetime*: a report to the Women's Unit, London: The Stationery Office.

Rapoport, R. and R.N. Rapoport (1978), *Dual-Career Families Re-examined*, London: Martin Robertson.

Rasmussen, B. (2002), 'Når jobben tar livet' (When your job takes your life), in U. Forseth and B. Rasmussen (eds), *Arbeid for livet*, Oslo: Gyldendal.

Rees, T. (1999), 'Mainstreaming equality', in S. Watson and L. Doyal (eds), *Engendering Social Policy*, Milton Keynes: Open University Press.

Rees, T. (2002), *The Helsinki Group on Women and Science: National Policies on Women and Science in Europe*, Luxembourg: Office for Official Publications of the European Communities.

Reskin, B.F. and P.A. Roos (1990), *Job Queues, Gender Queues*, Philadelphia, PA: Temple University Press.

RFV – Riksforsaknngsverket (2002a), *Brinnande dagar- en studie om fljraldrapenningdagar som inte tas ut*, 12, Stockholm: Riksforsakringsverket.

RFV – Riksforsakringsverket (2002b), *Spelade pappamanaden nagon roll? Pappomas uttag av fljraldrapennin*, 14. Stockholm: Riksforsaknngsverket.

Ribbens McCarthy, J., R. Edwards and V. Gillies (2002), *Making Families: Moral Tales of Parenting and Step-parenting*, Durham: Sociology Press.

Rifkin, J. (2004), *The European Dream: How Europe's Vision of the Future is Quietly Eclipsing the American Dream*, Cambridge: Polity.

Rones, P.L., R.E. Ilg and J.M. Gardner (1997), 'Trends in hours of work since the mid-1970s', *Monthly Labor Review*, 120 (4), 3–14.

Rønsen, M. (2004), 'Kontantstøtten og mødres arbeidstilbud: Større virkninger på lengre sikt' (Cash-for-care and mothers' working hours. Long term effects are larger), *Samfunnsspeilet*, 18 (6), 24–30.

Rose, D. and K. O'Reilly (1998), *The ESRC Review of Government Social Classifications*, London: ESRC/ONS.

Rose, D. and D. Pevalin (2002), *A Researcher's Guide to the National Statistics Socio-Economic Classification*, London: Sage.

Rosenberg, K. (2004), *Värdet av arbete – arbetsvärdering som en lönepolitisk process* (*The value of Work – Job Evaluation as an Instrument for Wage Policies*), Göteborg: BAS.

Rubery, J. and C. Fagan (1995), 'Comparative industrial relations research: towards reversing the gender bias', *British Journal of Industrial Relations*, 33 (2), June, 209–36.

Rubery, J., H. Figueiredo, M. Smith, D. Grimshaw and C. Fagan (2004), 'The ups and downs of European gender equality policy', *Industrial Relations Journal*, 35 (6), 603–28.

Rubery, J., M. Smith and C. Fagan (1999), *Women's Employment in Europe: Trends and Prospects*, London: Routledge.

Rubery, J., M. Smith, H. Figueiredo, C. Fagan and D. Grimshaw (2004), *Gender Mainstreaming and the European Employment Strategy and Social Inclusion Process*, Oxford: Blackwell.

Rubery, J., K. Ward, D. Grimshaw and H. Beynon (2005), 'Working time, industrial relations and the employment relationship', *Time and Society*, 14 (1), 89–111.

Rubin, L.B. (1994), *Families on the Fault Line*, New York: Harper Perennial.

Rübsamen-Waigmann, H., R. Sohlberg, T. Rees, O. Berry, P. Bismuth, R. D'Antona, E. De Brabander, G. Haemers, J. Holmes, M. Jepson, J. Leclaire, E. Mann, R. Needham, J. Neumann, C. Nielson, C. Vela and D. Winslow (2003), *Women in Industrial Research: A Wake Up Call for European Industry*, Luxembourg: Office for Official Publications of the European Communities, http://europa.eu.int/comm/research/wir.

Russell, P. (2003), '"Access and achievement or social exclusion?" Are the government's policies working for disabled children and their families?', *Children and Society*, 17 (3), 215–25.

Sainsbury, D. (1994) (ed.), *Gendering Welfare States*, London: Sage.

Sainsbury, D. (1996), *Gender, Equality and Welfare States*, Cambridge: Cambridge University Press.

Sainsbury, D. (1999), *Gender and Welfare State Regimes*, Oxford: Oxford University Press.

Sassen, S. (2001), *The Global City: New York, London, Tokyo*, Princeton, NJ: Princeton University Press.

Sastry, A. and F. Lee (2000), 'Pairing stability with change: rules, operations, and structures in an enduring organization', presented at the ICOS Seminar, University of Michigan, 28 January.

Savage, M. (2000), *Class Analysis and Social Transformation*, Buckingham: Open University Press.

Säve-Söderbergh, J. (2003), 'Are women asking for lower wages? – Individual wage bargaining and gender wage differentials', *Essays on Gender Differences in Economic Decision-Making*, Swedish Institute for Social Research 59, Stockholm: Stockholm University.

SCB (2002), *Women and Men in Sweden*, Stockholm: Statistics Sweden.

Schiebinger, L. (1999), *Has Feminism Changed Science?* Cambridge, MA: Harvard University Press.

Sen, A. (2000), *Development as Freedom*, New York: Anchor Books.

Sennett, R. (1998), *The Corrosion of Character*, New York: W.W. Norton & Co.

Sennett, R. (2000), 'The new political economy and its culture', *The Hedgehog Review*, 12 (1), Spring, 1–13, http://www.virginia.edu/isac/hh/ThrTocsvol2-1.html.

Sennett, R. (2003), http://www.lclark.edu/~ria/Richard.Sennett.html.

Sevenhuijsen, S. (2002), 'A third way? Moralities, ethics and families: an approach through the ethic of care', in A. Carling, S. Duncan and R. Edwards (eds), *Analysing Families*, London: Routledge.

SFS (1991), Ändringar i jämställdhetslagen, 443.

SFS (2000), Jämställdhetslagen, 773.

Sheridan, A. (2004), 'Chronic presenteeism: the multiple dimensions to men's absence from part-time work', *Gender, Work and Organizations*, 11 (2), 207–25.

Shorthose, J. (2004). 'Like summer and good sex? The limitations of the work–life balance campaign', *Capital and Class*, 82, 1–7.

Siaroff, A. (1994), 'Work, welfare and gender equality: a new typology,' in D. Sainsbury (ed.), *Gendering Welfare States*, London: Sage.

Siim, B. (2000), *Gender and Citizenship: Politics and Agency in France, Britain and Denmark*, Cambridge: Cambridge University Press.

6, P., D. Leat, K. Seltzer and G. Stoker (2002), *Toward Holistic Governance: the New Reform Agenda*, Basingstoke: Palgrave Macmillan.

Skeggs, B. (1997), *Formations of Class and Gender*, London: Sage.

Skinner, C. (2003), *Running around in Circles: Coordinating Childcare, Education and Work*, Bristol: Policy Press in association with Joseph Rowntree Foundation.

Skolverket (1998), *Beskrivande data om barnomsorg och skala 98.* Skolverkets rapport nr 157. Stockholm: Skolverket.

Skolverket (1999), *A vgifter i fljrskola och fritidshem 1999.* Skolverkets rapport 174. Stockholm: Skolverket.

Skolverket (2000a), *Bamomsorg och skala i siffror 2000: Del 2- Barn, personal, elever och ltirare.* Skolverkets rapport nr 185. Stockholm: Skolverket.

Skolverket (2000b), *Beskrivande data om barnomsorg och skala 2000.* Skolverkets rapport nr 192. Stockholm: Skolverket.

Skolverket (2001a), *Barnomsorg, skala, vuxenutbildning. Skolverkets ltigesbedomning 2001.* Rapport 2001-10-22. Stockholm: Skolverket.

Skolverket (2001b), *Barns omsorg. Tillgang och efterfragan plz/bamomsorgfOr ham 1- 12 ar med olika social bakgrund.* Skolverkets rapport nr 203. Stockholm: Skolverket.

Skolverket (2002), *Plats utan oskiiligt drOjsmal. UppfOlining av tillgiingligheten till bamomsorg i mal 2002.* Skolverket: Stockholm.

Skolverket (2003a), *Gruppstorlekar och persona/tathet i fOrskola, fOrskoleklass och fritidshem*. Stockholm: Skolverket.

Skolverket (2003b), *UppflJlining av reformen maxtaxa, allmdn fOrskola m.m.* Skolverkets rapport nr 231. Stockholm: Skolverket.

Skolverket (2003c), *Bamomsorg, stola och vuxenutbildning i siffror 2003: Del 2 - barn, personal, e/ever och l{irare*. Skolverkets rapport nr 233. Stockholm: Skolverket.

Skolverket (2004), 'Barn, elever och personal – Riksnivå avseende år 2003. Officiell statistik för förskoleverksamhet, skolbarnsomsorg, skola och vuxenutbildning, Del. 2, Skolverkets rapport nr 244, Stockholm: Skolverket.

Sletvold, L. (2000), *Kontantstøtteordningens konsekvenser for yrkesaktivitet og likestilling (The Consequences of Cash-for-Care for Employment and Equality)* Report 15/00, Oslo: NOVA.

Slotkin, R. (1986), *The Fatal Environment: the Myth of the Frontier in the Age of Industrialization*, Middletown, Conn.: Wesleyan University Press.

Smith, D. (1999), *Writing the Social: Critique, Theory and Investigations*, Toronto: Toronto University Press.

Smith, S.J. (1986), 'The growing diversity of work schedules', *Monthly Labor Review*, 109 (11), 7–13.

Smith-Doerr, L. (2004), *Women's Work: Gender Equality vs. Hierarchy in the Life Sciences*, Boulder, CO: Lynne Rienner Publishers.

SOU (1990) *Tio år med jämställdhetslagen – utvärdering och förslag*, Stockholm: Allmänna förlaget, 4.

SOU (1998), *Ty makten är din ...* , Stockholm: Fritzes, 8.

Staines, G.L. and J.H. Pleck (1983), *The Impact of Work Schedules on the Family*, Ann Arbor, MI: Institute for Social Research, University of Michigan.

Statham, J. and A. Mooney (2003), *Around the Clock: Childcare Services at Atypical Times*, Bristol: Policy Press.

*Statistisk årsbok (*1994–99), Stockholm: Statistiska Centralbyrån.

Stewart, K. (2005), 'Changes in poverty and inequality in the UK in international context', in J. Hills and K. Stewart (eds), *A More Equal Society*, Bristol: Policy Press.

Still, M.C. and D. Strang (2003), 'Institutionalising family-friendly policies', in P. Moen (ed.), *It's About Time*, Ithaca, NY and London: Cornell University Press.

Strauss, A. and J. Corbin (1998), *Basics of Qualitative Research*, London: Sage Publications.

Streeck, W. (1999), 'Competitive solidarity: rethinking the "European Social Model"', MPIfG Working Paper 99/8, Köln: Max Planck Institute für Gesellschaftsforschung.

Sullivan, O. (2000), 'The division of domestic labour', *Sociology*, 34 (3), 437–56.

Sundström, M. and A.-Z. Dufvander (1998), 'Föräldraförsäkringen och jämställdheten mellan kvinnor och män' in Inga Persson and Eskil Wadensjo (eds), *Valfardens Genusansikte*, SOU 1998:3, Stockholm: Fritzes.

Sweet, J., L. Bumpass and V. Call (1988), 'The design and content of the national survey of families and households', NSFH working paper no. 1, Madison, WI: University of Wisconsin.

Taylor, R. (n.d.), 'The future of work-life balance', London: Economic and Social Research Council.

The New York Times (1999), 'Management: a network of their own: from an exclusive address, a group for women only', 27 October, Wednesday late edition – final section C.

The New Yorker (1957), 'Talk of the Town'.

The New Yorker (1976), 'Financial women', 6 September.

Time and Society (2005), Special edition on *Work, Life and Time in the New Economy*, 14 (1).

Toynbee, P. (2005), 'Gender inequality: old patterns, new challenges', Ralph Miliband Lectures on *Inequalities: Dimensions and Challenges*, LSE, 3 February.

Transport for London (2003), 'London travel report 2003', http://www.tfl.gov.uk/tfl/ltr2003/road-related-trends-2.shtml].

Traube, E. (1992), *Dreaming Identities: Class, Gender, and Generation in 1980s Hollywood Movies*, Boulder, CO: Westview Press.

TUC (various), 'Changing Times news bulletin', www.tuc.org.uk/changingtimes.

TUC (1998), *The Time of Our Lives*, London: TUC.

TUC (2001), *Changing Times: A TUC guide to Work–Life Balance*, London: TUC.

TUC (2002a), *About Time*, London: TUC.

TUC (2002b), *Partnership Works*, London: TUC.

UNDP (2003), *Millennium Development Goals: a Compact Among Nations to End Human Poverty*, Oxford: Oxford University Press.

UNICEF (2004), 'Children under threat: the state of the world's children 2005', New York: United Nations Children's Fund, http://www.unicef.org/sowc05/english/sowc05.pdf.

US Census Bureau (2001), *Statistical Abstract of the United States: 2001*, 121st edition, Washington, DC: US Government Printing Office.

US Congress (1991), *Biological Rhythms: Implications for the worker*, Office of Technology Assessment, OTA-BA-463, Washington, DC: US Government Printing Office.

US Department of Labor, US Bureau of Labor Statistics (1981), 'Workers on Late Shifts', Summary 81–15, September, Washington, DC: US Government Printing Office.

US Department of Labor, US Bureau of Labor Statistics (1998), 'Workers on Flexible and Shift Schedules', *Labor Force Statistics from the CPS*, USDL98-119, Washington, DC: US Government Printing Office.

US Department of Labor, US Bureau of Labor Statistics (2002), 'Labor Force Statistics from the Current Population Survey: household data annual averages', Table 19, http://www.bls.gov/cps/cpsaat19.pdf.

Valentine, G. (1999), 'Doing household research: interviewing couples together and apart', *Area*, 31 (1), 67–74.

Viard, J. (2002), *Le sacre du temps libre: la société des 35 heures*, Datar: Editions de l'Aube.

Vincent, C. and S. Ball (2001), 'A market in love? Choosing preschool childcare', *British Educational Research Journal*, 27 (5), 633–51.

Wade, R. (2001), 'Is globalization making world income distribution more equal?' *London School of Economics DESTIN Working Paper*, No. 01-01.

Wainwright, D. and M. Calanan (2002), *Work Stress: The Making of a Modern Epidemic*, Milton Keynes: Open University Press.

Wajcman, J. and B. Martin (2001), 'My company or my career: managerial achievement and loyalty', *British Journal of Sociology*, 52 (4), 559–78.

Walby, S. (1994), 'Methodological and theoretical issues in the comparative analysis of gender relations in Western Europe,' *Environment and Planning*, 26, 1339–54.

Walby, S. (2002), 'Gender and the new economy: regulation or deregulation?' Paper presented at the *ESRC Seminar Work, Life and Time in the New Economy*, London School of Economics, October.

Wedderburn, A. (ed.) (2000), 'Shift work and health', special issue of *Bulletin of Studies on Time*, Vol. 1, Luxembourg: Office for Official Publications of the European Communities, and www.eurofound.ie.

Westergaard, J. and H. Resler (1975), *Class in a Capitalist Society*, London: Heinemann.

Wheatley, R. (2000), *Taking the Strain: A Survey of Managers and Workplace Stress*, London: Institute of Management.

Wheelock, J. and K. Jones (2002), '"Grandparents are the next best thing": informal childcare for working parents in urban Britain', *Journal of Social Policy*, 31 (3), 441–64.

White, L. and B. Keith (1990), 'The effect of shift work on the quality and stability of marital relations', *Journal of Marriage and the Family*, 52, 453–62.

White, M., S. Hill, P. McGovern, C. Mills and D. Smeaton (2003), '"High-performance" management practices, working hours and work–life balance', *BJIR*, 41 (2) 175–95.

Whitehead, B. and D. Popenoe (2004), *The State of Our Unions, National Marriage Project*, Piscataway, NJ: Rutgers University, and http://marriage.rutgers.edu/Publications/soou/soou2004.pdf.

Wichert, I.C. (2002), 'Job insecurity and work intensification: the effects on health and wellbeing', in B.J. Burchell, D. Ladipo and F. Wilkinson (eds), *Job Insecurity and Work Intensification*, London: Routledge, pp.92–111.

Williams, C. (2002), 'A critical evaluation of the commodification thesis', *Sociological Review*, 50 (4), 525–42.

Williamson, J. (2004), 'A short history of the Washington consensus', paper commissioned by the Fundación CIDOB for a conference 'From the Washington consensus towards a new global governance', Barcelona, http://www.iie.com/publications/papers/williamson0904-2.pdf.

Wilthagen, T. and F. Tros (2004), 'The concept of "flexicurity": a new approach to regulating employment and labour markets', *Transfer*, 10 (2), (summer), 166–86.

Winfield, F.E. (1985), *Commuter Marriage: Living Together, Apart*, New York: Columbia University Press.

Working and Caring in London (2002), 'Survey summary findings', Early Years Development Partnership in partnership with the City of London, http://www.parentsatwork.org.uk/asp/employer_zone/e_wcl_survey.asp, last accessed June 2005.

Index